*Action for Rural Change*

WITHDRAWAL

# *Action*
## *for*
# *Rural Change*

### Readings in Indian Community Development

**MUNSHIRAM MANOHARLAL, NEW DELHI**

MUNSHIRAM  MANOHARLAL
*Oriental Publishers*
54, Rani Jhansi Road, New Delhi 55

*Sales-Counter* 4416, Nai Sarak, Delhi-6

*First  Published  November,  1970*
ⓒ India International Centre, New Delhi.

Issued under the auspices of Council for Social Development,
India International Centre, Lodi Estate, New Delhi-3.

*Printed in India*
At The Raisina Printery, Delhi and Published by Devendra Jain
for Munshiram Manoharlal, New Delhi.

# PREFACE

THE COUNCIL FOR Social Development was set up by the India International Centre in 1964 with the hope that the cardinal aim of promoting mutual understanding and amity among the different communities of the world would be best achieved if the Centre undertook the study of social development alongwith the study of the past and present cultures of different countries. The deliberations and recommendations of two important seminars organised at the India International Centre—*Social Welfare in a Developing Economy* and *Social Administration in Developing Countries*—have also stressed the need for establishing a Centre to undertake studies: (*i*) in the national/ regional policies of social development, (*ii*) in the process of planning in social development, and (*iii*) in the interaction between social and economic development at various stages of national growth in developing 'countries.

One of the first important tasks that the Council has undertaken after its establishment is the preparation of a social policy statement by a group of experts in the field of social welfare. This was followed by a Seminar on *Social Policy for India* in late 1965 wherein the need for a clear and coherent social policy for India was discussed thoroughly. After the Seminar, the Social Policy Statement was forwarded to the National Government and the Planning Commission for their consideration.

Among the first studies undertaken by the Council is the study of *Human Factors in Community Development* by Miss Elmina Lucke (a former U.N. Consultant) in early 1965. This study is to form part of a larger study of community development in different countries of the world undertaken by Miss Lucke and Prof. Beldon Paulson of the University of Wisconsin. The study in its turn led to the recognition of the acute need in the field of social welfare training for carefully collected and organised teaching material for use in the various teaching and training institutions.

The present publication is an attempt on the part of the Council to meet the long standing need for appropriate teaching materials in the field of rural community development. I sincerely hope that this collection will prove to be of use to the trainees and the students in schools of social work, departments of sociology and anthropology, agricultural universities, orientation and study centres, social education organizers' training centres, Gram Sewak training centres, Panchayati Raj training centres and other similar institutions. I hope that our present effort will be followed by many others to systematically compile and publish suitable indigenous teaching material in other areas of social welfare and social development. In accordance with the objects of the Council mentioned at the outset, the Council is at present engaged in a study of *Cost Benefit Relations in Selected Beggars' Homes* (sponsored by the Research Programmes Committee of Planning Commission) and a study of *Communication in Urban Community Development Projects*. The Council has also several proposals under active scrutiny and consideration, particularly in the areas of urban community development, social aspect of family planning, social surveys of individuals states, rural urban migration and problems of non-student youth. I earnestly hope that as these proposals take concrete shape, the Council will be filling an acknowledged need for serious study and research in social development.

In the end, I take great pleasure in acknowledging the generous support received from our parent organization, India International Centre, and the Asia Foundation which has financed this project. Our grateful thanks are also due to the members of the advisory committee of this project, Sarva-Shri Sugata Dasgupta, V. Jagannadham, M.C. Nanavatty and S.N. Ranade and, finally, to all the authors and publishers of the extracts included in this publication.

<table>
<tr><td>40, Lodi Estate,</td><td>Dr. (Mrs) Durgabai Deshmukh</td></tr>
<tr><td>New Delhi-3.</td><td>*Honorary Director*</td></tr>
<tr><td>May 5, 1966.</td><td>*Council of Social Development*</td></tr>
</table>

# CONTENTS

*Personnel*

# INTRODUCTION

## K. MUKUNDARAO
### *Project Director*

IT IS NOW widely accepted that programmes aimed toward bringing substantial change in individual and social patterns in any given society should be in harmony with the basic cultural traits of that society. This is not to deny that programmes involving planned individual and social change do sometimes run counter to many existing behaviour patterns and in fact have often as their principal aim a change in these traditional behaviours. While change may be seen as desirable and even necessary, the efforts to bring about these changes should be so directed as not to violate the fundamental value system of the society concerned.

The Post-war era has seen a great spurt in efforts to enhance the quality of living in the less developed areas of the world and among these efforts, the community development movement certainly deserves the place of pride. Although it is true that the community development movement has borrowed heavily from many earlier rural reconstruction efforts and from professional social work methods, the community development programmes have suffered, for all their idealism, from a severe lack of a body of knowledge of tested techniques and more specifically from a dearth of appropriate indigenous teaching material drawn from local experience. This problem has assumed serious proportions in the light of a very rapid—according to several social scientists, too rapid expansion of the innumerable training programmes for the various types of community development workers. The Indian schools of social work who train workers for professional service in various branches of social work have also reported similar problem in regard to the dearth of indigenous teaching material. From the reports of several regional and international meetings, this problem seems to be common to all the developing countries.*

*TAA/AFF/4, United Nations : Asia and the Far East Seminar on Training for Community Development and Social Work. Lahore, 1957.
ST/TAO/WER. C/56. Family and Child Welfare Seminar for Asia and the Far East. Kualalumpur, 1960.
E/CN. 11/L 116(E)/CN. 11/FCW/L.2). Asian Seminar on Training for Family and Child Welfare. Bangkok, 1962.

The present source-book owes its origin to an earlier project conducted in early 1965 under the auspices of the Council for Social Development by Miss Elmina R. Lucke—a former U.N. Consultant. Miss Lucke's project was concerned with human factors in community development and was intended to provide material for a proposed book to be jointly co-authored by her and Prof. Beldon Paulson of the University of Wisconsin. On the conclusion of Miss Lucke's study it was strongly felt in the Council that the valuable material collected so far can form a base for the preparation of a source-book geared toward Indian training needs in community development and professional social work. The Asia Foundation which has sponsored the study by Miss Lucke, enthusiastically supported this idea and provided the needed funds for the additional work connected with the preparation of the source book.

The report of the working group on development of indigenous teaching material for social work (Ecafe Bangkok, 1964) deals with this problem exhaustively and contains valuable suggestions as to how it may be tackled. In regard to community organization and community development, the report states that "for the teaching of community organisation no indigenous text-books are available in this region. Teachers of the subject lean heavily on written text-books as well as articles appearing in foreign journals but have had to adapt most of this literature to suit the socio-cultural patterns of their countries . . . . For the teaching of the course on rural community development, however a large number of text-books are available in the region and serve an excellent teaching material. In addition, reports of programme evaluation organizations and governmental committees on rural development provide a wealth of critical analytical material. It was felt (however) that special attention should be given to the production of suitable teaching material on community organization and community development. (*op. cit.*, pp. 51, 52, 92).

In India, teachers and instructors in the various schools of social work have voiced for a long time the need to develop more and more teaching material that is appropriate to the Indian conditions. No doubt, India perhaps leads other developing countries in the amount of written material that is published dealing with problems connected with planned social change. There are some text-books on community development but the bulk of the material is in the form of articles in magazines and journals, unpublished mimeographed reports, students' field work records and similar sources. Much of this material is not easily accessible to the busy instructor and the need for carefully selected readings from various sources and available in the form of a source book is keenly felt and expressed variously. This is the primary justification for the present publication.

The importance of human factors in bringing about economic and technological changes is now widely accepted, although there is considerable difference of opinion as to how far this recognition is translated into concrete terms at the level of implementation in a programme like community development. To quote Battern "Although the community development worker may need to acquire some technical skills, for example, in developing countries he may need to know something about agriculture or methods of road making or building construction, his basic and primary skill is in working with people. No one community or community group is quite the same as any other, and therefore the worker cannot even be sure that what he has succeeded in doing in one community he can do with equal success in another; and one lesson that all the cases teach is that in this field of work it is the people, not the worker or his agency who are in control."* Human factors particularly refer to the psychological and cultural dimensions of change including attitudes to change and innovations and the nature and degree of flexibility available in a given range of cultural norms. Human factors also include the consideration of the nature and process of interaction between persons and groups, the forms of various hierarchical relationships, self-images and aspiration levels. In short, human factors in the context of the present source-book refer primarily to the impact of the community development programmes on the individual and group and their reaction to the same. This was the major criterion employed in the selection of the extracts, although it is readily admitted that the significance of human factors described as above is not easily discernible in all the extracts. In some extracts, the issues and problems arising out of human factors are explicit and in many others, they are implicit and need to be drawn out by the student and the teacher through discussion.

As mentioned earlier, the extracts were drawn from different sources—published and mimeographed papers. It is readily admitted that the extracts are of varying quality. Some provide only information, some others explore the implications of a given programme and there are other extracts which critically examine the deeper conceptual issues involved. It is hoped that the variety provided in this collection will help in providing not only the basic information regarding community development but also provide an insight into the basic dilemmas inherent in inducing change in rural India. In

*T. R. Batten, *The Human Factor in Community Work*. London, Oxford University Press, 1965, pp. 181.

all cases, the sources are clearly mentioned and acknowledged.

In addition to the above, five field-reports from five different National award winning village level workers are included in the Section IV : Process of Change. These reports were collected after a prolonged period of search from the village level workers who have won the national awards for outstanding performance. It is hoped that this effort to get first-hand field experience will be continued and case records from different types of functionaries in community development will be collected systematically and made available to the training institutions.

Some time ago, in the field of community development one heard often the slogan—Man—the destination. It is earnestly hoped that the present publication will serve to underscore that fundamental ideal and the diverse skills involved in the process of helping people to make a conscious use of their own selves in effecting changes in their inner and outer environment and in choosing the pace and direction of their own growth.

In the end, we gratefully acknowledge the generous support of the Asia Foundation, the advisors Sarvashri Sugata Das Gupta, V. Jagannadhan, M. C. Nanavatty and S. N. Ranade who have provided valuable guidance in the preparation of the source-book, and finally all the authors and publishers of the extracts which are included in the present collection.

# Action for Rural Change

## SETTING FOR CHANGE

### The Village

*In recent years, many viilage studies have been completed by several Indian and foreign social scientists. Most of them describe the social structure, inter-group relationships, the changing role of caste, the nature of hierarchical patterns in the village and other features.*

*Prior to any discussion of the programmes of change and their impact, it is obviously necessary to have an understanding of the nature of the Indian village. The selections in this section discuss some of the salient aspects of the village and its inhabitants.*

## CONTRIBUTORS

1. Hugh Tinker, "The Village in the Framework of Development," in *Administration and Economic Development in India*, Edited by Ralph Braibanti and Joseph J. Spengler, Durham, Duke University Press, 1963, pp. 94-133.

2. K. William Kapp (in collaboration with Lore L. Kapp.), "The Retardation of Economic Development," in *Hindu Culture, Economic Development and Economic Planning in India*, A collection of essays, Bombay, Asia Publishing House, 1963, pp. 41-66.

3. Robert O. Tilman, "The Influence of Caste on Economic Development," in *Administration and Economic Development in India*, Edited by Ralph Braibanti and Joseph J. Spengler, Durham, Duke University Press, 1963, pp. 213-223.

4. Morris Carstairs, "Hindu Personality Formation Conscious Processes", in *The Twice Born*, London, The Hogarth Press, 1961, pp. 137-151.

5. Dorothy Willner, "Community Leadership," in *United Nations Series on Community Development*, New York, United Nations, 1960, pp. 12-14.

6. Evelyn Wood, "Leadership in Community Development," in *International Review of Community Development*, Vol. 8, 1961, pp. 66- .

# THE VILLAGE IN THE FRAMEWORK OF DEVELOPMENT

## *Hugh Tinker*

THE APPROACH OF this essay (as with every other study of the Indian village) is external to the subject. The writer has had practical experience of local government institutions in India and in Britain, but his view of village life is inevitably that of a spectator : one, moreover, who views the 500,000 villages of India as somehow amenable to the artificial description of "the Indian village". In other words, his outlook is that of a historian or political scientist, attempting to deduce a general hypothesis from a wide area of evidence, rather than the observation of the anthropologist, building up his conclusions from a detailed knowledge of a limited area. In this essay we shall consider the attempts (largely by government agencies) to mobilize village society for economic, social and political activities whose ultimate purpose is national. Of course, these attempts to put government policy into practice hinge entirely upon the response of the village folk. All the government activity of the last fifty years or so in this direction has been based on persuasion rather than compulsion (the line of demarcation is sometimes a little hazy, and has, therefore, succeeded or failed only so far as it has won the co-operation of the villagers. But the initiative for all these efforts has been external. There has been nothing to compare (for example) to movements during the last century in Britain, originating entirely among the people, such as the Sunday School movement for adult education, the co-operative movement, or the trades union movement. The twentieth-century Indian village has yet to produce its own panacea for its own needs: even *Bhoodan* is an external force.

However, most observers will agree that Community Development is a massive attempt to enable the ordinary people of India "to want what they need, and do what they want."[1]

During the last ten years the Indian village has been the subject of three main types of investigation. There have been anthropological

---

[1] J.S. Furnivall, *Colonial Policy and Practice*, London, 1948, p. 470. This essay tries to assess the impact of this programme upon village India.

studies—pure research enterprises—which have deepened our understanding of relationships between different social groups within the
village and have explored extra-village ties. There has been work (it
may be described as "social engineering") by political scientists and
others who have developed theories of community behaviour by means
of the application of certain values to actual experience ; in this field
the name of the American town-planner, Albert Mayer, is pre-eminent.
Finally, there has been the activity of administrators, politicians, and
social workers, concerned largely in an ad hoc manner with the practical task of building a new India. These three groups have been
almost exclusively concerned with analysing and evaluating the Indian
village as it is today. They have almost all begun by accepting a
certain model of the village—the village as it has emerged from the
ages—as axiomatic. It is agreed that the Indian village throughout
ages has been a corporate body, guided and guarded by a council,
the panchayat. There is tacit agreement that the functioning of the
panchayat provided a kind of prelude to democracy, even if almost
all careful to qualify their words. Sooner or later Charles Metcalfe's
celebrated phrase about the "little republics" comes out, endowed with
overtones that would astonish Metcalfe himself. Many go on to
suggest that these republics were destroyed by the British; some assert
that this was a deliberate policy of extermination.[1]

The conclusion which generally follows is that the village republic
must be revived as the foundation of the new India; here, it is said, is
a living tradition from which will grow a grass-roots democracy that
is native to Indian soil.

This modern Indian belief in the special political genius of the
people, stemming from times long past and drawing its strength from
local associations, had a parallel in nineteenth-century England.
Toulmin Smith, and those of his school, in urging the importance of
local self-government went back to the Anglo-Saxons and saw in their
Moots and Hundreds the origins of parliamentary democracy.[2]

They affirmed that this community spirit had been passed on to
their descendants, so that Victorian Britons possessed as their birth-
right an innate talent for local organization. Out of this political
mysticism came the spate of late Victorian local government legisla-

---

[1] Thus, V.B. Raju, in Kurukshetra, Oct., 1958 (p. 57), writes, "Panchayats have
been in existence from the Vedic Age .... They continued to be live bodies ....
till about 1800 A.D. when they were mercilessly destroyed by the British."

[2] "It is forgotten that Parishes and our other Local Institutions do not owe their
origin to Parliament; but that, quite the reverse, Parliament itself is a result
derived from out of the pre-existing action of these institutions." Toulmin
Smith, *The Parish*, London, 1857, p. 10.

tion; but few nowadays would rate the achievement of British local government in the twentieth century as fulfilling the faith of the nineteenth.

Present-day Indian belief in the village as the political bedrock stems, of course, largely from the preaching of Gandhi. Forty years ago, Indian political theorists, looking back to their past, considered the village only as the base of royal authority; today, they view the ancient village as a self-governing community.[1]

Gandhi had a semi-mystical vision of the village and ascribed to his ageless (and perhaps idealized community the qualities he sought to inspire in the India of his dreams. His philosophy, drawn from Tolstoy and Kropotkin, rejected the modern state as a foreign accretion upon the true India which he regarded as a federation of village republics, Panchayat Raj. "That state will be best which is governed least," declared Gandhi, and "Society based on non-violence can only consist of groups settled in villages in which voluntary co-operation is the condition of dignified and peaceful existence. . . . The nearest approach to civilisation based on non-violence is the erstwhile village republic India."[2]

Gandhi's teaching has become the accepted doctrine of India's public men. Very few are bold enough to stand up against this idealized concept of village society. During the debates upon India's constitution, Gandhian speakers constantly reiterated the necessity to base the new Indian system of government in "the old plan of Panchayat Raj or decentralised democracy."[3]

Only Dr. Ambedkar, leader of the *harijans*, was bold enough to call these arguments obscurantist: he declared, "The love of the intellectual Indian for the village community is of course infinite if not pathetic. . . . I hold that these village republics have been the ruination of India. . . . What is the village but a sink of localism, a den of ignorance, narrow-mindedness and communalism? I am glad that the Draft Constitution has discarded the village and adopted the individual as its unit."[4]

---

[1] As a factual illustration of the change, the treatment given to a passage from the *Sukraniti*, a medieval political treatise. In the standard translation by B.K. Sarkar (Allahabad, 1914) the six chief officials are clearly shown as servants of the king p. 76. In 1954 a Congress committee which included scholars of repute could refer to these officials as examples of "composite leadership for management of village affairs." See Report of the Congress Village Panchayat Committee, New Delhi, 1954, p. 19.

[2] Cited in S.N. Agarwal, *Gandhian Constitution for Free India,* Allahabad, 1946, pp. 39, 58.

[3] Indian Legislative Assembly, Debates, XI, 690.

[4] *Ibid.*, VII, 39.

However, Dr. Ambedkar found few supporters in the Constitutional Assembly, and the belief in "the self-sufficient village community" remains an article of faith with most Indian intellectuals.[1]

Recent American anthropological work has sought to revise that oft-accepted view of the village as a self-sufficient unit. The multiplicity of ties (social, economic and religious) which have made the village part of the "great society" have been elaborated. Yet, two of the most perceptive of such studies agree that an Indian village is "a living thing . . . . a system," with "a well-defined separate entity and an individual quality."[2]

Most Indians are subject to a whole series of interlocking communities, but the only territorial tie that is really compulsive is the village. The district, the state (now that this is everywhere based upon linguistic grouping) are both important, it is true; but the village is the sheet-anchor of a man's sense of place, of home. This becomes sharply clear with regard to those who appear to have cut loose from the village. The professional man, cosmopolitan and urban, clings to his piece of ancestral village land, although it yields him nothing but trouble and expense, because it is his link with home. The factory worker in the distant city still calls himself a member of X village.[3]

The purpose Marwari banker on industrialist maintains his connections with his ancestral village in Rajasthan.

There is no space here to trace out the remote origins of this intense loyalty to one particular huddle of houses and patch of ground (this loyalty, we may note, is in sharp contrast to the much looser village ties of Burma and Malaya). Certainly this loyalty was intensified by the eighteenth-century Time of Troubles (the Gardi-ka-Wakht) when central authority collapsed and local communities had to fend for themselves against marauders and the exactions of local tyrants. This factor is identified by a modern British anthropologist with regard to Malwa. Quoting accounts he was given of inter-village

---

[1] See, for example, A.H. Desai, *Social Background of Indian Nationalism,* 3rd ed, Bombay, 1959, p. 7. "The Self-sufficient village as the basic economic unit had existed for centuries in India." Desai cites, in support of his belief, Metcalfe's Minute: it is typical of this cogent, forceful, but slipshod book that he does not cite the Minute accurately.

[2] McKim Marriott, ed ; *Village India: Studies in the Little Community,* Chicago, 1955, p. 176; and Morris E. Opler, "The Extensions of an Indian Village," Journal of Asian Studies, XVI, No. I (1956), p. 5.

[3] A Christian missionary, working among industrial labourers in suburban Calcutta spoke of his difficulties in welding the Christians into a real congregation: "None of them regard this as their church," he said. "The church is somewhere in Bihar or U.P., even though some of them have lived all their lives here in Calcutta."

relations, he says, "Formerly, it seems, villages were separate units, linked only by the ties of kinship between their inhabitants of the same sub-caste. In the unsettled days of the early nineteenth century, villages were maintained by the courage and acumen of their headmen who had to defend the place from marauders."[1]

This quotation brings us back to the question of village leadership. In matters requiring immediate action and decision a committee cannot lead; in the Indian village today there is usually one outstanding individual who leads, because of hereditary status or personal ability.[2]

And so it was in the Gardi-ka-Wakht, from the evidence of contemporary writers such as Sir William Sleeman. The headman is sometimes represented as a creature of the British administrative system, but there was an older type of headman (the patel, chaudhuri, desai) who corresponded more to the English squire, or perhaps the Burmese myothugyi. Such men the villagers recognized as their leaders. But what of the panchayat? Here we must attempt to disentangle legend from historical evidence. There is a clear record of the village panchayat in ancient India, but it is far from certain that it was found everywhere.[3]

In south India there is some evidence that the panchayat was composed of the representatives of the different castes.[4]

During the Middle Ages the panchayat virtually disappears from the record. The Muslim historians who portrayed the Indian scene in such careful detail give it no mention. Indeed, for this long period references to village life are scanty; among these few is the picture of Bengali rural life depicted by Mukunda Ram.[5]

The absence of evidence has not prevented historians from assum-

---

1 Adrian Mayer, "Local Government Elections in a Malwa Village," Eastern Anthropologist, XI (1958), 193. Mayer stresses the separateness of individual villages.

2 Cf. J.T. Hitchcock, "Leadership in a North Indian Village," in *Leadership and Political Institutions in India,* ed.; Richard L. Park and Irene Tinker, Princeton, 1959, pp. 395-414.

3 Even such a careful historian as A.L. Basham can write, "The village council is rarely referred to in most sources, though it certainly existed all over India... We have no record of the composition of the village council in the North." *The Wonder That Was India*, London, 1954, pp. 105-106.

4 Cf. H. Tinker, *The Foundations of Local Self-Government in India Pakistan and Burma*, London, 1954, p. 19. It may be significant that the same practice is followed in south India in modern times op. cit., p. 198.; see also Park and Tinker, *op. cit.*, p. 430.

5 See, J.N. Das Gupta, *Bengal in the Sixteenth Century*, Calcutta, 1914, based upon Mukunda Ram and other contemporary writers. Das Gupta produces no evidence for the existence of the village panchayat; he does not even mention it.

ing that "village committees" were functioning throughout the Mughul period. The first really firm references to the panchayat were made by British administrators like Munro and Elphinstone at the beginning of the nineteenth century. Perhaps too much has been adduced from what they said. Englishmen (and Americans) look at the world through political spectacles; in their society any kind of organized activity tends to be a reflection of the town meeting or the parish council. It seems possible that the British pioneers in describing the panchayat saw it first as a reflection of their own accustomed municipal institutions. Certainly, mistake assumption were made.[1]

For what it is worth, the following formulation is suggested. The word panchayat describes form, not purpose—a technique of seeking agreement through consultation, hallowed, according to tradition, by divine sanction: *panch men parameswar*. This technique was mainly employed in social or economic organisms (the closest Western parallels are the medieval trade guild or the Victorian friendly society) but it was also extensively used for the arbitration of both caste and village disputes.[2]

With possible reservations regarding south India, the panchayat was not an administrative body in the usually accepted sense, but it was sometimes employed to apportion the village land revenue assessment and may have had a role in regulating the duties of the village servants. Most probably, when its members assumed this quasi-administrative role, they belonged to the dominant *zamindar* or proprietor group, descendants of the putative founder of the village.

If the panchayat first found a place in the records of administration thanks to the field-work of pioneer British officials, such as

---

[1] In Bengal the early British administrators concluded that the "village" watchman they found must be the servant of the village; he was actually the agent of the absentee landlord. See W.W. Hunter, *Annals of Rural Bengal*, London, 1868, p. 334. One of the best accounts of north India in the early nineteenth century is the narrative of *A Journal through the Kingdom of Oude in 1849-1850*, by Sir W.H. Sleeman, 2 Vols., London, 1858. Sleeman, a master of observation, makes one reference to a judicial panchayat. He constantly produces evidence to show that the Oude peasants followed their landlords' orders without any kind of village consultation: see I, 253-254.

[2] One Indian writer, at least has reached the same conclusions. K.S.V. Raman, in Kurukshetra, Jan. 26, 1961, p. 26, writes: "There seems to be hardly sufficient ground to maintain that Panchayats as institutions of self-government for an area, are indigenous to India. A few public works committees organised in the South, and a few *Janapadas* in the North may have worked in the past. Otherwise Panchayats seem to have been organisation mainly for adjudication of disputes of a particular profession or class, sometimes distributed over fairly large areas."

Munro and Elphinstone, their successors turned their attention else-where. For a quarter of a century the British in India were imbued with a belief in reform and the beneficent influence of Western ideas and institutions: Indian law and custom were regarded as super-annuated. This movement largely came to an end with the Mutiny. Thereafter, British policy was conservative. From believing that India could be changed within a generation, the British came to be-lieve in "the unchanging East". Matthew Arnold wrote at this time:

The East bow'd low before the blast,
In patient, deep disdain.
She let the legions thunder past.
And plunged in thought again.[1]

The British administration was, as it were, a dome over the life of India. Traditional Indian institutions were permitted to function; but an aloof, *laissez-faire* philosophy did little to stimulate activity. An excellent illustration of contemporary policy is Lord Lawrence's Resolution on Local Self-Government of 1864: "The people of this country are perfectly capable of administering their own local affairs. The municipal feeling is deeply rooted in them. The village communi-ties are the most abiding of Indian institutions. . . . Holding the posi-tion we do in India, every view of duty and policy should induce us to leave as much as possible of the business of the country to be done by the people".[2]

Yet, while this was the declared policy, the forces which the British had set in motion (what Lord Dalhousie called "The engines of progress") were sapping ancient institutions and ways of life. A recent Indian survey observes, not unjustly, that "While on the one hand the Britishers created tier upon tier of course of law they also tried to revive in their peculiar half-hearted manner the panchayat system of judicial administration."[3]

Throughout the nineteenth century there were spasmodic efforts to succour the panchayat and relate it to the structure of government. In the 1880's Lord Ripon sought to raise his new system of local self-government upon the ancient village system; typical of the legislation which followed was the Madras Village Courts Act of 1888. During the parliamentary debates upon the Indian Councils Act of 1892 (the measure which introduced elected members into the Indian legislatures), Sir W. Plowden moved that the new legisla-

---

1 From "Obermann Once More."
2 Tinker, *op. cit.*, p. 36.
3 G.S. Chooramani, *Nyaya Panchayats and Panchayati Adalats in Uttar Pradesh* (Bureau of Agricultural Information), Lucknow, pp. 2-3.

tors be selected throughout India by panchayats.[1]

But there was no sustained support for the panchayats, and every trend of the times served to complete the disintegration of traditional custom and influence. The pressure of the courts of law, the railways, new patterns of trade, and the shift of power to new classes all had their effect on traditional village society. Tarlok Singh, out of the breadth of his knowledge, sums up thus:

For several decades, as a well-knit social organisation the village community has been slowly but steadily declining. As the pursuit of individual interest within and outside the village has become more common, the influence of the community over its members has diminished. The growth of inequality in the ownership of land, land transfers to non-cultivators and migration to towns are evidence of these trends. . . . The old leadership in the village has been losing its position and influence without substantial signs of a new leadership stepping into its place. The institution of caste has less of social incidence, but it may well be that the economic incidence of caste . . . is being accentuated. . . . In this situation conflicts of interest within the village community have sharpened and the process continues. There are now few values which can be said to be common to the whole community, and certainly there is no common purpose which inspires all sections equally.[2]

This historical sketch has attempted to establish that, while the panchayat is an ancient institution of unique prestige, it provides no precedent for the village council of today. During the greater part of recorded time panchayats were ignored by officials and official chroniclers until after the arrival of the British. Thereafter, attempts to endow the panchayat with some kind of formal status failed, partly because the British had no firm policy, but mainly because the panchayat could not resist the assaults of the modern age. These points have been made at some length as a reminder that the assumptions that the present-day village council has a historical antecedent, and that village solidarity exists as a social force ready to be tapped, are both without foundation.

From the early 1900's the role of government in India began to be diversified. The old style of village contacts with the machinery of government—and the kind of leaders which it had brought forward —can be glimpsed in this cameo of village leadership in Punjab, delineated by a reforming British district officer: "Socrates came into the

---

[1] House of Common Debates, London, April 25, 1892. His amendment was defeated 94 to 47.
[2] Tarlok Singh, *The Village Panchayat and the Pattern of Village Development* (mimeographed, 1955), pp. 2-3.

village and found the patwari and the kanungo and the zaildar and sufedposh sitting with the lambardars, discussing the new jamabandi . . . 'Good morning' said Socrates . . . 'Silence' said the patwari. 'Can't you see the hakims are taking counsel together? Who are you, old man, to interfere with your croaking?' "[1]

Who are these folk? They are the petty revenue officials (petty in their superiors' eyes, but all-important to the villagers) and the village bigwigs who are responsible for insuring that the land revenue is paid, and that law and order are maintained. Their discussion is concerned with the revenue record (jamabandi: literally, "binding and tightening") and if any outsider dares to interrupt their grave counsels he is peremptorily repulsed. This was the old order, but as the twentieth century opened, social welfare and political education received higher priority. The Decentralisation Commission, reporting in 1909, insisted that a whole-hearted attempt must be made to build up village councils: "the foundation of any stable edifice which shall associate the people with the administration, must be the village". Panchayats must be constituted, with petty civil and criminal jurisdiction, and responsibility for village sanitation, education, and minor public works.[2]

In the following years legislation was passed to implement these reforms, such as the Punjab Panchayats Act of 1912; but it was not until after World War I that this legislation became effective, so far as it was effective. The period bears the same relation to the present that an overture does to an opera. Every problem that has exercised Indian opinion since independence was first sounded during the Dyarchy years.[3]

Perhaps the dominant problems was the uneasy balance between established autocracy and immature democracy in a time of transition. Is it possible for the high official to hand over power to elected representatives of the public while at the same time retaining a measure of residuary power and responsibility in the expectation that the elected leaders will conform to the same code that he follows? A tall order, but it might be done, given good will on both sides. During Dyarchy the Congress was dedicated to the principle that there could be no co-operation with the British administration; so the only contribution of the chief political party to local government was to

---

[1] F.L. Brayne, *Socrates in an Indian Village* (London, 1937), p. 47. Socrates is, of course, the author, Patwari is the village accountant, *kanungo*, the (superior) circle revenue officer. The others are "squires" or yeomen, presented in order of diminishing importance.

[2] Tinker, *op. cit.*; p. 85.

[3] Tinker, *op. cit.*; pp. 116-118 and 197-213.

further its disruption. But, leaving aside politics, there was an inescapable ambivalence in this transitional situation. The traditional attitude to the administration was aptly summarized by an experienced Pakistani official:

In one important respect the British regime before a strong resemblance to the regimes that had preceded it. It was essentially a Mai-Bap (Mother-Father) regime. The King-Emperor was not averse to be viewed as a benign and kindly being who had replaced the Grand Moghal and had been ordained to look after the interests of his subjects. A certain psychological atmosphere was created. A belief was assiduously fostered that the Government was capable of doing everything under the sun . . . A school wall is cracking up in the rural area; well, the Government will set it right. A small bund is needed to save the people from seasonal floods; why not address a representation to the Government? That will do the trick . . . Such an attitude killed initiative.[1]

The newly constituted panchayats functioned against this background—and also against a barrage of adverse propaganda from the Congress. Despite certain good work (particularly in the traditional sphere of judicial arbitration), they disappointed expectations; especially, they failed to create a sense of belonging to the village.[2]

Because the villagers thought of themselves as separated from an aloof and beneficent government, they were exceedingly reluctant to introduce new taxes or to collect taxes actually introduced; "Government will provide." With absurdly small financial resources they were able to accomplish little.

In the 1930's emphasis was transferred to rural construction or rural uplift, the precursor of Community Development. This idea was first launched by individualism of whom F.L. Brayne and M.L. Darling are the best known. In the early days, their activity "was regarded (by higher authority) as a heresay practised by crazy district officers".[3]

But in time these ideas became official orthodoxy. Brayne, in arid, parched Gurgaon, tried to awaken the villagers to possibilities of agricultural and domestic betterment; he devised a scheme of Village Guides, as a kind of bridgehead whereby the activities of the "nation

---

[1] *Village Aid in West Pakistan* (Village Aid Administration, Lahore, 1957), pp. 20-21.

[2] When in 1958 the writer visited villages which (according to the records had set up panchayats in the 1920's, he was sometimes met with denials that a panchayat had ever existed there, perhaps because it had been so ineffective or perhaps because, to the villagers, it had never been "their" panchayat.

[3] *Village Aid in West Pakistan*, p. 56.

building" departments might be more effectively brought into touch with the villagers. Brayne's approach was empirical. He intended that in each individual village, the people should work out their own solution to social and economic problems. But Gurgaon District was an especially difficult area in which to make progress. Partly because of its appalling climatic uncertainty, partly because of its long history of invasion and disturbance, the people were suspicious and unresponsive. Brayne found himself in a dilemma familiar to the social reformer: he had to win over a hostile audience. Among his official colleagues there were many who cast doubt on his motives and denied the validity of his theories, while among the people of the district there was an equal disbelief in the new ideas. He had to show results; and that meant forcing the pace. Brayne probably tried to push through too much too quickly; he himself realized that his approach relied to a dangerous degree upon his own personal leadership and example. His detractors (of whom there was no shortage alleged that the "Gurgaon Experiment" left no permanent legacy, and unfortunately for students of Community Development it is to no one's interest to attempt an objective assessment of Brayne's work.[1]

The rural reconstruction programme did achieve a distinct measure of success, but mainly in material terms: new wells, drains, paved lanes. All this depended heavily on higher direction.[2]

Following independence, Congress's plans for regenerating local administration began from two main premises. There was the Gandhian doctrine which led to including among the Directive Principles of the Constitution a provision for the formation of village panchayats as "units of self government" (Article 40). There was also a conviction that autocratic administration and public passivity were exclusively derived from British rule and would now disappear with independence.[3]

There was renewed activity in devising a legislative framework for administrative panchayats.[4]

---

[1] Cf. Brayne, *op. cit.*; pp. 116-119; see also Albert Mayer and associates, *Pilot Project India*, (Berkeley, 1958), p.19: "Brayne's work, it seemed, had not in any permanent way affected village well-being, life or outlook." No evidence is offered that Mr. Mayer actually visited Brayne's Gurgaon villages.

[2] In visiting villages where development work is flourishing today, the writer was impressed with the number which had been prominent in the programme of the 1930's. But the "sample" was too small to show whether this correlation was significant.

[3] Cf. Albert Mayer, *op. cit.*; p. 8 Nehru wrote in 1946 to Mayer, "Our people have naturally developed a number of complexes during these past generations of foreign rule and foreign exploitation. But we can get over them. . . . "

[4] See Report of the Congress Panchayat Committee, Appendix B (Panchayat Organisation in India).

One important consideration was the size of the proposed administrative unit: should this be the nucleated village (the actual village community which might comprise a small market town of three thousand or a hamlet of fifty souls) or should it be manufactured out of combinations of villages and hamlets to make an area which would be viable in terms of competent leadership and adequate financial resources ? This question had been debated through the Dyarchy period, and both solutions had been found to have disadvantages. In Uttar Pradesh under the 1947 Act, the countryside was divided into Gaon Sabha (administrative) circles, containing a population of about a thousand and comprising an average of three or four villages; the executive committee of the Sabha was the elected Gaon Panchayat. Three or four Gaon Sabha circles formed a Panchayati Adalat (local court). With the abolition of landlordism in Uttar Pradesh village management committees (Gaon Samaj) were formed in every village, leading to "chaotic conditions" of conflicting jurisdiction.[1]

Subsequently, the area of the administrative panchayat was narrowed so that each village with a minimum population of 250 had its own panchayat. The other states can be divided into a "big panchayat" group (Madras, Andhra, Orissa, Bihar, Rajasthan, Kerala, and Himachal Pradesh) and a "small panchayat" group (Bombay, Madhya Pradesh, Punjab).[2]

The trend towards a larger unit appears to predominate.[3]

This is applauded in what is probably the most influential survey of local administration which has appeared since independence—the Mehta Report:

Little panchayats constituted for small villages are generally swayed by narrower considerations and sometimes dominated by caste interests which are toned down in a bigger body, comprising a number of villages inhabited by practically all castes. Membership of such a body infuses a wider outlook and a sense of responsibility which transcends narrow and parichial considerations.[4]

In general, the panchayat experiment showed the same discouraging

---

[1] Report of the U.P. Panchayat Raj Amendment Act Committee (Lucknow, 1954), p. 14.

[2] West Bengal, Mysore, and Assam "have not made any appreciable progress" in establishing panchayats; see Fifth Evaluation Report, Programme Evaluation organisation, Planning Commission (New Delhi, 1958), p. 17.

[3] According to the Fifth Evaluation Report, the average population of each panchayat circle in a sample survey was 2,600.

[4] Report of the Team for the Study of Community Projects and National Extension Service (Balvantray G. Mehta, Leader) (New Delhi, Committee on Plan Projects, Government of India, 1957) Vols. I and II (Nov., 1957); Vol. III (Parts I and II) Dec., 1957 II, 3.

refusal to "get off the ground" as before independence. Reporting in November, 1957, the Mehta team declared that "the available information indicates that possibly not more than 10 per cent of the total number of panchayats are functioning effectively."[1]

Their poor performance stems directly from the circumstances of rural life. Faction dominates most Indian villages, and "the number of panchayats which are torn by factions or in which squabbles are rampant is large. In fact in some States they are in a majority."[2]

"Panchayat elections have resulted in creating or aggravating factional rivalries in about one-third of the villages in which there was a contest."[3]

Also, "separatism arising out of caste distinction" is said to be on the increase, and "caste becomes a political division of society at the same time it is losing its position as a ritual division.[4]

The remedy often urged is a return to the ancient tradition of choosing village leaders by general agreement. "It is this principle of unanimity which was the soul of panchayats in ancient India, and it... requires revivification."[5]

Many committees are formed with an appearance of unanimous support, but frequently the absence of an election merely "indicates lack of interest in the community."[6]

Committees are usually dominated by the conservative, upper-caste prosperous elements in the village; one survey reported that, on an average, 60 per cent of members were over forty years old, and 90 per cent were landowners.[7]

"The economically weaker sections have as yet little voice in the affairs of the panchayat."[8]

The Minister for the Local Self-Government in Uttar Pradesh observed (in 1954) that "the panchayats and district boards alike suffered more from poverty than from any other evil or disease."[9]

Of course, Indian villages are desperately poor, but the poverty of the panchayats is at least partially self-inflicted. They have been given powers to impose taxes, but do not apply them; taxes in force

---

1 *Ibid.*, II, I.
2 *Ibid.*, II, 7.
3 *Ibid.*, I, 18.
4 *Ibid.*, I, 18; and Adrian Mayer, *op. cit.*, p. 202.
5 Report of the Congress Village Panchayat Committee, p. 22.
6 Fifth Evaluation Report, p. 18. Six of the eight panchayats investigated by Adrian Mayer in Malwa were constituted by unanimous choice of the villagers. Mayer, *op. cit.*, p. 210.
7 Fifth Evaluation Report, p. 18.
8 Mehta, Report, II, 2.
9 Report of the U.P. Panchayat Raj Amendment Act Committee, p. 18.

are not collected; average collections are less than 50 per cent and in some states less than 30 per cent. Panchayat members are themselves frequent defaulters.[1]

The majority of panchayats have a total annual income, inclusive of grants, of less than Rs. 500 ($100). Of the funds collected, at least half is absorbed by administrative costs.[2]

A large proportion of the panchayats fail to render an account of their financial stewardship to the general body of the Gaon Sabha as required by law.[3]

It is not surprising that their over-all record is unfavourable. A survey of sixty panchayats at work revealed that only about twenty made provision for lighting and sweeping the streets, while "Their role in economic development is negligible."[4]

Reports of this kind began to mount up in the early 1950's but attention had already shifted to another sphere (Community Development) reproducing almost exactly the sequence of the 1920's and 1930's. During the first decade of independence there was an increasing degree of official and centralized control throughout the whole range of local affairs. The Mehta Report speaks of "the gradual eclipse of district boards from the social polity."[5]

In many states the boards were relieved of their main functions, such as education, the highways, and medical care. All over India, individual boards and municipalities were superseded and their functions vested in appointed government officials. The new constitutions drafted for such major municipalities as Greater Poona and Greater Delhi transferred the actual powers of management to a Municipal Commissioner, a senior administrator. In consonance with this national trend, rural reconstruction was placed almost exclusively in the hands of government officials. The purpose of the Community Development Programme is thus defined by V.T. Krishnamachari:

To create in the millions of rural families a burning desire to change their old-time outlook and arouse enthusiasm in them for new knowledge and new ways of life. This "will to live better" is to be brought about by ensuring that every family has a programme for increased employment and production for which it is assisted: that every family is represented on at least one multi-purpose cooperative society in its own right: that every family makes its voluntary contribution to works

[1] Mehta, Report, II, 7; and Fifth Evaluation Report, p. 20.
[2] Report of the Congress......Committee, p. 47.
[3] Report of the U.P.......Committee, p. 28.
[4] Fifth Evaluation Report, p. 23.
[5] Mehta, Report, II, 12.

of benefit to the community as a whole.[1]

The new movement was set in motion in 1952, and in conception and organization drew heavily upon the Etawah Pilot Project. Albert Mayer, the overseer of this project, had laid great emphasis upon assisting the village folk to realize "felt needs"—to attain ends which they themselves desired rather than what the government thought was good for them; to create a co-operative effort, with villagers and government technicians pulling together as a team, dissolving the age-old division between aloof officials and docile villagers. Mayer made no claim to have discovered new principles but did claim to have "systematized" previous methods and to have enrolled all concerned in a sense of shared decision and effort.[2]

The Etawah Project started with the advantages of consistent support from the highest in the land, a hand-picked team of workers, and an area that was manageable and had a tradition of local initiative. Great emphasis was laid on the role of the Village Level Worker (Gram Sevak) as a "multi-purpose worker and friend of the village people."[3]

The aim was to establish a new kind of relationship between the Gram Sevak and the small group of villages with which he was linked —that of a social worker rather than of a minor government servant. The success of the Etawah Project was undoubted, but this was ue (more than Mayer and his colleagues cared to admit to their own single-minded leadership. And as the scope of the project was enlarged, the "felt needs" of the people became submerged in the larger plans of the government. The autonomy of the development organization and staff, to which Mayer attached great value, was increasingly sapped away; the control of the administrators was extended until, in 1954, the District Officer became directly responsible for development work in his district.

However, long before this, the Etawah Project had become merged in a national programme. In 1952 fifteen pilot projects were inaugurated in different states on the Etawah model of a "block" of 60 to 100 villages, the block being divided into circles of 5 or 6 villages under the Gram Sevak. By the end of 1958 there were 2,361 blocks covering about 300,000 villages with a population, of 162 million (about three-fifths of rural India). Yet this immense achievement was accompanied by an ever-increasing volume of criticism. The Mehta Report, which appeared in November, 1957, brought this to a head, insisting

1 V. T. Krishnamachari, "The National Extension Movement and Community Projects," Sainik Samachar, Jan. 1957.

2 Albert Mayer, *op. cit.*, p. 65.

3 *Ibid.*, p. 82.

that the programme was right off its course; it had been meant to kindle a new sense of community and assist in launching the "take-off" in economic development, but instead it had been diverted into an officially controlled "bricks and mortar" programme of public works, devoid of almost any popular dynamic.[1]

The Govind Sahay Committee, appointed by the government of Uttar Pradesh came to a similar conclusion: it reported "The whole programme has suffered from a lack of vitality and is tending to degenerate into a number of material benefits for a limited few. In the absence of a proper perspective and an ideological bias, the programme has not so far developed into a people's movement with a purpose. It is mostly spoon-fed, and lacks a purpose."[2]

A review prepared by the Development and Planning Division of the Reserve Bank of India estimated that the contribution made by the people, during the period of the First Five Year Plan, came to 34.9 per cent of total expenditure; it rose in 1956-57 to 40.8 per cent of the total, and then steadily declined to 28.4 per cent in 1959-60. The Bank review adds: "there is also a tendency to overvalue this contribution. Anyway, it seems the programme has lost its original attraction".[3]

What were the reasons, in detail, why the "government programme" failed to evolve into a "people's programme," as the publicists insisted it would? The following is offered as a very tentative analysis.

The block has been the working unit for development, but the level of effective administrative decision has been that of the state or district. The First Five Year Plan forecast that the "first effect......of development will be to increase the district officer's work and responsibility still further".[4]

The district officer is the bottleneck of the government process: loaded with new duties, compelled to fulfil a quasi-political role (like the French prefect yet still burdened with all his former responsibilities, he is now expected to coordinate and inspire development. He is supposed to share this task with a district advisory committee but everywhere this committee has been little more than a formality. The First Plan urged that the district boards should have "a vital part to play" but "in practice these recommendations have not been carried out to any great extent".[5]

---

[1] *Cf.* Kurukshetra, April, 1959, p. 11: "Successive evaluation reports have pointed out that community development programme in India is Government's programme carried out with people's participation and not people's programme."

[2] Quoted in Kurukshetra, March 1961, pp. 17-18.

[3] Reserve Bank of India, Bulletin, Jan., 1961.

[4] First Five Year Plan (New Delhi, 1952), p. 131.

[5] First Five Year Plan, p. 131; and Second Five Year Plan, 1956, p. 160.

The district officer remains the keystone of the development structure but has been unable to make this his principal concern. He has often to delegate his work to the district planning officer, and the departmental district-level officials resent the interposition of this officer (often their junior in service). They often persist in pursuing the policy laid down by their department. Block Development Officers (BDO's) find they are under a system of "duplicate control" and have to refer to two sets of superiors; some BDO's talk of "a Cold War among the higher ups. . . . Administrative coordination as it exists at present is only a pious word."[1]

The BDO is the actual supervisor of activities in the field.[2]

Sometimes he comes from the Agricultural or the Veterinary Department; some are directly recruited university graduates; a few are promoted Gram Sevaks; and in several states all BDO's are appointed from the Revenue Service. In Bihar and Bombay the Tahsildar or Mamlatdar (subordinate revenue officers) has to run a block in addition to his regular duties. The block programme planning, budgeting, etc. is supposed to be decided by the Block Advisory Committee, but this body has all too often had the same shadowy existence as its district counterpart. Membership of the committee is commonly sought and awarded purely for reasons of status and prestige.[3]

In most blocks at least a year elapses—the most critical year—before a committee is constituted. In size they vary from over 150 in Uttar Pradesh down to 18 in Kerela. Where the committee is unwidely it is difficult to get through the business, and where it is small the official component is too strong to permit an effective local voice to be heard.[4]

Attendance of non-officials averages a little over 50 per cent.[5]

---

[1] Mehta Report, II, 44.

[2] The block headquarters staff also includes assistant development officers, one for agriculture, one for social education, and one for panchayats and co-operatives. There is usually an engineer one or two health visitors, a veterinary officer, and others; *see* Mehta, Report, II, 38.

[3] (Fourth) Evaluation Report, 1957, p. 18.

[4] Of the 150-160 U.P. members, 138 on average are non-officials and 21 officials; in Madras there are twice as many official members as non-officials; in Bihar there is an average of 15 officials to 13 non-officials. Mehta Report, II, 90.

[5] Where attendance figures of non-officials are worst (in U.P. with 40 per cent), the highest proportion (90 per cent) "felt they could effectively influence decisions". In Bihar, where the attendance record is the best (72 per cent) the proportion who thought they could influence decisions was lowest (30 per cent). This paradox seems to indicate that statistics based upon reported opinions should be accepted with caution. It is inconceivable that if the Bihar representatives thought they could do no good, they should continue to turn up in large numbers. See Mehta, Report, II, 93.

To the village representative, attendance at block headquarters means a journey of many miles over rough roads, out of his familiar environment into an alien, official milieu. Most block headquarters are modest enough—bare brick buildings with no luxuries—but they are laid out in traditional official "contonment" style, with the traditional office peon, symbol of petty extortion, at the door. At the meeting the villager is uneasily aware that he is not on his home ground but is dealing with officials very much on their ground; his instinct is to defer, to "play it safe".[1]

And so the officials make the decisions—for the good of the people, of course, but without their active participation. Instead of Community Development being built up out of rural needs, it is dispensed from above, often concentrated into a few major projects which are easier to plan and administer and yield concrete results. Of course it is practical policy not to scatter the never plentiful funds around in penny packets—a few rupees in this village, a few in that, and nothing permanent to show for it anywhere. But an unduly large share has gone into bricks and mortar, sometimes into office buildings; "apart from being waste, (this) has an unfavourable effect upon the people's minds and widens the gulf between the people" and administrators.[2]

That gulf has remained in the mind of the village folk, and the original intention of development, whereby the administrator's role would be to "prime the pump"—to insure that a venture was fairly launched and then transfer authority to the people—has been disappointed. In many areas, when the impulse from above has weakened, the people's contribution has dwindled away.[3]

The originators of Community Development envisaged the Village Level Worker (Gram Sevak) as the vital link between government and people, the means whereby popular initiative might be awakened and sustained; but the Gram Sevak has not always been able to fulfil these expectations. To a highly status-conscious society, his status remains peculiarly ambivalent.[4]

Is he on the side of the villagers or that of the government? He is not received as a social worker, as the Gandhian village workers were; but it is entirely correct to assume that the Gram Sevak "earning less

[1] The phrase comes from Evelyn Wood, "Patterns of Influence in Rural India," In Park and Tinker, *op. cit.*, pp. 372-390. This study of peasant psychology should be required reading for all concerned in Community Development.
[2] Mehta, Report, I, 117.
[3] Mehta, Report, I, 115.
[4] For a detailed analysis of his position, see S.C. Dube, *India's Changing Villages* (London, 1958), p. 177.

than Rs. 100 a month is a new bureaucrat whether he likes it or not."[1]

His role is such a novelty that he is often able to create his own *persona*. This partially depends upon the number of villages for which he is made responsible; the greater his area, the less of a "villager" he will be. His jurisdiction has varied widely, but the average appears to fall between 10 and 17 villages, with a population of 8,000 to 14,000.[2]

In the Etawah scheme the Gram Sevak had been responsible for only four villages. It seems that most of his time is spent in the head-quarters village; those more distant (45 per cent of the total) are visited less than once a month.[3]

However, the Gram Sevak is the most frequent visitor among the village level government agents.[4]

Another important element influencing his position is, of course, his caste. Official reports are silent on this matter, and one can only surmise that many Gram Sevaks are *brahmans* or members of the higher agricultural caste (such as rajputs and jats): non-agriculturalists (such as kayasthas or banias) will be few and harijans even fewer.[5]

In this situation the Gram Sevak will tend to work with upper-caste, conservative village leaders, leaving the "have-nots" outside. But his personality will be of greatest consequence: what does he himself make of the job? His list of duties is Herculean: it includes agriculture, animal husbandry, and irrigation; "human development" or welfare activities; help to youth, women, and section of the community needing special assistance; and in general "he should function as the sevak, or servant of the village and help individual villagers."[6]

But it is reported that many Gram Sevaks acquired a place in village esteem not so much for acting as a universal Mr. Fixit but because, when the programmes were first launched, ample government funds became available and the Gram Sevaks were able to arrange for subventions, supplies, and credits for their villagers.[7]

When this "give away" phase tapered off, some Gram Sevaks found their position had altered and their role in village society became nebulous.

Some reacted by "getting more 'official' in their behaviour" and acquiring a tendency "to prefer desk work to field work."[8]

1  Park and Tinker, *op. cit.,* p. 385.
2  Mehta, Report, III, Pt. II, 105.
3  Fifth Evaluation Report, p. 12.
4  Mehta, Report, III, Pt. II, 102.
5  See Dube *op. cit .,* 159.
6  Fourth Evaluation Report, p. 27.
7  Fourth Evaluation Report, p. 28.
8  Fourth Evaluation Report, p. 26-27; and Mehta, Report, I, 120.

The Gram Sevaks began to "expect the villagers to come to their 'offices' for their requirements," but they in turn were put in their place by their superiors: "at the least provocation, the Gram Sevak was required to visit the Block headquarters for small odds and ends in which the BDO and his extension staff were interested."[1]

There was an almost total eclipse of the "team" concept of development by the traditional "hierarchic" bureaucratic relationship. The Gram Sevak is not treated as the key pioneer in a new adventure of nation-building but as the lowliest figure in yet another branch of administration, to fetch and carry for official or political bosses.

The diminution of the status of the Gram Sevak is related to the minor role assigned to village leaders in Community Development. It is scarcely credible that, after all the talk about panchayats and village democracy, they were given no effective place in the new enterprise; yet such was the case. Despite long passages in both the First and the Second Five Year Plans on "Village Planning and Village Panchayats" it was still necessary in 1957 to acknowledge that" they have not come into the (development) field to any appreciable extent."[2]

Instead of incorporating the already established panchayats, in most areas ad hoc development committees (Vikas Mandal) were set up, bringing a fourth committee into the village to be set alongside the administrative panchayat, the co-operative, and the land management committee. In some states, the development staff are linked with the Panchayat Raj, and elsewhere the work of the two parallel departments is brought into some sort of alliance, but in many areas the panchayats were entirely by-passed by those in charge of Community Development on the grounds that they were "dormant, inactive and ineffective."[3]

The situation is analogous to that which elicited F.W. Maitland's celebrated aphorism concerning the old unreformed English boroughs: "untrusted because untrustworthy, untrustworthy became untrusted."

One survey, designed to assess village responsiveness, declared that:

Suggestions for raising income and for increasing taxes are forthcoming much more readily from those blocks where the panchayats

---

[1] Mehta, Report, II, 172.

[2] *Ibid.*, 1, 5.

[3] Kurukshetra, April, 1959, p. 13. See also Sixth Evaluation Report, (June,59), pp. 16-18. A sample survey of 190 villages situated in 38 blocks, scattered all over India, revealed that 37 villages had no panchayat ; the remaining 153 villages were covered by 145 panchayats. Of these, only 13 are reported to have undertaken some planning and execution of programmes. In 24 out of the 36 blocks in which panchayats exist they have failed to levy taxes.

have levied taxes, mobilised resources and shown some activity. On the other hand, in block where the panchayats are not active, or the resources mobilised by them are meagre, the response is poor. The correlation is by no means perfect but the trend does suggest that the very fact of effective functioning the panchayats for some time might prove a stimulus for further progress.[1]

In the same vein, while the Mehta team's members found in general "excessive dependence on continued Government initiative," they report that a "few panchayats have been successful in a small measure in mobilising voluntary labour for community work. In such villages a new leadership is emerging, indicative of a new attitude to local welfare and local development and a realisation of the value of local institutions."[2]

On the basis of this faith in local leadership, Balvantray G. Mehta and his colleagues recommended broad measures of "democratic decentralization". The main responsibility for development should be transferred to a local representative body at the block level, the Panchayat Samiti, to be composed of members indirectly elected, by the village panchayats and certain other bodies. The samiti is to take over "the development of agriculture, improvement of cattle, promotion of local industries, public health, welfare work, administration of primary schools . ." and "other functions." Its income is to include a proportion of the land revenue. The staff is to be strengthened; BDO's are to be put on the junior administrative cadre, and all junior revenue officers are to be posted as BDO's after their initial training, before they are imbued with the "revenue bureaucratic spirit." Gram Sevaks are to be increased in numbers, and the area of the circle limited to cover a population of four thousand; they should establish closer links with village panchayats, for whom they will serve as development secretaries.[3]

The Mehta Report was endorsed by a National Conference on Community Development, which met at Mount Abu in May, 1958, and subsequently by the Conference of Local Self-Government Ministers of all the state meeting at Hyderabad in October, 1959; but perhaps of greater significance than this support by politicians and officials was the appearance of a similar proposal for local community action evolved by Jayaprakash Narayan. His draft Pleas for Reconstruction of Indian Polity is a restatement of Gandhian principles which, as he says, has "much in common" with the Mehta Report: Jayaprakash Narayan, one-time revolutionary Marxist, and now

[1] Fifth Evaluation Report, p. 24.
[2] Mehta, Report, I, 44.
[3] The full list of recommendations is given in Mehta, Report, I, 125-161.

*jivan-dani*' "life devotee" and leader of the Bhoodan movement and exponent of Sarvodaya, or "ideal harmony," finds himself alongside the hard-headed Gujerati businessman and chairman of the Estimates Committee of the Union Parliament, Balvantray G. Mehta. This merging of the philosophies of the idealist and visionary, and the practical man of affairs, in a mutual insistence upon the necessity for genuine local self-government may be one of the seminal influences in the emergence of Indian democracy.

Jayaprakash sees this as a "problem of social reconstruction", to be attained by means of co-operative or "communitarian" society. He insists that neither society nor the state can be an aggregation of individuals: the community remains the foundation-stone of India. His goal is gram dharma: the function of dharma is law rooted in social ethics. Jayaprakash contrasts his communitarian society with the present regime: democracy in name, but centralized bureaucracy in practice. His solution draws heavily on Gandhian teaching, but he insists that the community must be wider than the village. He builds his polity around what he calls the "regional Community", *i.e.*, a group of associated villages. This regional community would be the basic unit for planning and for joint activity and even for agricultural and industrial production. The whole of his argument is directed against what he describes as "the divisive influence of the existing atomistic policy." The villagers merge into the village, the village merges into the regional community into the district, the state, and the nation.[1]

Both Balvantray Mehta and Jayaprakash Narayan have discarded the hoary myth of the "self-sufficient Indian village," which Gandhians have nurtured right to the present day. And their ideas have been taken up and have become the orthodoxy of Community Development. The Minister, S.K. Dey, in his somewhat rotund way, has preached the new doctrine many times. For example:

A self-sufficient village republic, even regionally, is a myth in the sputnik age where the world has already shrunk to the virtual size of a peanut and life is springing forward for a leap into the wider cosmos. . . . The revolution already under way in the means and processes of production makes it quite obvious that self-sufficient village republic can at best be a dream.[2]

To symbolize the transformation, in place of the phrase used so often by Gandhi, Panchayat Raj, the usage Panchayati Raj has

---

[1] Quotations from the "draft for private circulation" of Plea for Reconstruction of Indian Policy, Banaras, Sept., 1959.
[2] S.K. Dey, *Community Development: A Movement is Born,* Allahabad, 1960, p. 173.

supervened. It is, perhaps, not just an exercise in semantics to suggest that "Village Council Government," and "Government of the Village Councils" are subtly differentiated.

The new system has been introduced in a number of states. The procedure varies. In some states; enabling legislation has been followed immediately by inauguration of the new councils. In others, the legislation was implemented at leisure, elections preceding the actual constitution of the councils by many months. In Mysore, Panchayati Raj was introduced by phases; the Madras method was similar. The inauguration of Panchayati Raj in Assam did not result in any early change of note. Subject to these variations, which affected the progress of the new system, the following states were the pioneers of Panchayati Raj: Rajasthan brought the new scheme into operation, on October 2, 1959; Andhra followed on November 8, 1959. In 1960 Madras formally inaugurated the scheme on October 2 and Mysore on December 21. During 1961 Panchayati Raj came into being in Orissa on January 26 and in Punjab on October 2. The pattern is roughly the same. The old district boards are abolished, and a new structure arises. At the base are Gram Panchayats for each large village or for a group of villages or hamlets. Above are the Panchayat Samitis, coterminous with the Community Development Block, or the revenue Taluka, and forming the main executive unit, the focus of activity. Over all is a district council, termed the Zila Parishad in North India and the District Development Council in the south. Its functions are least well-defined; it is intended to act as a co-ordinating body. Only one state, Gujerat, has signified that it intends to continue to utilize the district as the main unit of administration.

At the time of writing (August, 1961) any assessment of the trend of Panchayati Raj is premature. Two evaluation reports have indeed appeared. A parliamentary study team, led by Raghubir Sahai, M.P.; was asked by the Congress party to assess the working of the new system in the two pioneer provinces of Rajasthan and Andhra. The team spent nine days in Rajasthan in October, 1960, and ten days in Andhra Pradesh in December, 1960. Their conclusions (necessarily limited to surface impressions) were published soon after.[1]

A second survey was made under the auspices of a private venture known as the Association of Voluntary Agencies for Rural Development (AVARD); their teams visited Rajasthan in November, 1960.[2]

In the main, both reports present a similar picture. On the credit side they pronounce that the new elected chairmen, endowed with

---

[1] Summarized in Kurukshetra, and Panchayat Raj (formerly Gram Sevak), March, 1961.
[2] Summarized in Kurukshetra, April, 1961.

executive authority are working well with their chief officers, formerly their leaders and now their coadjutors. The AVARD report has some reservation and notes a "mild tussle for power" between the block development officer (now called Vikas Adhikari) and the Pradhan, the chairman; the Raghubir Sahai team detected only a small amount of friction between the official and the elected heads—mainly attributable to the misconduct of a small minority of the Pradhans. Both reports state that the Panchayat Samiti is the principal centre of activity. The role of the Zila Parishad in Rajasthan is only vaguely defined, while in Andhra the continuing presence of the District Officer as chairman inhibits non-official enterprise, though the Andhra District Councils have inherited most of the powers of the old District Boards.

Concerning the village panchayats the AVARD team found that the success of the Panchayat Samiti has been achieved at the expense of village-level institutions. The village panchayats are inclined to look up to the Panchayat Samiti as the fount of power (a new variant of the old Ma-Bap attitude? The village councils have failed to attempt any extension of economic activities. They have also failed to exploit the resources within their grasp by levying the taxes which they are empowered to introduce. The Raghubir Sahai team noted that "general meetings of the Gram Sabha (the assembly of the whole village) were not called, and therefore the village people as a whole were not apprised of the activities of the Gram Panchayat." Both reports emphasized that, because of Panchayati Raj, faction and division within the village life had been intensified. Most panchayats were split into factions, some on political party lines. In the same way, caste conflict had been intensified: in Rajasthan, the principal struggle appears to be that of *jat* cultivators and *rajput* traditional leaders; in Andhra, the new system served to define the gulf which lay between harijans and caste Hindus. On the credit side, the village panchayats had lessened the power of petty officials to exact petty levies from their village "clients," even if this petty corruption had to some extent been appropriated by the arrivistes, the elected bosses.

It would be unwise to deduce from this evidence that the pattern of village power and leadership has been transformed by Panchayati Raj. Past experience, both in the Rural Reconstruction and Community Development movements, provides warnings of the false impression of change which the first impact of a new movement seems to portend. The novelty of the activities even the novelty for the village folk of being suddenly promoted from the back row of the audience to the front row of the show generates a temporary dynamic which can appear quite impressive. In the past this dynamism has evaporated when the outside interest has dwindled and the village folk have been left to themselves again. The time to form a balanced estimate of the new system may not arrive for another five years. However, it may be worth attempting to examine some of the trends which appear to be emerging. First, there is the widespread decision to make the block the principal unit for development. On practical grounds much can be said in its favour. In the view of the Mehta team, "The block . . . . offers an area large enough for functions which the village panchayat cannot perform and yet small enough to attract the interest and service of its residents."[1]

But the average block has a population of sixty to eighty thousand and contains from twenty to a hundred villages. Experience has demonstrated that between the village or neighbourhood and the district there is no intermediate area that provides a basis for a sense of community. The object of local government planners from the time of Ripon onwards has been to get away from the district down to a more cohesive area, such as the subdivision or the *tahsil*; but the pressure of local circumstances has always frustrated such intentions. The administrative district, merely through having functioned for a hundred years or more, has acquired a certain meaning. At district headquarters are the Law Courts and the lawyers; here is located the only decent hospital, the government high school, perhaps an intermediate college; here is all the mechanism of commerce and exchange. The administrative centre has taken on the character of a social centre, at any rate for the middle classes. The *tahsil*, headquarters is nothing—a treasury, a police station, a dispensary and that is about all. A block headquarters is even less a potential nucleus of the local community, except where by chance it is situated on a market town serving the surrounding villages. As the centre of the principal unit of the new local administration, block headquarters will not only be artificial, but will actually have a negative quality. Social, political, and administrative pressures will combine to make district headquarters the focus of Community Development—at any rate until middle-class leadership gives way to a broader democracy which includes the underprivileged classes, when an area evolved out of a neighbourhood (perhaps coterminous with the Gram Sevak's circle) may become the local unit. In this regard the proposals of Jayaprakash Narayan to constitute "regional communities" of neighbouring villages in an "integral" community is more in keeping with the nature of Indian village society. Marriage ties and economic connections do often provide a neighbourly nexus which could provide the basis of

[1] Mehta Report, I .9.

inter-village co-operation, which the block can never hope to emulate.

Of course, it is artificial to consider the balance of rural leadership and influence except in relation to the over-all pattern of power. The initiative in planning and programming still comes from above; the rural folk still look up to government, or to the new block councils as the emanation of government for purposes of fund-raising. Moreover, the pull of the central government, the state governments, and even the pull of the district administration, still insures that the "centre of gravity" of politics is at high level. So long as this government from above persists, the attempt to build up Panchayati Raj as a counter-attraction will not prevail against the general political trend. The forces of centralisation have been actually increasing as S.K. Dey has made clear: "In administration, despite the provisions of our Constitution demarcating the relative spheres of States" and Central subjects, there is a tendency of more and more powers concentrating in the centre. The States in their anxiety not to be left behind are dealing in the same way with the local bodies. Though the panchayats remain they are being used mainly as organisations for offering receptions to V.I.P.'s and ministers. The people in India . . . are doing just the opposite of what ideals the Mahatma stood for all his life, *viz.*, that the village should be treated as the base for the democratic structure in this country."[1]

The budget debates in Parliament in April, 1961, revealed anxiety at the mounting control over local activity. Thus Kamal Singh, M.P.: "The sense of dependence and helplessness is increasing in our villages. Villagers look to the government for every little thing. There is also lack of co-operation. The result is the constructive work is hampered. Village factions and power politics add to the problem."

Similar qualms were expressed by Munishawar Dutt Upadhyay, M.P., among others: "Regarding Panchayati Raj, we have to see whether decentralisation has really taken place or not. One still feels that nothing can be done without orders from above. It was seen at one or two places that the local people collected some money for certain schemes. Yet approval from above came after years."[2]

The retention of political power in the hands of few was the keynote of the presidential speech which Jayaprakash Narayan delivered to the All-India Panchayat Parishad which convened at Jaipur in May, 1961. He likened Indian democracy to "an inverted pyramid that stands on its head," as opposed to the broad-based pyramid of a genuine democracy. In assessing the potentialities of Community Development for broadening the base in India and creating what Jayaprakash called "participating democracy," he pointed to

[1] Kurukshetra, Jan., 1961, p. 4.
[2] *Ibid.,* May, 1961, pp. 11-12.

the cramping effect upon the programme of its initially limited purpose, which he defined as "a procedural reform of the administration at the lower levels." It would be necessary, he intimated, to introduce "a real devolution of power, and not a make-belief." To implement this radical change, Jayaprakash wanted the District Magistrate to "disappear or remain only as representative in the district of the State Government. . . . Panchayati Raj even in Rajasthan where it began, is yet a far cry from this consummation."[1]

Of the tiers of the new structure, the Gram Panchayat must be the solid foundation; and the village community must be the source of the authority of the Gram Panchayat. The Gram Sabha of the whole village must become a reality: at present Jayaprakash declared, Gram Sabhas "do not function, and the panchayats or sometimes only their presidents usurp all authority, naturally inducing a sense of indifference among the people. . . . The gram sabha should meet as often as possible, say, quarterly. . . . Then it would be that the people would awaken to their responsibilities and opportunities, and the gram panchayats cease to be convenient tools in the hands of officers of the State or the vested and selfish interests in the village communities themselves."

If under the new order, the public services are to become advisers and supervisors instead of direct administrators, a change of attitude will become more than ever necessary. Today it is probably true to say that the senior district official is more aloof and out of touch with the general public than was his British predecessor. The old style British District Officer spent anything up to half the year in camp, from September to May. It is easy to ridicule the almost Mughal style in which he moved: the elaborate camp, the ceremonial entry into a village on horseback, surrounded by a posse of notables; the inspection of village accounts and the hearing of disputes under the banyan tree. The snipe shooting, the memsahib's dispensary—how dilatory, how pompous it all was. But in 1850 or 1900 this was often what the villager wanted. He was able to receive the *hakim* on his own native ground, he could speak to the great man face to face; he was able to make proposals or register grievances and expect an answer. If all this has become an anachronism, it has not been replaced by anything new: there is just a vacuum.

Today, few District Officers go out on lengthy tours. Certainly, they are tied to headquarters by all the reports they have to compile and the ministers and other visitors whom they have to please. So today's inspections are perfunctory and unsatisfactory.[2]

1 Panchayati Raj, June, 1961, pp. 3-8.
2 Mehta, Report, I, 40-41.

There is no leisurely entry into the village demesne on horseback, giving time for the village folk to absorb their visitor into their own environment. He arrives, in a storm of dust in a jeep, a visitor from another world, and he keeps his other-world aura with him. There is a hasty walk around, a conference with the leaders, a propaganda speech, a cup of tea, and he is off to another village, and another.[1]

It is unheard of to stay more than one day in one village. A District Officer said to the writer, "I am trained to find out all I need to know in one day," and another younger official said, "Frankly I do not like to spend a night in a village. I have nothing to say to the villagers, nor have they to me."

Much of the British Indian Civil Service tradition has been adopted by the Indian administrators of today, but the legendary British District Officers have bred no Indian successors. A few Indian officials cling to a still older tradition: they take with them the aura of Mughal *Mansabdars*; men of power, men of rank, they still see rural society in terms of rulers and ruled. But the younger Indian administrator sees government in terms understood at the London School of Economics and Political Science, or the University of California. He is something of an economist, statistician, and political scientist; he readily finds his way about the Secretariat or the Planning Commission in New Delhi where his accomplishments will stand comparison with any. But Houghton Street or Berkeley have not prepared him for the district world of Indian peasant and landlord. Perhaps the old British idea of the father of the people (who toiled and sweated to give them justice and prosperity, whose memorial was an equitable revenue assessment, an irrigation canal, a hospital, and a reputation for fair dealing) was always more of an ideal than a reality; anyhow it was fast becoming an anachronism, and one need not have lamented its disappearance too much if it had given way to something better. The young Indian Administrative Service probationer still has to learn to ride a horse; but this is little more than a gesture to tradition, like the Latin grace said in hall before dinner in a Cambridge college. The old gear, the saddle, the gun, tent, medicine-chest are brought out no more. But a new technique of face-to-face encounter has still to be created. The young Indian administrator is well endowed with a sense of public service, but in an abstract rather than a personal sense. His approach is inclined to be clinical; the villagers appear as suitable material for analysis by means of I.B.M. cards. He rejects the relation-

---

[1] The Mehta Report recommended that jeeps be withdrawn from use by BDO's. Because the jeep can go so fast and so far, "The result (has been) that visits to the villages, even for the junior-most officers, become affairs of a few minutes, rather than the work of a few days."

ship of squire and villain which many British officials seemed to cultivate, but he has no new pattern to adopt. One recalls the spectacled,
stooping pilgrim who trudged patiently from village to village, lodging
where he could, quietly listening and talking with the village folk. Is
not this perhaps the pattern for India?

It seems that in the future IAS probationers appointed to Rajasthan will begin work on BDO's. This echoes the former practice of
making the fledgling ICS officer spend his first year carrying out the
work of subordinate officials, from the level of the *Patwari* or *Lekhpal*
(the village accountant) upward. It is to be hoped that these young
IAS men will, like their ICS predecessors, live away from headquarters
in touch with rural life, learning the rustic speech and thought, and
developing a philosophy that is not just handed down by their seniors.

Desirable though it is that today's officials should evolve a new
relationship of confidence and understanding with the country-dweller,
this does not mean that their role as leaders is finished, despite the
forthcoming "democratic decentralization." The new situation will
not be democracy but another, mere positive, attempt to bridge the
awkward transitional period when autocracy and democracy are trot-
ting along in dual harness. It will be years before the present administrative framework (still essentially that created by the Mughals) is
finally dismantled. The administrators now beginning their service
must try to succeed where their British and Indian predecessors did
not, in creating a new image of government and its relation with the
people. It was somewhat in this spirit that Raghubir Sahai addressed
the Lok Sabha during the April 1961 budget debate: "We found that
the District Collector was an non-voting member of the Zila Parishad
in Rajasthan; in Andhra he presided over all the standing committees
of the Zila Parishad. In Madras and Mysore he presided over the
Zila Parishad directly. I think the time has come when his role should
be defined. I personally feel that the best role for the District Collector would be that of a friend, philosopher, and guide. He should
remain away from these institutions, but still near them."[1]

If the younger generation of civil servants can rise to this challenge
they will have an invaluable part to play.

But of course they can only do so much: the interested onlooker
will be looking most for signs of a change in the heart of village
India. The refurbished panchayats, despite enlarged powers and
better finances, will still depend heavily upon the voluntary co-operation of all their village brethren. The panchayat has to do so much
more than village councils in other lands—to run schools and repair
roads; it has to expend the wealth of the community, for only so can

---

[1] Kurukshetra, May 1961, p. 8.

India attain higher living standards. It is difficult to know how the community spirit can be whole-heartedly awakened under the existing system of agriculture in which there are marked inequalities. It is arguable that the result of the first phase of the Community Development programme was to accentuate these inequalities. "Caste and class distinctions are so acute that the feeling of belonging to one community has not yet come. Self-help, therefore, has amounted to helping certain sections or individuals only."[1]

The *harijans* especially feel that they have had little benefit from Community Development, though they are compelled to give their labour for Shramdan.[2]

Within a neighbourhood, development funds are likely to have been applied to one village only. The programme has tried to encourage self-help, and the only villages capable of showing initiative are those which are reasonably prosperous. The poorer villages and hamlets see funds and benefits going into perhaps the one village which was already prosperous. Is there an escape from this impasse? Tarlok Singh believes in a total solution:

Village society has to be transformed so that, on the one hand it offers equality of status and opportunity to all its members and, on the other, it offers gainful employment to individual workers. . . . The village panchayat must take upon itself the responsibility for creating and maintaining sufficient work opportunities, in other words for development of resources and employment. . . . The concept of joint or cooperative village management is important for the further development of the rural economy. It means that the land and all the resources of the village are to be managed and developed in the interest of the entire village community. That is to say, the village as a whole is an economic unit in which agriculture and other occupations are organised by or on behalf of the community.[3]

It is possible to agree wholeheartedly with this analysis and yet to doubt whether this total co-operation can ever become effective on a voluntary basis.

American sociologists, such as Carl C. Taylor, have been important advocates of group participation in development: yet American history offers interesting evidence of the limitations which voluntary community projects must accept. The small town in America offers

---

[1] Kurukshetra, April, 1959, p. 12.
[2] A study of harijan response to Community Development found that 11 per cent felt they had definitely benefited; 53 per cent said, "they were not exactly aware" of any benefit; and 36 per cent said, "they had definitely received no benefit." Mehta, Report, II, 88.
[3] Tarlok Singh, *op. cit.*, pp. 4-6.

one of the most striking examples of the community spirit anywhere. In the small country town, the wealthy lawyer, fifth-generation descendant of the original settlers, and the threadbare newly arrived Hungarian janitor are both united by this spirit in supporting new buildings for the high school or better amenities for the park; but even this close sense of community operates only over definite areas of common interest. It vanishes in other areas where religious or social divisions intervene, and in the economic sphere all experiments in total community development on a New Harmony model have sooner or later collapsed. The Mormons have provided an exception to the individualism of American life with their emphasis upon close community organization, but they, equally, have rejected communal economic effort.[1]

When Americans have proved that the community as a voluntary economic unit does not work, it is difficult to understand why they should expect Indian experience to be different. If compulsory co-operative or collective farming is not accepted—and it would undoubtedly cause greater social and economic disruption in India than in the Russia of the 1920's—then there remains the slow way of social change. What are the prospects for a more unified village society?

The prevailing trend of opinion expects to find the key in the concept of unanimity, applied particularly to the process of choosing the members of the panchayats. The people's choice, it is averred, must be unanimous, or when complete agreement is not possible then the choice must be left to fate—as signified in the drawing of lots. Many have argued the need for unanimity, but none so consistently as the proponents of Sarvodaya, led by Jayaprakash Narayan.

The more I have thought over this question, the more I have discussed it with others and the more I have learnt of the workings of the village panchayats, the more convinced have I become that if Panchayati Raj is to succeed, contests at village elections must be avoided. . . . A community spirit must be created before there could be proper community development. To introduce electoral contests into the village is to throw a monkey-wrench into the works. . . . Self-government through faction fighting will not be self-government but self-ruination . . . Electoral contests have already produced such tensions that there is a virtual stalemate in the affairs of the panchayats.[2]

The All-India Panchayat Parishad, meeting at Jaipur in May, 1961, with Jayaprakash in the chair, passed a resolution urging the

[1] For example, the Orderville Mormon community collapsed from a combination of internal and external pressures; see R. B. West, *Kingdom of the Saints*, (London, 1958), pp. 311-315.

[2] Panchayati Raj, June, 1961, pp. 9-10.

holding of "unanimous elections". This being the climate of opinion, it is instructive to consider some of the actual results in the elections of Gram Panchayats. Elections were held in Punjab in December, 1960, in preparation for Panchayati Raj. Out of 13,439 panchayats, 3,779 were chosen by unanimous consent. The Punjab Government awarded grants-in-aid equivalent to one year's land revenue to all villages where the Sarpanch (chairman) and members were returned unopposed. Yet despite this notable inducement, only 29 per cent of the elections were unanimous. The villagers of Uttar Pradesh showed themselves less contumelious. Elections held at the same time included the unopposed return of 42 per cent of the Pradhans (chairmen) and over 50 per cent of ordinary members. However, only in the case of the Pradhans were these the result of elections by ballot.[1]

Panchayat Samiti elections in Orissa showed about 30 per cent of "unanimous elections".[2]

Mr. Nehru has indicated that the All-India proportion of uncontested elections is also about 30 per cent; it therefore does not appear probable that the concept of unanimity through electoral agreement will quickly take hold in the villages. Nor is it obvious that this concept assures all the beneficent effects anticipated by Jayaprakash Narayan. In a characteristically perfervid passage, S.K. Dey has denounced unanimity as a synonym for apathy: "Heat and cold, light and darkness, saint and devil are opposites which make for life and its continuance. A self-sufficent village republic consisting of God-fearing people, thinking, believing and acting all alike, is a village dead before it is born. Life cannot spring from such an inanition. Democracy demands ideology and ideals in a perpetual but healthy clash. Only dead people do not compete." S.K. Dey goes on to argue that it is better to channel the competitive instincts into the service of the Panchayat, rather than to leave them to fester in caste and class conflict.[3]

It would be a travesty of the thesis of Jayaprakash Narayan to suggest that he expects to resolve conflict by pretending it does not exist: he clearly indicates the necessity for digging deep into the socio-economic causes of tension in order to eradicate them. But the popularizations of the "unanimity" idea do not recognize these root causes of tension: they insist that unanimity can work in the village as it exists today. In the present-day village it is more realistic to recognize the power of faction and caste and attempt to institutionalize conflict, to some extent, by means of local self-government, through properly constituted organs of procedure.

1 Kurukshetra, May, 1961, 38.
2 *Ibid*, March, 1961, p. 28.
3 Dey, *op. cit.*, p. 173.

This article in its early pages insisted upon two apparently conflicting propositions: first, that the villager is uniquely aware of his village as his own place; second, that the village's capacity for leadership and its corporate sense have generally proved inadequate to make the village of today a better place. The two propositions are not irreconcilable. The villager is attached to his village because rural India is still, after centuries of change, a society dominated by tradition and, in an important sense, static. Villagers have a strong sense of antiquity, of the primordial origins of their community, which may go far beyond any historical basis.[1]

The ancient bonds of caste are frequently forget out of local village custom.[2]

In the present-day class struggles within village society, caste solidarity can be of greater advantage than individual enterprise. Most villages have their own godlings and local cults; religious custom (for example, veneration for certain beasts and birds) is one of the severest inhibitions upon agricultural improvements. So one could go on, demonstrating that village associations are powerful but mainly negative, working against corporate action and initiative.

Attempts to bring together the villagers for common purposes made during the past forty years have all been external, from above; this is just as true of the "democratic" Panchayati Raj as of any other scheme. The traditional view of government as external has continued to apply to the new statutory panchayats. Today, India's political leaders try to bring the rural population to realize that village and nation and government are all one. The causal visitor to a village involved in a development programme may well be irritated by the amount of energy which is devoted to propaganda. Perhaps the first project in the village will be to build a Gandhi *chabutra* (a meeting platform)—what could be more superfluous? Yet this provides a symbolic link between the village and India's greatest leader. Playgrounds, wall newspapers, slogans, songs—all these often precede work of a really solid character. This may be right if it brings the epic of India's planning and development right down into the village.

But this dramatization of the national effort has to be mirrored by an effort within the village. It may be necessary to stimulate the process from outside, to shatter what Gandhi called the "pathetic contentment" of the villager; but this process must become self-sustaining, if only because there are insufficient national resources to

1 Bernard S. Cohn reminded the writer that many Gangetic village settlements, which by their own traditions are a thousand years old, were actually founded in the sixteenth or seventeenth century.

2 Adrian Mayer, *op. cit.*, 193.

support an all-out programme of rural reconstruction. Signs are not wanting that in some villages a new spirit of self-confidence is building up. Perhaps this is more striking to the visitor returning after a long absence that to those closely involved with events. Today Indian women are taking part in village affairs to an extent unimaginable only fifteen years ago. Untouchables' children, if not their parents, are receiving a more equitable share of facilities; they are accepted in village schools without being penalized, so that they will be better equipped in the future to obtain that equality which is legally their right. In the small percentage of "developed" villages the visitor detects new sense of self-confidence, a new awareness that change can be made where there is determination and sticking power. Of course, the visitor who strays away from the "developed villages will discover, only a few dusty fields away, the age-old village world. There will be no school and no panchayat; lanes are foul and homes are desolate; all is apathy and men can only await the will of God. India's plight would have broken the hearts of any people less forbearing, less patiently determined to go on.

It is easy to enumerate changes which would strengthen community feeling, but unfortunately that obstacles to such desirable changes are all too plain. Village leadership would be strengthened if the flight of the educated to the towns could be reversed. For fifty years a small minority of village boys have been going on to higher education, but as soon as these young men pass the matriculation or intermediate examination, the village sees them no more. If they could be retained, they could usefully contribute to fighting obscurantism, bringing order into the business of the panchayat, speaking more equally to the agents of the government. But nothing about the village of today makes it any more attractive to the educated; it is still a place to get away from.[1]

Village solidarity would be strengthened if the lower castes were recognized by the higher-born as having equal rights; if the really shared in the fruits of co-operative action, they would not grudge their share of the labour. Yet almost everywhere the attempts of the lower castes to raise their status are strenuously resisted. The civic sense of the villagers would be strengthened if the rich would accept the obligation to utilize part of their wealth for the good of the community. In former days rich men made charitable contributions for religious purposes and for such quasi-religious objects as rest-

---

[1] "With the[progressive spread of education, there can be seen emerging . . . a new class of educated youth, many of whose members are unemployed, not fully occupied or just not fit absorption into village life". Fourth Evaluation Report, p. 66.

houses, wells, or bridges. This tradition was somewhat strained during the British period when rich men were more or less compelled to contribute towards good works like hospitals and schools in order to remain in official esteem. Today, the ancient tradition of charity and selflessness has become faded, and the wealthy Indian (like his counterparts throughout southern Asia) is increasingly dazzled by the glittering gadgets of the West. Finally, there is the rising spirit of individualism which permeates the village, especially in the economic sphere. Despite the abolition of *zamindari* (in some ways, because of abolition) there has been no improvement in the lot of the small peasantry. The beneficiaries are the capitalist farmers, some drawn from the classes of absentee landlords, some from the more enterprising, prosperous peasantry. The activities of these farmers are quite separate from the rhythm and routine of traditional agriculture. They employ their own machinery and plan their crops for a definite market. Their technique is leading directly to the individualist farming of Northwest Europe or North American. A recent study of the agricultural co-operative movement throughout India emphasizes this division between the big farmers, the "village oligarchs" as the writer calls them, and the smallholders and labourers. The big farmers were able to manipulate the land reforms, and they also manipulate the co-operatives.

Control of the co-operatives tends to vest in the hands of a few of these landholding families. Often they do some informal moneylending, and sometimes they carry on trading as well. In a striking number of cases the members of these same families also serve as headmen in their villages, or hold other posts of local or district importance. The membership of the State legislatures and the State ministries is drawn largely from their ranks. In the village world, these families are the big people . . . As against them, the ordinary people of the village are little folk, small people.[1]

It may well prove the paradox of the era of Community Development that, while all the forces of government authority have been directed together the mass of the village folk and improving their general lot, economic forces have led to the elevation of *kulak* farmers and the liquidation of the marginal peasantry. If this hypothesis should unhappily prove correct, it will stimulate still further the flood of migrants into the cities. We have all become so used to thinking of "village India" as the bedrock of Indian society that we may be in danger of failing to appreciate the significance of Indian urbanization today. For a century the great metropolises were steadily expanding; but this new urbanization is upon an entirely different scale. For

[1] Daniel Thorner, *Prospects for Cooperation in Indian Agriculture*, advance copy, mimeo., p. 24.

example: Delhi had a population of some 400,000 in 1947: is now a city of nearly 2.5 million. This phenomenon is accompanied by a rootless squalor which is worse than that of the early industrial revolution in England. Here, if anywhere, communism will feed and flourish; as it has in the wretched suburbs of Calcutta.

The Congress governments will be compelled to change their priorities, to focus attention upon the city slums which hitherto have been neglected by all: central, state, and municipal governments. Emphasis, both in politics and development, could shift from the countryside to the cities, leaving Community Development to die of neglect.

The list of factors which prejudice the success of village co-operation is seen to be formidable : the continuing counter-attraction of centralization, government from above, the divisive forces of caste and faction, the decay of the sense of community and the growth of individualism, and the gradual sapping of rural life by the drift to the cities. But village Community Development is by no means a lost cause. The village remains the most vital social factor in the India of today, as yesterday. One Indian writer of a pragmatic and practical sort, having honestly acknowledged the stresses of village disunity, is led to insist: "The common needs of environment and the sharing of problems of living are the essence of community development and the mechanical age in breaking through it. Our country has not yet gone as far as the West. Individual and social happiness with all the things it involves is the ultimate goal. Social desires will have to be created which will result in small self-managing communities. It seems as though it could still be achieved in India and her 'backwardness' is one definite advantage from this point of view."[1]

But a policy of village reconstruction must, necessarily, be accompanied by a deliberate policy of dismantling the whole superstructure of control. This same writer sees this clearly and adds: "The time seems to be getting ripe in our country for a shift of power from the State level to the Panchayat". This is also the view of the writer on co-operation previously cited: "the government must become the instrument of the ordinary people and must be considered as such by the ordinary people."[2]

This, of course, is the essence of the philosophy of Gandhi and Jayaprakash Narayan: the need to make democracy a reality by bringing it into the lives of ordinary village folk. Hard-headed Balvantray G. Mehta came to the same conclusion:

It is not theory or dogma which is impelling us to make these

---

[1] K.S. V. Raman, Kurukshetra, Jan. 26, 1961, p. 26 (italics inserted).
[2] Thorner, *op. cit.*, p.27.

recommendations but practical considerations. Democracy has to function through certain executive machinery but the democratic government operating over large areas through its executive machinery cannot adequately appreciate local needs and circumstances. It is, therefore, necessary that there should be a devolution of power and a decentralisation of machinery and that such power be exercised and such machinery directed by popular representatives of the local area.[1]

If the philosophy of village-level democracy is to succeed, then it is surely important that the Community Development movement itself should faithfully reflect the "leveling down" of the locus of power to the village level. Present evidence suggests that the trend is towards just that "inverted pyramid" which Jayaprakash condemned as the failing of parliamentary government in India. The issue of Kurukshetra for June, 1961, was a Special Training Number. It is virtually an unconscious indictment of present-day Community Development. Parkinson's Law has nowhere been applied with such assiduity as in independent India. The employees of the central government (excluding the "productive" servants of government, posts and telegraphs, railways, and the armed forces, increased from 49,000 in 1939 to 669,439 in 1956. Community Development has proved one of the most flourishing fields for bureaucratic empire building, and the June Kurukshetra gives us a big parade of its minions. Orientation and Study Centres, Reorientation Centres, the Central Institute of Study and Research, the Planning Research and Action Institute: these are a few of the rarer fields in which the Community Development experts happily graze. One article is significantly entitled "Training of the Trainers," one feels that in a year or so, a sequel, "Training of the Trainers of the Trainers" will be required. All this forth might be dismissed as a sensible solution for India's problem of graduate unemployment (and a useful device for enabling Americans to visit India were it not necessary to recall that this vast *papeterie* is all carried on the back of the peasant. He is the producer: all the rest are consumers. And the Indian peasant, like peasants everywhere, is no fool. He can figure out who is actually pitching in with him, and who is just getting a ride. One day he may protest. To alter the context of G.K. Chesterton's lines:

We are the people of India; and we have not spoken yet.
Smile at us, pass us.
But do not quite forget.[2]

It would be irony indeed if the collapse of Community Development came about not from external causes but because of the increa-

[1] Mehta, Report, I. 20.
[2] From The Secret People.

singly Byzantine characteristics of the Community Development empire itself.

The concept of Panchayati Raj runs counter to all the traditions of a thousand years of Indian government. India's principal inheritance from the British period was an administrative service of unrivalled integrity and efficiency. Is the tried and tested steel frame to be dismantled to give room to the mud and thatch of village democracy? The whole idea may appear to be a gamble; a gamble; which deliberately discounts the known failures and disappointments in village reconstruction in the recent past. Yet, if India is to be true to her declared purpose of creating a society based upon consent, moulded together by voluntary co-operation, with the ordinary people working together as equal citizens, then Panchayati Raj is major step forward upon this road.

# RETARDATION OF ECONOMIC DEVELOPMENT

## K. William Kapp

*in collaboration with Love L. Kapp.*

THE GENERAL PURPOSE throughout the preceding analysis has been to appraise the existing social and economic institutions of India in relation to their role in the nation's economic development. We must now set forth in greater detail the impact of Hindu culture and Hindu social organization on economic growth and development. We shall try to answer this broad question by proceeding in an order of increasing concreteness from a discussion of the effects of Hindu metaphysics to an analysis of the impact of the major social institutions on economic change. Essentially, we shall try to appraise existing institutional arrangements in the light of the declared goals of increasing production and productivity of the Indian Five Year Plans. Needless to say that we are not here concerned with the question of the superiority or relative value and truth of any particular belief systems and social arrangements.

## I. Cyclical Time and Cosmic Causation

The notions of cyclical time and cosmic causation tend to relate man to a cosmology of such vast dimensions in time and space that they can only increase the feeling of human helplessness in the face of nature by reducing man's confidence in his own powers. Furthermore, circular time and cosmic causation give causality a fatalistic time and pen they way to astrological speculations of all kinds. By spreading cause and effect over durations of time which exceed the lifespan of the individual—indeed by spreading causation over many human existences—the relation and the continuity between cause and effect tend to become not only vague but may ultimately be lost altogether. The causal relationship certainly assumes and retains a supernatural and mystical character not subject to rational comprehension and human control. Under these circumstances acceptance and obedience become the only meaningful and appropriate attitude toward life. *Karma* and the iron law of retribution in effects deny that history, social reform and economic development are essentially matters of our own choice and depend upon human will and social action.

Indeed, this commitment to the concept of cosmic causation may explain the role of astrology in the daily life of contemporary India. The continued strength of the belief in the influence of the constellations of the stars at birth can be accounted for only in terms of a basic acceptance of cosmic causation and circular time.[1] Such commitments will lead either to the use of magic or to resignation and acceptance of the *status quo*, or whatever may befall the individual.

Moreover, when the present is viewed as causally related, in a cosmological sense, to the past and the future the actual condition of human existence loses much of its significance. It becomes transitory and illusory or at least relatively if not absolutely unimportant as compared to the postulated supreme reality. As a result, not only life and death but all forms of human suffering as well as social institutions in general assume a transitory and in this sense secondary character. Indeed, all things, that happen on this transitory stage, all social and economic change, are matters of the moment and partake of the generally transitory character of the world. By providing a ready-made explanation and justification for the unequal distribution of fortunes in a society based upon hereditary status, traditional Hinduism may be said to weaken the impulse to ameliorate social conditions. It includes its adherents to endure what after all is considered to be only transitory. In short, cyclical time and cosmic causation coincide with and support the ethics of endurance, contentment, submission and withdrawal. In the last analysis this is only another way of saying that the core of Hindu thought makes it less urgent and less meaningful than a Western world outlook to improve the conditions of social and economic existence. On the contrary, in the light of Hindu thought acceptance of an imperfect world is likely to be more attractive than any desire to master and improve it. On the whole "Eastern civilizations are interested not so much in improving the actual conditions as in making the best of this imperfect world, in developing the qualities of cheerfulness and contentment, patience and endurance. They are not happy in the prospect of combat. To desire little to quench the eternal fires, has been their aim."[2]

In fact, by placing a premium on acceptance of one's *Dharma*, on

---

[1] The powerful role of astrology and even palmistry in the daily life of contemporary India needs no documentation for anybody who has lived in the country for any length of time. Detailed studies of the dependency of decision-making on the auspicious day and hour could throw light on the strength of this belief in cosmological causation, See G.M. Carstairs, *The Twice-Born*, London, 1957, pp. 51-52.

[2] S. Radhakrishnan, *Eastern Religions and Western Thought*, London, 1939, p. 257.

sacrifice and contemplation, and by inducing its devotees to view the course of events within a scheme of cosmological causation Hinduism tends to lower level of human aspirations. It leaves man in a more helpless position than he would be if his world outlook and his social institutions were such as to encourage an attitude more in harmony with the scientific temper and the use of existing scientific and technological knowledge.

It will be, and indeed it has been, argued that in Hinduism the temporal and the spiritual (cosmological) concerns are not as inter-related as is here assumed and that what really destroys man's confidence is nature's relentless enmity to man in the tropics.[1] It may be true that while the Hindu is in the world he is also of the world, but it is hardly plausible that the belief in rebirth, Karma and cyclical time and cosmic causation do not pervade and influence the temporal sphere including man's attitudes toward the amelioration of the actual condition of human and social life. Cyclical time and cosmological causation belong to those basic categories of Hinduism which stand in the way of the emergence of one basic prerequisite of economic development, namely, the conviction that man does make his own history and that, while the conditions under which he makes history are given, social and economic progress are not a matter of blind destiny but depend upon human choices and social action.

## II. Desireless action and the level of Aspiration

We have indicated that the moral ideal of the *Gita* is a logical conclusion drawn from the notion of circular time and cosmic causation. The moral imperative that "to action alone hast thou a right and never at all to its fruits; let not the fruits of action be thy motive" must have the most far-reaching consequences on the level of aspiration and motivation. When the *Gita* insists that man should perform the work that has to be done without attachment to the fruits of action it supports, as we have tried to show earlier, the unresolved dualism which overshadows every economic activity and which tends to relegate efforts of social and economic reforms to a secondary and subordinate role in the Hindu scheme of things. What are some of the further consequences of this moral doctrine?

If perfection can be reached by obedience to Dharma, *i.e.*, by fulfilling one's ascribed and inherited duties, the level of aspiration and motivation, however high or low, tend to be confined to the field of one's prescribed traditional activities. This is to say, the desire for change, mobility and improvement must be seriously curbed. Furthermore, it is at least an open question whether the stress on non-attach-

[1] N.C. Chaudhuri, "On Kipling's India," Encounter, April 1957, Vol. 43, p. 51.

ment to the fruits of one's action does not deprive man of the necessary motivation and involvement needed to act purposively and productively either in the economic or other spheres. For such a doctrine may not only promote lack of interest in the formulation of proper plans of action but may ultimately lead to indifference to the results of one's action altogether. Hence action may well become half-hearted and abortive. Indeed, action either without an adequate plan or without continuous concern for its outcome may remain altogether ineffective. We are aware of the fact that the doctrine of disinterested and selfless action calls for the full application of one's skill and workmanship. However, while this may well be part of the moral imperative the emphasis on skill and workmanship is seriously weakened by the injuction against attachment to the results of action in this transitory world of appearances. Indeed, it is doubtful whether action in a world believed to be transitory can ever be as strongly motivated as action in a world in which man finds the meaning of existence in purposeful work. In other words, in a transitory world of appearances desireless action without attachment to its fruits runs the risk of degenerating into ritualistic performances of one's duties. Such performances born of renunciation and non-attachment will not generate the strong aspirations and motivations required for the hard and systematic work carried out with precision and punctuality, without which there can be no increased productivity and efficiency.

Another question is whether the doctrine of non-attachment and work done for sacrifice can perhaps be reinterpreted in such a fashion as to serve as an ethic of development under conditions of economic planning. Gandhi's reinterpretation of the ideal of disinterested action into any act of service including bodily labour (sacrifice, austerity[1] and the channelling of Yoga in Japan into a discipline of self-training for greater personal efficiency are significant in this connection.[2] A

---

[1] M. Singer, "Cultural Values in India's Economic Development", Annals of the American Academy of Political and Social Science, Vol. 305, May 1956, pp. 81-91 and M. Singer: in "India's Cultural Values and Economic Development," Economic Development and Cultural Change, Oct., 1958. Vol. 7, pp. 10-12.

[2] "The Japanese . . . wipe the slate clean of the assumptions on which Yoga practices are based in India. Japan, with a vital love of finitude which reminds one of the ancient Greeks, understands the technical practices of Yoga as being a self-training in perfection, a means whereby a man may contain that 'expertness' in which there is not the thickness of a hair between a man and his deed. It is a training in efficiency. It is a training in self-reliance. Its rewards are here and new, for it enables a man to meet any situation with exactly the right expenditure of effort, neither too much nor too little and it gives him control of his otherwise wayward mind so that neither physical danger from outside nor passion from within can dislodge him." R. Benedict, *The Chrysanthemum and the Sword*, 1946, p. 241.

reinterpretation of the traditional ideal of desireless action and renunciation designed to make it support an ethic of frugality and action for a common purpose could indeed be important for the development effort by providing the incentive and ethical justification for hard work and greater saving and abstinence from ostentatious (unproductive) consumption. It is significant that despite the teaching of Gandhi no successful effort seems to have been made by India's political and intellectual leadership to reinterpret the doctrine of action without desire for the fruits of one's labour so as to support an ethic of social action and of austerity by the wealthy in the interest of greater savings and a higher rate of capital formation. This, it must be said, would be in harmony with Nehru's dictum to combine the best of both the old and the new.[1]

However, even if this were done it is still likely that renunciation and non-attachment within the context of *Karma* would support at best only limited or static levels of aspiration and achievement as compared with the inner drive which harnesses the energies of man and makes him accept the discipline, orderliness and punctuality required for the highly differentiated tasks in modern industrial society. Thus, the cultivator who fails to take the water from the new irrigation canal because it may rain or who delays the building of field channels, the villagers who despite many droughts have not bothered to sink a well, or the peasant who will not make use of improved techniques because he is convinced that increases in yields are not due to improved seeds and fertilizer but a fate and *Karma*, may fail to act because of limited static aspirations which have their root in traditional beliefs and value systems.

### III. Caste, Social Segmentation and the "Faction Society" :

The impact of the caste system on economic development can hardly be overestimated. Indeed, it goes far beyond what is usually acknowledged by economists and other social scientists. It has long been realized that caste affects the supply of labour and interferes with the adjustment of supply and demand on the labour market. In fact,

"...caste and joint family are important social institutions affecting the available supply of family labour. Among the advanced castes (so-called upper castes) there is, at least in Bihar, a considerable restriction on and prejudice against field work on agricultural operations like ploughing. Except for a few operations on which the members of these castes may do manual labour, they usually engage mostly

---

1 "We cannot discard the past. Nor can we live in it, surrounded by rituals. We must combine the best of both the orders." Nehru's statement before the Inter-University Youth Festival, The Hindustan Times, October, 26, 1961.

in supervision of hired labour, often staying in the field all through the day."[1]

Changes in occupation although not impossible are rendered difficult by the fact that they may endanger one's status and may even lead to outright degradation and ostracism. Caste rules work against the acceptance of occupations normally followed by lower caste and Untouchables; in farming areas they have often held up and actually prevented the introduction of improvements of techniques such as the use of certain types of manure (bones, fish or nightsoil) and the maintenance of compost piles. In fact, by organizing society into closed economically non-competitive groups, caste frustrates the creative powers and lowers the aspirations of large numbers of people, thereby causing a serious waste of individual capacities and labour resources, Caste puts a premium on traditional occupations by preventing the development of personal initiative; it works against the emergence of a relationship between individual aptitude, performance and earnings.[2] Cast may then be said to restrict and determine consumption standards which are open to each individual in accordance with various caste rules. Not only are a man's social relations prescribed by caste, but what he is permitted to eat and drink and how to dress are objects of caste rules. Caste may thus be said to achieve what Western advertising aims at: it differentiates demand schedules and makes them less elastic.

More recently, the recruitment policy pursued within the private sector of the economy is said to follow caste lines especially as far as the higher and middle administrative positions are concerned. Thus, personnel belonging to the same caste or region as the founder of the concern may be "imported" from places hundreds of miles away from the seat of the company. Employment policies may thus degenerate into a form of caste or kinship charity which is liable to cause serious undercurrents of resentment among those aspirants who do not belong to the "right" caste-quite apart from the fact that the positions are not filled by the most competent persons available.[3] For all these reasons, caste, much more than to Western counterpart—racial discrimination and segregation—has always been an important obstacle to socio-economic change and as such has played not only a major

---

[1] J.P. Bhattacharjee, "Underemployment among Indian Farmers," in Artha Vinjnana, Vol. 3, No. 3. September 1961, p. 266. See also K. Nair, *Blossoms in the Dust*, London, 1961, pp. 91, 150.

[2] G.B. Jathar and S.G. Beri, *Indian Economics*, London, 1949, Vol. I, p. 83.

[3] For a general discussion of this subject see R. de Nitish, "Business Organisation and National Integration," The Economic Weekly, XIII, No. 42, October, 21, 1961, pp. 1639-42.

part in the economic stagnation of pre-independence India but today is still a major impediment to economic development.

However, the impact of the caste system on economic development goes far beyond these more or less generally recognized effects. In order to understand its full impact it is necessary to probe into the effect of caste on intergroup relations and the resulting segmentation of village life. Let us recall in this context that the village is essentially an agglomeration of castes, subcastes and joint families and that joint families and "Sovereign" castes live in a ranked order which determines the patterns of behaviour, *i.e.* what members of the different castes can and cannot do together is dependent upon caste rules and prohibitions.

The effect of these rules on the nature of intergroup relations may be illustrated by the results of a survey of intergroup relations in three villages in Maharashtra.

According to this survey not a single marriage had occurred outside caste; even Untouchables were not willing to exchange brides with another untouchable caste (of lower status); hospitality (invitation to a meal, going to other for a meal, visiting for a few days) were confined in nearly 90 per cent of the cases to kinship groups with the remaining 10 per cent within the caste group; friendships outside caste groups were not only rare but were generally accompanied by much shame and feelings of guilt; gift giving (except in business relations) was confined almost exclusively to the kinship group; while giving and receiving of food and clothing to or from people of a caste other than one's own was not uncommon, not a single case of sheltering or nursing an ill person of a caste other than one's own was recorded. And while major emergencies, like the burning of a barn or shed used for storing crops call for help by all regardless of caste, minor emergencies call for help only from the members of the victim's caste.[1]

Even more significant for an understanding of the role of caste on social isolation in rural India is the fact that ideas of purity and pollution also are responsible for segregation in housing, restriction on access to wells and even the use of village streets. Segregation of castes within distinct clusters of houses particularly for the Untouchables, seems to be a common characteristic even today.

"The habitation area . . . of the untouchables is always separate. If a village situated on a bank of a river or stream, the untouchables must use the water only from the lower reaches while the place for bathing, fetching water . . . of the touchables was always on the upper

---

[1] As reported by Y.B. Damle in staff seminars at the Gokhale Institute of Politics and Economics in Poona; and by I. Karve, "What is Caste?" The Economic Weekly, January, 1959, pp. 149-50.

reaches. In some villages the village street is divided into two parts, one higher and the other lower and only the later can be used by the untouchables."[1]

According to a survey in Bombay State not even one out of 70 villages had allowed the Harijans to take water from the common well.[2] Thus, as we have pointed out before, the actual position of the Untouchables is determined not by their legal rights but by their social and economic dependency which makes insistence on their part to be treated in accordance with constitutional guarantees problematical. While Untouchables may not be serfs of individual families in the legal sense of the term, as a group they tend to remain attached to the village, at least as long as there are no jobs in industries and urban centres. The practice of untouchability thus persists after its legal abolition because economic conditions have not changed sufficiently and because members of the higher castes refuse to undertake certain activities which they consider to be unclean or polluting.

"Nothing illustrates the dilemma of the Untouchables more vividly than the problem of the scavengers in some areas and that of the tanners and leather workers (Chamars) of North India. Whereas installations of facilities which do away with scavenging may run into opposition of the scavengers themselves, the refusal of the Chamars Panchayats to remove the dead cattle even without alternative employment in sight may lead to retaliation which 'is immediate often cruel and there have been ugly outbreaks of violence in the countryside'![3]

The foregoing discussion anticipates what is probably the most important effect of the caste system, viz., the segmentation and widespread antagonism which mark all intergroup relations in a caste society. Caste and kinship organizations tend to be among the primary factors which prevent the emergence of larger loyalties and the development of a spirit of solidarity and participation without which neither economic development nor political democracy can be achieved. In fact, in a society of scarcity and acute shortage of land, caste and kinship not only limit social relations and loyalties but also divide the groups into factions. When this happens almost every source of friction may become the reason for disputes and can easily give rise to strife and conflict. The distribution of canal water, irrigation rights, ownership of land, cases of inheritance, competition for rank, quarrels over marriages and dowries, violation of caste taboos, election

[1] *Ibid.*, p. 157.
[2] B. Venkatappiah, "Some Problems of Transition of a "Traditional Society," in N.V. Sovani and V.M. Dandekar, (eds.) *Changing India*, Bombay, 1961 p. 310.
[3] Lelah Dushkin, "Removal of Disabilities," The Economic Weekly, Vol. XIII, Nov. 4, 1961 m O. 1696.

to the panchayat, sex offences, rivalries for caste supremacy any one of these, but primarily land problems, seem to be the cause of major splits between the various kinship and caste groups which consequently tend to form themselves into more or less hostile factions.

In such a "faction-society," as it has been called, people will "react sharply and unfavourably to any new idea or change for the simple reason that they always fear and suspect that a change may place their opponents and rivals in a more favourable position than their own or in which they are placed now. Each group, therefore, respects, and fights for the *status quo* so that the members of the opposite faction may not gain or improve. Progress itself becomes unwanted because while it may benefit them it may also benefit their opponents and that they would like to prevent at any cost or a sacrifice."[1]

Under these circumstances many attempts at social and economic improvements may lead to the formation of new factions or old factions may close ranks. A network of inter-factional alliances may be formed with a view to dominating others. Factions composed of the higher castes and groups owning land may attempt to gain supremacy by attaching the poorer groups to their "cause" either by threats or by lending them money or by letting them have land.

Indeed, unable to develop the identification with objectives and interests which transcend those of their family, their caste, and their faction, many villagers seem to be incapable of establishing and maintaining an effective machinery or self-help. Even the attempts of economic and social reform introduced by Community Development Projects have, in some instances, led to a deterioration in the existing relations within the village and to an increase of tension between rival factions.[2]

We may conclude, therefore, that caste, social status by descent, segregation and hierarchy give rise to modes of reaction and a general climate of suspicion which makes most forms of social action difficult if not impossible.[3] Indeed feelings of solidarity with other groups which are a prerequisite for any effective concerted social action are

---

[1] Baljit Singh, "*Next Step in Village India*," Bombay, 1961, p. 14. For detailed evidence see the village studies referred to *supra* p. 33. On casteism or the exploitation of caste for political and regional interests and the vulnerability of India's political unity *see* S.S. Harrison, *India, The Most Dangerous Decades*, Princeton, 1960. See also E.E. Sehattaschneider, *Party Government*, New York, 1942, Ch. I.

[2] For evidence see Fourth Evaluation Report, On workings of Community Projects and N.E.S., Blocks, New Delhi, Planning Commission, 1957, Vol. 1, p. 65; Vol. II, pp. 29, 60, 65.

[3] A revealing illustration of how the fundamental distrust and mutual fears between villagers are being resolved in specific cases became clear during the

not likely to arise under such conditions.

The foregoing conclusions are not refuted by the fact that on special occasions the Indian villager is quite capable of common action. Thus religious festivals and ceremonies, or the construction of a shrine of temple, do require considerable community efforts. However, closer analysis of these community efforts confirms rather than refutes our hypothesis that caste and hierarchy in Hindu society are responsible for the inability to act in a concerted fashion as a means of improving the economic situation of the village. First, cooperation in religions is usually prescribed and mediated through one's membership in a joint family and caste and is, moreover, marked by the same ranked participation which characterizes all social life in the village. Secondly, the objectives of those common efforts are religious in character; they have nothing to do with such secular common objectives as the building of a road or a well which may benefit different villagers and castes unequally.

### IV. Caste and Moral Aloofness :

So far we have dealt with the general nature of intergroup and interpersonal relationship in the Hindu social system ... We have analyzed the social factors which make for distrust, suspicion and mutual fear and generally give rise to factions. We must now raise the more fundamental question as to the nature of human relationships in a social system in which notions of purity and pollution on the one hand, and detachment on the other are important values. More specifically, what are the effects of caste on the perception and acknowledge of the moral qualities of others? What are the consequences of caste and detachment on human relations and the efficiency of action? What role do affection and the feeling of sympathy and compassion for one's fellow men play in a caste society? We are concerned here with the relationships between members from different castes rather than with the interpersonal relations within kinship and caste groups.

Caste and the ideal of detachment tend to have similar moral consequences : they create and support an attitude of moral aloofness. This is perhaps clearest in the case of perfect detachment which although it may be impressive "as a moral achievement ... has a disconcerting moral corollary: for perfect Detachment casts out Pity,

author's visit to a village in Maharashtra. In commenting on the fact that there seemed to be only one storage place for certain crops in the village, we were told that this was the only way in which the individual owner could protect himself against arson by hostile neighbours. By storing their crops together they were able to achieve an effective mutual protection against deliberate destruction.

and therefore, also Love, as inexorably as it purges away all the evil passions."[1] Caste, with its ritual purity and fear of pollution, has similar corroding effect on sympathy and compassion especially as far the members of other castes are concerned.

"(Caste) cuts human beings off from each other. It inhibits the growth of those sensibilities which are required for the perception of the moral quality of other human beings. It is the caste system which cuts human beings off from each other by denying to them the possibilities of conubial and commensal intimacy and their more basic affinity as moral entities. It is the caste system which deadens the imagination to the state of mind of other human beings. It is the caste system, perhaps even more than the other factors like poverty and the crushing ubiquality of other human beings which makes the upper caste Hindus, from whose circles most Indian intellectuals are recruited, fundamentally and humanly insensate to the mass of the population who belong to lower strata."[2]

We have no desire to overestimate or to idealize the strength and the prevalence of compassion and love in contemporary Western societies. Undoubtedly there has always been a wide gap between the verbal acknowledgement of love and compassion as positive values and the practical measures taken to alleviate the distress of the underprivileged. But it will scarcely be denied that the feeling of affinity with all human beings and the perception of their moral quality has played a major role in all movements of social protest and social reform in the West. It is the perception of needless human suffering and cruelty which has sustained the feeling of moral indignation without which all movements of social and political reform would have remained ineffective.

Moreover, this moral aloofness as a state of mind which fails to perceive the underlying moral affinity of human beings may be the basic explanation also for the relative ease with which promises and commitments are made and not kept. While this phenomenon has been explained in terms of the importance attributed to signs and bad omens which make it appear inauspicious at the last moment to keep the promise we feel that such a change of mind is made easy by an attitude of moral aloofness. For if the moral quality and affinity of other persons were unequivocally recognized and accepted either on the basis of moral law or as a religious commandment the breaking of a promise would be regarded as a moral failure. It is clear that moral aloofness in this sense affects not only the quality of interpersonal relations but

---

[1] A. Toynbee, *A Study of History*, London, 1939, Vol. VI, p. 144.
[2] E. Shils, "The Culture of the Indian Intellectual," Sewanee Review, Vol. 67, 1959, pp. 257-58.

also undermines efficiency and performance at all levels.

Furthermore, if we contrast the equalitarian climate of the West centered as it is on the principle of the moral quality of all human beings regardless of status with the principles of caste, purity and pollution, it becomes clear why it has proved so difficult in India to mobilize human energies for the eradication of poverty and human suffering. Indeed, as long as it is possible to see in the suffering and the disabilities of the Untouchable, the beggar or the leper—a demonstration of fate or the iron law of retribution, neither compassion nor indignation can become strong social forces.

It is true that moral aloofness has been recognized and castigated in strong terms by Indian reformers. Thus, Vivekananda pointed out: "In India there is a howling cry that we are very poor, but how many charitable associations are there for the well-being of the poor ? . . . . Are we men ? What are we doing for their livelihood, for their improvement? We do not touch them, we avoid their company; Are we men ?"[1] But moral aloofness has withstood many attacks by social reformers and great leaders who like Nehru deplored "those wretched don'ts-don't do this, don't touch that, don't go out, don't marry outside caste and the like."[2] The difference between Vivekananda and Nehru lies in the fact that the former accepted the caste system, where Nehru rejects it. Thus Vivekananda writes: "Caste is a very good thing. Caste is the plan we want to follow . . . The plan in India is to make every body Brahman, the Brahmin being the ideal of humanity . . . . Indian caste is better than the caste which prevails in Europe or America. I do not say that it is absolutely good. Where will you be if there were no caste ? Where would be your learning and other things if there were no castes ?"[3]

It may be argued that since Hinduism stresses the oneness of all life and rejects the killing of animals it cannot be said to be devoid of pity and compassion. But this argument overlooks the fact that the religious prohibition of the killing of animals is not absolute but a matter of degree; it is particularly strong in the case of cows and other sacred animals. And neither this prohibition nor the feeling for the oneness of all living things implies a protective attitude towards animals in general or has led to the provision of shelter, food and water for the large herds of decrepit and helpless cattle that roam the countryside. Even a man of the stature of Gandhi at a time when he enjoyed already widespread esteem provoked a storm of protest abuse

---

[1] Swami Vivekananda, "The Elevation of the Masses," in the Mission of the Master, Madras, n.d. p. 361.

[2] The Hindustan Times, October, 6, 1961.

[3] Vivekananda, *op. cit.*, p. 365.

in Ahmedabad when he attempted to reinterpret the doctrine of *ahimsa* so as to permit the taking of life of a sick and suffering calf. He encountered the same opposition when he approved of the killing of rabid dogs and he hesitated to take a similar position in the case of monkeys which threaten crops and fruit trees with destruction.[1]

## V. Joint Family and Fertility :

The economic and social effects of the joint family can be understood only within the context of Hindu culture. For the joint family is in harmony with the Hindu world view and religion, the caste system and the hierarchical principle which characterizes most interpersonal relationships. What is particularly important for the purpose of our discussion is the fact that the joint family encourages the high fertility rates which were functional as long as high mortality rates remained unchecked by modern medical techniques. By bringing up the child and by transmitting to it the essential elements of Hindu culture, the joint family perpetuates a model personality type which is more or less well adapted to its environment. It is within this broad context that the social scientist can find a relevant answer to the question of the impact of the joint family on economic development.

Before examining some of the negative effects of the joint family on economic development it may be useful to analyze briefly some of its positive aspects. Indeed to ignore these positive aspects would leave us in ignorance concerning the reasons which account for the relative strength of the institution of the joint family. The Hindu family serves two important positive functions. First, it provides some degree of security to those of its members who may lose their earning capacity due to illness, unemployment or other misfortunes. As such it may be said to bear some of the social costs which the economy as a whole leaves unpaid, it serves as a cushion against the consequences of chronic poverty. Secondly, it acts as a form of corporate structure for the pooling of resources required for joint ventures; for instance, it helps to maintain relatively more efficient economic units especially in agriculture, than a nuclear family would be able to do. This is of considerable importance especially under conditions of heavy population pressure. Not only can meagre capital funds be pooled but small and fragmented holdings can be combined and cultivated together. Thirdly, the joint family is able to pool the earnings of all its members and distribute them to each in accordance with needs as defined and

---

[1] See Louis Fisher, *The Life of Mahatma Gandhi*, New York, 1950, pp. 236-239 and D.G. Tendulkar, *Mahatma*, Life of Mohandas Karamchand Gandhi, Bombay, 1951, pp. 420-26.

sanctioned by custom and tradition.[1]

At the same time, however, the joint family has important effects which can only be described as negative in relation to economic development. Take for instance those customs and traditions which combine to promote high fertility, such as the high value placed on male offspring, the custom of marrying early, the comparatively low status of childless women or of the young woman before the birth of a son, all of which encourage a tendency to have offspring as early as possible and in considerable numbers. Considerations of the economic costs of rearing children need not act as restraints because the burden and effort of having additional children do not fall on the biological parents alone but are borne by the joint house-hold.[2]

Indeed, from the point of view of young married persons, or, for that matter, even from the perspective of the rural joint family, an increase in the number of children cannot be regarded as irrational—no matter how self-defeating and deleterious the effects of a high birth rate may be on the average level of living.

There are countless peasant families who "have never had either the opportunity nor the capacity to 'invest in land, or other productive' things . . . and who have been able to achieve security in old age only by rearing a family . . . ."[3] Viewed in this light the rearing of children may in fact be regarded as an investment decision in the double sense that it draws upon and reduces actual as well as potential savings (since it cuts into consumption) and that it adds to the supply of the potentially productive factor labour (even though in fact it may only swell the ranks of the underemployed or the unemployed). For the cultivator the resources devoted to the rearing and the care of children is a kind of forced saving and investment combined, which competes—at least where both cannot be fed properly—with the breeding and feeding of the cattle population or other productive investments. It is hardly necessary to point out that high fertility, declining death rates and a rapid expansion of population hamper the development effort by absorbing increasing percentages of savings and capital required for demographic investment. These factors also increase the proportion of unproductive persons in the population who have to be maintained.

---

[1] Whether this reliance on the reciprocity and redistribution principle (Polanyi) in the joint family necessarily reduces incentives to work and promotes idleness is a question which deserves further empirical investigation. See M.F. Nimkoff, "Is the Joint Family an Obstacle to Industrialization"? International Journal of Comparative Sociology, March, 1960, Vol. 1, No. 1.

[2] K. Davis, "Institutional Patterns favouring High Fetility in Underdeveloped Areas, in L.W. Shannon, (ed) *Underdeveloped Areas*, New York, 1957, pp. 88-95.

[3] K.H. Parson, *op. cit.*, p. 12.

Other customs and traditions connected with the joint family have the tendency of retarding the rate of economic growth by inhibiting the utilization of the nation's potential surplus for productive purposes. Take for instance the use of considerable surpluses for purely ostentatious consumption such as expensive celebrations of weddings, dowries, death feasts, ornaments, and the hoardings of gold and silver.[1] These customary outlays, just as the time and money spent on a host of tradition-bound functions and festivities of a religious and secular character have the same effect: they reduce the flow of savings and divert potential capital surpluses from productive to non-productive uses. While no reliable estimates of the relative and absolute magnitude of expenditures for non-productive purposes are available, it is noteworthy that they have been considered of sufficient significance as to warrant the enactment of legislative restrictions.[2]

## VI. The Hindu Personality :

No analysis of the effects of Hindu culture and Hindu social organization on economic development can afford to omit a discussion of the Hindu personality. What are the predominant traits of the Hindu personality which the child acquires in the process of enculturation? We raise this question in full realization of its controversial character. However, this is not the place to go into a lengthy discussion of the concept of national character or model personality; suffice it to point out somewhat dogmatically that any distinct selects and validates some personality traits while it rejects others.

The acceptance of this thesis does not rule out the emergence and existence of diverse and autonomous personality types.[3]

We have referred earlier to one important element of the Hindu personality; the submergence of the individual in the group which accounts for a group-directed pattern of values and aspirations. Desires are accordingly shaped by the group and any failure to fulfil them does not necessarily lead to frustration and neurosis, or at least not to the same extent as would be the case in more individualistic personalities. Furthermore, a person who is governed by group aspirations and traditions may be said to be more regimented than the

---

[1] It is hardly necessary to add that the low status and insecurity of childless women, widows and divorces in India makes it not necessarily irrational from the point of view of the married woman to accumulate ornaments, gold, or bullion.

[2] For example, in Rajasthan where a Minister is reported to have remarked "the money spent on these death and marriage feasts in Rajasthan would suffice to finance its Five Year Plans," K. Nair, *op. cit.*, p. 127n.

[3] For a full discussion of the issues raised in this connection see K. William Kapp, *Toward a Science of Man in Society*, The Hague, 1961, pp. 169-71.

individual in the West without necessarily feeling that he is oppressed.[1]

In the Indian extended family which is itself for all practical purposes a hierarchically organised network of interpersonal relations,
enculturation is mediated by a greater number of persons and continues over a much longer period of time than is the case in a nuclear
family. As a result affection is usually spread over several members of
the large family and identification with particular persons is likely to
be less close and intense.[2] While this may reduce the 'oedipal' antagonism between parents and children it may also have the effect that
the child "cannot identify himself with any one particular person . . .
The big family acquires somewhat the position of an impersonal
system from where he can never be altogether rejected but to which
he never wholly belongs. This weak foundation and the absence of a
clear-cut-personality for identification and initiation must be hamper-
ing the growth of the Hindu child towards maturity."[3]

The patriarchal structure of the family (we are omitting here any
consideration of the remnants of matriarchy in some parts of Southern
India), with it strong central figure of authority as well as the omni-
presence of the ancestors does, however, provide a sense of permanence and protection. Indeed, this feeling of permanence and protection may be sufficiently strong to create expectations of security and
to encourage a reliance on help from others—a behaviour pattern
which may be carried over into later life and may become part of the
Hindu personality. The result may well be the crystallization of a
dependency complex which leads the individual to expect to be taken
care of in a manner reminiscent of childhood.

Additional factors which may make for and strengthen the

---

[1] "The majority . . . do not feel regimented . . . And not all Indian women either . . .
feel. . . opressed, suppressed, repressed and depressed! Our conception of freedom is different because our conception of man is purusha and not the individual,
or vyakti." D.P. Mukerji, "Indian Sociology and Tradition." in R.N. Saksena,
*Sociology, Social Research and Social Problems in India*, Bombay, 1961, p. 26.

[2] "A man born in a joint family in the northern zone has a very large number of
playments of his own generation. He may be with the mother during the
feeding times only. At other times he may be looked after by one or two
aunts or grandmothers. He and the other little ones, once they were weaned
from the mother's breast may also be sleeping with their grandmother. His
initiation ceremony is generally performed together with cousins of his own age.
In India it used to be not the proper thing for a man to fondle his own child in
the presence of other members of the family or when strangers are present. So
a child is generally fondled by the grandfathers or younger uncles. He is thus
not dependent on his own parents physically and psychologically as is a child
in a modern European household. His sisters are generally with the women
folk." I. Karve, *op. cit.*, 1953, 0.13.

[3] D. Narain, *op. cit.*, p. 179.

dependency complex are the feeling of helplessness generated by the iron law of retribution and other supernatural influences, the existence of powerful social and political forces such as the landowner, the village headman, the district collector, and occupying power or a colonial and paternalistic administration. Whether in addition there is also an identification with a strong mother or father figure which supports the emergence of a dependency complex is a question which must be left open in this context.[1] The hypothesis of such a dependency complex would provide an answer to many perplexing psychological and sociological phenomena. Thus, it would explain not only guru-pupil relationship and the extent and intensity with which dependency on the family is maintained, but it would also suggest an explanation for the reliance on, and expectation of, outside help. One may speculate on the emotional effects which a dependency relationship may have on the Hindu personality. Disappointment in expectations of help and denials of dependency and protection are particularly apt to give rise to strong feelings of bitterness, anger and violent emotional reactions. Even more important, the emergence of a dependency complex would have the effect of delaying and even preventing the child and young person from reaching the stage of a fully developed and independent individuality.

The hypothesis of the dependency complex and the related personality type is of considerable interest for the analysis of economic development in a traditional society. In the first place, it throws additional light on the ease with which villagers come to rely on outside help rather than self-help. This was so under the British system of district and local administration and, to judge from the experience of the Community Development Projects, it still applies today. In fact, a dependency complex tends to relieve the individual of the necessity of developing, to a significant extent, self-reliance, self-confidence and initiative.

Secondly, it may be argued that the dependency complex and the submergence of the individual in the group will be carried over into all performances and professional relationships. A person whose springs of action are predominantly group-determined and whose feelings of security are derived from his dependency on his group will experience difficulties in developing an impersonal work discipline and commitments to an impersonal organization such as a firm

[1] *Ibid.*, 183, See also W.S. Taylor, "Basic Personality in Orthodox Hindu Culture Patterns, "Journal of Abnormal and Social Psychology, Vol. 43, No. 1. Jan., 1948; pp. 3-12. On the dependency complex in a colonial setting see O, Manoni, Prospero and Caliban: *A Study in the Psychology of Colonization*, New York 1956.

(whether private or public).   Indeed, discipline, orderliness, prevision and punctuality for the sake of such an impersonal organization may be rejected as pedantic, tyrannical and intolerable.

Thirdly, the hypothesis of a dependency complex together with the submergence of the individual in the family, kinship and caste would explain why and how his aspirations and values are strongly tradition-bound. In fact, goals and behaviour patterns are shaped and governed by these group traditions which are set by the culture rather than by individual needs, and desires. While this adherence to traditional patterns of group action may have the effect of reducing the feeling of regimentation and repression and may diminish the experience of frustration, it also strengthens the hold of tradition over individual aspirations and motivations. That is to say tradition in a society with group-orientated action patterns will have a greater power of resistance than tradition in a society in which individualistic action patterns are determined by voluntaristic strivings towards individual goals. Under such circumstances traditional value orientation and world outlook may not only withstand the impact of social change but may actually remain powerful enough to absorb and assimilate such changes and reshape them along traditional lines.

For all these reasons we must conclude that the model Hindu personality type is that of a tradition-oriented person rather than that of an innovator.

## VII. Summary and Conclusions

What then are the conclusions which can be drawn from our analysis of the impact of Hindu culture and Hindu social organization on economic development?

Hindu culture and society are caught between conflicting and contradictory forces: the forces of tradition and the forces of modernization. The former manifest themselves in such basic thought patterns as cyclical time and cosmic causation the doctrine of rebirth and Karma, the ethical ideals of selfless action, sacrifice and renunciation, the interpenetration of the supernatural, the temporal and social, the continued strength of the caste system and the disabilities of the Untouchables, the role of the joint family and the traditional personality structure. The forces of modernization are represented by the introduction of universal suffrage, policies of land reform, the channelling of investment funds into industrial production, the creation of social overhead capital such as the provision of educational facilities, the constructions of dams and irrigation facilities, administrative reforms special treatment of backward castes and classes and a host of similar measures. The critical question remains as to which these forces are likely to prove stronger in the long run. It is needless to say that such a question can be answered only in a highly speculative fashion. No answer is likely to command unanimous consent.

While the attainment of Independence has given India the opportunity to shape her political and economic policies and to embark upon a deliberate programme of national economic development, it cannot be said that Independence has removed any of the deep-seated obstacles to economic development which are rooted in Hindu culture. The independence struggles seems to have left no significant impact on Hinduism as a world outlook and a religious interpretation of the world. If anything, the struggle for independence may have left the country a heritage of populist nationalism which has not weakened the forces of traditionalism. Indeed populist nationalism and traditionalism may well have the effect of reinforcing the basic world view and value orientations represented by Hinduism. While it was inevitable that aspirations for national independence found their expression in praise for the wisdom of traditions and the sagacity of the ancestors, these appeals to the past offer no solution for the problems of the present. On the contrary "they simply prolong the predominance of generalities and nebulous standards and ideals which, though they may be ineradicable from the political platform, contribute little to the hard world of making economic institutions function effectively."[33]

The introduction and maintenance of universal suffrage remains the most powerful agent of social change. However, even the effectiveness of this agent is, as we have seen seriously affected by a heightening of factional tensions with its fissiparous and disintegrating tendencies. While factions and tensions are unavoidable, and indeed are part of social change, casteism (in the sense of exploiting caste for political purposes) may defeat the goal of bringing about an integrated society and self-sustained economic development.

Apart from the casteism and factionalism, the most important obstacles to modernization and secularization have their root in what we have identified as the core of Hindu culture: the traditional thought and value pattern which underlie the Hindu interpretation of the universe and man's role in it. Hindu culture shares with other pre-scientific civilizations a basic acceptance of cyclical time and cosmic causation and the related interpenetration of the supernatural with the temporal-social. This is in open conflict with a secularized society and the scientific temper. India has never experienced the religious, political, scientific, intellectual and technological reorientation which prepared the West for intellectual, agrarian and industrial revolutions of the last centuries. While there have been several attempts at religious and social reform, none of them have apparently succeeded in seriously undermining the principle of caste or the hierarchical organization of society, or the ideals of purity and pollution. Indeed, it cannot be too strongly emphasised that none of the earlier reform movements ever effectively challenged the underlying distinction between an illusory world of appearances and that of an ultimate reality or, for that matter, the idea of rebirth in accordance with an iron law of retribution.[1]

Furthermore, neither Gandhi's opposition to untouchability nor the constitutional guarantees and special treatment of Untouchables nor Nehru's unequivocal rejection of the caste system have so far had any serious impact on the ideas and attitudes upon which the caste system is based and which it promotes and enforces.

It would be wrong to assume that secularization requires only the separation of church and state and that it can be achieved by proclaiming freedom of religion. If this were the case India would always have been a secular state for it has never had an organized church and has always enjoyed freedom of religion. Secularization in the context of economic development, calls ultimately for the abandonment of the concepts of cyclical time and cosmic causation and their replacement by the notions of linear historical time and natural (physical) laws. This must be the ultimate measure of secularization and modernization. For as long as cyclical time and cosmic causation and its metaphysical implications are not abandoned there remains room for the supernatural, the stars and the occult to intrude into the temporal sphere and to override natural causation and natural laws. That is to say, under such conditions man cannot develop the necessary confidence in his ability to master a hostile environment and his pride of living will be undermined. Instead of relying on his own strength and the application of natural laws he will be continuously tempted to appeal to supernatural forces and to propitiate occult powers.

Despite many verbal declarations to the contrary there seems to be little evidence that India's political and intellectual leadership is unequivocally committed to a secular interpretation of the human and social situation. On the contrary, there is good reason to believe that many of India's political and intellectual leaders, with the notable exception of Nehru, are as yet uncommitted to the scientific temper

---

[1] While the various Hindu reform movements of the nineteenth and twentieth century doubtless contributed to secular reforms (such as the abolition of sati, the legislation on child marriages and the promotion of education), it can hardly be said that they were widely accepted as a religious renaissance of Hinduism. For an account of the opposition of Hindu orthodoxy to Arya Samaj and Brahmo Samaj, both of which are pictured as a spent force which never caught the imagination of larger masses, see D.S. Sharma, *The Renaissance of Hinduism*, Benaras, 1944.

and have remained traditionalistic in their orientation. To the foreign observer it seems as though only limited and half-hearted efforts have so far been made to reorientate and reinterpret Hindu tradition in order to make it part of the great venture of modernization and socio-cultural change. Indeed it appears that there are no religious or intellectual reformers on the Indian horizon who may do for India what Luther and Calvin, or Galileo and Newton, did for the modern interpretation of the world in the West. And yet, such a reinterpretation is required for the transformation of a tradition-bound culture into a new society.

What would be the first step toward such transformation is precisely what India has always found most difficult to do, viz., to select and reject rather than to preserve and to change only by agglomeration. Indeed, this traditional tendency to permit change by agglomeration rather than selection and rejection seems to continue to guide the process of social development. While conservative groups call for the revival of old values, Nehru insists that India cannot live in the past surrounded by rituals but adds rightly, that we must combine the best of both the old and the new." India has yet to make these fundamental choices and to clarify what constitutes the best of the old and the new. Her intellectual leaders must also find ways to integrate tradition with the new ways of living. Only when this painful but creative intellectual process of adaptation has found acceptance will it be clear that India is willing to pay the price of economic development in terms of abandoning those elements of her pre-technological civilization which stand in the way of the necessary secularization and modernization.

In the light of the results of our analysis it can hardly be doubted that Hindu culture and Hindu social organization are determining factors in India's slow rate of development. It is not only the lack of capital resources or skilled manpower which impedes the process of economic growth but non-secular and pre-technological institutions and values such as the hierarchically organized caste system, the limited or static levels of aspirations, moral aloofness, casteism and factionalism—to name only a few of the major barriers. Since these socio-cultural elements are growth-determining factors it will be necessary to take them into account in economic planning, otherwise the expected rate of economic development will constantly be slowed down by persistent discrepancies between expected and actual increases of output and productivity.

A lasting solution of the problem of economic development can be found only by a gradual but systematic transformation of India's social system, of her world outlook, and levels to personal aspirations. This does not mean that India must copy every step which the West or the Soviet Union have taken on their long and successful road toward a modern society. However, to a considerable extent such transformation calls for the application and maintenance of criteria of technical efficiency. There can be no progress in India's agriculture and food production unless social institutions are adapted to the technical requirements of scientific agriculture just as a large-scale irrigation and drainage system, or a network of modern transportation, or a system of flood protection require institutional arrangements in harmony with technology. Western Europe, the United States and the Soviet Union have been able to make the necessary adjustments in their socio-cultural arrangements in the past. As a matter of fact, they are continuously abandoning old traditions by adapting their institutional arrangements to new economic and political requirements. The difficulties of such adjustments should not be underestimated, particularly when we consider the magnitude of such changes as the shift to automation, the establishment of a European Common Market, the abandonment of submarginal farms, the consolidation and concentration of farms and plants, and the mergence of megalopolis to mention only a few major transformations.

Undoubtedly the problem of social change is infinitely more difficult in a pre-technological society in which desires and goals are group-and hence tradition-directed. What is required is a reinterpretation of the core of Hinduism and a clear separation between the social and the supernatural as well as social and political reforms and their implementation by public administration in order to prepare the ground for the emergence of institutions and aspirations which foster creativity and individuality in the great mass of ordinary people. For a traditional culture which is not open to socio-economic change while the rest of the world, including its powerful neighbours, are adapting their institutions to new technologies, pursues in effect a policy of cultural parochialism. Such insolation did not protect India in the past; today it invites political disaster.

Finally, there can be no doubt that socio-cultural change is primarily an internal problem. While financial aid from abroad may help to ease the transition in a similar manner in which relative abundance has facilitated social reform in the American economy, institutional change is not dependent upon foreign aid and foreign loans. Indeed no matter how much foreign capital may be sunk into an economy, economic development will become a cumulative process only if institutional obstacles to economic growth are overcome. In this sense, investments in modernization and institutional change constitute the most promising outlets for India's limited real savings.

# THE INFLUENCE OF CASTE ON ECONOMIC DEVELOPMENT

### Robert O. Tilman

## The Emerging Synthesis

THE ATTEMPT HERE will be to predict the emerging synthesis by determining the reaction of the caste system under environmental conditions different from those in which caste developed and flourished. It is of course readily apparent that an infinite number of variables are at play and that to each conclusion many exceptions may be cited, but, based on evidence pointed out below, the following tentative generalizations are suggested.

**I. Social mobility has increased; craft-exclusiveness has declined; and these changes may be expected to continue.**

It has already been noted that through the practice of *apaddharma* some occupational mobility existed for the individual even in the traditional system. In addition, for the group, society in India has not been so static as it is often supposed. Sir Denzil Ibbetson, who was responsible for carrying out the census of the Punjab in 1881, noted that the whole theory of society is that occupation and caste are hereditary; and the presumption that caste passes unchanged to the descendants is exceedingly strong. But the presumption is one which can be defeated, and has already been and is now in process of being defeated in numberless instances. As in all other countries and among all other nations, the graduations of the social scale are fixed; but society is not solid but liquid, and portions of it are continually rising and sinking and changing their position as measured by that scale; and the only real difference in this respect is, that the liquid is much more viscous, the friction and inertia to be overcome infinitely greater, and the movement therefore far slower and more difficult in the former than in the latter.[1]

---

[1] Sir Denzil Ibbetson, *Panjab Castes*, Lahore, 1916, p. 9. For a recent statement pointing out the same conclusion, see D.N. Majumdar, *Caste and Communication in an Indian Village*, (Bombay, 1958, pp. 330 ff.

As the impact of the British on the subcontinent became felt, the process of change was accelerated. It was the West that introduced influences that were ultimately to disrupt craft-exclusiveness and shake the very foundations of the existing economic order. When the Indian economy became linked to the expanding world economy, new occupations were introduced and old trades attracted new workers by promises of greater financial rewards. Thus, Buchanan observed in 1934 that the *camars* (leatherworkers), a caste extremely low in the Hindu hierarchy, had gained considerable prestige because the sale of hides to European countries had produced a new source of wealth out of all proportion to their traditional income. Similarly, the *teli* (oil pressers) of Bengal had profited greatly from the new markets, and many of their numbers had become wealthy bankers and merchants.[1]

In a more recent study (1947) of twenty-eight *jati* in a rural Bengal village, it was found that only twelve were still performing their traditional occupations exclusively five were in a state of transition between traditional occupations and new functions; and eleven no longer performed any part of their traditional roles.[2]

Kingsley Davis, in his study of the Indian census reports of 1921 and 1941, furnishes the following table showing the percentages of Indians (including the areas of the subcontinent that are now Pakistan) still engaged in their traditional occupations:[3]

|  | *Per cent* |
|---|---|
| Dealers in food and drink | 37 |
| Agricultural | 21 |
| Labourers and village menials | 14 |
| Pastoral | 20 |
| Learned professions | 20 |
| Boating and fishing | 9 |

[1] Daniel H. Buchanan, *The Development of Capitalist Enterprises in India*, New York, 1934, p. 24.

[2] These figures were compiled from the tables appearing in Bose, *op. cit.*, pp. 398-99. It might also be pointed out that, according to one report, "the untouchable castes . . . represent the majority of the labour force at Ahmedabad and Nagpur. See Radhakamal Mukerjee, *The Indian Working Class*, 3rd ed., Bombay, 1951, pp. 8-9. Since the two centers mentioned are involved in the manufacture of textiles, it is not surprising, therefore, that a large percentage of the labour force should be of the lowest strata. Many tasks in textile mills are considered defiling to caste Hindus. Nevertheless, the untouchables are provided with jobs providing incomes out of proportion to those of their traditional roles. Also see Bernard S. Cohn, "The Changing Status of a Depressed Caste," in McKim Marriott, ed., *Village India : Studies in Little Community*, Chicago, 1955, pp. 53-77.

[3] Kingsley Davis, *The Population of India and Pakistan*, Princeton, 1951, p. 170.

|                        | *Per cent* |
| ---------------------- | ---------- |
| Trade and industry     |            |
|    Unspecified | 70 |
|    Specified   | 51 |

Similarly, N.K. Sharma, basing his conclusions on the study of a village about ten miles from Kanpur, shows statistically that a large percentage of the membership of each caste has forsaken its traditional occupation.[1]   Clearly, craft-exclusiveness has yielded to the pressures of changing times. As Davis concludes, mobility can be seen up and down the hierarchy, and with the mobility there is emerging a new middle class that draws from all castes, "some more than others to be sure, but certainly from no particular caste."[2]

2. **Other major characteristics of the caste system are proving increasingly vulnerable to mutation and rationalization.**

As we have note, endogamy and commensality have shown the greatest resistance to change in traditional Hindu Society, but there is ample evidence today that these barriers are rapidly weakening. The informal atmosphere of rapidly expanding urban centres has placed a great strain on traditional endogamous rules, and, in addition economic factors are increasingly rendering endogamy impractical. For example, in one of many interviews in the industrial centre of Kanpur, it was found that a *brahman* was prepared to permit the marriage of his daughter to a member of lower *varna*, not out of sympathy for the lot of the young couple, but because the *brahman*, now working as a clerk in a factory, could not provide the necessary dowry for a *brahman varna* marriage.[3]

Commensality and taboos related to the handling of food and water are also undergoing many changes, especially in the urban industrial areas. It has been shown that Hindus who observe rules of commen-

---

[1] Sharma presents detailed charts summarizing his findings in the field. See "Occupational Mobility of Castes in a North Indian Village," Southwestern Journal of Anthropology, XVII (Summer, 1961), 146-64 at 148-49.

[2] The Population of India and Pakistan, p. 176. The transformation from caste-consciousness to class-consciousness has been noted by several authors. See, for example, Ghurye, *Caste and Class in India*; Humayun Kabir, *The Indian Heritage*, 3rd ed., New York, 1955, pp. 140-42; and K.M. Panikkar, *Hindu Society at the Crossroads*. Bombay, 1955, pp. 6-26.

[3] Basuder Narayan, "Changing Caste Distances in Urban Industrial Community, "in Radhakamal Mukerjee, *Inter-Caste Tensions*, Lucknow, 1951, p. 94. A similarity might be pointed out lining the experience of nineteenth-century France, where the nobility intermarried with the new commercial aristocracy for much the same reason.

sality at home in the village often do not hesitate to break the same rules when visiting the cities.[1] For the permanent residents of the cities, Mukerjee has pointed out that the water taps (which are usually very scarce, especially in the slum areas) have become great social levellers. All classes frequently must draw water from the same source, and, although in queueing up for water much discrimination still exists at some taps, at other taps a late-comer, regardless of caste, puts his vessels near the fountain and awaits his chance.[2]

Rituals and taboos associated with the preparation and consumption of food have also felt the pressures of present-day life. As in any other country, urbanization has given rise to hotels and restaurants, and as it was said even several decades ago, the exigencies of office work have forced city people to put aside the old ideas of purity. Caste-Hindus have to eat articles of food prepared by Christians, Musalmans, or Persians, because Hindu restaurants have not been easily or equally accessible during office hours. In Hindu hotels, they have to take their meals in the company of people of almost any caste—as the hotel keeper cannot manage to reserve accommodations for members of different castes. What was originally done under pressure of necessity has become a matter of routine with many in their city life.[3]

When old taboos come in conflict with new patterns of life there is the tendency initially to seek rationalizations that might render the old and the new more compatible. For example, when caste Hindus are compelled to use the same tap from which untouchables also draw water, a supply of clay may be kept close at hand by which the tap may be ceremonially cleansed before use.[4] Another interesting example of this process of rationalization is related by M.N. Srinivas. According to the author, *brahmans* exposed to Western influence soon discovered the advantages of bicycle riding, but there was a serious' religious difficulty involved. Bicycle seats were covered with the hide of the sacred cow and were therefore defiling to the touch. This taboo was at first rationalized by concealing the leather beneath a protective cover of pure deerskin, but later this deerskin disappeared and the exposed leather seat was used. Similarly, Srinivas notes that running water in homes was at first rejected even by those who could afford the luxury because the water had to pass through a leather washer on the valve. Soon however, the temptation became too great and ritual gave way

---

1 Mayer, *op. cit.*, pp. 47-49.
2 Mukerjee, *Inter-Caste Tensions*, pp. 27, 84.
3 G.S. Ghurye, *Caste and Race in India*, London, 1932, p. 173.
4 Mukerjee, *Inter-Caste Tensions*, pp. 27, 84.

to convenience.[1]

### 3. While caste debilitation are diminishings, the lingering effects of caste remain.

Although the observance of caste prejudices add rituals seems to be on the wane, the ties of caste, on a much broader scale, are becoming increasingly important in Indian life. The Indian Constitution undoubtedly gave some support to this trend by reserving seats for the "backward classes" in the House of the People, in the legislative assemblies of the states, and in the public services (consistent" with the maintenance of efficiency of administration).[2] While the definition of "backward classes" may be vague,[3] the agitation for increased benefits is not.

Recent debates in the Lok Sabha have pointed up well the demands of the scheduled castes and tribes for a better than-even break for the backward classes. One member was critical of admission policies to colleges based on merit, arguing that these procedures discriminated against the backward groups. To this another member added that those of the depressed classes satisfying matriculation requirements should automatically received scholarships. Several members criticized Government for not doing more for the depressed classes in government service; one suggested the holding of a special examination for these groups for recruitment into the all-India services, and further suggested that special reservations should be made for them in promotions.[4]

This broadening emphasis on the ties of caste has given new life to India's caste associations. Caste associations, in addition to fulfilling a number of fraternal purposes, originally served as centralized bodies for directing the attempts of their castes to achieve higher status in the caste hierarchy. With the coming of popular elections, however, their value as political organizations soon came to be recognized. Although reliable statistics on caste voting are difficult to obtain, it seems to be accepted by most political observers that caste

---

1 Srinivas, "A Note on Sanskritization and Westernization," p. 489.
2 Articles 330-36. The Constitution provided that these reservations should end on January 26, 1960, but by the Constitution (Eighth Amendment) Act, 1959, these provisions were extended for an additional ten years. Provisions has also been made for the reservation of scholarships for the backward classes.
3 The appropriate provisions of the Constitution (Articles 15, 46, 335, and the Fifth and Sixth Schedules) do not define "backward classes of citizens." In Venkataramana v. State of Madras (A.I.R. 1951, S.C. 229), the Supreme Court, without defining backward classes, found it impossible to include groups other than harijans and backward Hindus in this category.
4 This debate is fully reported in The Statesman, Delhi, Aug. 10, 1961, p. 9.

associations play a primary role in most local and state elections.[1]

Whatever may be the long-range disadvantages of this political use of caste, this very trend itself is increasing social mobility by breaking down the debilitating restrictions traditionally imposed on the lower castes. Commenting on a recent village election in which an *ahir* defeated a *brahman* and a *thakur*, it has been pointed out that it "was a revolution for the village-one that demonstrated most eloquently the decline of the caste hierarchy and the rise of casteism." The writer concludes that "what is dying is caste hierarchy, (that is,) that acceptance of superior and inferior status with concomitant social obligations and restrictions."[2] Two Western political observers, perhaps too optimistically, have recently reached similar conclusions.

The caste associations bring political democracy to Indian villages through the familiar and accepted institutions of caste. In the process it is changing the meaning of caste. By creating conditions in which a caste's significance and power is beginning to depend on its numbers, rather than its ritual and social status, and by encouraging egalitarian aspirations among its members, the caste associations is exerting a liberating influence.[3]

Upward social movement, crucial for economic modernization, has been made easier, although possible at the expense of long-range political stability.[4]

Although the political implications of caste deserve increased attention by social scientists, of more immediate concern to this essay must be the continuing influence of caste restrictions in the Indian economic sphere. It has often been observed that in Indian industry high-caste workers are frequently employed in supervisory, skilled, or semi-skilled positions, while lower-caste labourers usually gravitate toward unskilled tasks, often finding roles similar to their traditional

---

[1] For the most thorough treatment of this point, see Harrison, *op. cit.*, pp. 96-136. Also see Lloyd I. and Susanne H. Rudolph, "The Political Role of India's Caste Associations," Pacific Affairs, XXXIII (March, 1960), 5-22. For an illuminating insight into the political sophistication of some representative villagers, see Majumdar, *op. cit.*, pp. 297-300. Viewing Majumdar's findings, it is easy to understand how voting could be influenced by traditional ties. For an incisive analysis of the conflicts of local issues in state elections in Orissa, see the series of nine articles by F.C. Bailey in The Economic Weekly, Bombay, Aug. 29, Sept. 12, 19, 26, Oct. 3, 10, 17, 24, and Nov. 7, 1959).

[2] This paragraph is based on an excellent analysis of several panchayat elections contained in The Statesman, Delhi, June, 20, 1961, p. 6.

[3] Rudolph and Rudolph, *op. cit.*, p. 9.

[4] The long-range consequences of the political manipulation of caste associations is one of the objects of Harrison's scrutiny, *op. cit.* passim.

occupations.[1] For example, in the factories of Kanpur, Mukerjee's UNESCO research group found that 90 per cent of all the workers performing duties classified as unskilled were drawn from the four lowest classes ; the same classes filled 24 per cent of the semi-skilled jobs and only 13 per cent of the skilled jobs.[2] It has also been pointed out that entrepreneurial as well as managerial personnel are drawn chiefly from only certain castes and groups. In Indian business and industry, one will most often find these positions filled by *Marwaris, Gujeratis, Chettiars, Sindhis,* and *Parsis*.[3]

Outside the factories of Kanpur, there are many evidences of a social levelling. To be sure, the residential areas still show the marks of caste consciousness : the better housing is usually occupied by the upper castes, inferior quarters are taken by the lower castes, and the untouchables are frequently found living in squalor some distance from all caste–Hindus. The situation is especially true of slum areas, where, the UNESCO report adds, "caste distance and segregation are writ large." But in general the signs are encouraging for the proponents of social change. Averaging the figures for all residential areas, for example, we find that approximately 30 per cent of the members of the lowest three castes now reside in common wards with the upper castes.[4]

The lingering effects of the traditional caste system will undoubtedly remain in Indian society for an indefinite time. But the question remains : What effect will these have on attempted economic modernization in India ?

## Conclusion

Almost every sociological, economic, and political study of India today takes note of at least some degree of social unrest. In the south, along the historic Malabar coast, the area first touched by European merchants and adventurers, changes have occurred more rapidly than probably even the Indian Government would have desired: (Industry) threw open not only many avenues of getting a living but also made necessary certain adjustments on the part of old ways of getting a living.

[1] There are of course the two factors of education and caste to consider here, and one feeds upon the other. High caste Hindus are the best educated and thus qualify for the best jobs. Having the best jobs they are then able to provide their children with the best education. The continuation of this cycle will undoubtedly be observed for many years to come.

[2] Mukerjee, *Inter-Caste Tensions*, p. 23. Cf. *ibid.*, p. 82. Actually, the figure 13 per cent indicates a hopeful degree of vertical mobility.

[3] Vakil, *op. cit.*, pp. 47-48. Also see Oscar A. Ornoti, *Jobs and Workers in India*, Ithaca, 1955, pp. 40-41.

[4] Mukerjee, *Inter-Caste Tensions*, p. 25.

The wider dissemination of technical knowledge was to a great extent responsible for breaking the spell of the hereditary nature of occupation . . . The industrial economy has brought with it the working class and the capitalists . . . The emergence of these classes modifying the caste system is dominant strain in the changing pattern of society . . . With the contact of a foreign culture, mainly the Western, there is a great shifting of values in the older and new modes of thinking and behaviour. The pattern of culture receiving the traits acts, reacts and operates like a sieve in the process of assimilation . . . Malabar . . . has grown sensitive to change.[1]

To be sure, the primary areas of change are the large urban centres,[2] but the villages are not immune. For the first time in India's history large numbers of restless labourers are moving back and forth between city and village, in search of work in the cities but still impelled to return to the villages by strong familial and cultural ties. As has been succinctly written:

in the city the villager is free to live as suits him. Thus the city acts as a centre of new ideas and of new experiences as well as of a new freedom from customary controls and beliefs. Going back to the village, the peasant carries elements of an "urban" intellectual ferment and disseminates this ferment among those who have remained tied to the soil.[3]

Humayun Kabir, discussing the conflict of social inertia and social progress, has similarly observed the importance of increased intercourse between villages and cities:

the tendency toward change and progress was accelerated . . . not only in the circulation of goods, but also in that of ideas. Towns were brought nearer the villages . . . The impact of the towns on the village has shaken the compliance of traditional modes of life.[4]

The result of this transplanted social ferment has been felt to some degree in almost every aspect of village life. Writing in 1952 of a rural village of about 1,800 population in south-eastern Uttar Pradesh, Morris Opler noted that significant changes had occurred since 1947 in

---

1 M.S.A. Rao, *Social Change in Malabar*, Bombay, 1967, pp. 202-6.
2 However, cf. Mckim Marriott, "Some Comments on William L. Kolb's 'The Structure and Functions of Cities' in the Light of India's Urbanization, "Economic Development and Cultural Change, III (Oct., 1954), 50-52. According to Marriott, citing several field studies, "that a kind of extended primary group organization has in fact remained strong—perhaps grown stronger—along with the growth of cities, in India is attested by the lively existence of urban caste councils and associations," p. 51.
3 Robert I. Crane, "Strata Disruption and Social Change in South Asia," United Asia, VI (Nov., 1954), 223.
4 *Op. cit.*, p. 142.

modes of transportation, the use of agricultural implements, farming methods, the diet, the household, communication, and education. An observation of particular relevance to this study is that
with the coming of independence two trends developed. The first was an organization of the low castes in opposition to the Brahmans, Thakurs, and Kayasthas; the second trend was an alignment on a political basis regardless of caste. Both kinds of groupings are present still but grouping on a caste basis is growing weaker while alignment on a wider political basis is growing stronger.[1]

According to Opler, the village he observed is typical of its region, and in a general sense typical of rural India.[2]

Seeking to discover the most significant charges in Indian village life, Opler finds them not in technology but in the field of political and social relations.[3]
The mass education of "untouchable" children, the introduction of co-education, the toleration of widow re-marriage, the wresting of political power from the land owners and high caste groups–these are momentous changes that penetrate to the core of village life. They bespeak the end of an era and a reorganization of intellectual and social energy.

While casteism may be on the rise, there seems to be no reasons to assume that this can seriously impede economic development so long as the new ideas associated with casteism do not include an emphasis on acute social immobility. In fact, there seems to be mounting evidence that caste might be reinterpreted fit in with the needs of industrialism. In a brilliant field study of the Seetaa Raam Sugar Mill, located in a village of almost one thousand in Uttar Pradesh, Joseph W. Elder has illustrated that Hinduism is sufficiently elastic to include within its fold the intrusion of Western technology.
There was evidence to indicate that the ease with which village Hindus became Mill labourers . . . indicated more than mere accommodation or compartmentalization and more than simply the pressure of financial necessity to support their families. They seemed to be able to fit their participation in the Mill meaningfully into their world view. In other

---

[1] Morris E. Opler and Rudra Datt Singh, "Economic, Political and Social Change in a Village in North Central India," Human Organization, XI (Summer, 1952), 5-12 at II. The Momentous change occurring in India's villages have occasioned one anthropologist to conclude pessimistically that "in perhaps ten years . . . it is questionable whether the village will any longer be useful isolate for study." See E. Kathleen Gough, "The Social Structure of a Tanjore Village," in Marriott, *op. cit.*, pp. 36-52 at 52.

[2] *op. cit.*, p. 12. However, for a contrary view expressing the continuing rigidity of caste restrictions in the village, cf. Lewis, *op. cit.*, pp. 83-84.

[3] *op. cit.*, p. 12.

words, as Hindus they could have a certain type of commitment to their jobs in the Mill. This commitment was not absolute. . .But, given the fact that these labourers were employed by the Mill, they seemed able to fit their jobs in the Mill into a larger religious frame of reference.[1]

Almost all writers would agree that "the old order still has a good deal of life in it,"[2] in the sense that India is no more likely than Keji Japan to abandon its own traditions completely for those of the invading culture. It may be all but certain, however, that one of the most significant casualties in the struggle between inertia and change will be social restrictions associated with the traditional Hindu-caste stratification. It may appear unduly optimistic to predict that "if industrialization proceeds rapidly in . . .(India), the caste system will have essentially disappeared by the end of the century,"[3] but there is impressive evidence that its religious-ritualistic hold is rapidly loosening on the minds of men. It is this hold that was likely to pose the most serious threat to economic modernization.

---

[1] Joseph W. Elder, "Industrialism in Hindu Society; A Case Study in Social Change" (Harvard University, unpublished Ph.D. Thesis, 1959), p. 151, by permission, Also see *ibid.*, p. 308.

[2] W. Norman Brown, "Class and Cultural Tradition in India," Journal of American Folklore, LXXI (July-Sept. 1958), 245. For a less hopeful appraisal of the viability of the caste system see M.N. Srinivas, "Castes : Can they Exist in India of Tomorrow ?" Economic Weekly (Bombay), Oct. 14, 1955, pp. 1230-32. Srinivas concludes, however, that modernization "should remove the more obnoxious features of the caste system gradually," p. 1232. Also see Elder, *op. cit.*, pp. 152-53, 167, 304-7.

[3] Davis, *The Population of India and Pakistan*, p. 176.

# HINDU PERSONALITY FORMATION CONSCIOUS PROCESSES

## *G. Morris Carstairs*

(IN THE PRECEDING chapters an attempt has been made to delineate certain recurring patterns of behaviour, of belief and of emotional reaction which could be indentified in the notes of my interviews with informants supplemented by actual observations of domestic life in Deoli. To have presented the dates in this form already implies acceptance of the view that the individuals belonging to any culture will exhibit in their personalities certain regularities which are the heritage of their particular community, and which in turn can provide a key to the understanding of the psychological characteristics of that community as a whole. This view is the basis of a branch of anthropology which has come to be known as the study of culture and Personality or (as Margaret Mead prefers to put it) of personality in culture.)[1]

The concept of the integration of the diverse elements which are found in any culture has long had a place—though not an undisputed acceptance—in anthropological theory. Malinowski, who inaugurated a new era of research by carrying out field work of unprecedented thoroughness in the Trobriand Islands,[2] was the leading exponent of the functionalist point of view. He maintained that cultures are like living organism in which every part is meaningfully related to the functioning of the whole. Many subsequent field studies have demonstrated the functional integration of multiple elements in a society.[3]

It has remained a matter of debate whether the regularities discernible in various cultures are the relatively fortuitous result of impersonal material and social influence or whether they are intimately related to the psychological make-up of individuals who compose each society, and reflect their personal needs and affirmations. Many eminent anthropologists have shown themselves to be wary of attri-

---

[1] Mead, M. and Metraux, R (1953), p. 18.
[2] Malinowski, B. (1922, 1929).
[3] Examples are: Richards, A.I. (1939); Evans-Pritchard, E. (1945, 1949)., M. 1941.

buting too much importance to a factor so elusive of definition as human personality. Opler speaks for them when he asserts that "to borrow terms and concepts from art, psychology and philosophy may add flexibility and sparkle to the social scientists descriptive offerings, but it has its limitations for serious analytical work."[1]

More recently David Mandelbaum has marshalled the arguments which make him sceptical of attempts to base the interpretation of social forms upon predominantly psychological theories.[2]

It is noticeable, however, that interest in culture and personality studies is acute even among their critics, and this may be because they do, however imperfectly, advance a consistent theory to account for the existence of culture-patterns, and for the genesis of national character. This branch of anthropology is also one which has had a very wide appeal to the educated public: the early works of its leading exponents, Ruth Benedict and Margaret Mead.[3] reached a vast circulation. Both of these writers combine analytical insight with exceptional imaginative and literary gifts. Geoffrey Gorer, the leading British exponent of culture and personality is also a stylish writer— and perhaps this is no coincidence: he himself has suggested that for success in such studies "a quasi-aesthetic ability to recognise patterns is probably a pre-requisite."[4] He goes on, however, to emphasise that this aesthetic sensibility can be exercised to advantage only upon the basis of a thorough knowledge of a people's natural environment and their social structure.

The first step in attempting to analyse the social influences at work in personality formation must be to indicate those elements which operate "in the open," for all to see. These are the processes involved in conscious learning, and in the acquisition of overt habits of behaviour (which may be picked up through involuntary imitation as well as through explicit instruction): but as will be shown in the next chapter, they are far from being the only ways in which a people's cultural heritage is transmitted.

Personality development stems from two sources, one being the individual's biological inheritance with its potentialities and limitations and other his learning experiences. The latter in turn may be considered as of two kinds: deliberate and involuntary. Of these, the first concerns the mastery of facts and of techniques, both practical and social, which have been consciously formulated and are explicitly conveyed to the growing child; the second includes a number of

1 Opler, M.E. (1945)
2 Mandelbaum D. (1953)
3 Benedict, R. (1934), Mead M. (1928), (1930), (1935), (1939).
4 Gorer, G. (1953), p. 62.

deep-seated convictions, held on emotional and not intellectual grounds, which have been conveyed implicitly in the constant give and take of relationships with the persons who look largest in the infant's early years. The former correspond with the ideal patterns of cultural behaviour, and with the deviant patterns which are recognised by the community. The latter relate to the dynamic complexes into which instinctual drives are channelled during each individual's slow progress from dependent babyhood to maturity, complexes which find expression in his phantasy life, in his irrational quirks of behaviour, and in their concealed influence upon his supposedly rational decisions.

From the dynamic viewpoint the formal patterns of behaviour adopted by a community can also be regarded as defences against the expression of anti-social libidinal urges. The implicit, emotionally-charged influences are taken to be the more basic ones: certainly, a description of a culture which deals solely with its articulate ideal values is bound to be misleading–but the reverse is also true.

It is, of course, the work of psycho-analysts which has in recent years emphasised the importance of the unconscious promptings of behaviour, although recognition of the dualism of passion and reason, the rider and his steed, the Appollonian and the Dionysiac aspects of man's nature, is as old as philosophy itself. Freud was well aware of this duality. Because so much of his effort was directed to pointing out the unconscious elements in what people did and said, it tends to be forgotten that he also respected the proper function of rational control. This was made explicit in his therapeutic maximum: "Where it was, let Ego be": and in his abundant appreciation of literature and art it was not merely the exhibition of the artists 'veiled libidinous urges which he admired, but the successful harnessing of these urges to provide a communicable and eloquent statement about experience.

Some psycho-analysts, in approaching the study of cultural phenomena, tend to minimise the importance of ideal patterns, of institutions, and of historical events as against the interpretation of unconscious instinctual drives whose operation can be seen most clearly in dreams, myths and phantasies, but which can also be shown to find veiled expression in the formal custom of a society. This is to forget that the Ego is no less a part of the personality than the Id ; and that communication between these sides of a person's nature is a two-way process. Just as, in considering the individual, Ego-psychology as well as the elucidation of unconscious complexes must be taken into account, so it is with the analysis of cultures. A people's history represents its attempts to control its environment, its relations

with neighbouring peoples, and its own unruly tendencies. Its institutions may have originated as "mechanisms of defence" in the
psycho-analytic sense, but they assume a degree of stability and relative
permanence which causes them to represent also an important part of
the reality situation to which each new generation must learn to
adapt.

The present chapter has a restricted purpose, namely to indicate
the sources in their environment from which my informants learned
the consciously formulated facts, opinions and attitudes proper to
their society. In order to emphasise that these "deliberate" influences
continue to operate throughout their lives, I propose to reverse the
usual order by first considering those experiences which occur latest
in their adult career and then retracing the consecutive types of
learning situation, back through adolescence to childhood. It will be
appreciated that this division into periods and "areas of influence"
is an abstraction from the real situation, in which the different spheres
continually overlap one another.

To start at the periphery, then, with contemporary influences: by
far the most important of these is the political transformation which
has been taking place in Deoli, as throughout Rajasthan, since the
Rajahs surrendered their absolute powers in favour of the democratically organised Congress government in 1948. This revolution was a
bloodless one, carried through on behalf of, rather than by, the common people. In outlying districts the change of ruler meant very little to
the ordinary people: their chief contact with authority was through
the tax-collector, and he remained unchanged although under a
different employer. In Deoli, however, because of the close integration
of village society with the prestige of the Ruler in his castle, the
change had profound repercussions. In 1951 the villagers were still
groping their way in the new situation it was becoming apparent only
gradually that the Ruler's centuries-old position of dominance had
come to an end, but as yet the characteristics of the new civil authorities were not understood. Within the village community new foci of
power were beginning to be recognised, not in the official panchayat
or village council (which had not yet succeeded in commanding
popular respect) but rather in the personal influence of a few wealthy
and aggressive citizens.

These contemporary changes were the subject of constant debate,
and they were discussed in the light of recent local history. For
example, every government-inspired public meeting excited reminis-
cences of the Rajah's prolonged hostility to Congress ideas, to Indian
nationalist propaganda and to the reformist teachings of Mahatma
Gandhi, a hostility which had caused the several States of Rajasthan

to lag far behind the rest of India in political education. It was remembered that only since 1940 had Congress views been discussed openly in Deoli, and that their first proponents (who included Gopi Lal and Vikram Singh) had run the risk of being beaten by the Ruler's servants. A small minority of the upper-caste villagers had ventured to identify themselves with the new ideas. They had attended meetings in neighbouring towns and had brought back news of the rapid growth of Congress influence there; but even now, in Deoli itself, a political meeting carried with in an atmosphere of bravado and defiance, which appealed especially to the younger men and boys.

In the innumerable informal discussions in which these changes were deliberated, a prominent part was taken by those men who had travelled abroad to do business or to find work in advanced cities like Bombay or Ahmedabad. Hitherto, village conservatism and the paralysing hand of palace rule had prevented these returned travellers from contributing anything new to the accepted way of life–as Bhagwat Singh put it: "Too many grey-beards, that's what's wrong with this place"–but now that rapid changes were taking place they were consulted as authorities on the new way.

There were few in Deoli who could speak English, but this ability or, to a less degree, evidence of familiarity with Western inventions—such as electrical machinery, radios, gramophones, motor cars, wrist-watches and fountain pens–was displayed proudly and recognised as a mark of social distinction.

The impact of Western material culture upon the village was much less than in the town. Perhaps the most important feature was the daily bus service, passing the outskirts of Deoli. Its fitful progress and long delays protracted the journey to Udaipur to about four hours: but this still was a great advance in communications. In Hari Lal's youth, this had been a day's journey, calling for the engagement of armed guards to see the travellers safely through a bandit-infested pass.

A conspicuous demonstration of Western technology was given to the village when the Ruler of Deoli installed an electricity plant in his palace, in order to add to the magnificence of his sister's wedding; but for some years it had lain in disuse. His was the only house in which bright lights burned at night; the others might borrow or hire a Petromax for special occasions, but were content with frugal oil-wick lamps for the rest. The only radio was in the palace and it was usually out of order. The ruler and the Ayurvedic physician were the only persons who subscribed to periodicals, in the bazaar, a few young men liked to show off their European style trousers, jackets and shoes, but soon found that here this dress was not admired as in the cities but rather despised. European shirts, however, worn with the tails flapping over pyjamas or a dhoti were now a usual form of dress. Many of the villagers had seen films in the nearby towns, and were familiar with sound of popular Indian dance music blaring from radio loudspeakers in the bazaars there, but only the young men seemed to hanker after these novelties.

The detailed impacts of recent social, economic and political changes are too diverse to be enumerated, but they fall under two heads; those challenging the established authority of the old order, calling into question religious and caste rules of conduct; and those offering opportunities (in new occupations, in business and administration and in politics itself) for social mobility never known before.

The current political changes were a reflection of the passing of two long-established types of authority, that of the Rajahs and that of the British Raj. Each of these had made their mark in popular lore. History, as known in the village, was concerned with the rule of Rajput princes, stretching back through historical events like the storming of the village fortress, the battle of nearby Haldi Ghat and the fortunes of the ruling house of Udaipur, to become continuous with legendary anecdotes drawn from the Ramayana or Mahabharata. Informants often described stories in which the Gods entered and played an active part. They explained that this used to be a common occurrence but now, because the world has entered into Kalyug, the era of deceit, such interventions have become rare.[1]

The fame of some of the outstanding Ranas of Mewar lives on in popular anecdotes inspiring Rajputs and other castes alike with a vicarious pride in their chivalry and heroism. This was seen both in the place, where Charans intoned their heroic ballads, and also in the village school where children of all castes learned locally-patriotic songs. The Mewar culture—here is Rana Partap, whose life history is as well known here as is that of King Robert the Bruce in Scottish villages—and in a similarly romanticised version.

In addition to their familiarity with local history and legend, my informants were aware of a community of interest with all fellow-Hindus: but this was expressed in terms of religious rather than of political values. It was made evident in shared recognition of the gods and goddesses of the Hindu patheon. Identification with their wider community was given expression in the throngs which assembled at

[1] It was a shrewd political calculation which, in 1951-52 during the first general election ever to be held in Rajasthan inspired the conservative Rajput Mahasabha to describe itself as the Ram Raj Party. This conjured up an ideal picture of just and pious government, as when Ram Chandarji ruled on earth. It did not, however completely succeed in swaying the electorate although the opposition parties led by Ram-Raj held the Congress to a very narrow majority.

holy festivals; and remote parts of India were known by name because of their sacred associatio is. On the other hand, until the present day the concept of a single government representing and ruling the whole of India has not been part of popular history. In the epics of the past, there was no single supreme ruler, but only Rajahs contending among themselves for a temporary ascendancy. It was left to the Moghuls and subsequently the British to introduce a centralised administration. It may have been for this reason that so many country people, in 1951, still found it difficult to believe that India had really achieved self-rule. One old blind blacksmith asked me if it were true that the British had left Delhi. When told that this was so, he thought deeply and then said: "I suppose, then, the Moghuls are in power again." He remained politely incredulous of my assertion that the Government was Indian now. Others were prone to believe rumours that the British had come back, or that American or Russian troops were about to invade their country.

This indifference to politics and sense of remoteness from the "Raj", or government, was undoubtedly accentuated in Deoli, as in other villages of Rajasthan, because of their forced isolation from the "freedom movement" so long as the Rajahs were in power. Elsewhere in India political consciousness and fervent nationalism have for long been synonymous with popular education: but in Deoli they still carry the excitement. . .of novelty—which condemns them in the eyes of the elders of the village.

The years of remote British rule left, in Rajasthan as elsewhere in India, a legacy of improved communications, of a bureaucratically organised civil service and educational system, and the Indian Penal Code. These Western institutions were subtly Indianised, and yet they never lost their alien quality. As a result every detail of civil, or railway or postal administration had to be arrived at with rigid adherence to the written regulations. The Penal Code came nearest to being assimilated, perhaps because it lent itself to the prevailing passion for litigation. In Mewar, the expression: Wuh pakka char-sau-bis hai— "He is a regular 420," had passed into the vernacular, 420 being the Section of the Code under which people were charged with "loitering with nefarious intend." Other Sections, such as 307 ("attempted murder") and 336 ("aggravated assault") were freely bandied about in village gossip.

The contemporary political and economic changes were thus being assimilated in a process of referring them constantly to what had gone before, whether in public meetings or in the daily gossip of the bazaar. They represent instances of new learning imposed upon adults and children of all castes alike. Religion also was feeling the impact of change, though a more gradual one. The older men agreed that in their lifetime they had seen a casting off of many religious restrictions, and deplored the process, which still continues.

Religion is not taught systematically, but rather is picked up piecemeal. As in the West, most people are content to leave philosophy and theology to those who have a professional interest in those subjects, and rub along with an imprecise unsystematised collection of beliefs. The most basic of these concern the inevitability of fate, the need to acquiesce in all that comes, calling upon God's name. This is learned from the repeated examples of older men's sayings. More specific beliefs are picked up as a result of listening to the songs in praise of particular Gods and Goddesses which are sung at their several feast days and to the dissertation with which they are accompanied. As an onlooker at the temple, the villager soon learns the gesture of obeisance, and the modes of address proper to these Gods. Sometimes he will have an opportunity to listen to a Brahmin reading aloud from the sacred poems (which only members of the three high castes are supposed to hear): sometimes he may see incidents from the Ramayana or Mahabharata enacted in popular versions by travelling players. Part of this religious life is common to all but much of it is conducted separately in each caste's panchayati nothera or meeting place. That of the Brahmins was in a Vishnu temple; the Banias had two notheras, each a miniature caravanserai with rooms to accommodate those of their wandering "saints" who elected to stay in Deoli during the four months of the rains. Rajputs met together in the Ruler's palace, and each of the lesser castes had a temple of their own which was their place of assembly.

As they showed in their conversations with me, each villager in this way came to acquire the fundamentals of Hindu belief, which are epitomised in the concepts of karma, dharma and moksh.* They knew without question that their life was only one of a long series of rebirths, they must conform to right behaviour in order to advance their spiritual progress towards the desired aim of Release; and they knew that the hierarchy of castes and the gradations of sub-human life are a reflection of the soul's progress in working out its karma. They learned to accept a time scale, and an impersonal ordering of existence which minimised the importance of individual existences; and to regard the material world as maya, a shifting illusion. In this teaching morality was linked with abstinence, with celibacy, and with a disengagement from desire of sensual or emotional gratification. Selflessness and equanimity were the qualities which they came to identify with progress in the religious life. In repeated instances they were told that the way to enlist divine help is to abuse oneself unreservedly before God and to call on him with faith—because such an entreaty, if it is earnest enough, never remains unanswered.

Besides these shared elements of Hindu doctrine, each caste had social and moral rules of its own. In former years, the conferences of all male members of each caste were most important. It was here that joint decisions were taken, and these meetings had the power to out-caste offenders against their accepted customs—a very potent sanction. Nowadays, however, such caste-decisions no longer have the force of law, and formal assemblies seldom take place; but still, when a crisis occurs, or when many members of a caste are assembled for a wedding or a funeral feast, matters of common interest are discussed, and the expression of the elders' disapproval is still something to be reckoned with. On a smaller scale every meeting of several adult members of one caste is made the occasion for reviewing current events in the light of caste values. Listening to these repeated deliberations, children and young men become familiarised with the prejudices and preroga-tives of their respective caste groups.

Acceptance of one's place in the caste system was unquestioning. It was a part of the order of nature. As a consequence of this, there was little room for ambition. A Rajput might be (and generally was) proud of the reputation of his clan; but only rarely could he hope to add to it with a conspicuous feat of valour. A Bania might hope to amass a fortune and to have his death celebrated with prodigiously meritorious feasts, but he would always remain a merchant: whereas a Brahmin was born already a god, and his only ambition was to attain Release. The new non-hereditary occupations cut across these old forms, but in the village at least each person has the assurance of knowing that if he refuses to compete, preferring to conform a task which is not exacting and can rely on the approval, and ultimately the support of his fellows even though his material rewards may be piti-fully small. The old system puts a premium on conformity at the expense of personal initiative; the individual achieves integration and stability in his life habits by adhering to the pattern of his enveloping society, rather than by asserting his own personality.

At the lower end of this scale, the caste-meeting becomes a confer-ence of members of an extended family. In these family gatherings—as indeed in every kind of meeting children are not excluded but wander in and out among the guests, sometimes sitting to listen, sometimes playing and chattering or lying down to sleep. They are expected from an early age to show respect and obedience towards their elders. Now and again, when they get in the way, they are sternly told to be quiet behave, but for the most part they are ignored. As onlookers they see demonstrated the proper greetings, the forms of address to be used towards each class of relation, and in the repetitions talk they learn to recognise the approved behaviour expected from each member of the family group. In contrast, and frequently in conflict with this sphere of caste is the influence of new, foreign (and therefore casteless roles and occupations in Westernised industries and public services. Although few villagers have yet been able to enter them these careers offer unprecedented opportunities for social mobility to members of all but the lowest castes; but they introduce new complexities at the same time—such as fixed wage rates, competition for promotion, and the envied prestige of self-made men. The mere possibility of being able to "make good" in the big cities has already destroyed much of that sense of inevitability which was formerly a mainstay of the caste system.

For the majority of men whose education will not proceed beyond a few years at the village school the most important part of their learning occurs within the extended family. Sometimes a father will personally instruct his son in his own calling. This is seen most often among the Banias, a son helping in his father's shop for several years and continuing to receive advice and supervision thereafter, if he sets up in business on his own. Among Rajputs and Brahmins, this is not the rule. The restraints between fathers and sons is such that it is found preferable to leave it to others to act as the boys' instructors, though their fathers will watch their progress jealously. The inhibition of any open expression of affection between father and son means that the former's instructions are usually negatively phrased, in terms of admonition and reproach rather than of encouragement. In particular, there is a reiteration of the demand to be controlled in behaviour, never to betray spontaneous emotions—"like animals" until this is firmly impressed upon the growing boy. To a western observer, high-caste Hindu children seem unnaturally wellbehaved.[1]

In a family life, as in religion, great stress is laid on submission, resignation and obedience. Emotional relationships are played down, but one's obligations towards other family members are underlined. Security consists, within the family as in the society as a whole, in an acceptance of one's limited role with the knowledge that all one's kin will participate in every crisis of one's life.

Formerly (and still to some extent), a Rajput boy's tutor in riding, use of weapons and in pride of social position, would be a Rajput feudal subordinate, or lower-caste servants of his family, and a Brahmin pandit would come to instruct him in book-learning: whereas

---

[1] Dr. Lois Murphy, viewing Indian children with the insight of an authority upon Western child psychology, remarked upon their smiling spontaneity in infancy and their relative unresponsiveness, and lack of initiative in later childhood. (G. and L.B. Murphy, 1952, p. 48.)

a Brahmin boy might be sent away from home, to an uncle's house or to the ashram of a religious teacher for several years. Today, however, all castes except the lowest meet in the same class of the village school, and are equipped if they pursue their studies long enough, for the new clerical, commercial and administrative posts which are replacing the old hereditary forms of employment.

In Deoli a public school has been in existence for some fifteen years. Here children are indirectly exposed to Western ideas, because both the principles and the content of the teaching curriculum were inspired by the example of the British educational system, upon which he Indian schools were based. This was evident in the bias in favour of practical accomplishments—still, the apparent aim of the majority of students who reach matriculation is to become government clerks —and received open expression in the fact that higher students trained for the "Cambridge entrance" examination. Even so, certain peculiarly Hindu modifications entered the system; for example children were taught to know the names, and to admire the example, not only of celebrated teachers of Hinduism, but also of the Buddha, of Mahmmed and of Jesus Christ. It is open to question whether an equal degree of tolerance is inculcated in classes of religious instruction in the West. Because the school is now an institution of the Congress government, and its teachers are for the most part "new men," the curriculum emphasises national history and new ideals of social progress and reform.

During playtime at school, and in the neighbourhood gangs of his playfellows, a boy rehearses those items of adult learning which he is in the process of making his own; and he also debates those topics which he has overheard, but which his elders will never directly discuss with him such as sex, and child birth, and the exciting connotation of swear words. According to several of my informants, sexual play and experimentation, both hom- and heterosexual was common among pre-pubertal children when they were young, and is no less common now; but it is always concealed from their elders, who would not approve of it.

Although it is particularly through his participation in the adult male world of caste and family discussions that a child receives the imprint of his community's values, the process has begun even before this, during his earliest years when he spent more time in the women's side of the household than in the men's. Brahmins commonly mentioned that it was their mother, or their grandmother, who first impressed upon them the need to bathe if they touched a low-caste person, until the response became second nature to them. It is women, also, who give a boy his early toilet training, first by attending to his needs and later by teaching him how to clean himself. In later years he comes to see that this learning is especially related to his high-caste status. From his mother and his substitute-mothers, a boy learns also how and what to eat, how to dress, what constitutes good manners and what is to be avoided as indecent or shameful. Their example as well as their warnings impress upon him the obligation, to defer unconditionally to the male head of his family. Even in families where the husbands were reputed to be bullied by their wives, the public behaviour of each member of the household always confirmed to the "proper" pattern.

From his mother, grandmothers and aunts a child learns the concrete details of religious observance at all the multitude of holy days in the calendar. Women are said to be more conservative than men, and to insist on the performance of such duties. A part of the experience of every child in Deoli is to be taken by his mother to a bhopa when he is sick: he is made familiar from an early age with the belief in possession by witches and evil spirits, and in their exorcism by the power of the mother-goddess. As he grows older, the possibility of such occurrences will be confirmed by the magical healers who are consulted in cases of sickness in the family. From them, as from all his older relatives, he will learn of the many supernatural dangers believed to exist in his surroundings, and how to circumvent them.

The child's sources of verbal instruction can now be viewed as a serious problem of concentric circles, the innermost representing the women's world ; then that of the extended family in which his father, if himself a younger son, may seem to play a minor part. Through the family come contracts with village neighbours, in their respective caste roles, and with religious and magical beliefs which are shared in common with them; then comes the contact with the wider network of kinsmen which becomes evident at times of family crisis such as wedding or a death, and finally, with the interests of the caste as a whole. As he grows older, goes to school, and mingles in the life and play outside his home, he acquires the historical, religious and social knowledge and prejudices which are the common heritage of his fellow-villagers and shares their experience of having to adjust to the changing times.

Besides these "areas of influence," the process of deliberate learning can also be considered as occurring in three temporal stages. The first is a gentle prelude, because very small children are not forced or scolded, are not held responsible for their actions until "they begin to understand." This dawn of understanding is believed to occur when the child can speak a few words, and respond to simple instructions; and this coincides more or less with his weaning at some time between one and a half and two and a half years of age. From now on, verbal demands and social expectations become somewhat more insistent, but a small boy is still regarded as irresponsible until he begins to perform an adult role, which happens much sooner in India than in the West; children of seven or eight commence to help with adult tasks. In Brahmin and Rajput families this is formalised by the ceremony of adoption of the sacred thread, after which any breach of caste rules is regarded as a serious matter. A Bania youth demonstrates his "putting away childish things" by working long hours in the family shop and by displaying an appropriately serious attention to money matters. The final step towards adulthood consists not in his marriage, which may be arranged early or late according to the state of his family's finances, but in his becoming the father of a son.

Every aspect of orthodox Hindu society is well integrated and yet retains its conscious formal rules, so that the complex interactions of economic and ritual relationships, can be demonstrated with great clarity.[1] Similarly, attitudes towards each other, towards the social order, and towards the supernatural are all explicitly formulated. The cumulative effect of these learned attitudes upon the adult personality was discussed some years ago by a Western scholar who had lived and worked in Madhya Pradesh, a State adjacent to Rajasthan.[2] Basing his analysis upon the explicit values to which high-caste Hindus subscribe, Dr. Taylor gives a penetrating account of the inter-relations of Hindu patterns of custom and belief, stressing the impersonality of a social order where status and formal obligations outweigh personal relationships. There is little in his argument with which I would quarrel, and yet I believe that it is possible to take the analysis a stage further.

Dynamic theories of development assume that adult personality structure has its roots in emotional events and relationships which precede by several years the capacity to define concepts in rational terms. These emotional relationships are formed in a child's first years of life and they determine in large part his patterns of response in his subsequent encounters with people and events. They can be recognised most clearly when he is behaving irrationally, or indulging in phantasy; and once recognised, they can be shown to underlie a great deal of his apparently rational activities and beliefs as well.

It would be absurd indeed for me to claim to have fully comprehended the emotional springs of motivation of this group of high-caste Hindus after so short and so relatively superficial an acquaintance with them and their community. Nevertheless, I believe that I did find

[1] As has been done for example by Opler and Singh (1948) by Srinivas (1952) by Dube (1954) and by the contributors to Indian Village, edited by Mckim Marriott (1955).

[2] Taylor, (W-S. 91948).

clues to a number of deep-seated emotional complexes, shared by most if not all of my informants; and in the next chapter I shall attempt to elucidate them. I approach the task with caution, as an alien interpreter must be emboldened by the realisation that my own personal psycho-analysis has revealed that I share not only the same mother-tongue as my informants but some at least of their characteristic unconscious phantasies as well. Before outlining these basic phantasies, however, it is necessary to discuss the theory of personality development upon which their interpretation is based.

# COMMUNITY LEADERSHIP

*Dorothy Willner*

## Leadership as a factor in cultural change

IN EVERY SOCIETY, certain individuals, by the force of their personalities, may widen this margin between behaviour that is accepted and behaviour that is prohibited in the statuses which they occupy. They may introduce modifications and bring about the acceptance and institutionalization of these modifications as part of the role. In this regard, it has been found that in certain democratically-organized societies, modifications of certain attitudes, habits and patterns are truly accepted and adopted by members of the society only when they have been introduced democratically, that is when the members of the group have been given the chance to discuss them freely and decide on their relative merits and demerits. This observation must also, however, be qualified; such modifiable beliefs and habits did not belong to the core of beliefs, values and rituals central to the culture and its perpetuation in regard to which persuasion rarely works. Under the threat of force or for opportunistic reasons, individuals and groups may outwardly change, while nevertheless guarding their previous values, beliefs, attitudes and habits, to express them again when conditions make this possible.

Systematic pressure backed by sanctions, or the sudden introduction of fundamentally different ways of earning a living and meeting everyday needs, may change these core elements of the culture over several generations, especially when the younger generations are systematically educated to a tradition different from that of their parents. This produces real culture change; it also may produce social and cultural disorganization and an uprooted generation, whose members, lacking deeply ingrained values, may be susceptible to a variety of influences which they have no criteria for assessing. This is especially likely when beliefs and values are undermined without new ones to replace them and in situations of sudden and widespread disorganization.

Under conditions of more gradual change, however, especially change in the wider world, many traditional beliefs, values and habits begin to lose their binding force. They no longer have the same symbolic importance to the group. Under such conditions, directed change can more easily be effected through making new knowledge available, and through example, persuasion and democratic group leadership.

## Community development programmes as factors in cultural change

All these considerations should be taken into account by the community agent appointed to work in little communities and in the setting up of programmes of community development. The general purpose of such programmes is to bring about social and economic improvements and to integrate the communities into the national life. More specific objectives of specific programmes include improving health, nutrition, agricultural production, establishing and/or improving handicrafts, industries, marketing arrangements, means of communication and public utilities, raising the level of literacy, and so on. These objectives involve changes in the behaviour, beliefs and attitudes of the members of the community and may involve changes in their established network of relations. Community development may be seen as goal-oriented change.

According to the principles of community development, such change is not to be imposed from above, but rather to be effected through the active involvement and participation of the community members. This demands their recognition that the projected change will indeed improve their lives and add to their material and spiritual well-being. Such recognition may not be easily forthcoming, for many deeply-embedded traditions, patterns and social arrangements may be challenged by the new ideas and projected activities.

The culture of a peasant society, however, has much in common with that of neighbouring communities and the surrounding countryside. Means of communication for the transmission of news and ideas invariably exist. The little community has its social structure; but in peasant societies this is linked with that of the region and with the nearby centres of trade and administration. Similarly, its specific tradition has elements filtering in, supplementing and, in certain cases, replacing older ideas, ideals and practices. The peasant society may be considered a "part-society" with a "part-culture"; and the wider culture indicates avenues through which modifications can be introduced.

## The leadership role of the community development agent

The community agent may represent a new factor in the life of the community. He may be carrying out a role unfamiliar in the culture. His status in regard to the social structure is uncertain. Unwittingly he may compete with established leaders in one or another field of activity; unless he can locate them, identify the source and nature of their authority, determine the extent of their influence and gain their cooperation or at least their neutrality, his efforts may be ignored or resisted by the community. Or else, he may be equated with traditional representatives of governments organizations who come to the community to collect taxes, impose levies and effect a series of interventions regarded by the community as recurrent and inevitable misfortunes. Traditional modes of dealing with such representatives have generally been devised, which may be extended to him. These can range from apparent servility and compliance masking passive resistance to open defiance. The first task of the community agent may be to win personal acceptance; once seen as a good person, *i.e.* as one who does not threaten the community, he can begin to carry out a more active role.

This role is rarely easy. On the one hand, the community agent is the representative of an organization which has a particular goal and in which he occupies a specific status with certain duties determined by the organization. On the other hand, his activities in carrying out these duties must win the acceptance of the community. He has a double set of obligations; those towards the organization, and those towards the community which involve adding to its well-being. His rights, at least as regards the community, are less defined. He cannot demand the co-operation of its members in bringing about the changes desired by his organization, but must achieve this co-operation through influencing the community to want to change.

In this regard, the community agent is by definition a leader, as indicated in paragraphs 5 to 8 above. He is, however, a leader who may begin without a clear-cut leadership status within the group he is to lead, and without the recognition and/or acceptance of its functions as defined by his organization by this group. Within the community, his leadership will be informal. Generally, he has to create new groups and gain a position of prestige and influence within established groups. His leadership functions will be primarily those associated with setting group goals, providing the group with an ideology, serving as a source of expert knowledge, often as an example. In so doing, he will avoid competing with established community leaders since this threatens community solidarity, or setting the groups he may create against existing and institutionalized ones. Sometimes, this cannot be avoided; for few little communities lack long-established functions, which may try to use the community agent, or with which he unwittingly may become involved. A way to try to overcome this is to promote projects desired by the whole community, and to help the community achieve them even if they are somewhat marginal to the programme. Long-established factions may be united on such projects, with the skilful community agent establishing a truce for the joint consideration and carrying out of other activities.

Given the ethic he represents, democratic modes of leadership are the only ones possible to the community agent. Also, they may be the only ones open to him in terms of his ambiguous position in the social structure and his goal of effecting real change. Such modes of leadership may be relatively unknown in the community's culture. In this case, by introducing them, by serving as model and possibly by teaching them, the community agent, whatever his concrete achievements may be, will be effecting changes of the utmost importance.

In so doing, he should, however, be careful not to disparage established modes of leadership. Certain segments within the community, such as those who are underprivileged in some respect or the young, may be most open to the new ideas and practices. They should be cultivated with circumspection in order not to antagonize the rest of the community. The community leader is not an agent of social disorganization to foment rebellion or turn one generation against another. By consciously or unconsciously discrediting traditional statuses or turning traditional "father figures" into "scapegoats," the hasty or imprudent community development agent may set into motion processes which he can rarely control. He may later find that both himself and the programme he has come to represent are discredited; the new leaders he helped to establish themselves may aspire to greater power and have their own programmes; or the traditional leaders he antagonized may reassert themselves. In the former case, disorganization may be progressive, with the community members now vulnerable to all kinds of agitation; in the latter, a deeper distrust towards innovation and change becomes established. It may even happen that some combination of both processes may split the community. Truly democratic leadership avoids this by guiding the community rather than building up specific segments or factions to push a programme that affects to total group.

The training and development of local leaders includes communicating specific insights and techniques in regard to group behaviour that the community agent himself should possess. These techniques may also have to be adapted to the local culture. Some of these have been indicated in this paper. Basic to their application is a clear understanding of what leadership involves. It is hoped that the paper will contribute to this understanding.

# LEADERSHIP IN COMMUNITY DEVELOPMENT

## Evelyn Wood

THE CHIEF TROUBLE about the leader—principle is that it means something rather different to almost everyone who uses it as a base for
action. It also has further, different meanings for those who are so
frequently the subjects of attempted group action—the peasants of the
so-called under-developed countries.

### The excellent leader

We have grown up in the Western world with the idea that the man
who excels in any field must be some kind of leader there. Perhaps the
Americans make the most of this principle; certainly they appear to
promote leadership through competition more deliberately than other
people do. The British are not far behind for competitiveness, but they
do not perhaps have quite the same confidence in this device for selecting dominant individuals. The British genius for compromise has
matured the selective idea of competition to a method of picking teams.
This comparison may be unfair to Americans. Perhaps the Anglo-
Saxons as a whole value the captain of the team or of the ship most
highly. He is the real leader who is the co-ordinator of other people's
efforts and the consolidator of their opinions. This is a very advanced
state of social development, and probably no other national groups
have reached such a stage of abnegation of personal power.

The writer has lived among Indians in circumstances of great
intimacy for over thirty years. An aggregate of over four years of this
period has been spent by him as a village-resident. He is married
into one of the old families of Western India. He has thus seen Indian
attitudes towards leaders, competition and other disputed social
mechanisms from both extremes of the Indian social ladder.

It is very clear that the people of India divide into two large groups
about such matters. Those who have had something of a Western-
style education incline to adopt the Anglo-Saxon valuation of leadership. But often Indians with only fractional westernization, in their
school or college, misread the Western concepts of a leader, and consequently they tend to exalt the individual, the Fuehrer. This attitude is

particularly common in Bengal. But the second, and many times principal group, throughout the country, is the traditionally based India, now best represented by the peasant in an ordinary Indian village.

The Indian peasant does not approve the man or woman who tries to excel others. This behaviour is regarded as either childish or dishonest, and a person who aims at superior performance is invariably distrusted. All the basic culture-patterns of India repeat this levelling tendency. It follows that competitions are regarded by villagers with grave suspicion.

Where there is an adventurous streak in peoples' temperaments, there is more individual license to remake tradition. This is the situation in the Punjab; but, even there, the group—usually a large kinship group—must sanction the new way which departs from tradition. Competitions can be accepted with less difficulty by Punjabi villagers. They are however, swallowed piecemeal rather than whole. It always remains an open question in a Punjabi, as in other Indian villages, as to what forms of persuasion moral or financial, the successful competitor has secretly, and by devious ways, brought to bear on his judges.

### Effects of American Aid

Consequently, when the massive American Point Four aid programmes decanted large numbers of enthusiastic, competitive U.S. citizens into rural India, a clash of cultures was inevitable, at any rate at the level of motives. Fortunately, most of the misunderstandings were funny rather than otherwise. The most comic occasion in the writer's experience was when an earnest amateur sanitarian solemnly led the elders of a village to inspect the maggots of disease-carrying flies breeding in uncovered human excreta. The horror of the villagers when they realized that they would have to peer through a magnifying glass at something ritually as well as naturally filthy was infinitely puzzling to the scientific American. Anyway, the village people had a good laugh about it later on, when their friend retired to his air-conditioning.

It was, however, natural that the Indian administrators and the high level counterparts of the American technicians should be fired with their infections, constructive enthusiasm. The reader should also recollect that everyone of such exalted Indians is largely the product of a Western education; the best example is of course the Harrow-and-Cambridge Prime Minister.

Crop-competitions were therefore launched to determine the best farmers. These skilful peasants have duly been rewarded, both in cash (which makes their fellow-villagers regard them with even deeper suspicion), and with honours such as Presidental pats on the back, and the title of Krishi Pandit. Now the next stage is being entered: setting-up as leaders the successful competitors in crop and other competitions.

Neighbouring farmers would, in their own slow way, be very glad to examine and learn from the superior work of their Krishi Pandit colleague; but there would be a protocol about the learning process which is not officially encouraged today. The traditional manner of learning new skills from a neighbour demands a certain humility on his part. The social mechanisms in traditional India which is comparable to competition in Western cultures is emulation. This is best expressed in the words spoken by a village-elder to the writer: Look! Lord Ram is a great king, a perfect husband, a mighty hunter and warrior. . .and He is a god. So no man should try to be equal to Ram. Nor should any man try to be superior to another man, in skills or wisdom. Every man should try to make himself a little more like Ram, and he may try to learn something of the superior man's skills and wisdom. . .but not to be better. O No! So we think about farming, the results of which are in any case in the hands of God: it is not healthy to try and be nor to do the best of anything.

This old farmer friend was a bit of a cynic, too. The village in which he lives has been touched by the influence of metropolitan Delhi. It is within fifty miles of the capital. Yet this old farmer is definitely afraid of the Krishi Pandit being installed as a *neta*. This word has almost the exact connotation of Fuehrer. The people of this village are quite conscious of serving as laboratory guinea-pigs to official experiments in rural development. The old farmer remarked on this, observed that the situation had proved profitable to several villagers, and predicted the intensive promotion of Krishi Pandit as Pradhan, or head of the new, statutory village council.

It has happened just as he predicted. Pressure was applied to the voters in the village to elect the best farmer so established by crop-competition, as the Pradhan. He was an ambitious fellow, anyway, so he was ready to stand, and he got the job. Then his official backers urged him to lead his followers in the village onwards to progress. The first target the experimenters indicated was the installation of latrines, which were unknown in the village. But the people were not at all disposed to follow the Krishi Pandit's lead.

### The village idea of a leader

Their idea of a leader is a more sober type. He must be a pliable sort of man, and his family should be distinguished in the village. The Krishi Pandit was probably pliable enough, but his family had no particular distinction. The village people expect any internal boss, administrative or political, to call meetings of the whole village about such a revolutionary matter as latrines. Literally everyone who is interested must have a chance to talk, if he wants to, and certainly listen. There are always plenty of children at such meetings, and the women are present, but usually lurking in the shadows. They would be far more in evidence in Maharashtra, for example. At such a meeting, the leader is expected first to state his view of what people should do; but, unless the interminable arguments which must follow such a statement result in a unanimous decision, no action will be taken. There is no counting of heads. Perhaps argument is not the right word for the speeches which are made at such a meeting. There is no give and take. The speeches are punctuated with general sounds of approval or disapproval. There is plenty of *sotto voce* discussion among people sitting next to each other, and sometimes furious, loud argument at that level. But the main line of speeches is purely didactic.

No person who addresses the whole meeting ever retracts a word of what he has said. There is no public discussion, or conceding of points, in a process of questioning after a speech. As soon as one man has spoken another jumps up and makes his contribution—which may be for or against. Fifty disparate exhortations to do or not to do the thing proposed by the Pradhan may flow over the heads of the audience during the weeks or months which such a meeting often occupies. Everyone of the speakers will have some claim to some kind of leadership, recognized by some group or the other in the village.

No one expects any decision to be taken verbally. The voting on resolutions is a pattern of talk-work which is quite foreign to Indian villages. The verbalization of a decision is not wanted by anyone. It can, of course be known, more especially from the small conversations which go on between the sessions of the meeting, just when 99% of the people in the village—or in one neighbourhood in a large village—are ready to build and use latrines. The true leader, in the eyes of village people, is the man who is never so crude as to say Build latrines. No, after some days a good pradhan will have assessed the unanimity of feeling. If and when he knows it to constitute a real decision for action, he will then call quite a brief and final session of the meeting, in which those people who are going to start building latrines will get up and say so. Then everyone congratulates everyone else, and the job is done. The leader is the man with the rare discernment to operate this whole process.

The writer must add that this happy solution[1] has not yet been

---

[1] This paper was written almost entirely from experience during five years of widespread attempts at Community Development in India. The writer had been previously concerned with rural development in India, which had naturally

(Continued on next page

reached in the village given as example. The unfortunate Krishi Pandit, as pradhan, is still struggling to work the oracle on Western lines. And his people won't play: his use of this unfamiliar bag of tricks only deepens their distrust in the poor fellow—who is actually an excellent man as well as an excellent farmer.

### The desire for personal rule

Yet, democracy has come to stay in India, at any rate as a catch-word. To implement democracy in any form, persons with ability to rule by co-ordination have to be found who will replace the rejected Brahmins and Kshatriyas. Such new, personal ruler-types must be genuinely accepted by village people as well as townsfolk. It is however, dangerous to import foreign leadership-concepts to confuse that necessary search for acceptable rulers. It is, of course, equally dangerous to palter with foreign concepts of democracy's mechanical processes, especially while the old, total-village panchayat is still available as a working model. It may be that the ballot-box and other corruptible devices from abroad are now in India to stay. If so, new ways of using these devices have got to be formed by persons who are not blinkered by new-Gandhian or other reflections of Western social and political mechanisms.

*Continued from last-page)*
fallen into patterns that encouraged the development of community action, but without making a principle of it. This experience extends over the whole of the decade previous to 1952, of which more than three years were spent as a village resident.

# PHILOSOPHY AND GOALS

*What are the major goals in community development? How are they expressed ? What are the shifts that take place in content as well as emphasis in times of crises? What is the image that is projected by the philosophy and goals in community development ? How feasible are the goals in terms of implementation?*

*These are some of the questions that arise when one considers the objectives in community development. The extracts included in this section also refer implicitly to the often expressed dichotomy between human versus economic goals or as one author put it—between 'things' and people.*

## CONTRIBUTORS

1. Jawaharlal Nehru, "Men: The Ultimate Objective," in *Community Development, Panchayati Raj and Co-operation*, Delhi, the Publications Division, 1965, pp. 1, 7 and 90, 92.

2. S.N. Jha, "Planned Economy on Gandhian Principles," in *A Critical Study of Gandhian Economic Thought*, Agra, Lakshmi Narain Agarwal, pp. 236-257.

3. Rabindra Nath Tagore "Rural Reconstruction," March 1962. pp. 60-66.

4. Asoka Mehta, "Development" (Address to the Community Development and Panchayati Raj, New Delhi, July 1964), Kurukshetra, Conference Number, August 1964. pp. 6-7.

5. Chester Bowles, "The Making of a Just Society," University of Delhi, 1963. pp. 59-62.

6. B. Rudramoorthy, Extracts from "Extension in Planned Social Change" *The Indian Experience*, Bombay, Allied Publishers Private Limited, 1964.

7. Extract from *Community Development: A Handbook*, London, H.M. Stationery Office, 1958. pp. 1-9.

8. Extract from "*A Guide to Community Development*," Delhi, Ministry of Community Development and Cooperation, Government of India. pp. 3.

9. Extract from Presidential Address of Shri Jayaprakash Narayan, "Seminar on Fundamental Problems of Panchayati Raj," All India Panchayat Parishad, New Delhi, January 1964, pp. 34-42.

# COMMUNITY DEVELOPMENT PANCHAYATI RAJ AND CO-OPERATION*

*Jawaharlal Nehru*

## Man : The Ultimate Objective

IT ALL DEPENDS on how you and I and all of us approach the question. Is it just another of our many schemes—good schemes, no doubt—in which we shall do our day's work and leave the rest to chance or is it something more than that? Is it something which you will direct from above as an administrator, as a Development Commissioner, as a Central Committee or as the Planning Commission and so on, or is it something which will enable you to unleash forces from below among our people to do the work? Forces unleashed without definite aims and without proper co-ordination sometimes yield good results and sometimes bad. A good lead and a good organisation from the top is obviously necessary and essential yet it may be completely useless if the forces from below are released.

Sometimes, I begin to suspect and become a little afraid of these leads from the top that we, including myself, are always giving. We have got into the habit of doling out good advice to the country, to our people, to everybody. Nevertheless, my own experience has shown that people who give too much advice are unpopular. They are irritating. At any rate, such advice does not conduce to the good of others, as it is intended to. That is to say, if we act too much from the top without adequate foundations and without that intimate relation with the lower rungs, we can hardly achieve any great results. We will achieve something, of course. So the problem becomes one of how to bring about a union of these two elements.

Obviously, it is necessary to plan, to direct, to organise and to co-ordinate; but it is even more necessary to create conditions in which a spontaneous growth from below is possible. I wonder if this Community Development scheme is something which is likely to bring about a union between the top and the others. By the term top, I do not mean that some people are superior; I mean those who guide,

---

* Inaugural speech at the Development Commissioners' Conference Delhi, May, 1952.

the organisers; and by others, I mean the millions who will participate in the work. In fact, ultimately there should be no top and no grada- tions. Nevertheless, I feel that even the organisational lead should not be tossed like a ball from what is the top to what might, if you like, be called the bottom; that is to say, even the initiative for the Community Projects should come, wherever possible, from the people who are most affected by them.

Often, we like to sit in our chambers and decide everything accord- ing to what we consider to be good for the people. I think the people themselves should be given the opportunity to think about it and thus they will affect our thinking as we affect their thinking. In this way, something much more living and integrated is produced, some- thing in which there is a sense of intimate partnership not in the doing of the job but in the making of the job and the thinking of the job. Those of us or those of you who are more trained, who have given more thought to the problem and might be considered, to some extent, especially suited to that kind of work are better qualified for thinking and giving the lead than you or I; at the same time, it is equally true that unless those, who may not be specialists but for whom you are working and who ultimately are supposed to work for themselves, feel that mental urge, that impact of the creative spirit within them to think and act, they will not work in the way that we all want them to work.

I do consider that the scheme of Community Projects is something of very great importance and it is so not merely because you can sum up and write down on paper the material achievements of such a project, which I hope will be considerable—all the additional food grown, the houses built, schools and dispensaries, better roads, tanks, wells and so on. You can make a list of them and it is pleasing to see that list but somehow my mind goes beyond to the man, woman and child. The house may be good but it is the builder of the house that counts ultimately, not the house or even the occupant of the house. Therefore, it is to the builder that my mind goes; we want to make the people of India all builders. These Community Projects appear to me to be something of vital importance, not only in the material achievements that they would bring about but much more so because they seek to build up the community and the individual and to make the latter a builder of his own village centre and of India in the lar- ger sense.

Now, how are you going to proceed? Naturally, not by vague talk and discussion. One cannot have those plans without a very great deal of careful discussion and I am glad to say that there has been a good deal of these discussions in the last two or three months and they have borne some fruit already. Yet a slight fear seizes me when I see all this planning and organisation that, perhaps, we might begin to think that this is the major part of our work. We might begin to think, as many of us are apt to do, that, sitting in big buildings and big offices, it is we who are doing the job. We are doing nothing of the kind. We are only indicating how the job is to be done; it is the others who will have to do it. But, somehow, as things are, the persons who do the job are rather different. How to give the initiative to the people in these things? How to invest them with that sense of partnership, that sense of purpose, that eagerness to do things?

Looking into my own mind and trying to revive old memories, I remember how at some periods of our existence, individual and national, we did think that way, we did feel that way and act that way. It is this sense which adds to one's stature. Although that kind of thing has happened in this country, whether anything similar can happen again in our life-time, I do not know. We may not achieve our former standard because conditions are different. Anyhow I am of a generation that belongs more or less to the past and cannot, therefore, speak for others—the younger generation, who ought to feel as we did. Whether we feel that way or not, it seems to me quite obvious that if the tremendous task of re-building India is undertaken, it will have to be undertaken with something much more than the books and statistics, papers and directions and planning and organisation that we may put into it. It will have to be undertaken with something fiery and with the spirit that moves a nation to high endeavour. Well, can the Community Projects be looked at that way? Perhaps, I am putting it too high and it is dangerous to put a thing too high, because if you do so you are liable to react the other way.

I suppose, there is hardly a country—and I mean no disrespect to other countries—which has such high ideals as India. And I may add that there is hardly a country where the gap between ideals and performance is so big as in India. So it is a dangerous thing to talk big and then not be able to come anywhere near your objective. Nevertheless, occasionally one has even to gaze at the stars even though one may not reach them. Merely to lower your ideals because you think they are too high is not right, even though you might not quite achieve those ideals. How far can we take the Community Projects out of the setting of our offices and make them a scheme for living men and women inspired by something worthwhile to do? That is the problem. We measure and calculate rightly and inevitably about the finances and the resources involved; one has got to do it, one cannot act irresponsibly. However, if I may say so, all these are secondary matters. The primary matter is the human being involved, the man who is going to work, the man who is going to feel it and translate that feeling into action. Are you going to try to create that type of human being? The human being is there of course: you have only to reach his heart and mind. You cannot do that only by doling out advice. Take it from me, do not advise too much; do the job yourself. That is the only advice you can give to others. Do it and others will follow. Why do you think it is our business to sit in a big office and issue orders because you are the Development Commissioner? If I may say so with all respect, you are no good if you do that. Better go somewhere else and do some other job. Let us be clear about this.

Whether it is the Development Commissioner or the Administrator, he must not sit in his office and issue decrees all the time. He must take the spade and dig or do something else. No man connected with the scheme, who merely sits in his office, is good enough, as far as I am concerned. If you work, you will make other work. That is the only way of giving a lead and calling upon others to work. We are becoming a lazy people, especially with our hands and feet, and often enough intellectually lazy, too. I regret to say, although it has nothing to do with our present work here, that our university standards are going down and if this is not checked, I do not know how we are to make good in anything big later. However, that is another matter.

Wherever you are, I expect that you should begin your work every morning with a little manual effort, if possible, in furtherance of the Community Projects. You must develop a sense of partnership.

I do not know what our Development Commissioner or the Administrator has done thus far in regard to the production of leaflets, pamphlets, etc., explaining the schemes. I have seen a pamphlet here. It is in English. It is rather businesslike and good. I hope that such pamphlets will be issued in the various languages of India. But much more is required. I want this matter to be explained, not in this businesslike way but in a more human way, so that somehow it may catch the imagination of the people concerned. But what is more necessary is that you, the Development Commissioners, should function in a human way with the people, should talk to them in a friendly way, get to know what they want and explain to them what you propose to do, how it is their work, how it is not something imposed upon them and not even something that is a gift from above. You should explain to them that it is going to be a project of co-operative endeavour, how they will benefit by it and then their children and their children's children. See that you get to know them, somehow, reach their minds and hearts and invite them to work with you; not under your command but with you, so that you gradually form some kind of brotherhood, a fraternity of workers.

I speak, naturally, with some knowledge of my people. I am not afraid of criticising my people. I have just called them lazy and all that. And yet I do believe quite honestly that the human material we have in India is very fine and, given the opportunity, it can achieve big things. How to give an opportunity to this vast mass of human material—that is the problem. You cannot suddenly give it to all. however much you may plan for it. Of course, you must plan for everybody. No planning which is not for all is good enough. You must always have that view before you and you must prepare the the foundations for the next step towards the final goal. And so, you ultimately start a process which grows by itself. Suppose you take fiftyfive Community Projects today; you plan next year to take another hundred or whatever the number and so on. You want the number to grow so that in the course of five or six years you may have from 500 to 600 or more centres.

That itself is a tremendous thing covering as it possibly will, a very large proportion of our population. But I was thinking of something slightly different. Take a centre in one place comprising about a hundred villages; what you do there in a concentrated way will percolate through to the surrounding villages. If the work is too officialised, this will not happen. It will never spread beyond your immediate vision. It must not become something too rigid but be something which has an element of spontaneous growth within it, And that can only happen when you catch the imagination of the people. Then it grows automatically. There is always a danger—I am myself guilty of it often enough—that by direction and authority we may make a thing rigid, not flexible, making it a part of the official hierarchy. Now, official hierarchies are, I suppose, necessary. But with all the good they do, they have a certain deadening influence on anything that is spontaneous or vital. The Community Projects will never grow if they are approached in that way. You must always think of the element of spontaneity.

This kind of project will succeed or fail in the measure that you achieve results within stated periods. There is, of course, a certain amount of vagueness when you approach the people but there must be precision about one thing: about the time in which a thing must be done. That target must be continually before you. And if you do not reach it, well, you fail to that extent.

Really, what we are committed to is not a few community centres but to working for the biggest community of all and that is the community of the people of India, more especially those who are down and out, those who are backward. There are far too many backward people in this country. Besides the Scheduled Castes and the Scheduled Tribes organisations, there is an organisation called the Backward Classes League. As a matter of fact, you can safely say that 96 per cent of the people of India are backward. Anyhow, we have to think more of those who are more backward because we must aim at progressively producing a measure of equality in opportunity and other things. In the modern world today, you cannot go on for long having big gaps between those who are at the top and those who are at the bottom. You cannot make all men equal, of course. But we must at least give them equality of opportunity. So, I hope that these community centres will not merely pick out the best and most favourable spots and help them develop but also try to work out the problems of the other respects and thus gain a wealth of experience of various types and conditions in India, so that this tremendous problem of backwardness may be tackled in the best and quickest way possible.

**Full Confidence in the people[1]**

Ever since the beginning of the Community Development programme I have taken deep interest in it. It did much good but it became clear, later on, that something else should be done to give fresh vitality to our work in rural areas.

This was the panchayati raj programme. This was not only an extension of Community Development, but was also qualitatively somewhat different and it went deeper into the roots of our village structure. Therefore, I was deeply interested in it and attached great importance to it. It struck me as an attempt to strike at the roots of our weakness, specially in rural areas. The measure of success it may attain depends on the workers connected with it as well as the large number of others, such as sarpanches, panches, who are closely associated with it.

To what extent it has succeeded it is difficult for me to say without much more detailed information, but I am convinced that it is working on right lines and if the people connected with it realise its inner significance, its success is assured.

On achieving Independence, we inherited not only various psychologies and habits of British times, but also an administrative apparatus which though good in its own way for the purpose the British Government had in view, did not fit into the new order that we were trying to build. Many of our officials were well trained and good but naturally they were too much tied up with the old order.

---

[1] Message for the eleventh anniversary number of Kurukshetra, October 2, 1963.

We came to realise gradually that the whole outlook of our administrative structure has to change if real progress was to be made. In particular, it has to change in the lower ranks and in rural India. The old 'Ma Baap' attitude was not good. It had to be replaced by full indentification with the masses of our people and a growing responsibility being cast on the people themselves. After all, the main aim of Community Development and panchayati raj was to develop this outlook and a spirit of self-reliance amongst the people. The fact that those people were quite often not trained and had other failings was obvious. Nevertheless, the only way to train them and to lessen their failings was to give them the chance of shouldering responsibility and learning by their own mistakes. We have to undertake many development schemes but the biggest project of all is to build men and women.

I should like to judge the success of panchayati raj from this point of view. Sometimes I have heard, to my great regret, that our Village Level Workers, BDOs, etc., instead of helping to change others have been themselves influenced by the old official mentality and acted only as officials. If that is so, it means the failure of our work, because, essentially, we have to fight that old official mentality and replace it by something entirely different. We talk of the co-operative method. That can only succeed provided it is not officialised.

Unfortunately, today the aim of the average public worker is to get elected to Parliament or State Assembly or to the chairmanship of zila parishad or sarpanch, etc. This has vitiated the public life. Little attention is paid to work done and the results achieved. It is the achievements that should put the object to the test.

It is with this objective that we looked upon the panchayati raj as giving the millions of our people the chance to share responsibility, do good work and grow in the process.

This much should be understood not only by our BDOs, Village Level Workers and others but also essentially by those who hold offices elsewhere. Indeed, we should create an atmosphere which is very different from an official atmosphere where one is always searching for posts. All our officials must realise this fully and earnestly and enthusiastically work to this end. They are in a position to lead people and they must exercise leadership not to suppress others but to encourage them also to develop qualities of leadership in their own spheres. The officials, while helping in every way, must remain in the background and make the people realise that the job is theirs and that the success and failures will also be theirs.

It is in this manner that I should like the panchayati raj to function. I have full confidence in its success because I have full confidence in the Indian people.

# A CRITICAL STUDY OF GANDHIAN ECONOMIC THOUGHT

## S. N. Jha

### Planned Economy on Gandhian Principles

THUS WE HAVE to make a choice between India of the villages and India of the cities. We will find that there is no escape for us but the choice to go to India of the villages. Gandhi examines the economic efficiency and social significance of self-employment and describes its virtues. "We have to make a choice between India of the villages that are as ancient as herself and India of the cities which are a creation of foreign domination. Today the cities dominate and drain the villages so that they are crumbling to ruin. My Khadi mentality tells me that cities must subserve villages when that domination goes. Exploiting of villages is itself organized violence. If we want Swaraj to be built on non-violence we will have to give the villages their proper place."[1]

If we decide to reconstruct the villages and go to them our duty would be to teach self-help and we will find, then, the glory of the villages: "Men or women who would go to the villages would tell the village people that it would be their duty to keep their village clean and make them self-supporting. They must not expect the Swaraj Government to do these things for them. Our villages are on the verge of destruction owing to the disappearance of village industries. They can be revived only by a revival of village industries. Among these industries the spinning wheel occupies the centre. The others easily arrange themselves around the wheel. Thus everybody will learn the value of industry, and if all will engage in industries conductive to the welfare of the State, several lakhs of rupees will be saved, for the people by the people. And it can be shown that by putting into practice the ideal of self-help and self-sufficiency they will have to pay the lowest taxes and realize a greater degree of happiness in the sun than is possible under any other system. Under Swaraj based on non-violence nobody is anybody's enemy, everybody contributes his or her due quota to the common goal, all can read and write and their know-

---

[1] M.K. Gandhi, *Rebuilding Our Villages*, p. 3.

ledge keeps growing from day to day. Sickness and diseases are reduced to the minimum. No one is a pauper and labour can always find employment. There is no place under such a government for gambling, drinking and immorality or for class hatred. The rich will use their riches wisely and usefully, and not squander them in increasing their pomp and worldly pleasures. It should not happen that a handful of rich people should live in jewelled palaces and the millions in miserable hovels devoid of sunlight or ventilation. Hindu-Muslim differences, untouchability, vertical differences between high and low, these must not be."[1]

Gandhi justifies this organization to be harmless to every interest: "Let no one suppose, that the practice of swadeshi through khadi would harm the foreign or Indian mill owners. A thief, who is weaned from his vice, or is made to return the property that he has stolen, is not harmed thereby. On the contrary, he is the gainer, consciously in the one case, unconsciously in the other. Similarly if all the opium addicts or the drunkards in the world were to shake themselves free from their vice, the canteen keepers or the opium vendors, who would be deprived of their custom, could not be said to be losers. They would be the gainers in the truest sense of the word. The elimination of the wages of sin is never a loss either to the individual concerned or to society; it is pure gain."[2]

Thus the village will be the unit of planning and the family will be the working unit ; "A village unit as conceived by me is as strong as the strongest. My imaginary village consists of 1000 souls. Such a unit can give a good account of itself, if it is well organized on a basis of self-sufficiency."[3]

The structure of such unit will be: "My idea of village Swaraj is that it is a complete republic, independent of its neighbours for its own vital wants, and yet interdependent for many others in which dependence is a necessity. Thus every village's first concern will be to grow its own food crops and cotton for its cloth. It should have a reserve for its cattle, recreation and playground for adults and children. Then if there is more land available, it will grow useful money crops, thus excluding ganja, tobacco, opium and the like. The village will maintain a village theatre, school and public hall. It will have its own water works ensuring clean water supply. This can be done through controlled wells or tanks.

Education will be compulsory up to the final basic course. As far

---

[1] M.K. Gandhi, *Rebuilding Our Village,* p. 4-5.
[2] M.K. Gandhi, *Economic and Industrial Life and Relations,* Vol. II, p. 60.
[3] M.K. Gandhi, *Rebuilding Our Villages,* pp. 6-7.

as possible every activity will be conducted on the co-operative basis. There will be no castes such as we have today with their graded untouchability. Non-violence with its technique of Satyagraha and non-co-operation will be the sanction of the village community. There will be a compulsory service of village guards who will be selected by rotation from the register maintained by the village. The government of the village will be conducted by the panchayat of five persons annually elected by the adult villagers, male and female, possessing minimum prescribed qualifications. These will have all the authority and jurisdiction required. Since there will be no system of punishments in the accepted sense, this panchayat will be the legislature, judiciary and executive combined to operate for its year of office. Any village can become such a republic today without much interference, even from the present Government whose sole effective connection with the village is the exaction of the village revenue. I have not examined here the question of relations with the neighbouring villages and the centre if any. My purpose is to present an outline of village government. Here there is perfect democracy based upon individual freedom. The individual is the architect of his own government. The law of non-violence rules him and his government. He and his village are able to defy the might of a world. For the law governing every villager is that he will suffer death in the defence of his and his villages' honour."[1]

Gandhi considers this type of rebuilding the villages quite possible; "There is nothing inherently impossible in the picture drawn here. To model such a village may be the work of a lifetime. Any lover of true democracy and village life can take up a village, treat it as his world and sole work, and he will find good results. He begins by being the village scavenger, spinner, watchman, medicine-man and school-master all at once. If nobody comes near him he will be satisfied with scavenging and spinning."[2]

The functions of such unit, *i.e.*, village, will be all-round development, "The villagers should develop such high degree of skill that articles prepared by them should command a ready market outside. When our villages are fully developed there will be no dearth in them of men with high degree of skill and artistic talent. There will be village poets, village artists, village architects, linguists and research workers. In short there will be nothing in life worth having which will not be had in the villages. Today the villages are dung heaps. Tomorrow they will be like tiny gardens of Eden where dwell highly

[1] M.K. Gandhi, *Rebuilding Our Villages*, pp. 5-6.
[2] *Ibid.*, p. 6.

intelligent folk whom no one can deceive or exploit. The reconstruction of the village along these lines should begin right now. The reconstruction of the villages should not be organized on a temporary but permanent basis. Craft, art, health and education should all be integrated into one scheme. Nai Talim is a beautiful blend of all the four and covers the whole education of the individual from the time of conception to the moment of death. Therefore I would not divide village uplift work into watertight compartments from the very beginning but undertake an activity which will combine all four. Instead of regarding craft and industry as different from education, I will regard the former as the medium for the latter. Nai Talim therefore ought to be integrated into the scheme."[1]

The whole scheme of village reconstruction and working should not be based on money: "You cannot bring a model village into being by the magic wand of money . . . It has got to be earned when it required."[2]

The various items of village development will be as under:—

## 1. Village Sanitation

Cleaning of the village:

(*a*) Tanks and wells to be cleaned and kept as such.

(*b*) Lanes and streets have to be cleaned of all the rubbish which should be classified into two categories

(*i*) Portion which can be turned into manure including excreta by composting.

(*ii*) Portion which can be used for industrial purposes, *viz.,* bone, from which useful articles can be made or crushed into manure, rags and waste-paper can be turned into paper.

(*c*) Manure pits—to bury all the refuge for the double purpose of promoting the villagers' health and their material conditions.

(*d*) Night-soil pits—When night-soil is superficially buried, according to Poore's formula, it may be converted into manure in about a fortnight. Its disposal should be regulated in such a manner as to stop defiling of streets. Each villager may put up fences a few feet inside his boundary leaving the marks intact. The few feet he may leave will by the end of the season be richly manured strips of his fields.

## 2. Village Health

The primary care is educative in matters of health as well as of economy. Health is closely connected with wealth. Investigations have

1 M.K. Gandhi, *Rebuilding Our Villages*, p. 7.
2 *Ibid.*

to be made to find out what the villages can supply in the shape of drugs. Where one is certain of the diagnosis, there is no doubt that the bazar medicine is the cheapest and best. Amongst the stocked medicines, a few like castor oil, quinine, tincture of iodine, soda, and boiling water are the best medical agents. When the workers do not know for certain what to do, they must allow the local vaidyas to have full sway. The most effective way of dealing even with disease is to attend to sanitation. The practice of "The Nature Cure" should be adopted, as it does not require high academic qualifications or much erudition. Simplicity is the essence of university. Observance of the rules of personal, domestic and public sanitation and dietetics should be imbibed to eliminate most of the diseases. "I hold that where the rules of personal, domestic and public sanitation are strictly observed and the care is taken in the matter of diet and exercise, there should be no occasion for illness or disease. Where there is absolute purity, inner and outer illness becomes impossible. If the village people could but understand this they would not need doctors, hakims or vaidyas."[1]

### 3. Village Diet

"Right diet and balanced diet are necessary. Today our villages are as bankrupt as we are ourselves. To produce enough vegetables, fruits and milk in the village, is an essential part of the nature cure scheme. Time spent on this should not be considered as waste. It is bound to benefit all the villagers and ultimately the whole of India."[2]

Gandhi emphasized on the balanced diet to be obtainable to each, which should be within the means of the villager, and advocated use of green leaves: "Take up any modern text-book on food or vitamins, and you would find in it a strong recommendation to take a few edible green leaves uncooked at every meal, of course, these should always be well washed half a dozen times to remove all dirt. These leaves are to be and in every village for the trouble of picking. And yet greens are supposed to be only a delicacy of cities. Villagers in many parts of India live on dal and rice or *roti* and plenty of chillies, which harm the system. Since the economic reorganization of villages has been commenced with food reform, it is necessary to find out the simplest and cheapest foods that would enable villagers to regain lost health. The addition of green leaves to their meals will enable villagers to avoid many diseases from which they are now suffering. The villagers' food is deficient in vitamins; many of them can be supplied by fresh

---

[1] M.K. Gandhi, *Rebuilding Our Villages*, p. 20.
[2] *Ibid.*, p. 21.

green leaves. An eminent English doctor told me in Delhi that a proper use of green leaves was calculated to revolutionize the customary notions of food and that much of what was today being supplied by milk might be supplied by green leaves. That of course, means elaborate research and examination in detail of the nourishing properties of the innumerable leaves that are to be found hidden among the grasses that grow wild in India."[1]

## 4. Village Education

Basic education from pre-primary to University stages will be the national education suited to India. Gandhi commended it. "The scheme I am adumbrating does not exclude literary training. No course of primary instruction would be considered complete that did not include reading, writing and arithmetic. Only, reading and writing would come during the last years when really the boy or girl is the readiest for learning the alphabet correctly. Handwriting is an art. Every letter must be correctly drawn, as an artist draws his figures. This can only be done if the boys and girls are first taught elementary drawing. Thus side by side with vocational training, which would occupy most of the day at school, they would be receiving vocal instruction in elementary history, geography and arithmetic. They would learn manners, have object lessons in practical sanitation and hygiene, all of which they would take to their homes in which they would become silent revolutionists."[2]

## 5. Village Industries and Agriculture

*Cloth.* Gandhi wanted the villages to be self-sufficient in respect of cloth requirements: "The ideal no doubt is for every village to spin and weave for itself just as today most villages grow corn for themselves. It is easier for every village to spin and weave for itself than to grow all its corn. Every village can stock enough cotton and spin and weave without any difficulty."[3] He regarded spinning wheel as a symbol of corporate life and none could escape without undergoing this discipline: "The spinning wheel for us is the foundation for all public corporate life. It is impossible to build any permanent public life without it. It is the one visible link that indissolubly binds us to the lowest in the land and thus gives them a hope. We may or must add many things to it but let us first make sure of it even as a wise mason makes sure of his foundation before he begins to build the

---

[1] M.K. Gandhi, *Rebuilding Our Villages*, p. 28.
[2] *Ibid.*, p. 24.
[3] *Ibid.*, p. 29.

superstructure, and the bigger the structure the deeper and stronger the foundation. For the result to be obtained therefore spinning should become universal in India."[1] Spinning for wages should be introduced only in those villages where people are in perpetual want but spinning for one's own requirements should be introduced in all the villages irrespective of poverty. They must be taught all the processes—ginning, carding or spinning etc.

*Place of Charkha.* Charkha is regarded by Gandhi as the spirit of village life as it provides various jobs, in addition to supplying the needs to direct pliers: "The spinning wheel represents to me the hope of the masses. The masses lost their freedom, such as it was, with the loss of the charkha. The Charkha supplemented the agriculture of the villagers and gave it dignity. It was the friend and solace of the widow. It kept the villagers from idleness. For the charkha included all the anterior and posterior industries—ginning, carding, warping, sizing, dyeing and weaving. These in their turn kept the village carpenter and the blacksmith busy. The charkha enabled the seven hundred thousand villages to become self-contained. With the exit of the charkha went the other village industries, such as the oil press. Nothing took the place of these industries. Therefore the villages were drained of their varied occupations and their creative talent and what little wealth these brought them. Hence, if the villagers are to come into their own, the most natural thing that suggests itself is the revival of the charkha and all it means."[2]

*Village Industries.* Gandhi visualized the fact that agriculture today, on account of many factors like small holdings, its sub-division and fragmentation etc., is not a paying preposition. Evil practices like that of the village moneylenders, and exploitation etc. add salt to injury. Hence he thought salvation of Indian villages lies in the revival of village industries, according to the village methods, *i.e.*, the villagers working in their own cottages what we have referred to as self-employment: "Few know today that agriculture in the small and irregular holdings of India is not a paying proposition. The villagers live a lifeless life. Their life is a process of slow starvation. They are burdened with debts. The moneylender lends, because he cannot do otherwise. He will lose all if he does not. This system of village lending baffles investigation. Our knowledge of it is superficial, inspite of elaborate inquiries. Extinction of village industries would complete the ruin of the 7,00,000 villages of India. I have seen in the daily press criticism of the proposals I have adumbrated. Advice has been given to me that

[1] M.K. Gandhi, *Rebuilding Our Villages*, p. 29.
[2] *Ibid.*, p. 30.

I must look for salvation in the direction of using the powers of nature that the inventive brain of man has brought under subjection. The critics say that water, air, oil, and electricity should be fully utilized as they are being utilized in the go-ahead West. They say that control over these hidden powers of nature enables every American to have thirty-three slaves. Repeat the process in India and I dare say that it will thirty-three times enslave every inhabitant of this land, instead of giving everyone thirty-three slaves. . .Hence the function of the All-India Village Industries Association must, in my opinion, be to encourage the existing industries and to revive, where it is possible and desirable, the dying or dead industries of villages according to the village methods, *i e.*, the villagers working in their own cottages as they have done from times immemorial. These simple methods can be considerably improved as they have been in hand-ginning, hand-carding, hand-spinning and hand-weaving. . .

"Though articles may be manufactured by villagers in their cottages, they can be pooled together and profits divided. The villagers may work under supervision and according to plan. The raw material may be supplied from common stock. If the will to co-operative effort is created, there is surely ample opportunity for co-operation, division of labour, saving of time and efficiency of work. . .

"The idea behind the village industries scheme that we should look to the villages for the supply of our daily needs and that, when we find that some needs are not so supplied, we should see whether with a little trouble and organization they cannot be profitably supplied by the villagers. In estimating the profit, we should think of the villager, not of ourselves. It may be that in the initial stages we might have to pay a little more than the ordinary price and get an inferior article in the bargain. Things will improve if we will interest ourselves in the supplier of our needs and insist on his doing better and take the trouble of helping him to do better. . .

"There is hardly anything of daily use in the home which the villages have not made before and cannot make even now. If we perform the mental trick and fox our gaze upon them, we immediately put millions of rupees into the pockets of the villagers, whereas at the present moment we are exploiting the villagers without making any return worth the name. It is time we arrested the progress of the tragedy. . .

"We are guilty of a grievous wrong against the villagers, and the only way in which we can expiate it is by encouraging them to revive their lost industries and arts by assuring them of a ready market. . .If we neglect our duty to our villages, we shall be courting our own ruin. This duty is no onerous one. It is incredibly simple. We have to be rural-minded and think of our necessities and the necessities of our household in the terms of rural mindedness. . .The task does not involve much expenditure either. . .It is in consonance with the true economies of our country."[1]

*Agriculture.* The plan about food production has been dealt with in the chapter 'Gandhi on Productive System'.

## 6. Village Self-Government

*Panchayats.* In a prayer meeting Gandhi expressed the view that distinguished travellers from the world came to India in the days of yore from China and other countries. They had reported that in India there was no theft, people were honest and industrious. They needed no locks for their doors. In those days there was no multiplicity of castes as at present. It was the function of the Panchayats to revive honesty and industry. It was the function of the Panchayats to teach the villagers to avoid disputes, if they had to settle them. That would ensure speedy justice without any expenditure. They would need neither the police nor the military. Then the Panchayats should see to cattle improvement. The Panchayat should also see to an increase in the quantity of foodstuff grown in their village. That was to be accomplished by properly managing the soil. The excreta of animals and human beings mixed with rubbish could be turned into valuable manure. This manure increased the fertility of the soil. Then they must see to the cleanliness of their village and its inhabitants. They must be clean and healthy in body and mind. Gandhi hoped that they would have no cinema house. People said that the cinema could be a potent means of education. That might come true some day, but at the moment he saw how much harm the cinema was doing. They had their indigenous games. They should banish intoxicating drinks and drugs from their midst. He hoped that they would eradicate untouchability if there was any trace of it still in their village.

## 7. Village Workers

To carry out village development programmes in each village a large number of suitable workers are required. Gandhi describes the qualifications and duties of village workers upon which the whole edifice of village revival pivots: "The centre of the village worker's life will be the spinning wheel. The idea at the back of Khadi is that it is an industry supplementary to agriculture and co-extensive with it. The spinning wheel cannot be said to have been established in its own proper place in our life, until we can banish idleness from our villages

[1] M.K. Gandhi, *Rebuilding Our Villages*, pp. 31-37.

and make every village home a busy hive.

The worker will not only be spinning regularly but will be working for his bread with the adze or the spade or the last, as the case may be. All his hours minus the eight hours of sleep and rest will be fully occupied with some work. He will have no time to waste. He will allow himself no laziness and allow others none. His life will be a constant lesson to his neighbours in ceaseless and joy-giving industry. Our compulsory or voluntary idleness has to go. If it does not go, no panacea will be of any avail, and semi-starvation will remain the eternal problem that it is. He *who eats two grains must produce four.* Unless the law is accepted as universal, no amount of reduction in population would serve to solve the problem. If the law is accepted and observed, we have room enough to accommodate millions more to come.

The village worker will thus be a living embodiment of industry. He will master all the process of Khadi, from cotton growing and picking to weaving, and will devote all his thought to perfecting them. If he treats it as a science, it won't jar on him, but he will drive fresh joy from it, everyday as he realizes more and more its great possibilities. If he will go to the village as a teacher, he will go there no less as a learner. He will soon find that he has much to learn from the simple villagers. He will enter into every detail of village life, he will discover the village handicrafts and investigate the possibilities to their growth and their improvement. He may find the villagers completely apathetic to the message of Khadi, but he will, by his life of service, compel interest and attention. Of course, he will not forget his limitations and will not engage in, for him, the futile task of solving the problem of agricultural indebtedness.

Sanitation and hygiene will engage a good part of his attention. His home and surroundings will not only be a model of cleanliness, but he will help to promote sanitation in the whole village by taking the broom and the basket round.

He will not attempt to set up a village dispensary or to become the village doctor. These are traps which must be avoided. It happened during my Harijan tour to come across a village where one of our workers who should have known better had built a pretentious building in which he had housed a dispensary and was distributing free medicine to the villages around. In fact, the medicines were being taken from home to home by volunteers and the dispensary was described as boasting a register of 1200 patients a month! I had naturally to criticize this severely. This was not the way to do village work, I told him. His duty was to inculcate lessons of hygiene and sanitation in the village folk and thus to show them the way of preventing illness, rather than attempt to cure them. I asked him to leave the palace-like building and to hire it out to the Local Board and to settle in that chad huts. All that one need stock in the way of drugs is quinine, castor oil and iodine and the like. The worker should concentrate more on helping people realize the value of personal and village cleanliness and maintaining it at all costs.

Then he will interest himself in the welfare of the village Harijans. His home will be open to them. In fact, they will turn to him naturally for help in their troubles and difficulties. If the village folk will not suffer him to have the Harijan friends in his house situated in their midst, he must take up his residence in the Harijan quarters.

A word about the knowledge of the alphabet. It has its place, but I should warn you against a misplaced emphasis on it. Do not proceed on the assumption that you cannot proceed with rural instruction without first teaching the children or adults how to read and write. Lots of useful information on current affairs, history, geography and elementary arithmetic, can be given by word of mouth before the alphabet is touched. The eyes, the ears and the tongue come before the hand. Reading comes before writing, and drawing before tracing the letters of alphabet.

If this natural method is followed, the understanding of the children will have a much better opportunity of development than when it is under check by beginning the children's training with the alphabet.

The worker's life will be in tune with the village life. He will not pose as a litterateur buried in his books, loath to listen to details of humdrum life. On the contrary, the people, whenever they see him, will find him busy with his tools—spinning wheel, loom, adze, spade etc.—and always responsive to their meanest inquiries. He will always insist on working for his bread. God has given to everyone the capacity of producing more than his daily needs and, if he will only use his resourcefulness, he will not be in want of an occupation suited to his capacities, however poor they may be. It is more likely than not that the people will gladly maintain him, but it is not improbable that in some places he may be given a cold shoulder. He will still plod on. It is likely that in some villages he may be boycotted for his pro-Harijan proclivities. Let him in that case approach the Harijans and look to them to provide him with food. The labourer is always worthy of his hire and, if he conscientiously serves them let him not hesitate to accept his food from the Harijans, always provided that he gives more than he takes. In the very early stages, of course, he will draw his meagre allowance from central fund where such is possible.

Remember that our weapons are spiritual. It is a force that works irresistibly, if imperceptibly. Its progress is geometrical rather than arithmetical. It never ceases so long as there is a propeller behind. The background of all your activities has, therefore, to be spiritual. Hence the necessity for the strictest purity of conduct and character.

You will not tell me that this is an impossible programme, that you have not the qualifications for it. That you have not fulfilled it so far should be no impediment in your way. If it appeals, to your reasons and your heart, you must not hesitate. Do not fight shy of the experiment. The experiment will itself provide the momentum for more and more effort."[1]

### Government's Role in Gandhian Economic Planning

It is legitimate to ask as to what our Government can do in respect of the Gandhian Economic Plan of reviving the Indian Villages. Gandhi himself has thrown light in this respect thus, "The Governments should notify the villagers that they will be expected to manufacture Khaddar for the needs of their villages within a fixed date after which no cloth will be supplied to them. The Governments in their turn will supply the villagers with cotton seed or cotton wherever required, at cost price and the tools of manufacture also at cost, to be recovered in easy instalments payable in, say, five years or more. They will supply them with instructors wherever necessary and undertake to buy surplus stock of Khaddar, provided that the villagers in question have their cloth requirements supplied from their own manufacture. This should do away with cloth shortage without fuss and with very little overhead charges.

The villages will be surveyed and a list prepared of things that can be manufactured locally with little or no help and which may be required for village use or for sale outside, such, for instance, as ghani-pressed oil and cakes, burning oil prepared through ghanis, hand-pounded rice, tadgud, honey, toys, mats, hand-made paper, village soap etc. If enough care is thus taken the villages, most of them as good as dead or dying, will hum with life and exhibit the immense possibilities they have of supplying most of their wants themselves and of the cities and towns of India."[2]

But the difficulty is, "When our own approach is not quite clear and there are different viewpoints and pulls, then it becomes even more difficult to deal with the problem."[3] We require robust faith in the ideals as Gandhi himself had, writing under the caption "Is He Buried Alive?" Gandhi replied in Harijan: "I cling to the hope that I am not

---

1 M.K. Gandhi, *Rebuilding Our Villages*, pp. 66-69.
2 *Ibid.*, pp. 100-101.
3 Pyarelal Nayar, *Mahatma Gandhi—The Last Phase*, Vol. II, p. 31.

yet buried alive. The hope rests on the belief that the masses have not lost faith in them (his ideals). When it is proved that they have, they will be lost and I can then be said to have been buried alive. But so long as my faith burns bright, as I hope it will even if I stand alone, I shall be alive in the grave and what is more, speaking from it."[1] The reason for the apathy towards Gandhian Economic Thought is, "You seem to forget that after 150 years of slavery, it would not be too much to presume that we shall need atleast half that much time to cleanse our body politic of the virus that has infiltrated every cell and pore of our being during our subjection. Far greater sacrifices will be needed after the attainment of swaraj (people's government) to realize Suraj (the era of good government or happiness of the people) than were required for the attainment of freedom."[2]

To conclude in the words of Richard B. Gregg, "here was the great wise man, Gandhiji; who showed India and the world the wise way to go. He was wise in economic affairs as well as in moral and political affairs. He was a great economist and businessman as well as a great statesman. Do you really understand his wisdom and his ways of doing things and why? Have you taken time to study his life and think it over and over? He belongs especially to India but there are increasing signs that some other parts of the world, especially in America whose ways seem wholly opposed to his. Perhaps that is because Americans have experienced the futility of unchecked industrialism and are beginning to realize that it is a blind alley leading to a desert.

Make your own choice. Live up to the light that is in you. But realize that for every effort or lack of effort one has to pay a price. If India adopts unqualified industrialism, she and her people will pay a heavy price. If she follows Gandhiji's advice, she will have to pay a different kind of price, but it will be hard for it will require changes of thinking and feeling. The price of a mistake is always heavier than that of a wise choice.[3]

The wisest choice under Indian conditions is to follow Gandhian Economic Thought to bring about an economic and social order, perhaps undreamt of, yet giving sufficient light to our track ahead and promising conclusively. But men by instinct inherit a variety of fears and therefore oppose such independent and new thoughts. To put in the words of Bertrand Russell, "Men fear thought as they fear nothing else on earth—more than ruin, more even than death. Thought is

[1] Pyarelal Nayar, *Mahatma Gandhi—The Last Phase*, Vol. I, p. 649.
[2] *Ibid.*
[3] Richard B. Gregg, *A Philosophy of Indian Economic Development*, p. 115.

subversive and revolutionary, destructive and terrible; thought is merciless to privilege, established institutions, and comfortable habits; thought is anarchic aud lawless, indifferent to authority, careless of the well-tried wisdom of the ages. Thought looks into the pit of hell and is not afraid. It sees man, a feeble speck, surrounded by un-fathomable depths of silence; yet it bears itself proudly, as unmoved as if it were lord of the universe. Thought is great and swift and free, the light of the world, and the chief glory of man."[1]

But if thought is to become the possession of many, not the privi-lege of the few, we must have done with fear. To put again in words of Bertrand Russell, "It is fear that holds men back—fear lest their cherished beliefs should prove delusions, fear lest the institutions by which they live should prove harmful, fear lest they themselves should prove less worthy of respect than they have supposed to be. So the opponents of thought argue in the unconscious depths of their souls. And so they act in their churches, their schools, and their universities.[2]

No institution inspired by fear can further live. Hope not fear, is the creative principle in human affairs. If the thoughts are permeable in heads and hearts the details of working may be worked out on the basic principles of the thoughts.

---

[1] Bertrand Russell, *Principles of Social Reconstruction*, p. 115.
[2] *Ibid.*, pp. 115-16.

# RURAL RECONSTRUCTION

## *Rabindranath Tagore*

### Basic Inspiration for Rural Reconstruction

WHEN I FIRST bought this house I had no special plans. I was occupied with Santiniketan was far from crowed life, and while it helped its students to pass examinations, it gave them something more than the ration stipulated by the Education Department.

But even in the midst of my Santiniketan work another current flowed in my mind. Living in the villages of Shelaidah and Patisar I had made my first direct contact with rural life. Zamindari was then my calling. The tenants came to me with their tales of joy and sorrow, complaints and requests, through which the village discovered itself to me. On the one hand was the external scene of rivers, meadows, rice-fields, and mud huts sheltered under trees; on the other was the inner story of the people. I came to understand their troubles in the course of my work.

I am an urban creature, city-born. My forefathers were among the earliest inhabitants of Calcutta and my childhood years felt no touch of the village. When I started to look after our estates, I feared that my duties would be irksome. I was not used to such work-keeping accounts, collecting revenue, credit and debit—and my ignorance lay heavy on my mind. I could not imagine that, tied down to figures and accounts, I might yet remain human and natural.

### ☐ The Dynamic Approach

As I entered into the work, it took hold of me. It is my nature that, whenever I undertake any responsibility I lose myself in it and try to do my utmost. When I once had to teach, I put my whole heart into it and it was a great pleasure. Setting myself to unravel the complexities of Zamindari work I earned a reputation for the new methods I evolved: as a matter of fact, neighbouring landlords began to send their men to me to learn my methods.

The old men on my staff grew alarmed. They used to maintain records in a way that I could never have grasped. Their idea was that I should understand nothing more than what they chose to explain. A change of method would create confusion, so they said. They pointed out that on anything becoming a subject matter of litigation, the court would be doubtful about the new way the records were kept. I persisted though changing things from top to bottom, and the result proved to be satisfactory.

The tenants often came to see me. Morning, noon, evening or night my door was always open to them. Sometimes I had to spend the whole day listening to their representations, and mealtimes would slip by. I did all this work with enthusiasm and joy. I had lived in seclusion since boyhood and here was my first experience of the village. I was filled with the pleasure of blazing new trails.

## Acquaintance with Village Problems

I was anxious to see village life in the minutest detail. My duties took me from village to village over long distances by rivers, large and small, and across heels, thus giving me a chance to see all aspects of village life and to satisfy my eager curiosity about the daily tasks of village-folk and the varied cycle of their work. Slowly the poverty and misery of the people grew vivid before my eyes and made me restless and I began to wish that I could do something for them. I was struck with shame that I was a zamindar, impelled by the money motive, absorbed in revenue returns. With that realisation I awoke to the task of trying to stir the minds of the people, so that they could shoulder their own responsibilities.

## The Basic Ideal—Cases Illustrated

To try to help villagers from outside could do no good. How to kindle a spark of life in them—that was my problem. It was so difficult to help them because the people had so little respect for themselves. "We are curse," they would say; "only the whip can keep us straight."

One day a fire broke out in a village nearby. The people were so utterly dazed that they could do nothing. Then the men from a neighbouring Muslim village came rushing and fought the fire. There was no water and the thatched roofs had to be pulled down to prevent the fire from spreading. The striken ones had to be beaten up before they would let this be done. Afterwards they came and told me how fortunate it was, "our roofs were dismantled—that is how we have been saved." They were happy that the beating benefitted them; but I filled myself with shame.

I planned to put up a small building for them at the centre of the village, where at the day's end they could get together, read newspapers, listen to recitations from the Ramayana and the Mahabharata— it would be a sort of a club. For, I had been unhappy, thinking of their cheerless evenings, as cheerless as if the same tedious line of a verse was erected. But, then it was never used. I engaged a teacher, but pupils kept away on all kinds of excuses.

In contrast, the Muslims from the other village came to me and said, "Will you give us a teacher? We are ready to bear the expenses." I agreed and a school was set up in the village and probably it is still there. In my village, nothing could be done its inhabitants had lost all faith in themselves.

The habit of dependence has come down to us from time immemorial. In the olden days one rich man used to be the mainstay of the village and its guide. Health, education and all else were his responsibility. In this way an indirect tax was levied in Indian society upon the wealthy and they submitted to it because in India the individual could not use the whole of his wealth according to his whims. There was a time when I bestowed much praise on that system, but it is also true that because of it the common man's capacity for self-reliance was enfeebled.

In my estate the river was far away and lack of water was a serious problem. I said to my tenants, "If you dig wells, I shall have the masonry work done." They replied, "You want to fry a fish in its own oil! We shall dig the wells and you will go to heaven through the merit of having provided water for the thirsty, all by our labour!" The idea, obviously, was that an account of all such deeds was kept by the gods and while I, having earned great merit, could go to the seventh heaven, the village people would simply get some water. I had to withdraw my proposal.

Let me give another example. I had built a road from our estate office up to Kushtia. I told the villagers who lived close to the road, "The upkeep of this road is your responsibility. You can easily get together and repair the ruts." It was, in fact, their ox-cart wheels that damaged the road and put it out of use during the rains. They replied, "Must we look after the road as that gentlefolk from Kushtia can come and go with ease?" They could not bear the thought that others should also enjoy the fruits of their labour. Rather than let that happen, they would put up with any inconvenience themselves.

The poor in our villages have borne many insults, the powerful have done many wrongs. At the same time, the powerful have had to do all the welfare work. Caught between tyranny and charity, the village people have been emptied of self-respect. They ascribe their miseries to sins committed in previous births, and believe that, to have a better life, they must be reborn with a greater fund of merit. The conviction that there is no escape from sufferings makes them helpless.

Once upon a time the rick regarded it as an act of merit to provide water and education. Through their goodwill the villages were well off. But when the rick started to move away to towns, the water-supply ceased, malaria and cholera struck hard, and the springs of happiness dried up in village after village. It is hard to imagine a life as cheerless as that in our rural areas.

I could see no way out. It is far from easy to do something for people who have cultivated weakness for centuries and do not know what self-help means. Still I had to make a start. In those days my only helper was Kalimohan. Fever used to grip him morning and evening. With my medicine box I treated him, and never thought that I could get him to survive.

The Shastras say: Shraddhaya deyam—if you give then give with care and respect. This is how I set to work. From my office building I had often watched the farmers going afield with their bullocks and ploughs. Their land was in small strips and each man tilled his own holding. That, I know, was a great waste of energy. So I sent for the men and said, "Plough all your land jointly. Pool the strength and resources of all. Then you can even use tractors. If you all work together, small differences in personal holdings will not matter, Whatever the profit, you will share it equitably. Store all the produce of the village at one place and you will get a fair price from the middlemen." They listened and said, "The idea is good, but how are we to work it out?" If I had the knowledge and the training, I would have said, "I will take the responsibility." They all knew me. But one cannot do good simply be wanting to; there is nothing so dangerous as ignorant help. Young men from town once went to a village to help the people. These young men knew neither the language of the villagers nor the workings of their mind. No wonder the people cried jeering. "Look, there come the quarter-rupee gentlefolk."

But something had to be done. I sent my son and Santosh abroad to learn agriculture and dairy farming. And in several other ways I started to work and to think.

It was about this time that I bought this house. I thought I would continue here the work I had begun at Shelaidah. The tumbledown house was supposed to be haunted! I had to spend a lot of money on its repair. Then, for a while, I sat still. Andrews said, "Sell off the house." But I thought to myself, "since I have acquired it, maybe there is some significance. Maybe one of my two objects in life will be fulfilled here." I had no idea, though of how and when. When seed is strewn in an auspicious moment even on barren land, it may sprout all of a sudden. At that time there was no such sign. Everything needful was scarce. However, slowly the seed started to put forth shoots.

My friend Elmhirst helped me a great deal. It was in his hands that this place grew into an independent field of work and made steady progress. It would not have been right to lump it with Santiniketan.

### The Self-Help Factor

I have one more word for you. We must see that a force from within the people starts functioning. When I was writing Swadeshi Samaj the same idea had struck me. What I wanted to say then was that we did not have to think of the whole country; we could make a start with one or two villages. If we could free even one village from the shackles of helplessness and ignorance, an ideal for the whole of India would be established. That is what occurred to me then and that is what I still think. Let a few villages be rebuilt in this way, and I shall say they are my India. That is the way to discover the true India.

### Work in Festive Spirit

I am glad to read the report on the progress of your work. Your efforts will have attained their final success only when the habit of engaging one's abilities in works of common welfare becomes ingrained in every individual. It is my firm belief that once this happens at one place it will spread from village to village.

I would like to emphasise one point here. With our work we must also bring in a spirit of joy. Our villages have become utterly joyless. The drought must be removed from their lives. The welfare activities should as far as possible be given a festive look. You should observe one day in the year as a tree-planting festival. It will be suitable to choose some day towards the end of Vaisakh. It will be a holiday for the schools so that the boys can join in the replanting festival and you can take them out for a picnic. If the building of a road and such other welfare activities started with some festival-like ceremony they would acquire in the eyes of the people something of the character of our traditional socio-religious duties.

I have seen village life very intimately, I have seen its sorrows and its happiness. When I lived in the boat on the Padmanmy main work was to see, I just sat watching.

# DEVELOPMENT*

### Ashok Mehta

DEVELOPMENT, AS WE all know, is the product of psychological awakening, cultural efflorescence, economic stirrings and social flux. Development demands both discontent with the prevailing conditions. This tension between discontent and dedication is an essential element of community development.

A German poet, Ernst Toller, wrote in his autobiography: "I died, was reborn; I died, was reborn; I was my own mother." In my view, this constitutes the essence of the developmental revolution. However, only Titans can achieve this creative transformation by themselves, that is, individually and in isolation. The rest of us need the support and inspiration of others around us, and so development unfolds through community development, or not at all.

The new socio-cultural ethos that we are thinking of must be built up in both the rural and the urban areas. For over a decade we have paid considerable attention to the organisation of community development in rural areas; similar efforts by different authorities in the cities have been restricted to certain centres and on a much less ambitious scale. We cannot afford to think of the urban and rural areas as water-tight compartments. In fact, an eminent demographer has estimated that if population growth remains unchecked and the current social trends continue:

"the net number of migrants to Indian cities between 1960 and 2000 will be of the order of 99 and 201 million, and in 2000 the largest city will contain between 36 and 66 million inhabitants."

It seems necessary to think of community development as part of an integrated whole, with mutually-supporting programmes in the rural and urban areas. Perhaps, we could use the movement to make a dent on the problems of the migrants to the cities and the development of growth-centres in the rural areas as countermagnets.

The ability to achieve results on the part of the Community Development organisation, with its network of extension services,

---

*Address to the Annual Conference on Community Development and Panchayati Raj.

depends partly on its own efforts and partly on the general climate of opinion in the country. General atmosphere of hope and confidence, of understanding and efforts, can be created only if politicians and publicists, educationists and the elite groups jointly will it: "A will to will the common will." The widening of horizons, sloughing of old habits, release of energy, assertion of confidence—all these cannot be injected by any field staff; they emanate from a revolutionary elan in the country.

While the above statement is basically true, equally true is the fact that a major responsibility of the bureaucracy in a developing country is of supplying a long run, and broad time-horizon, and an expanding set of development objectives to be realised through input transformation in both the private and public sectors.

Those entrusted with the conduct of the Community Development movement cannot shirk the responsibility for the unsatisfactory nature of the impact, even in terms of bare awareness, made by the Movement on the rural people. A recent public opinion survey, carried out in the Delhi region by the Indian Institute of Public Administration, showed that a very few—a bare 5 per cent—had 'considerable' knowledge of the goals of Community Development, while over 50 per cent were almost completely ignorant. They did not know of any Community Development officials at any level. Simultaneously, when asked to explain what the accomplishments of Community Development officials at any level. Simultaneously, when asked to explain what the accomplishments of Community Development in their village were, only a third could mention any specific accomplishments, while a fifth said that nothing had been done and over 40 per cent said they did not know what the accomplishments were. A fifth saw a change for the better in Block administration, 10 per cent saw a change for the worse, while over 60 per cent considered that no change had occurred, or they did not know. Until we pierce the miasma of ignorance we cannot shake off the apathy.

It is significant to find that the same survey noted that among these who knew about Community Development work, only a fifth felt that it was doing a "poor job," while over two-thirds felt that the programme was worthwhile and only a small fraction felt that there was a great opposition to the programme. This shows that when our people are fully exposed to the programme, the response is encouraging. Why then does the exposure remain patchy? This question gains an edge when we note that for instance, in the current year, of Rs. 2,898 lakhs to be spent on some rural amenities, Rs. 1,468 lakhs, or over 50 per cent will be in and through the Community Development Movement.

You must forgive me for underscoring the obvious, but in our absorption with the routine of work, there is a tendency to lose sight of the ultimate objectives. A rather caustic commentator has drafted a variation for planners of Gresham's Law : "daily routine drives out plan purposes." In the course of maintaining administrative discipline and achieving certain physical and financial targets, we sometimes tend to forget the reason why we started the Movement at all.

# THE MAKING OF A JUST SOCIETY

## Chester Bowles

IN DEALING SPECIFICALLY with India's development I am treading difficult ground. The subject itself is complex and as a foreigner I necessarily speak with some hesitation. However, the fact that I have had an opportunity to observe rural development in Asia, Africa and Latin America over a period of many years, and in particular to study the Indian economy, encourages me to offer my views.

Although the problems of India's rural areas are still appalling, a substantial beginning has been made in meeting them. The community development programme was conceived in 1952 as a modest effort to show villagers how to help themselves in a way that would liberate their energies, make them active participants in their own development, and show them that their government was concerned about their future .

This concept of local cooperation and self-help has been given an important boost by the recent establishment of the Panchayati Raj, .... Another important objective of the original community development programme was to promote integrated growth by improving educational, health and sanitation facilities, and roads and communications, while placing special emphasis on agricultural production.

It was felt that an interdependent programme of this kind would give the villager a feeling of his own worth and that the values fostered would encourage him to work for the improvement of every aspect of his daily life. These new values, with the help of land reform, better seeds and improved techniques, were expected to improve his agricultural output.

Because of budget limitations, because of the newness of the approach, because of the obstacles which the tradition-ridden guardians of the *status quo* always strive to place in the path of change, and because of the massive administrative task of organizing such a complex effort in 500,000 villages, progress thus far has failed to meet the excessively optimistic standards of the programme's proponents.

Under the circumstances it is not surprising that a debate should develop between those who might be described as "community firsters" who believe in the balanced development of the whole rural community and the "agriculture firsters" who think primarily in terms of increased agricultural output.

In my opinion those who favour integrated development have the best of this argument. Experience in every developing country has demonstrated that the sustained increase of agricultural output simply cannot occur in a social and political vacuum. It must be at one and the same time a product and a cause of a general betterment in the life of the farmer.

In this context let us consider what is clearly the most formidable question of all-land reform. The Congress Party has been traditionally aware of the importance of individual land ownership as a basis for community development. In 1935 a party resolution adopted in Allahabad correctly stated that "there is only one fundamental method of improving village life, namely the introduction of a system of peasant proprietorship under which the tiller of the soil is himself the owner of it and pays revenue directly to the government without the intervention of any Zamindar or taluqdar."

In the first years after independence there was considerable progress towards this objective. The Zamindars, some of whom controlled thousands of acres, were eliminated. In several states ceilings were placed on land holdings with additional ceilings on land rentals, and tenure of rented land was made somewhat more secure.

However, the most difficult part of the task lies ahead. The zamindars were a small minority and the fact that their privileged status was created under colonial rule made them an easy political target. Even with their removal from the scene and some additional curbs on large holdings, ten percent of India's cultivators still own more than fifty percent of the land, while one percent of them own nearly one-fifth.

Here the debate in regard to India's rural development takes on a new dimension. Some agricultural authorities accept the existing pattern of land ownership as reasonably satisfactory and argue that the process of land redistribution has gone far enough. By and large, they assert, it is the larger landowner—the man who still controls 50 to 250 acres—who has the education, the skills, and the personal incentives which enable him to understand and accept new techniques and rapidly to expand his production.

According to advocates of this theory, the primary task is to identify a single cultivator in each village with the necessary qualities and then train him in modern farming techniques. He may then be expected rapidly to pass on his superior knowledge to his neighbours and thereby unlock the door to vastly greater agaicultural output for the entire nation.

Although this trickle-down concept of rural improvement may seem appealing at first glance, I submit that it ignores the fundamental principles of rural development. The reasons for my doubts may best be explained by a conversation which I had recently with just such a "door opener" in a village in South India.

This cultivator was greatly pleased with the increased yields per acre which he had achieved with the help of new techniques sponsored by the Village Level Worker. As the conversation continued, however, it became evident that his personal success was unlikely to have much effect on his fellow villagers.

When I asked him how many acres he owned and how he farmed them, he told me that he controlled 150 acres and that his land was farmed not by tenants but by "servants." Since only thirty-seven families lived in his village I found myself wondering how many of them worked as his "servants," and how many had any land of their own.

I also wondered how much good his increased yields were doing the other villagers, how much more they were able to buy and contribute to the economy, how much incentive they had to work the extra hours which are essential to increases in their own production.

Most important of all, I wondered how much personal dignity among the villagers generally would be developed under his guidance. As I looked at the subservient, insecure attitudes of those standing nearby, I knew there could not be very much.

Although the larger and often more productive farmers in Asia, Africa and Latin America undoubtedly have a role to play as leaders and initiators, there is, I believe, a strict limit to what can be accomplished under their sponsorship. Rural people the world over want land of their own and the fertilizer, better seeds, and credit required to till it more effectively. There are no short-cuts to the rural democracy which offers the only assurance of orderly political growth in the developing continents.

# PHILOSOPHY OF EXTENSION
# WORK IN INDIA

## B. Rudramoorthy

### Destination Man

'DESTINATION MAN' HAS been keynote in India's community development programme launched all over the country in 1952. Developing
the individual much more than his physical conditions of living has
been the primary objective, and is being frequently emphasized. Our
Prime Minister, Shri Jawaharlal Nehru made this very clear when he
said, "The Community Projects appear to me something of vital
importance not only for the material achievement that they would bring
about, but much more so, because they seem to build up the community and the individual and to make the latter the builder of his
own village, centres and of India in the larger sense." Quite appropriately, therefore, extension has been chosen to be the method and
community development the aim of Indian community development
programme.

### Indian Philosophy of Extension

A glimpse into India's past traditions and culture reveals that the
country could not have chosen any other method other than extension
for helping rural people to come out of their rut and to move away
from their traditional pattern of living to the one based on rational
and scientific methods. The Upanishads, the Bhagavadgita, and the
great religions nave made rich contributions to the development of
the concept of the individual, his role in the society, his relationship
with the universe, and development of all the faculties of the individual in harmony within the society of which the individual is an
inextricable part. The meaning of life, the desirable values which an
individual has to cultivate during his life in this world and the path
of progress he has to tread have all been beautifully explained in the
various scriptures and books of religions.

### Man, the Crown of Creation

Thus the Vedas, the Upanishads, the Githa, the Puranas as well as
the orthodox schools of philosophy had a marked impact on the educa-

tional philosophy and systems in India. This is based on the concept of man, and the values which it considered worthy of human pursuit. Almost all the schools of Indian philosophy have regarded man as the crown of creation, and thus having infinite capacity to gain knowledge and broaden experience consciously through education.

One of the most fundamental and distinctive features of Indian philosophy is in regard to the concept of inner life of man or the human spirit. The essence of man is his self or Atman, and this is a moment or manifestation of the Absolute. While the Absolute is the embodiment of truth, beauty and goodness, man suffers from ignorance. This is due to his ego and sense of separateness which is born out of ignorance. It is this ignorance, ego and sense of separateness which have enslaved him in fear and want, and the consequent misery and unhappiness. It is possible for every individual to rid himself of this ignorance. Since man is regarded as the crown of creation, and his self the manifestation of the Brahman there can be no limit to the heights to which he can reach through knowledge. Every individual can attain perfection or become one with the Absolute through education which helps him to develop his faculties to the fullest extent possible. Knowledge (vidya) and virtue (dharma) help the individual to free himself from the bondages of evil and limitations, from ignorance and ego. Thus, education can lift the veil of ignorance and help to draw out what is implicit in the individual.

The vedic literature has given us the concept of cosmic order, the moral order and the social order which lay down the basic principles to guide man's actions and behaviour not only in the world but also in relation to the universe. These three concepts form the starting point of the social philosophy in India. The Cosmic order (Rth) refers to a certain order in nature, in the cosmos outside man. There is no chaos anywhere. Everything in the cosmos happens according to certain laws. The Moral order (Sthya) refers to the relationship of man with others. The Social Order (Dharma) refers to the actions of man in the society. All these orders exist in harmony. There is no conflict. Man's life is governed by these orders, and it should be his endeavour to work in harmony with these orders.

The Upanishads describe man's self or the Atman as having been surrounded by five sheaths (Panchakosha), first by Anandamaya Kosha, next by the Vijnanamaya Kosha, the manamaya Kosha, the Pranamaya Kosha and last, Annamaya Kosha. There must be proper and adequate food or Anna to maintain the physical frame through daily physical work to develop and strengthen it. The vital principle or Prana should be properly trained through Asanas and Pranayama. Then there should be the training of Manas, or the lower sensuous

mind. The intellect or the higher mind, Buddhi should be well developed. A harmonious and successful control and exercise of all these
faculties and elements can bring Ananda. Education, thus, in ancient
India was primarily concerned with the development of the total
human personality. It was only thought integrated training of all the
elements of human nature that man could lift the veil of ignorance
limiting him from self-realisation.

### The Four Ashramas

Contrary to some misconceptions, most schools of Indian philosophy have never advocated total withdrawal of man from worldly
actions. He should live a full life in complete harmony in nature and
society, fulfil his obligations to the nature, society and his own
body, and thus attain liberation from bondage which ignorance
has imposed on him. The four Ashramas, the Brahmacharya, the
Grahastya, the Vanaprastha and the Sanyasa are essentially to help the
man to live a full life discharging all his obligations and to attain
perfection. The Brahmacharyashram was for education and preparation, the Grahastyashram for living a life of householder performing
his social duties and to work as a producing member of the community, the Vanaprasthashram for retirement and meditation, and for
gradual withdrawal from the active life in society, and finally the
Sanyasashram for complete renunciation from all his worldly attach-
ments and for his efforts to become one with the Absolute through
liberation from all bondages. A man was entitled to renounce the
world only when he has gone through the earlier three stages. Even
the four-fold aims of life, Artha, Kama, Dharma and Moksha are
essentially to help the development of the total personality of man.
It is this principle of comprehensiveness in the development of human
personality that is so often reflected in the ancient Indian philosophy
and systems of education.

### Yoga

The Bhagavadgita lays down the method of reaching the goal of
perfection—the way of knowledge (Gnanamarga) and the way of action
(Karmamarga). Gnana (Knowledge), Bhakti (Devotion) and Karma
(Action) are three different ways, but should be harmoniously blended
in action. Faith is the basis of Bhakti (Devotion). Bhakti (Devotion)
leads to Gnana or wisdom. Gnana included both the intellectual
knowledge and spiritual wisdom. Work, knowledge and action are
complementary, and this is Yoga.

Yoga prescribes disciplined culture and exercise to concentrate and
perfect knowledge. It is eight-fold in its aspects, namely, Yama (res-

traint in bad tendencies, passions in thought, speech and action), Niyama (cultivation of right habits and emotions) Asana (Physical exercise) Pranayama (Regulation of breath) Parthayahara (withdrawal of attention from undesirable objects), Dharana (fixation of attention on selected objects), Dhyana (contemplation, and Samadhi (Total absorption of the mind in that object).

The Bhagavadgita also sets down a programme of action for every individual to work to maintain the state of balance in nature society and body. Yajna making up for the harm that has been caused to creation by our own actions and to replenish loss, to purify things and to create new things in nature 'Dana', the service we render to free ourselves from our debt to society due to the various services we have received from the society since our birth, and 'Tapas' to remove the defects and distortions in the body are prescribed so that the work of the three orders—nature, society and the body—may go on smoothly and efficiently. "Through 'Yajna' we maintain equilibrium in nature, through 'Dana' in society and through 'Tapas' in the body."[1]

'Samjnan' or the knowledge of living together in society, or social education inspired us to understand each other better, to live together.

This idea is expressed in the 'Santhi Manthra' (Peace Chant) of the Vedic Philosophy:

Om ! May He Protect us both;
May He be pleased with us.
May We develop strength; illumined
May our study be. May there be no dispute.
Om ! Peace, peace, peace !
Harih Om!

The individual's well-being can be secured only by the individual identifying with the society in which he lives. But the group exists only to secure the complete unfolding of human personality. "By developing our inner spiritual nature, we gain a new kind of relatedness to the world and grow into the freedom, where the integrity of the self is not compromised. We then become aware of ourselves as active creative individuals, living not by the discipline of external authority but by the inward rule of free devotion to truth."[2]

The importance of the individual's freedom of choice and action is recognised and stressed in the 'Gita'. To Buddha as a man acts, so shall he be. He says "My action is my possession: my action is my inheritance: my action is the matrix which bears me: my action is the

1 Acharya Vinoba Bhave, *Talks on the Gita*, Akhil Bharat Sarva Seva Sangh Prakasan Kashi, 1958, p. 250.
2 Radhakrishnan, *The Bhagavadgita*, George Allen Unwin Ltd., London, 1960, pp. 44-45.

race to which I belong; my action is my refuge."[1] To Buddha, "What controls the universe is Dharma' the moral law. The world is made not by Gods and angels, but by the voluntary choices of man. The history of man is the total sequence of human lives, their decisions and experiences."[2]

The purpose of life, the way to knowledge, the way to action, the role of individual in the society, the concept of balanced personality and methods of achieving it through action have all been clearly outlined in the various scriptures in the past.

## Methods of Fold education in the Past

It is this knowledge which the saints and philosophers like Valmiki, Buddha, Shankaracharya, Gandhiji have spread, and more recently Vinoba Bhave has been spreading to the world. They visited the different parts of the country, established Ashrams, taught their disciples, and helped this knowledge to spread among the common people so that the latter could apply this knowledge to their own living.

Although direct access to this knowledge about life, purpose of life, ways through which man can get rid of his ignorance and attain liberation from bondage, was necessarily limited only to a few people because of lack of communication, printed material, etc., all efforts were made to spread this message to the people to help them to apply this knowledge to their everyday life. The need for educating people for the improvement of community life was very well realised. The community also administered law and justice through a council of elders. Nor were the cultural needs of the people ignored. They were trained to honour the ancient ideals and imbibe the ethical habits needed for the welfare of the community. The education was imparted through many ways. The system of Gurukulashrams is now well known. Pupils lived with Gurus in these ashrams and underwent training in all walks of life. It was practical knowledge besides a good background of philosophical knowledge they acquired in these ashrams. The pupils were encouraged to question the Gurus on many issues, and thus develop their individuality. Freedom of thought and action was encouraged.

The travels of saints and philosophers all over the country brought the people into intimate contact with the knowledge. Besides, Yathras became *A* must for those who were seeking knowledge. Learned men were invited by people to stay in villages and were treated with hospitality and respect; and this was taken advantage of by

1 Radhakrishnan, *The Dhammapada,* Oxford University Press, London, 1958, p. 17.
2 *Ibid.* p. 33.

people to listen to and discuss with them about various aspects of life. Epics were read and discussed during these occasions. Harikathas and Sivakasthas became popular. Besides these a variety of folk arts such as dramas, vakshaganas and dances developed, and all these conveyed to the people knowledge about life and its purpose, and the ways through which men could live happily and contentedly, and liberate themselves from the bondage of evil and consequent misery. The paintings and sculptures became widespread and provided an effective method of visual education for people. The Puranas and many other forms of folklore became popular.

The social channels also assisted this spread of education among people. The social institutions developed. The community administered law and justice through a council of elders. "the people were trained to honour the ancient ideals and imbibe the ethical habits needed for the welfare of the community."

Thus people, mostly rural in those days, lived peacefully. They managed their own affairs through their local institutions or councils of elders. They were self-reliant, managing their own affairs themselves, without depending on outsiders. The villages were mostly self-sufficient. And this was partly due to the fact the needs of the villagers were very few, and most of these needs were met or fulfilled with in the villages.

# COMMUNITY DEVELOPMENT*

## What is Community Development

IT IS OFTEN said that community development is an old idea in a new dress. There is truth in this, for it uses new methods to achieve objectives of long standing. Although community development workers know what the term means to them in practice, they would probably be baffled if asked to produce a definition of 'community development' which would be generally acceptable. This, contrary to what critics declare, is not evident that its workers suffer from warm hearts and woolly minds. Community development can, we believe, be defined in terms which are generally accepted, but it is a round subject, and changes in emphasis since its conception make it difficult to produce a text-book definition without tracing the evolution of the term. Therefore, before coming to a definition, it will be useful to summarize the history which lies behind it.

## History of the Term

Community development has grown out of the earlier concept of "mass education," a term used by the Secretary of State's Advisory Committee on Education in its report entitled "Mass Education in African Society." The publication of this report in 1944 can be taken as a starting point in the evolution of community development as an arm of Government policy. The idea behind mass education was, in the words of the report, that

"the realisation of citizenship begins in a small unit where common loyalty and common interests are expressed in daily activities,"

and that

"in focussing attention on the whole community as a unit to be educated, we are aiming at getting people everywhere to be aware of, to understand and take part in, and ultimately to control the economic and social changes which are taking place among them."

Mass education implied, rather than formal teaching in class, the use of modern techniques and equipment among people out of school. It

*Extracts from Community Development: A Handbook. London, 1958, pp. 1-9.

implied mass literacy campaigns, films, film strips, posters, displays and demonstrations reinforced by specially prepared pamphlets, newspaper articles, books, radio—in fact an onslaught on the mass of the people by imaginative informal methods. Mass education was an injection from outside: once stimulated the community was supposed to do the rest for itself.

There were various reasons why the term "mass education" was abandoned: for example, the word "mass" had undesirable political overtones; the word "education" gave rise to misconceptions when translated into the vernacular languages. In 1948, the Cambridge Summer Conference on African Administration recommended that the term "community development" should be adopted and defined it as

"a movement designed to promote better living for the whole community with the active participation, and if possible on the initiative of the community, but if this initiative is not forthcoming spontaneously, by the use of techniques for arousing and stimulating it in order to secure its active and enthusiastic response to the movement. (Community development) embraces all forms of betterment. It includes the whole range of development activities in the district whether these are undertaken by government or unofficial bodies; in the field of agriculture by securing the adoption of better methods of soil conservation, better methods of farming and better care of livestock; in the field of health by promoting better sanitation and water supplies, proper measures of hygiene, infant and maternity welfare; in the field of education by spreading literacy and adult education as well as by the extension and improvement of schools for children. (Community development) must make use of the co-operative movement and must be put into effect in the closest association with local government bodies."

In 1945, the Ashridge Conference on Social Development endorsed the Cambridge definition but preferred a shorter version which had just been adopted by a conference in Malaya

"community development is a movement designed to promote better living for the whole community with the active participation and on the initiative of the community."

The Conference also emphasised its relevance to urban conditions. A number of other definitions and descriptions of community development are reproduced in Appendix A and a study of these shows clearly that though, so to speak, the carpets are woven of the same colours and the same materials there is considerable variation in pattern. In some the emphasis is on material progress; in others community development is considered as a "movement"; elsewhere it is regarded as an "aspect of administration" in its broadest sense.

**What is Community Development?**

So much for the definition and its history. But the reader may well still ask "What is community development?" First it is an idea, the idea of a positive approach to the handling of affairs which aims at developing the initiative of the individual and the community and at obtaining the willing participation of the people in schemes for promoting their own betterment. It follows that all officers of Government in adopting such a positive approach accept the ideas underlying community development.

Community development has its own content in informal education and in the training of people. It includes such things as adult literacy, project work of a practical nature, informal adult education of men and women especially through the family, the fostering of youth movements, the encouragement of new skills, and last but not least leadership training. In addition to having its own content, community development participates in the extension work of technical departments or local government bodies when they ask for help, supplying its own skills to such work and using its own officers in it.

**Political, Economic and Social Ends**

The 1954 Ashridge Conference recognised community development as coming within the broader field of social development which it described as

"the whole process of change and advancement considered in terms of progressive well-being of society and the individual."

A social development policy will obviously reflect a general political theory. H.M. Government's policy for the dependent territories has been described as

"to guide the colonial territories to responsible self-government within the Commonwealth in conditions that ensure to the people concerned both a fair standard of living and freedom from oppression from any quarter" (Cmd. 7433).

The British people have found a brand of parliamentary democracy which has evolved through a process of trial and error in the United Kingdom to be the answer to political organisation seen in terms of human happiness and well-being rather than in efficiency for its own sake. Not unnaturally they hope to see a broadly similar type of political structure established and flourishing in the emergent territories. But a parliamentary democracy can only flourish when it has strong roots in a self-reliant community with a sense of social responsibility. It is in this context that the significance of the relationship between community development and democratic government—local and central—can be seen. Practical community development, by pro-

moting a measure of autonomy at village level, gives people the opportunity of practising self-government and learning its difficulties. The
people, working through their own representatives, become more
conscious of the connexion between the paying of rates and the provision of services. They soon learn that those representatives who
protest most loudly are not necessarily those who work hardest or
most successfully for the community. Opening the 1951 Cambridge
Conference on African Administration, the Rt. Hon. James Griffiths
said that local government and community development were really
two aspects of the same subject.

"Local government" he said, "is the building up of institutions
through which people can manage their own affairs and provide
the services they need. Community development is the betterment
of local conditions through community effort. The two tasks are
interrelated. Local government and community development must
go forward hand in hand."[1]

Successful community development will encourage economic
advance as well as political responsibility. It is sometimes said that
one territory or another cannot afford the expenditure required to
initiate a policy of community development. It would be more correct
to say that such a country cannot afford to neglect the possibilities of
economic advance that community development makes possible.
In such fields as agricultural extension or preventive medicine the
great problem of winning public acceptance of the changes advocated
by technical department is best solved by community development
methods.

Besides these political and economic ends, community development
has its own purpose of social construction. In most British colonial
territories the indigenous social structure is constantly being eroded
by a complex of influences—contact with western culture, transition
from a subsistence to a cash economy with the consequent substitu-
tion of individuality and self-interest for the older tribal loyalties,
industrial development resulting in the growth of towns, extension of
education and health services, the work of the Christian missions,
and the introduction of European systems of justice. The old tribal
society which grew up in response to quite different circumstances is
not capable of withstanding the stresses and strains of rapid change.
The accent must therefore be on the word "community" rather than
on the word "development," that is to say, development of communities rather than for, or even by, communities. As means are found to

---

[1] The working relationships between community development and local government are discussed in chapter V.

bring the community to realise its own creative potential, the community itself is strengthened and prepared to meet the need for adaptation in the face of change.

The process of creating a new community also implies creating ever-widening loyalties: first of the individual to his immediate group, then of this group to wider grouping, then of the wider grouping to the territory or country as a whole. Community development looked at in this way can be seen as nation-building from what is called nowadays the "grass roots." The political, economic and social aspects of community development meet in helping to establish a firmly founded nation. But there are communities which, for ethnic, historical or other reasons, concentrate all their efforts on themselves at the expense of a wider unity and the development of a sen:e of common citizenship. In sueh cases it will be necessary to concentrate on seeking out and using situations or experiences which evoke a common loyalty among several communities.

While the ends of community development may be analysed as political, economic and social, its means cannot be so conveniently summarised. But an essential characteristic is that they are not imposed from outside. Instead of an outside agency presenting the community with ready-made solutions, the community is encouraged to look at its own problems and to find solutions to them. At the same time, to avoid too sharp a break with tradition the community is encouraged to set about solving local problems using its own resources and local organisation, although outside help may be provided in the way of expert advice, materials and finance.

Once there fundamental characteristics of community development are understood, it becomes clear that it is not the exclusive concern of any special department of government manned by officers specialising in techniques of communicating ideas and skills and in working with people. It is the concern of government as a whole. It is particularly relevant to the work of the administrative officer or his equivalent whose responsibility it is to see that the people of an emergent territory acquire the right attitudes and organisations to fit them for the new situations they will have to face as they advance towards, and reach, full self-government.

One of the main drawbacks of community development has been in name, which is somewhat vague, sounds "high-falutin," is comparatively new and perhaps seems to stand out too sharply against the conventional activities of government. These impressions are sometimes voiced by government officers who allege that over the years much time has been spent in considering what community development is and in arguing about a definition of the term; also that there has been a proliferation of abstract terms appearing to mean roughly the same thing, such as "fundamental education," "mass education," and "social education." Like most new ideas, it seemed in the early stages to become the private property both in Britain and in international circles of intellectuals and theoreticians: in the eyes of the man on the job, they seemed to be more interested in inflating the subject into a theoretical discipline than in applying its possibilities in the field. From this period it emerged clothed with its own mystique and a specialised sociological jargon, such as "felt needs," "indirect approach," "working within a culture." Thus apparelled it proved, as might have been expected, somewhat less than attractive to the man doing the work.

In point of fact, though the aims of community development are admittedly very comprehensive and so in a sense intangible, the means used are eminently practical. It should be part of the task of each community development officer* to convince officers of all departments by every possible means, in practice as well as in precept, that community development is essentially a new approach to administration which uses special techniques of communication and of working with groups of people in achieving the ends of both the administration and the technical departments.

There are illustrations in every territory of projects failing because the community development approach was not used. Sufficient here is the one example of a maternity centre, built and staffed by a Department of Medical Services, which became in time through disuse a store for the tools of the District Development Committee. Such failures involve more than economic waste: they harden local opinion against later attempts at extension work in the same field. Had community development methods been employed the project would have been preceded by a child-care campaign involving group discussions with village men and women emphasising the need for maternity services and, by suggestion, stimulating a popular desire for a maternity centre. The people would then through their leaders have played a part in the siting, planning and construction of the centre and would subsequently have used it as their own creation.

## What Community Development is Not

While it is essential for the community development officer to know

* It is common practice, as will be seen in chapter V, for special departments of community development to be created working in the closest possible touch with the administration. The term 'community development officer', however, has been used throughout the handbook, to apply to those doing community development work, whether members of such a department or not.

what community development is it is equally important for him to be quite sure what it is not; and to understand very clearly the limits of his field. For one thing, if we accept that community development represents a positive approach to administration in all its branches, it follows automatically that this approach must be a co-ordinated one in which the administration, technical departments and the community development staff work as one team and with one mind. The community development officer is likely to meet with distrust for different reasons both from the administrative officer and from members of technical departments; the administrative officer, realising the political implications of community development work, may sometimes question the discretion of the community development officer; professional men in technical departments have an understandable suspicion of amateur's encroaching, in however elementary a fashion, on the technicalities of their fields. Experience shows that officers soon come to realise that their community development colleagues bring skill and advantages of their own to the common task of local development. By a punctilious recognition of the limits beyond which his own elementary technical knowledge of extension work in health, agriculture, public works etc. will not carry him, and a readiness to call in the expert on these occasions, the community development officer can convince the technical departments that he represents for them a useful ally in the difficult job of presenting technical problems to the people. In some cases he may provide a rudimentary extension service in, for example, agriculture, health or co-operatives. But the service he starts must not be carried beyond the point where follow-up services can be provided by the technical department concerned; nor must he try to control it after the appropriate department is willing and able to take it over.

Because the community development officer starts with the advantage of not being closely identified by the people with "they"—that is to say government in its more authoritative aspects—he in turn ought to resist pressure which will assuredly be put on him to use community development primarily as a way of carrying out economic development on the cheap. It can, in the aggregate, produce a formidable total of small-scale economic development and represent a not unimpressive total of "capital formation," *i.e.* the creation of real wealth, at the village level, and so profoundly affect the economic potential of the territory. But community development cannot be a substitute for the normal process of economic development on a massive scale which must still be carried out by government or private enterprise by the normal methods.

A warning might be given at this point of the dangers of becoming fascinated by a growing and impressive tally of material achievements. The community development officer, faced by a situation where his efforts are not producing immediate results will be subject to a great temptation to compromise with methods of compulsion. If he succumbs, his work will naturally fall short of the material standards which could have been achieved by more orthodox means while failing to bring about the social and political ends of community development, thus discrediting it in the eyes of the sceptical.

### How is it Recognised ?

It may be appropriate to end this chapter by attempting to answer the question "How do we recognise successful community development? The number of material projects completed cannot give the answer. Successful community development will bring about a change in attitude towards desirable ends, persisting to the point where the community can be said to appreciate its social obligations and responsibilities. Success in this direction will depend on how far the experience gained and the lessons learned by common effort have influenced each individual to realise his own needs and problems in relation to those of his community; also on his willingness to take part in, and accept responsibility for measures to better the condition of the community as a whole. In other words, the community development officer has to use all the means available to him to help the community to reach a stage of development where initial projects are maintained, used and often expanded, but where it can be said in addition that, as a result of his work, the community has become a stable self-reliant unit with an assured sense of social responsibility.

# OBJECTIVES OF THE COMMUNITY
# DEVELOPMENT PROGRAMME*

IN MORE SPECIFIC terms, the objective of the Community Development
Programme is to assist each village first in having effective panchayats,
co-operatives, and schools; and though these village institutions plan
and carry out integrated, multiphased family, village, Block and
District plans for increasing agricultural production; improving existing village crafts and industries and organizing new ones; providing
minimum essential health services and improving health practices;
providing required educational facilities for children and an adult
education programme; providing recreational facilities and programmes; improving housing and family living conditions; and
providing programmes for village women and youth.

To achieve the above-outlined broad objective, many more specific
objectives of the Community Development programme must, of necessity, be kept in mind. Some of the more important of these objectives
are:

1. Changing the outlook of all village people is an essential objective of the programme. Unless the people develop rising
   expectations for a higher level of living, there will be no motivation for the people to provide the required leadership to
   assure that village development will become and continue to be
   a people's programme.

2. The development of responsible and responsive village leadership, and of village organizations and institutions, must be
   accepted by all as being vital to the success of the programme.
   If the programme is to become a sustained, living, village self-
   help programme, it is essential that the leadership for planning
   and implementing programmes in the villages come from the
   present and yet-to-be-developed leaders of the villages. Likewise, much of the responsibility for continuous planning and
   development must come from village-created and village-led
   organizations, including particularly panchayats, co-operatives,
   schools and such groups as youth clubs, women's organizations,
   farmers' associations, recreation clubs, etc.

*Extracts from *A Guide to Community Development* (revised).

3. When all is said and done, the most important of India's resources are its people. It, therefore, logically follows that the Community Development programme must for ever keep in mind that the basic objective must be to develop the village people to become self-reliant, responsive citizens capable and willing to participate effectively and with knowledge and understanding in the building of the new Nation.

4. With the rising expectations of village people for more and better food, clothing education, health services, shelter, roads, wells, and recreation the community programme must keep, as a central objective, the necessity of helping the village people increase their income. This means first that continued and heavy emphasis must be focussed on improving and modernizing agricultural practices and methods essential for increased agricultural production. Second, it means that concerted attention must be focussed on improving existing and organizing new village crafts and industries to produce the new things villagers will want and need, and on providing employment opportunities for the present large number of idle hands.

5. In accepting the responsibility for helping to rebuild each of India's 5,58,000 villages as significant functional democracies, the community development programme must assume responsibility for training village youth to assume citizenship responsibilities through early and continuous involvement in youth programmes and activities and all-round village development.

6. If village people are to be guided in the expression of their rising level of living and aided in effectively converting their increases of incomes into better living, the Community Development programme must, of necessity, have as a programme objective organized assistance to village women and village families. Needs for food, clothing, shelter, recreation, health and religion are crystallized within the family and the motivation for their achievement comes from within the family.

7. Essential to the success of the Community Development programme is the close inter-relation of the village school and the village teacher with all phases of village development. If the community development programme is to succeed in making its maximum contribution to the recreation of a significant village culture, the full participation of the school and the village teacher is essential. If the village teacher is to be restored as a self-respecting citizen and eventual village leader, his socioeconomic status in the village must be upgraded. It therefore follows that the up-grading of the teacher's status must be

accepted by the community development programme as one of its objectives, and that related objectives must be to train the village teacher, and once he is trained, to assist him in playing an active role as village social educator, contributing effectively toward village development.

8. If India is going to cut down on the high toll caused by illness, and early deaths which are due to infectious diseases, then the villagers must be helped to learn the causes, to construct the simple facilities necessary and to practice clean habits which will prevent this deplorable and unnecessary misery. Facilities which are absolute musts are those for truly safe water supply, for disposal of human waste, for necessary immunisation against epidemics for house and village drainage and for abatement of smoke nuisance within houses.

# FUNDAMENTAL PROBLEMS OF PANCHAYATI RAJ*

## Jayaprakash Narayan

FRIENDS, IT IS now my task to introduce to the Seminar the main subject of discussion, namely, the Concept of Panchayati Raj and its Realization.

Before I speak on the subject, I should like to express my sincere thanks to you all for so kindly responding to my invitation to attend this Seminar organised by the All India Panchayat Parishad. I must express my disappointment that including Sukhadiaji only two out of the fifteen Chief Ministers are present. Most of them had written to me that they would attend. Apparently, work has prevented them from coming here.

You probably are aware how the idea of holding this Seminar arose. It came out of the last Panchayat Ministers' Conference. There I had made some remarks about the need of a seminar to discuss the fundamental problems of panchayati raj. That suggestion had a very favourable reception, and Sukhadiaji was very kind to invite the proposed Seminar and place at our disposal himself and the resources of the Government of Rajasthan. It was natural that a seminar to discuss fundamental problems of Panchayati Raj should be invited by Rajasthan, because this was the first State to have the courage to establish it in this country. I am deeply thankful to Sukhadiaji and the Government of Rajasthan for their kindness.

I would like to discuss this subject in two parts—one, the concept, the other, its realisation. The first part is of basic importance, because unless we know what we are going to do, what we want to do, we will not be able to get anywhere.

It is my experience acquired by moving about the country, by talking to the people, by talking to my friends and also by corresponding with them that even though this is the fifth year of the initiation of panchayati raj in this country, it is not yet clear what we want to do. Panchayati raj has come to stay as a slogan that one hears all the time;

* Presidential address at All India Panchayat Parishad held at New Delhi on January, 1964.

but what has come to stay is not very clear. I am sure, nothing will come to stay unless we know what it is that we want. Therefore, I should like to emphasise the need for clarity as to what we mean by Panchayati Raj.

I shall try to place before you my own thoughts on this matter. My first observation is that it is really for the Congress Party, which has inherited a very great tradition, the tradition of Mahatma Gandhi, to clearly define its programme, its policies. As I was reading the reports of the discussions at Bhubaneshwar. I was struck by one fact. I happened to be on tour in the interior of Bihar in connection with the Gramdan programme. One fact which struck me was that all those fine words which were being uttered at Bhubaneshwar had hardly any relevance to the people in the villages. Eighty two percent of the people of this country are more or less left out of it all. This is the one field, friends, the rural field, the agricultural sector, which even Marxism has not been able to tackle in spite of its having come to power in two large countries of the world and in several other lands. It should also be admitted that Indian socialism also has not been able to solve this question. We have not been able to spell out socialism in terms of the rural population.

I think the time has come when the Congress Party at its highest level should take up this question: what is its concept of democracy, what is its concept of the economic order, whether you nationalise the banks or not. I hope this Seminar would be a starting point for such a discussion which is essentially the task of the Congress Party, because it is the party in power.

Now, friends, it is not only clarity about the concept which is important. I think what is more important is whether there is conviction behind the words that are uttered, whether there is a will behind those words. On paper panchayati raj may be defined in the clearest possible manner. But, just because we put down our concept on paper, it is not going to be implemented in the field, unless we believe in the words we utter.

Panditji, when he inaugurated panchayati raj, called it a revolutionary step. Several other people have also described it as a revolutionary step. But I have not seen any results or even genuine efforts during these four or five years to justify such a description.

When the British Government was here, the departments were run in a certain manner, and some departments were considered to be of the highest importance. I do not think that that order of importance has changed since independence, either at the Centre or in the States. What is more important the task of creating something new, building a new India, or keeping the wheel or routine administration smoothly running?

Take another example. There is so much talk of "building from below." Building from the lower levels, planning from the lower levels. Everybody may repeat those phrases, because the Prime Minister has used them or the Parliamentary Board or the Working Committee. But who is there to build from below, to plan from below? Everybody runs to Delhi. Everybody runs to Jaipur. No one seems inclined to go down to the people, except at election time perhaps. So, words are being uttered without conviction.

Only the other day I had a rather sad experience in this matter. One of the topmost Congress leaders said to me that while he believed in a theoretical way in decentralisation, he had no faith in the present policy of democratic decentralization or Panchayati Raj. He said that with signs of disintegration around us he did not know if the present policy was a wise one. Here you have another instance of what I have been talking: lack of conviction in our professed principles and programmes.

I do not think I am one with Mr. Dey when he wants our civil servants to provide clarity of direction. I think they are in a position to deliver the goods to a large extent, that is to say, to carry out directions, but it is not their job to give clarity of direction. That must be done by the party in power.

Another thought I wish to place before you is that there should be uniformity about the concept of Panchayati Raj. The States are autonomous, no doubt. Therefore, they may say that, whatever the Prime Minister's view or of the Government of India, we shall go our own way. Constitutionally, it is possible for them to say so, and I for one would respect their autonomy and their right to decide for themselves. But when there is the same party in power in all the States, and that party, decides upon a basic policy, I do not think it is open for the Chief Ministers or the Congress Party in State Assemblies to deviate from that. There may be difference in details, but the basic policy must be the same in all the States. Such, I am sorry to say, is not the fact today.

This brings me to the central question before us here at this seminar: what do we mean by Panchayati Raj, what is our concept of it? Broadly speaking, there are two opposite or divergent views about it, and many kinds of mixtures of the two. One view is that the institutions of panchayati raj, *i.e.*, the village panchayats, panchayat samitis and zila parishads, are limbs and agencies of the State Government and no more. The other view is that these institutions are primarily governments at their levels, and secondarily also agencies of the State Governments. As far as I am concerned, I reject totally the first view: it is the second view that I consider to be the right one; and this seminar would have served a great purpose if it were to put an end to this confusion once for all. To have gone to all the trouble and expense of establishing panchayati raj merely in order to create new agencies of the State governments would appear to me to have been a foolish and wasteful enterprise. It was possible to create better, more efficient and cheaper agencies, if that was all that was desired.

As I look at it there is a well defined social and political philosophy, an ideal of social and political democracy, that is behind the programmes of panchayati raj. Let me briefly put that ideal before you.

First of all, I should like to stress that to treat the panchayati raj as a programme, unconnected with anything bigger or higher or more comprehensive, will have no driving force. Gandhiji had said that Government was the best that governed the least; but today we are moving in the contrary direction. In the name of socialism and in the name of the Welfare State, the Government is taking upon itself more and more functions and the people's minds are being corrupted so that educated people in this country are demanding that everything must be done by the Government. Gandhiji's philosophy was that people should be free State intervention, the restraints should be from within, they should be disciplined from within. Likewise, there was more to be done from below and less to do from above. But we in this country are committed to the establishment of a Welfare State. We might, in the name of creating a Welfare State, get a system in which the individual will lose his identity, in which there will be no freedom and the human spirit will be crushed. Gandhiji wanted that the whole of society should become as much like the family as possible. Beyond the family is the community, beyond that wider and wider association of communities till you reach, to use Gandhiji's words, the oceanic community of human beings, the world community. Such was the social concept of Gandhiji: I call it the communitarian concept of society.

The concept of panchayati raj, to my mind, is based on a combination of the above two Gandhian concepts of government and society. Panchayati Raj begins at the bottom with the primary community which is conceived as an association of families living together, sharing together, endeavouring together, managing their affairs together and cooperating with other communities for whatever they are not able to do themselves, thus forming wider associations of communities and other institutions of panchayati raj.

If this should be the true concept, it does not seem right, to give only one example to build the structure of panchayati raj on the basis of adult franchise—individual votes. Because then you disrupt the community, you cut across it. A representative of a community, a village community, in the panchayat samiti, has a community behind him, which has an organisation, that is, the Gram Sabha. But take an M.L.A. in Jaipur; what has he behind him. Is there an organised community behind him? No, only some thousands of individual voters. Now, zila parishads in Maharashtra are largely constituted of directly elected representatives of panchayat samitis. Thus a zila parishad is not an association of panchayat samitis as it should be according to my concept of panchayati raj, but a miniature Assembly.

I have been writing and talking about these ideas for the last few years. You must have come across them in the agenda notes. I have mentioned some of these, for instance, in my foreword to the book[1] "Panchayat Raj As The Basis of Indian Polity," a copy of which was sent to all the invitees. By the way, it is very interesting if you read the debates in the Constituent Assembly how this whole idea of panchayat raj came as an afterthought after the Constitution had already been drafted. The President of the Constituent Assembly wrote to the Constitutional Adviser whether the whole thing could not be re-examined and the Constitution redrafted from that point of view. The Constitutional Adviser replied that there would be much delay in making the Constitution and it was not advisable to do that. He further advised that it was after all for the State Governments to create these panchayat institutions, and therefore, it would be sufficient if the idea were put down in the Constitution in the form of directive. It is in this form that one still finds it in the Constitution.

I should like to suggest at this stage that if you agree that the three institutions of panchayati raj are governments at their respective levels and accordingly the Indian State has five limbs and not only two, the constitutional pundits amongst us should give serious thought as to how to amend the Constitution so as to embody in it this idea and give to panchayati raj its rightful place and status.

I should like briefly to consider now the relation of panchayati raj to the economic organisation of society. I personally feel that political decentralization is not possible without economic decentralization. I am afraid this is not clearly realised. It would be spelt out how the units of political self-government could also be made units of self-government economically. It is possible to do so fully. If not, to what extent can it be done and how? To delay the answer to these questions might amount to stultifying panchayati raj.

[1] Panchayat Raj as the basis of Indian Polity—an exploration into the debates of the Constituent Assembly—Association of Voluntary Agencies for Rural Development, New Delhi.

Now friends, as far as the realisation of the concept of panchayati raj is concerned, I think the most important thing for its realization is what I have said already. It is for the party which initiates this programme to infuse in its cadres the will to implement it. It is not by proper legislation alone that the end can be achieved. For its realisation, the people have to be educated. A hundred or two hundred years of slavery of a kind which this country had never seen before, completely destroyed the power of the people to think for themselves and to come together and face their tasks together. It is for the Congress party to see to it that once again the will and the power is restored to the people. This is more important than all the debates on socialism. If your cadres cannot go out among the people and some of you, the leaders, too cannot go out to them, go to the bottom, so as to build from below, plan from below, this programme will not succeed. If you make laws, frame rules and you leave it to your staff to implement them, the result will not be panchayati raj: its institutions will be little more than agencies of the government.

A few more words about realisation of the concept. I think Sukhadiaji also spoke about this. To my mind, the basic structure is the village panchayat in panchayati raj; gram raj is the basis of lok raj. Now if you take the village, as it is today, and introduce panchayati raj, I do not think it will succeed. There are disruptive factors in the village. They have to be removed as far as possible before gram panchayats can function effectively. Disruptive factors are social, economic and political. Now the social factors, such as caste, are very old and I do not know when this caste system will become a thing of the past. It should have died in course of time. Caste was not meant originally to be a disrupting factor; it was an integrating factor, because it fixed responsibilities. But today it has begun to perform a different function, that of a political party, and I do not know how long will this situation continue.

As far as the economic factors are concerned—land, money-lending and trade, I think, these interests have been brought under control to some extent by land reform and other laws; they are still powerful factors of injustice, inequality and exploitation—factors that do not permit a community of interest to develop, without which the village community remains a community in name. Self-government in such a "community" is bound to be a failure.

In spite of the Planning Commission's and the Central Government's emphasis, there has not been much progress with land reforms. Even where some land reform measures have been adopted, the people for whom they are meant are not in a position to take any advantage of it. Such is the position of under-tenants and share-croppers. In

Bihar, the Homestead Act, meant for agricultural labourers mostly, has remained on paper.

Please do not think I am becoming a sectarian or want to convert you, but in this connection I do wish to speak about the Gramdan movement, which is one of the ways in which some of those economic factors that divide the people and result in injustice and exploitation can be overcome, perhaps in stages. The Congress Party, the Praja Socialist Party and the Communist Party of India are already committed to the programme of Gramdan. This they did in Yelwal Gramdan Conference in Mysore in 1957. Now, a simplified version of Gramdan is in vogue, which promises to develop into a mass movement.

Here is one way, I think by which some of these revolutionary changes, not only in systems but also in the minds of men could be brought about. I wish to emphasise that it is as one of the means that is ready at hand; you do not have to invent or fabricate it. The instrument is there which you could use, if you wished. It seems to me that a political party, such as the Congress Party, that believes in land reforms and socialism should take up Gramdan with energy and enthusiasm.

With due respect to what Mr. Dey said today about unanimous panchayat elections in the Punjab and elsewhere I think it is important that there should be broad consensus in these elections. By all means let us stop the devious methods that may be used. But at the same time let us not under-estimate the value of consensus in the working of the village community. If a community has to function together as a united team, it does not seem wise, particularly in the situation in which we are placed to throw into its midst all kinds of bones of contentions, so that the team spirit and the team action could never grow and develop. I think, in Bihar at least the view is growing that if some method is not found to see that elections to village panchayats are held by general consensus, then these panchayats are going to be so torn by dissension and conflict that they will never be able to function properly and achieve anything.

In an election for the Assembly or Parliament, after the voting is over people go back to their villages, and whatever excitement there was is all forgotten. But in the primary community, where people have to live together their whole lives, they cannot work together for a common purpose if from time to time the whole community is thrown into an upheaval. I do plead very strongly that serious thought be given to this question. I am told that some committee or team is to be appointed to go into the whole question of election. I hope this committee's report too will also not be gathering dust in the archives, as so many other reports. I myself do not know what happened to my own report on the welfare of the weaker sections.* In any case, I hope well-defined issues will be referred to the contemplated committee. This seminar may also give some thought to the question of consensus.

There are other questions on which other committees had been appointed or committees have reported already. You will agree that there must be certain sources of finances available to the panchayati raj institutions which they could consider their own. In these respects they should not have to depend upon the State government if they are to function as self-governing units. I do not know if the Santhanam Committee has done full justice to this question. I had a glance at its report, but did not feel quite satisfied with some of the recommendations. Not only reserved and transferred sources of revenue are important, rules regarding drawl and disbursement of funds have also a very important bearing upon the powers and privileges of the panchayati raj institutions. In this connection my suggestion about setting up in every State a Panchayati Raj Finance Commission might be considered.

The question of a Panchayat Civil Service has been considered. Various kinds of experiments are being made in different parts of the country. It would be wise to await the results of these experiments, before the general pattern of such a service might be designed with confidence.

Lastly, I should like to take up the question of the respective powers of the three tiers of panchayati raj. Sukhadiaji mentioned the relative roles of panchayat samitis in Rajasthan and the zila parishads in Maharashtra. Here again, the confusion is due to lack of clarity regarding panchayati raj. To my mind, there is no room for confusion on this question. If each of the three institutions is a government at its level, each is equally important and each is competent to do all it can with its resources and to possess the corresponding powers. The gram panchayat should have all the powers that it is competent to administer; and likewise the other two. There is no reason why the zila parishad should be merely a coordinating or advisory body, or the panchayat samiti merely an executive arm for the zila parishad.

The whole question is one of scale. There may be certain jobs which the village panchayats may find too big for themselves; these should be handled by the panchayat samitis. Likewise, jobs beyond

---

* Report of the Study Group on the Welfare of the Weaker Sections of the Village Community—Ministry of C.D. & C., Government of India, New Delhi, 1961.

the competence of panchayat samitis have to be handled by zila parishads. I hope this seminar would clear up the confusion on this score.

These, friends, are some of the thoughts I wished to place before you in introducing the main subject of this seminar.

## ADMINISTRATION, PERSONNEL & TRAINING

*The basic problem of orienting a traditional bureaucratic pattern to develop mentally oriented tasks is a crucial one in the process of implementing the broadly stated goals at the grass root level. So is the task of the selection, training and proper development of personnel in their key role of sparking the latent energies of the village people.*

*Although there is much information available regarding the administrative structure, personnel selection procedures and the network of training programmes, it appears that an honest attempt needs to be made to explore the nature of motivation, commitment and the strains in hierarchical relationships and the adjustment that the worker (at all levels) has to or should make in his own attitudinal and behavioural patterns.*

CONTRIBUTORS

1. "Community Development and Local Government" in *Public Administration Aspects of Community Development Programmes*, New York, United Nations, 1959, pp. 62-63.

2. Reinhard Bendix, "Extract from *Nation-Building & Citizenship, Studies of Our Changing Social Order*," Berkeley, University of California, August, 1964, p. 293.

3. "Chart Indicating Relationship Between Govt. Local Authorities and Field Agencies," in three Pillars of Democracy, New Delhi, Ministry of Community Development & Cooperation, Government of India, 1964, pp. 42.

4. "Importance of Block Staff Team Work, in a Guide to Community Development, New Delhi, Ministry of Community Development and Cooperation, Government of India, 1962, p. 113.

5. S. Chakravarti, "Block As Unit of Planning," in Planning and Administration in Community Development, Kurukshetra, April, 1964, pp. 9-10.

6. "The Scope of Extension," Hyderabad, The National Institute of Community Development, 1962, p. 18.

7. A.P. Barnabas, "Reporting At the Block Level."

8. Reinhard Bendix, "Some Unresolved Issues of Public Cooperation in Rural Development," in *Nation-Building and Citizenship*, Berkeley, University of California, 1964, pp. 277-283.

9. "Report 1963-64," New Delhi, Ministry of Community Development and Cooperation, Government of India, 1964, p. 10.

10. "Panchayati Raj," in A series of quotations by Indian Leaders, New Delhi, Ministry of Community Development and Cooperation, Government of India, 1964, pp. 13-19.

11. "Panchayati Raj and Its Structure."

12. Shri Vasudeva Rao, "Problems of Panchayati Raj," Rajendranagar, Orientation and Study Centre, 1964.

13. "Reasons for disorganisation of the Gram Sabha," from the Report of the Study Team on the Position of Gram Sabha in 'Panchayati Raj Movement, New Delhi, Ministry of Community Development and Cooperation, Government of India, April, 1963, p. 13.

14. "Critical study of different patterns of Panchayati Raj" from a Brief Report of the Thirty Sixth Orientation Course, Hyderabad.

15. "Community Development—The Wider Implications" from Report 1963-64, New Delhi, Ministry of Community Development and Cooperation, 1963-64, p. 34.

16. Henry Maddick, "Panchayati Raj, Rural Local Government in India," in Journal of Local Administration, Overseas, Volume I, Number 4, October 1962, pp. 201-212.

17. C.N. Bhalerao and I.H. Khan, "Some Problems of Development Administration under Panchayat Raj," Award Vol. VI No. 6 Nov-Dec. 1964, pp. 14-15.

18. William & Charlotte Wiser, "The New," from *Behind Mud Walls 1930-1960*, Berkeley, University of California, 1963, pp. 199-212.

19. Reinhard Bendix, "Public Authority and the People in Community Development," in *Nation-Building and Citizenship*, Berkeley, University of California, 1964, pp. 268.

20. R S. Shiwalkar, "Problems of Community Development Workers," Kurukshetra, 1964, pp. 17-18.

21. "Weeding out of Unsuitable Staff," from Main Recommendations, Proceedings and Agenda Notes on Annual Conference on Community Development and Panchayati Raj, New Delhi, Ministry of Community Development and Cooperation, Government of India, 1964, p. 219.

22. "The B.D.O.'s role in programme planning," from Profile II Job Course (64-65), Rajendranagar, Orientation and Study Centre, p. 6.

23. "Study of the Work-Load of Block Development and Panchayat Officer in Punjab State," Nilokheri, Orientation and Study Centre.

24. Albert Mayer, "The Multipurpose Village Level Worker," from Pilot Project India, New Delhi, Oxford University Press, 1958, pp. 161-62.

25. Tam Chandra Tewari (translated by D.R. Goyal), "The Village Level Worker and the Cooperative Movement," New Delhi, Ministry of Community Development and Cooperation, 1963, p. 10.

26. "Mukhya Sevika as a Supervisor," from A Guide to Gram Sevikas and Mukhya Sevikas, New Delhi, Ministry of Community Development and Cooperation, 1961.

27. "Gram Sevika's Multiple Role, from A Guide to Gram Sevikas and Mukhya Sevikas, New Delhi, Ministry of Community Development and Cooperation, 1961, p. 5.

28. "Gram Sevika—The Useful Link," from A Guide to Gram Sevikas and Mukhya Sevikas, New Delhi, Ministry of Community Development and Cooperation, 1961, p. 11.

29. Albert Mayer, "An Appeal to Old Colleagues," from Pilot Project India, New Delhi, Oxford University Press, 1958, pp. 329-330.

30. M.J. Coldwell, R. Dumont and M. Read, "Problems of Staff and Supervision," from Report of a Community Development Evaluation Mission in India, New Delhi, Ministry of Community Development and Cooperation, 1959, pp. 41-42 and 45-46.

31. W.B. Rahudkar, "Relationship of Certain factors to the success of Village Level Workers," from Community Development Digest Vol. I No. 2, July-September, 1963, Uttar Pradesh, National Institute of Community Development, 1963, p. 20.

32. D.C. Dubey, "Village," in Village Level Workers their work and result demonstrations, National Institute of Community Development, Government of India, 1962, p. 131.

33. Usha Bannerjee, "Experience of a Village Worker." Award Vol. VI, No. 4, July-August 1964, pp. 22-23.

34. A. Sahasrabudhe, "Garanda—a commendable experiment," from A Report on Koraput Gramdans, New Delhi, All India Panchayat Parishad, p. 14.

35. "Some Considerations in Training for Community Development," from Study kit on training for Community Development, New York, United Nations, 1957, pp. 1, 4, 6, 11.

36. "In Service Training Essential," from A Guide to Community Development, New Delhi, Ministry of Community Development and Cooperation, 1962, p. 157.

37. "Training and Education," from Report 1963-64, New Delhi, Ministry of Community Development and Cooperation, 1964, p. 26.

38. "Training Programme—A Summary," from Report 1963-64.

39. J.S. Mathur, "Teaching—Learning Process in Institutional Training of Community Development Workers."

40. "Objectives in the teaching of community organization and community development," from Report of Working Group on Development of Indigenous Teaching Material for Social Work, ECAFE, Bangkok, 1964, pp. 50-51.

41. B. Mukherji, "Problems of Training," Kurukshetra, June 1961, p. 5.

42. "Problems of Trainees during and After Training," from Report on Training Centres visited by the High Level Team on Training, New Delhi, Ministry of Community Development and Cooperation, 1961, pp. 19-20.

43. "Importance of atmosphere in Training" from Report on Training Centres visited by the High Level Team on Training, New Delhi, Ministry of Community Development and Cooperation, 1961, p. 8.

44. N.R. Malkani, "Training of Non-Official," Kurukshetra, June 1961, pp. 10-11 and 33.

45. B.P.R. Vithal, "The Gap between Training and Field Conditions," Kurukshetra, June 1961, p. 10.

46. Carl C. Taylor, et all, "Training Personnel for Community Development," from *India's Roots of Democracy*, New Delhi, Orient Longmans, 1965, pp. 222-226.

# COMMUNITY DEVELOPMENT AND +
# LOCAL GOVERNMENT

### Public Administration Aspects of Community Development Programmes

COMMUNITY DEVELOPMENT AND local government have different features which can complement one another, assuming their objectives are similar. As a general rule, programmes to improve local government should be planned and executed simultaneously and in co-ordination with community development programmes.

(*a*) In India, the *Fourth Evaluation Report* (1957) on the community development programme expresses grave concern over the problem of maintaining facilities built during the intensive phase of the programme: "It is obvious that permanent reliance cannot be placed for this purpose on either individual or unorganized or *ad hoc* collective effort. Long term maintenance of these facilities has to be the responsibility of the village *panchayats.* A part of the unwillingness of the *panchayats* to undertake this work is due to the fact that the original construction programmes were undertaken without their being consulted and that these programmes benefited only either individuals or special groups of individuals and not the village community as such."

Some countries have even found it advisable to place responsibility for fostering community development activities and for improving local government in the same agency. The Ministry of Community Development and Co-operation in India was recently given responsibility for aiding states in improving the functioning of *panchayats.* Comparative study is needed of the effect of various organizational arrangements for discharging community development and local government responsibilities. In some areas where these responsibilities are vested in separate departments, rivalry has developed among the officers concerned; those responsible for local government feel that the community development programme detracts from the people's interest in and support of local government by doing many things which local government should do, and can do better. Traditional leaders and local government officials also oppose the community development programme where they regard it or its principal local contacts as a threat to their position. On the other hand, placing both programmes in the same department might, under some circumstances, subject the community development programme to undue political and other institutional restraints.

It is sometimes suggested that responsibility for fostering community development should be transferred entirely to the local government units themselves. With allowance for differences in systems of government, local governments might be expected to take over—as they become able to do so—some of the functions of community development programmes, such as helping communities to develop a safe water supply, and they should certainly be encouraged to take on the spirit and methods of community development. However, until the point is reached where the community development process is established within the government and society, it is unlikely that local governments can fulfil the need for outside stimulation of community development activities.

It appears that community development committees or other general purpose bodies may be used successfully as instruments of community development at levels where statutory bodies do not exist or as means of effecting basic changes in local government, but they are likely to fail if they exist alongside statutory bodies and there is no pre-conceived plan to relate them in a meaningful way to local government.

In the early years in India, considerable emphasis was placed on the creation of village welfare committees and advisory Committees at higher levels. The report of the planning Commission's Committee on Plan Projects states that " . . . few of the local bodies at a level higher than the village *panchayat* have shown any enthusiasm or interest in this work; and even the *panchayats* have not come into the field to any appreciable extent. An attempt has been made to harness local initiative through the formation of *ad hoc* bodies mostly with nominated personnel and invariably advisory in character. These bodies have so far given no indication of durable strength nor the leadership necessary to provide the motive force for continuing the improvement of economic and social conditions in rural areas."[1] The Committee recommended that *panchayats* be strengthened and linked organically to form a new unit of local government at the block level. India has now abandoned the creation of *ad hoc* village councils and is emphasizing the improvement of panchayats and the ultimate conversion of advisory development committees into statutory bodies.

1. India. Planning Commission, Committee for Plan Projects, *op. cit.* p. 5.

Urban community development programmes have features which are quite distinct from rural programmes. Several propositions are suggested for study which, if valid, may aid in designing urban community development programmes.

There is a long history of community organization work in urban areas, but the experience in Pakistan seems distinctive in the nature and range of activities which were stimulated in city neighbourhoods by a higher level of government. Several questions arising from a review of this experience merit study and possibly experimentation. They are set forth below in the form of hypotheses.

(*a*) The provision in a neighbourhood through community self-help effort of services which the city ought to provide on a city-wide basis, should, to avoid fragmentation of government, be regarded as a temporary measure and not formalized on a statutory basis. Of course, if the policy of government is to decentralize certain activities to neighbourhood areas, community development workers can be helpful in the execution of such a policy.

(*b*) In order to avoid confusion in inter-governmental relations and to achieve co-operation among interested departments of government, neighbourhood community development workers should, if employed by government, be either employed by, or attached to, the level of government which is expected to provide the governmental services that may be stimulated by their efforts or that may be required to support voluntary efforts.

(*c*) Community development workers in urban areas need not possess as diverse technical skills as workers in rural areas. With rare exceptions, they will not be called upon to perform rudimentary functions on a regular basis for several technical services, as are multipurpose workers in rural areas of India and Pakistan, because technical services are more highly developed in urban than in rural areas and their further development would normally lie in increasing the number of specialists rather than in using multi-purpose workers. Urban community development workers will serve primarily as catalysts of civic action and as a liaison between civic groups and government agencies. Thus, in selecting and training urban community development workers, emphasis must be placed on skill in dealing with people in various aspects of urban life. A more highly educated person with more specialized skills in community organization and group work will normally be required for urban than for rural work and conditions of service must accordingly differ.

(*d*) Community development methods are particularly suitable as a means of bringing civic, business, university and other leaders together with governmental officials for a concerted attack on city-wide or metropolitan area-wide problems. The inter-municipal planning programme in the metropolitan area of San Jose, Costa Rica, resulted in part from the application of community development methods in field work done by students at the Advanced School of Public Administration for Central America. A number of private organizations in the United States are providing funds and personnel to encourage metropolitan area development programmes. Provincial or state governments in developed and under-developed countries might well consider making available, on an experimental basis, similar assistance to city governments or inter-municipal bodies where the existence of substantial community organization and social and physical research facilities makes urban-wide community development programmes feasible.

Local government system differ among developed countries and must be substantially modified if they are to be applied at all in developing countries. New concepts and new systems, adapted to the circumstances in these countries, are likely to be required. Basic information on local government is lacking for some countries which have community development programmes A major effort, including research, training, and other activities, will be required to effect improvements in local government which are so essential to community and national development in many countries.

The range of cultural, geographic and other differences in India are such that the conclusions derived from experiences with local government in India will probably have practical applications in some other countries and would be of general theoretical value. Rural local government systems differ among industrialized countries and it is already evident that they must be substantially modified if they are to be applied at all in developing countries; new concepts and new systems, based on circumstances in these countries, are likely to be required.

A number of countries and territories have established courses to train local government personnel and elective officials and representatives. Some of these courses have been carried out in conjunction with community development training schemes. The British Colonial Office serves as a continuing centre for the exchange of information with respect to such training in territories which it administers, but there has been no broad assessment of local government training in developing countries that might serve as a guide to governments in this respect. Fellowships for local government officials and for instructors engaged in the training of such officials and regional seminars for officers responsible for local government training should be fostered.

# NATION-BUILDING & CITIZENSHIP STUDIES OF OUR CHANGING SOCIAL ORDER

*Reinhard Bendix*

IN INDIA, PUBLIC administrators are called upon to implement age-litarian policies in a social structure marked by great inequalities. Typically, two things happen. Subordinates tend to look to their superiors for further instructions or review and authorization to proceed; they shun responsibility and seek reassurance. This tendency arises from the low pay and prestige of many positions, the insecurity bound up with the excess of applicants over available government positions, the consequent efforts of officials to "play it safe." and the resistance encountered in dealing with the public.[1] Superiors frequently encourage the evasion of responsibility. In a poor and inequalitarian society subordinates are subject to great pressures. Their superiors may wish to guard against the resulting danger of corruption and policy sabotage, when they do not connive in promoting that danger. Accordingly, superiors request reports and initiate reviews which by their number interfere with or even jeopardize the work of subordinates, though the purpose is only to check and control. These practices suggest a lack of trust within the administration which appears to characterize not only superior-subordinate relations but also the spirit of administrative procedure.[2]

---

[1] Since resistance frequently involves demands for favours, the most obvious consequence is corruption. For documentation of such a corrupt "web of mutual involvement"—a phrase coined by Joseph Berliner in his study of Soviet factory management—see Report of the Railway Corruption Enquiry Committee, 1953-55 (Delhi, Government of India, Ministry of Railways, 1961), passim. It is worth emphasizing that the opposite of corruption is not just honesty, but the willingness of honest officials to assume responsibility for the decisions needed to implement policies even in the face of resistance. That considerable discretion is needed even at the lower echelons of the hierarchy, if planning is to succeed, has been emphasized by D.R. Gadgil, "Public Enterprise Administration" Journal of the National Academy of Administration (Mussourie) VI (July 1961). pp. 1-10.

[2] My reference here is to the abuse of advisory and reviewing functions. According to Paul Appleby, subordinate officials in various ministries tend to transform their "checking" functions into policy-decisions through excessively narrow

*(Continued on next page)*

Thus, the great inequalities of Indian society, the plebiscitarian insistence on a direct relation between the "weaker sections" and the state, the desire to maximize economic growth and equality at the same time, the demand for state assistance by weak and strong alike, and the excessive centralization of administrative controls in response to political and administrative pressures—these are interrelated tendencies of the political community which make for much government and much inefficiency. Above all, centralized controls and an excess of consultation and referral interfere with the effective delegation and exercise of authority.

Since this recommendation was made, implementing legislation has been passed or is under consideration in the several States. Although the details vary, the over-all objective is to replace administrative institutions below the state legislature with a three-tier structure of directly or indirectly elected bodies. At the bottom are the panchayats, elected from one or several villages depending on their size. Secondly, a new statutory body—the Block Panchayat Samiti—will be established, composed of elected heads of panchayats and coopted members representing women and scheduled castes. All administrative personnel at the block level and all government resources at this level will be at the disposal of this body, which will have responsibility for all community development and other governmental programmes within its jurisdiction. The presidents of all Panchayat Samitis together with members of the state legislature, the collector, and the technical personnel at the former district level will constitute the Zila Parishad, which will advise and assist the Panchayat Samitis, especially in articulating local with state and national plans, but without exercising control over them.

This drastic reorganization of local institutions has been in operation since 1959 in the two states of Rajasthan and Andhra Pradesh, it is being implemented rapidly in a number of other states, and there

*(Continued from pre-page)*

construction of their responsibility. For an over-all analysis of the mental agencies, and for documentation also of the tendency to substitute administrative procedures for decisions on policy, see Paul Appleby. Re-Examination of India's Administrative System (Delhi: Government of India, Cabinet Secretary, 1956) passim. Mr. Appleby emphasizes that the tendencies he analyzes critically are not only intrinsic to the executive branch, but arise in part from the "negative influence" of parliament.

[1] Only Rs. 150,000 were actually spent. The preceding summary is based on Planning—Commission (Public Cooperation Division) Summary Record of the Meeting of the National Advisory Committee on Public Cooperation (August 1960), passim.

[2] Mehta Report, I p. 5.

[3] *Ibid.,* p. 7.

is little doubt that it will soon cover the country. At the time of writing data for a comprehensive evaluation are not available, though a few surveys of the new system have been made already. However, the new administrative structure can be analysed in terms of the problems of "authority and public cooperation" discussed previously. To do this, it is necessary to characterize the basic institution upon which the new system rests—the village panchayat—which is seen as representing the entire village community and which is now to be given added powers and resources to exercise leadership in the implementation of the development programme. From this vantage point it will also be possible to obtain some perspective concerning the conflicting claims of planner and administrators on one hand, and of local and state politicians on the other, whereby the future relations between centres of government and village India can be studied.

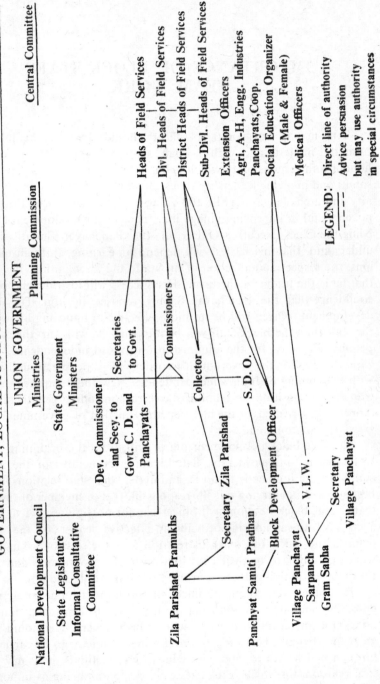

CHART INDICATING RELATIONSHIP BETWEEN
GOVERNMENT, LOCAL AUTHORITIES AND FIELD AGENCIES

# IMPORTANCE OF BLOCK STAFF
# TEAM WORK

... THE BLOCK DEVELOPMENT officer should approach his job with humility, modesty and with a high sense of appreciation for the honour and responsibility which is his helping guide in the panchayat samiti and in giving leadership to a staff which in turn has an opportunity and a challenge to assist 100 villages in removing conditions of poverty and in improving village life. The Block Development Officer being the Chief Executive Officer of the Panchayat Samiti should understand that his success will depend on earning, through his actions, the respect and affection of his staff and recognition by them that he is the leader of the team. His success will also depend on the confidence that the Panchayat Samiti reposes in him. The block development officer will be no more effective in imposing his will on the staff than the block staff will be imposing its will on the village people. The day for the administration to lead independence. Likewise, the day for the government to order village people around ended with the coming of India's independence. New India requires that all who occupy positions of administrative responsibility get themselves thoroughly oriented to the fact that the function of government is to serve, not to command.

The wise block development officer will, from the beginning, want to understand in considerable detail what each member of the block staff is to do, how he is to do it, and under what staff relations he can best succeed in carrying out his responsibility as a member of the staff team. The block development officer cannot possibly expect to be an acceptable, to say nothing of being an effective, leader of the block team if he does not start his relation with the staff by asking each what they think to be their contribution to the programme and how they suggest individually as a group they start to do the job.

The block development officer should himself immediately recognize and should let his staff that he has much to learn and that he hopes all members of the staff will be his teachers. He should recognize the obvious. He is new to development which is to be carried on through panchayati raj and with educational methods; he is new to a staff relationship which recognizes each person as being as important as every other person irrespective of administrative distinction. He is new to an administrative relationship where his success is dependent upon the informal response and respect he receives from the panchayat samiti and the other members of the staff. He is new to a programme that evaluates its accomplishments in terms of the contribution it makes in the development of the people to become responsive and responsible citizens.

While it is of particular importance for the block development officer to know the jobs of each member of the block staff, it is also necessary for each member of the staff to know and understand the jobs of the others. This means that all the block technical staff should know how the gram sevak has been trained, what he is expected to do in his group of villages, and the approaches and method he is expected to follow in working with the sarpanch and village panchayat. The gram sevaks in turn should, if they are to have an effective relation with the technical staff, know what each technician feels in his area of responsibility. While the gram sevak and the technical staff will have to, through experience, evolve an effective working relationship, they can greatly facilitate this if each knows what the other can do and how he hopes to do it.

To facilitate the definition and continuous re-definition of the staff's relations with the panchayats and the panchayat samiti and with each other will be the responsibility of the block development officer. This he can best do through systematic staff meetings democratically conducted. All staff meetings should encourage full and free expression from all. The gram sevak should feel just as free to express his point of view as the block development officer or any member of the technical staff. When any member of the staff expresses an attitude of either superiority or inferiority, the block development officer should note these and seek, through his personal contacts and other staff meetings, to eliminate such attitudes.

# BLOCK AS UNIT OF PLANNING

## S. *Chakravarti*

THE ADMINISTRATIVE UNIT for most purposes has hitherto been the district, with a population of 1.2 to 1.5 million and covering an area of 3,000 to 4,000 square miles. This unit was unwieldy and too remote from the village people for effective and intensive working. The Community Development programme, therefore, led to the creation of a new unit of planning and development, called the Community Development Block, comprising an area of 250 square miles with a population of nearly 80,000.

The concept of the Block as a unit of planning and development envisaged the pooling of all development funds at that level, including not only the schematic budget, but departmental funds and local community effort. The Block was to act as the common agent for all departments in the field of development, both for planning and implementation of programmes, evolving technically sound Block and village plans and executing them efficiently. The district plan is in part a summation of Block plans and in part a programme of activities affecting the district as a whole or areas comprising more than one Block. The district plan sets the tone for development work in the district as a whole, ensuring coordinated working of different Blocks, laying down priorities of work and establishing correct relationships between the technical and administrative services and the elected representatives at each level.

The acceptance of the concept of the Block as the chief operational unit of planning and development was, however, slow in coming. To start with the administrative pattern was developed on the basis of a single line organization consisting of the Development Commissioner at the State level, Collector at the district level, Block Development Officer at the Block level and Village Level Worker at the Village level. The exclusive attention given during the early years to the Block programme financed from the schematic budget, the entire reliance placed on the Block staff for its execution and the treating of the Block organisation as an almost self-contained set-up controlled by the Development Commissioner, kept the technical Departments at arm's length. It was only slowly realized that unless

X

the technical Departments were brought squarely into the programme and the Block developed as their common agency, the objectives of the programme could not be realized. This brought to the fore the problem or coordination at the level of policy-making and at the level of execution in the field.

At the policy level State, Governments have set up coordination committees both at Minister's and official level for the purpose of taking an integrated view of development programmes and taking decisions jointly. However, the approach of Departments is still governed by historical developments in respect of each Department and its capacity to spend. In spite of these deficiencies, coordination at policy level is fairly well established, even though joint planning in the real sense, that of taking an integrated view of the requirements of the rural sector, has still to take shape. At the implementation level the compulsions of the programme, namely inadequacy of the schematic budget, the need for coordination, the importance of pooling the resources of all development Departments, the inadequacy of technical content and technical support militating against efficient and economical operation of programmes, led to the acceptance of the principle of team work and joint responsibility, but brought in the problem of dual control. Dual control of implementation arose from administrative or operational control of technical officers by the Collector or the Block Development Officer and their technical control by their parent Departments. The problem of ensuring unity of outlook of work at different levels has been somewhat eased, but complete unity of approach has yet to be achieved.

# THE SCOPE OF EXTENSION

**Shortcomings in the Application of Extension**

THERE ARE A number of factors preventing the application of extension principles and methods at the field level, such as,

(*a*) Pressure for quick results and consequent hurry to fulfill the physical targets. This is due to the anxiety of the supervising staff to fulfill targets and achieve quick progress;

(*b*) Evaluation, having been based more on physical targets alone with the lack of self-evaluation among the workers has led to frustration and accumulation of pressure;

(*c*) Inadequate technical support and lack of necessary technical content related to local situations in the various directions given to field workers;

(*d*) Lack of adequate support by timely supplies and services;

(*e*) Lack of programme guidance for the field workers;

(*f*) The field workers are bothered with too much of office and file work, with "mere progress reports than progress";

(*g*) Overloading of the extension workers at the field level with miscellaneous works not related to the extension, such as collection of loans, collection of contributions, etc.

(*h*) The rigidity introduced by the schematic budget has left the field workers also rigid and has made them fall into a stereo-typed routine. Specified problems of the villagers are not being taken up to the desired extent, on this account;

(*i*) Lack of tenure and lack of prospects and other such personal problems have made the field workers worry about their career;

(*j*) With a view to achieve targets, there has been too much tendency for the workers to take decisions for the people.

# REPORTING AT THE BLOCK LEVEL

**Introduction**

THE COMMUNITY DEVELOPMENT programme was launched in India on
2nd October, 1952. The programme is implemented in Blocks with an
average population of about 60-70 thousand. A close watch has been
kept on its implementation right from the beginning through a system
of periodic reports. A well knit intelligence machinery has been provided at all levels to make available with minimum of delay dependable
information relating to planning, execution and progress of different
schemes. The programme has also benefited through evaluation by an
independent organisation namely the Programme Evaluation Organisation under the Planning Commission. The present paper, however,
does not discuss the role of evaluation which is outside its purview.

**Reports prescribed prior to 1959**

The Ministry called for a monthly and later on a quarterly
progress report on physical achievements in the Development Blocks
in regard to key indicators of progress which were generally selected
having regard to two basic considerations :—

(*i*) Only those items which were considered as key items for the
over-all assessment of the progress and here progress ought to be
watched continuously were included; and

(*ii*) The number of items included was kept as small as possible.
The items included in the list of key indicators were subject to revision
from time to time depending upon the relative shift in the emphasis
on specific items in the programme.

In addition, the ministry had prescribed a simple schedule for
Block Survey Report. The survey was undertaken immediately after
an area was selected for development under the programme. It provided basic information regarding the human and material resources
available in the area, the level of economic development and the
potentialities for further development.

A manual for village level workers' records was prescribed by the
Community Projects Administration (now the Ministry) to ensure
uniformity in the basic records maintained all over the country. The
Block Level reports were discussed in detail in the 'Manual on Administrative Intelligence.'

**Improvements introduced since 1959**

With the acceptance of the Block as the unit of planning and development, it was realised that the Blocks should report progress in respect of the total development activity in them. It was also considered necessary to bring about a co-ordinated approach in reporting. With this end in view, several measures have been adopted from time to time to improve the quality and content of the progress reports. The items on which information is required from the field have been broadly classified into two categories :—

(*a*) Those which lend themselves to reliable reporting by the V.L.W.'s or the other Block staff, by means of direct observation or local enquiry, or through compilation from existing village records; and

(*b*) those which could be satisfactorily obtained only by means of sample surveys.

Items of category (*a*) are further sub-divided into two groups according as they are to be collected (*i*) quarterly and (*ii*) annually, depending upon their importance; priority and the relative change over time. For campaign programmes, even weekly, fortnightly or monthly reports are collected.

Attempt has also been made to set out carefully the concepts and definitions of the various items of information, the source from which the information is to be collected and the manner of collection. This has considerably improved the uniformity in reporting in different States.

**Reports prescribed since 1959**

The Ministry introduced a revised set of schedules for Block level reports in April, 1959. (It is proposed to replace them shortly by a new set to meet the present requirements of the programme which has undergone considerable changes since 1959 particularly due to introduction of Panchayati Raj in different States and the complete coverage of rural India by the Blocks). The reports prescribed by the Ministry are :

(*i*) Block Quarterly Progress Report.

(*ii*) Block Annual Progress Report :

    (*a*) Part I for year ending 31st March. (It covers all fields except co-operation and Agriculture).

    (*b*) Part II for year ending 30th June. (It covers only Cooperation and Agriculture).

(*iii*) Block Survey Report. (Including the Village Schedule).

The above reports provide for information in regard to all important items relating to different sectors of rural development, the intention being that the information so collected will be sufficient to meet the requirements of all concerned. No other regular periodical reports are expected to be prepared by either the B.D.O. or the Extension Officers except a few special reports on ad-hoc programmes of specific activities for which they are individually responsible. A multiplicity of reports are, however, prepared by the Block staff in actual practice and this problem is discussed in detail in the following paragraphs.

A word about the relationship between the different types of reports. The annual progress report is essentially more detailed than the quarterly progress report. It indicates, for the important items, an advance over the bench mark position available in the block survey report. It calls for information only in "functioning" items thus taking care of the activities that have ceased to exist or works that have gone into disuse. An annual stock taking of the kind provides a more realistic picture of the programme.

The progress reports prescribed by the Ministry relate to the total actively under different sections of rural development taking place in the Block irrespective of the sponsoring agency *e.g.* Community Development, other Development Department in the States, semi-Government bodies etc. Private activity is also included for a number of items. The information on Block Budget in the Quarterly Progress Report relates, however, to only the expenditure from the schematic C.D. funds. The need for information on total expenditure in the Block has since become imperative. The revised Block Level Reports which are expected to be issued shortly by the Ministry will meet this requirement of the programme.

The Ministry of Community Development does not call for any monthly progress report, but it has no objection if such a report is prescribed by the States so that the Panchayat Samitis/Block Development Committees which are scheduled to meet every month in a number of States could be assisted in reviewing the progress of the Block programmes. (The preparation of a monthly report does not involve much difficulty as the village register provides for a continuous monthly record of statistics on all operational items).

The Ministry stream-lined in 1960 the system of basic records to be maintained by the Gram Sevaks. Each Gram Sevak was required to maintain a single Village Register (one for each village) and a Daily Diary (One for all the villages in the V.L.W. circle)...It was intended that these records would replace all other records maintained by the Gram Sevaks.

The Village register provides for all relevant information about the village, emphasis being laid on the accuracy of the data to be recorded and its amenability to verification. The Register has four parts mentioned below:

Part I     Basic Information.
Part II    List of Institutions and Community Organisations.
Part III   Community work taken up and the people's participation.
Part IV    Monthly achievements:
           (*a*) Schedule
           (*b*) Suggestive list of heads/sub-heads.

### Time lag in receipt of Reports

The time lag in receipt of progress reports by the Ministry is 2-4 months in the case of quarterly progress reports, 6-8 months in the case of Annual Progress Report (Part I) and 8-10 months in case of Annual Progress Report (Part II). The all-India reviews, on the basis of the information received from the States become available with a further lag of about one month.

### Utility of reports at the field level

The Panchayat Samitis/Block Development Committees are instructed to review the progress of work in their Blocks at their periodic meetings (monthly or quarterly as the case may be) and also chalk out their programmes for the next quarter.

A system of ranking the Blocks according to their performance, on the basis of the progress reports, has been evolved, and this has helped in focussing attention on Block which are particularly bad.

Assessment of individual Block performances based on statistical reports has become important in view of the decision to regulate the flow of funds according to the fulfilment of certain norms of self-help and self-reliance.

### Multiplicity of Reports

It has been mentioned that in addition to the periodical progress reports prescribed by the Ministry a large number of reports are being called from the Blocks. Some of these reports are required by the Central Ministries/Departments (*e.g.* Ministry of Food and Agriculture, Planning Commission, Home Ministry, etc.), but the large bulk of them are prescribed by the District Development Officers. The position regarding records maintained by Gram Sevaks also varies from place to place. The paragraphs below indicate the steps taken for rationalisation of progress reports and records.

(*i*) A team of officers from the Ministry of Community development and Cooperation and the Central Statistical Organisation visited all the States during 1958-60 to study the system of reporting and made detailed recommendations for rationalisation.

(*ii*) The Ministry of Food and Agriculture set up a Fact Finding Committee in 1962 to examine the schedules for progress reports relating to agricultural development prescribed by the Centre and to indicate the lines on which they could be streamlined. The committee has recommended a number of proformae for reports by the States. The committee found that in addition to periodical reports prescribed by the Ministry of Food and Agriculture, a large number of reports were being asked for, from time to time, on an *ad-hoc* basis. More often than not, the information could be extracted from the existing reports and records. Generally, such special enquiries created avoidable work-load for the block agencies. The committee also felt that there was need for bringing about a uniformity in the procedures, periodicity and content of the various proformae with a view to removing these defects. It may be noted here that some of the items in these proformae are already included in the Block reports prescribed by the C.D. Ministry. Besides, a number of items are not amenable to reliable reporting by the block agency.

### Case Studies

Following the recommendations of the Annual Conference on Community Development held in 1963, the Ministry undertook studies in regard to paper work in four blocks, namely, Gurgaon (Punjab), Meerut (U.P.), Sewar (Rajasthan) and Sanchi (M.P.). The purpose of the study was to assess the magnitude of the problem and to devise measures for improvement. The extent to which the instructions issued by the Ministry in this behalf had been implemented was also sought to be examined.

The study revealed that there was considerable avoidable duplication in the coverage of various reports. The block-wise position in the areas visited is given below.

Gurgaon block was required to submit regularly 15 monthly, 16 quarterly and 7 annual progress reports. The social education organiser/ panchayat officer and agriculture extension officer were the two most heavily burdened officers with paper work. The agricultural extension officer spent, on the average, 38 man-hours per month, on paper work. Four records were maintained by the Gram Sevaks though in a very perfunctory manner. It was estimated that a Gram Sevak spent, on the average, 15-20 minutes per day on paper work.

Meerut block submitted regularly 11 monthly 10 quarterly and 7 annual progress reports. Besides, 2 seasonal weekly progress reports and 3 seasonal fortnightly progress reports were also submitted by the block. A.D.O. (Agri.), A.D.O. (Coop.) and S.E.O./S.D.O. (Panchayat) were the most heavily burdened officers with paper work. The A.D.O. (Agri) in particular, spent 50 man-hours per month on paper work. The Gram Sevaks in the block maintained 14 records and spent on the average 55 man-hours per month on paper work.

Sewar block submitted 4 monthly, 10 quarterly and 4 annual progress reports. The paper work, on the whole, appeared to be light more due to absence of any systematic records rather than due to any rationalisation. The Gram Sevaks also did not maintain any systematic records.

Sanchi block was required to submit 1 fortnightly, 18 monthly, 12 quarterly, 1 four-monthly, 2 half yearly and 9 annual progress reports. E.O. (Agri), E.O. (Coop.) and to some extent the S.E.O. happened to be heavily burdened with paper work. The Gram Sevaks in this block were also much burdened with paper particularly because they had also to handle taccavi cases. The Gram Sevaks roughly spent 5-7 days per month on paper work.

## Reduction of Reports in Gujarat

It is interesting to note that the Government of Gujarat carried out of study of the various returns/reports in use in their blocks. Consequent on this study, 41 out of 78 periodical reports/returns called from the block have been discontinued, programme have been simplified for 4 reports and the periodicity changed in respect of 2 reports. This is expected to reduce the work involved in the submission of reports by the block by about 50%.

## Organisation for reporting

A post of statistically trained progress assistant is provided in the permanent staffing pattern of a Block. The post was sanctioned by all the States but it has since been abolished in Bihar, Punjab and Madras in the wake of the Emergency. Progress Assistants were in position in 3,658 Blocks out of 4,253 reporting Blocks in the country as on 30th September, 1963. The States of Madhya Pradesh, Orissa, Rajasthan and Manipur have almost full complement of progress assistants. In other states the shortages vary from 10 to 15 per cent. The progress assistant is borne on the technical cadre of the State statistical Bureau in all States except West Bengal and his work is directed and supervised by the Bureau and the District Statistical Officer.

Gram Sevak (incharge of about 10 villages) is the primary agency for reporting at the village level. The progress assistant imparts training to the Gram Sevaks in the Block in the methods of reporting and supervises their work; he himself participates in the collection of primary data (particularly on items covered by sample surveys); and prepares the periodic statistical reports of the Block. The compilation work of the Gram Sevaks is also supervised by the Block Extension Officers and the District Officers.

At the State level, the statistical reports emanating from the Block are processed and analysed by a statistical unit (called the Administrative Intelligence Unit) which is located in the State Statistical Bureau in all States except in the case of Punjab, Rajasthan and West Bengal where the Unit is located in the Development Commissioners' officer. The Administrative Intelligence Unit controls the programme of collection of data and prepares consolidated statistical reports for the State and also makes an appraisal of the progress on the basis of these reports. The Ministry of Community Development and Cooperation keeps a close liaison with the State Administrative Intelligence Units and prepares its own periodical progress reports on the basis of the data furnished by these Units.

## Problems

Three problems emerge clearly from the above analysis. Firstly, the gram sevaks in certain states are heavily over-burdened with paper work. Secondly, the appointment of progress assistant has not relieved the extension staff from the burden of unnecessary paper work. Lastly there is indiscriminate addition to the number of reports from time to time. How can these problems be solved ? The points which need special consideration are: (*i*) Will it be practicable to delegate the responsibility for reporting at the village level to the panchayat secretary, the Patwari or the school teacher instead of the Gram Sevak. If a workable solution could be found the Gram Sevak will be in a position to devote himself entirely to his legitimate function of agricultural development. (*ii*) How can the progress assistant be made more effective both in the matter of relieving the extension officers of the burden of paper work and also in ensuring the flow of accurate statistics. (*iii*) Will it be practicable for the States to put a ban on calling for additional reports of a periodical nature from the Block, unless they were screened and permitted by a committee on which the Development Commissioner and the Director of State Statistical Bureau are represented? It is pertinent that some authority should satisfy itself that the information required could not be extracted from the existing reports and records and that it would be possible for the Block agency to comply with the demand from the point of view of feasibility and work-load involved.

# SOME UNRESOLVED ISSUES OF PUBLIC COOPERATION IN RURAL DEVELOPMENT

*Reinhard Bendix*

MORE OFTEN THAN not, the faulty design or execution of community development and national extension is held responsible for the failure of India's villagers to respond "adequately" to the emergencies facing rural India. On such diagnosis puts the blame on the speed with which these programmes have been extended to all parts of the country and upon the rapid growth of staff that resulted. The programme has moved away "from the original impetus and clarity of vision;" while the "philosophy of community development" which was to have preserved the impetus has come to be "remote from village realities."[1] Another and related critique attributes the overemphasis on construction at the expense of extension activities to the fact that programme leaders do not believe in the willingness of the villagers to solve their own problems. Too many resources are devoted to the misguided attempt to motivate the people.[2] There is some merit and illusion in both comments, but they do not deal with the political ideologies and strategies which first led to the quest for public cooperation and has now led to the policy of "democratic decentralization."

The public cooperation sought by the Indian planners is not cooperation at any price. Although it is acknowledged that so far community development has benefited the upper sections of village society, it is constantly stressed that in this way the objective of community solidarity is defeated. National and local leaders should be troubled in their conscience by this failure to achieve social justice.[3] Nor does the objective of promoting rural economic development have exclusive priority. Rather,

Our Community Development approach stands for. . .the dual purpose of building democracy from the base and harnessing it to the cause of development. . .It is not so much a question of protecting the

1 U.N. Report, pp. 49-50.
2 Carl Taylor, "Two Major Evils," in Kurukshetra, p. 396. For several years Dr. Taylor has been advisor on community development to the Ford Foundation and the Indian Government.
3 Kurukshetra, pp. 28-29.

individual and the community from the evil effects of too much state action as of revitalizing the community and building up democracy from the roots upwards. The people have to be made conscious of their rights and responsibilities as citizens of a free country. They must be ready to bear the main burden of re-building the communities in which they live, which have been disintegrating over a period of centuries. To re-integrate the life of these communities must be an important objective of Community Development.[1] This explicit duality of purpose is related to the special meaning of "democracy" as used in this context. The rhetoric of the community development movement refers to "democracy" in the two senses of "equality" and "solidarity," and both meanings are linked with economic development.

It is said that development cannot succeed unless it has nearly universal and entirely voluntary support from the villagers. Officials are admonished to promote the solidarity of the village as well as "effective" leadership, since development will inevitably suffer where factions divide the village and local leaders fail to promote village development.[2] "Democracy" in the ordinary sense of a free competition for public office is not considered applicable or suitable at the local level. Rather, at the "lower levels of democracy" responsible political parts have an important "constructive role to play, and only at the "higher levels" should they play a "political role."[3] Again, political parties are characterized as "essentially undemocratic," because they foster ideological difference and "forment division at the village and Panchayat levels on every issue in order to form a rural political base for themselves."[4] To prevent both the natural and these "formented" divisions, an organisation representing the village as a whole is demanded. In its discussion of the new policy of "democratic decentralization" the Third Five Year Plan urges the village panchayat to encourage unanimity or near unanimity "so that various activities are undertaken with the general consent and goodwill of the community."

[1] *Ibid.*, p. 26. This statement may stand for many of its kind; I choose it because of its clarity. From a policy standpoint the same points are made in a statement by Tarlok Singh (Additional Secretary, Planning Commission) "Planning at the Village Level," *ibid.*, pp. 134-135.

[2] *Ibid.*, pp. 17, 19, 20, 23, 32, 70-71, and passim.

[3] *Ibid.*, p. 32. Note in this connection the statement by S K. Day, Union Minister for Community Development, Panchayati Raj and Cooperation, according to which village democracy should be safeguarded from the pressures of power politics. Although admitting that it would be difficult to isolate panchayat work from the activities of political parties, Mr. Dey said: "What we want to avoid is power politics," adding that there could be no objection to "good politics," See Economic Weekly, XIV (July 1962), p. 1106.

[4] Kurukshetra, p. 332.

In the absence of such unanimity and of an effective village organization "the approach to rural problems is (said to be) better organized from the side of the administration."

This drift toward centralized administration is a response of equalitarian officials to be stark inequalities of village life.[1] But the results of this "drift" have not always been salutary. Emphasis on centrally directed actions runs counter to the explicit demands for public initiative and cooperation at the local level. Plans for agricultural development are prepared at the state and central levels "independently of local plans" and hence lack responsiveness to local demands.[2] Local development officials are admonished to elicit cooperation, but they also have to prove their worth, which as we saw leads to concentration on physical construction and welfare activities in the absence of the desired cooperation in increasing agricultural production.

Moreover, achievements in both fields tend to accrue to the benefit of the better-situated segments of village society, so that the drift towards centralization which partly arises from the government's unwillingness to tolerate the inequalities of village society nevertheless intensifies these inequalities in many instances. The inadvertent effect has been instituted In practice planners and administrators proceed as if the public cooperation for which they ask and the caste diversions and inequalities which they denounce exist in two separate, watertight compartments. Yet the villagers are asked to cooperate today, not tomorrow, and today they are deeply divided by great economic inequalities and intense communal affiliations. The fact is that the "public" does not possess that capacity for a village-wide solidarity and organization which may arise in some distant future if and when the conditions of village society have been transformed.

In themselves these facts are clearly acknowledged. Solidarity is commended, factions are denounced, and it is frankly stated that "there is considerable weakness in the organization available in the village."[3] But the weakness referred to is the incapacity or unwillingness of villagers to organize themselves along equalitarian lines. Government leaders reject the capacity of villagers to organize along

[1] The plea for an organization representing the whole village and the statement concerning the administrative approach are contained in Tarlok Singh's statement of 1954 (*ibid.*, p. 134). The statement concerning unanimity and supporting arguments appear on p. 339 and passim of the Third Five Year Plan.

[2] Third Five Year Plan, p. 334.

[3] Tarlok Singh in Kurukshetra, p. 134. See also the statement by Raghubir Sahai in 1959 which declares that "we are woefully lacking in this kind of non-official element at each and every level" (*ibid.*, p. 354).

caste lines or in factions as an evil legacy of the past. Accordingly, Indian political one community is envisaged as consisting of organized government on one hand, and the masses of the Indian people on the other. Nowhere is this attitude more forcefully put than in this statement by Kaka Kalelkar, the Chairman of the "Backward Classes Commission."

National solidarity demands that in a democratic set-up Government recognize only two ends—the individual at one end and the nation as a whole at the other and that nothing should be encouraged to organize itself in between these two ends to the solidarity of the nation. All communal and denominational organizations and groupings of lesser and narrower units have to be watched carefully so that they do not jeopardize the national solidarity and do not weaken the efforts of the nation to serve all the various elements in the body politic with equality.[1]

The plebiscitarian framework is identical with the approach formulated at the end of the eighteenth century by such men as La Chalotais and Le Chapelier. It rules out any positive attention to the communal organizations which have sprung up with the advance of urbanization and the spread of communication facilities. In India, it has given rise to the quixotic effort if assisting voluntary organizations.

The government's purpose is to stimulate cooperation and initiative along non-communal lines.[2] Inevitably, this new scheme has raised major problems: the difficulty of making an officially sponsored "non-official" organization appear as a "voluntary effort" is only too apparent. At a meeting of the National Advisory Committee on Public

[1] Report of the Backward Classes Commission (Delhi: Government of India Press, 1956), I, p. iv. This commission was appointed pursuant to Article 340 of the Constitution authorizing the president to initiate an investigation of the conditions of socially and educationally backward classes. These classes are distinct from the scheduled castes (untouchables) and tribes which are provided for separately in the Constitution and the Government.

[2] The Planning Commission set up a "Public Division" which was authorized to give grants to the Bharat Sevak Samaj (Indian Service Society), a non-political and non-official organization that seeks to secure public participation in the work of the Five Year Plans. In 1958 the Bharat Sevak Samaj was invited to set up on an experimental basis Lok Karya Kshetras (areas especially designated for the purpose of enlisting cooperation). Through these special organisations voluntary labour and local resources were to be used to assist in local programmes of development, to create popular enthusiasm for the plan programmes, to draw out promising young workers from the masses and to strengthen local institutions like panchayats and cooperatives. For a period of three years each of these Kshetras would receive Rs. 5000 per annum. See Programme Evaluation Organisation, Planning Commission, A study of the Lok Karya Kshetras of the Bharat Sevak Samaj (New Delhi: Government of India, 1960), p. 1.

Cooperation a galaxy of public figures examined the government's role in sponsoring "voluntary" organizations. Since the need for public cooperation is all-pervasive, why should there be a separate allocation for this purpose ? If the government sponsors voluntary organisations, they will mushroom and the resulting rivalries will get out of hand. Voluntary agencies and their workers should strengthen existing institutions with their assistance rather than become another agency. One speaker states that the central government has publicized full particulars about the programme under which voluntary organizations could secure grants-in aid; now, the states should do likewise, and some criteria should be laid down so that the voluntary organizations applying for grants-in-aid can be properly assessed.

From here it is only a short step to the suggestion that all voluntary organizations should evolve a uniform programme on the national scale and that the government should encourage their activities since otherwise vested interests might outset them from their field of endeavour. These were, of course, warnings. Voluntary organizations maintained or run by the government would cease to be voluntary; that efforts to raise donations from the public are terminated when financial assistance by the government becomes available; the government comes to duplicate activities carried out by voluntary organizations already. But the tone is set by statements which refer to uniform training for all workers in voluntary organizations, to the periodic officials assessment of these organizations to make sure they have the desired results, to the required degree of planning and continuity in non-officials voluntary action, to the need to entrust voluntary organizations with certain specific responsibilities. The discussion reveals little awareness of its self-defeating character; it seems to take for granted that public cooperation can and should be organised from the side of the administration.[1]

But such plebiscitarian doctrines cannot disguise the failure of the Indian government to "evoke popular initiative" in its programme of community development and agricultural extension. In their exhaustive study of this programme, published in 1957, the authors of the Mehta Report state:

So long as we do not discover or create a representative and democratic institution which will supply the "local interest, supervision and care necessary to ensure that expenditure of money upon local objects conforms with the needs and wishes of the locality," invest it with adequate power and assign to it appropriate finances, we will

---

[1] But it is not surprising under these circumstances that of the Rs. 50 million set aside for "public cooperation" in the Second Five Year Plan.

never be able to evoke local interest and excite local initiative in the field of development.[1]

Such institutions have not been developed so far, because, "decentralization of responsibility and power has not taken place below the state level in recent years." Accordingly, it is recommended that in agriculture, animal husbandry, cooperation, minor irrigation works, village industries, primary education, local communications, health and medical relief, local amenities, and similar subjects the government would devolve all of its functions in these fields upon the local bodies, reserving to itself the functions of guidance, supervision, and higher planning.

# REPORT 1963-64

### Block as Unit of Planning and Development

THE BLOCK HAS yet to be developed fully as the unit of planning and development in many States. This has two aspects—local planning (which is dealt with in the next section) and implementation. Implementation would require that all expenditure of various development departments on schemes which can be implemented at the block level shall be routed through the block and implemented through the block agency. The Block Development Officer should also be the Drawing and Disbursing Officer for all such schemes wherever possible.

Madhya Pradesh, Mysore, Orissa, Rajasthan, Tripura and Manipur have made a provision of Rs. One lakh annually for each post-stage II Block out of their own plan and non-plan funds. Provision in the other States varies from Rs. 14,000 to Rs. 65,000 of their own plan and non-plan funds.

### District and Block Plans

For many years it has been hoped that integrated plans at the district and block levels would serve as an effective means for stimulating economic and social development. This hope has been realised only to meagre extent. In practice, neither districts nor blocks have well-knit plans. District and Block Plans are now essentially in the nature of a break-up of the State Plans on somewhat mechanical lines rather than well-integrated and forward looking plans of development, ensuring optimum utilisation of the resources including manpower.

In the context of the Fourth Five-Year Plan, it is necessary to ensure that District, Block and Village Plans serve both as a step in the formulation of the State Plans and as a means for more effective implementation of the State Plans.

These problems are being examined in consultation with the Planning Commission.

# PANCHAYATI RAJ

## A Series of Quotations by Indian Leaders

SELF-GOVERNMENT MEANS continuous effort to be independent of government control, whether it is foreign government or national. Swaraj-government will be a sorry affair if people look up to it for the regulation of every detail of life.

Gandhiji, Young India, 6 August, 1925

When the people come into possession of political power, the interference with the freedom of people is reduced to a minimum. In other words, a nation that runs its affairs smoothly and effectively without much State interference is truly democratic. Where such a condition is absent, the form of government is democratic only in name.

Gandhiji, Harijan, 11 January, 1936

Independence must begin at the bottom. Thus every village will be a republic of panchayat having full powers. It follows, therefore, that every village has to be self-sustained and capable of managing its affairs even to the extent of defending itself against the whole world. It will be trained and prepared to perish in the attempt to defend itself against any onslaught from without. Thus, ultimately, it is the individual who is the unit. This does not exclude dependence on, and willing help from neighbours. It will be a free and voluntary play of mutual forces. Such a society is necessarily highly cultured in which every man and woman knows what he or she wants and, what is more, knows that no one should want anything that others cannot have with equal labour.

Gandhiji, Harijan, 28 July 1946

If we would see our dream of Panchayati Raj, *i.e.*, true democracy, realized, we would regard the humblest and lowest Indian as being equally the ruler of India with the tallest in the land. This presupposes that all are pure, or will become pure if they are not. And purity must go hand in hand with wisdom. Not one would then harbour any distinction between community and community, caste and outcaste. Everybody would regard all as equal with oneself and hold them together in the silken net of love. No one would regard another as untouchable. He would hold as equal the toiling labourer and the rich capitalist. Everybody would know how to earn an honest living by the sweat of one's brow and make no distinction between intellectual and physical labour.

Gandhiji, Harijan, 18 January, 1948

Democracy required that everyone, man or woman, should realize his or her own responsibility. That is what is meant by Panchayat Raj.

Gandhiji's Message to a Prayer Meeting, May 18, 1947,<br>quoted by Tendulkar, Mahatma, Vol. VII, p. 470.

In democracy, the kisan should be the ruler. The speaker would certainly like to push forward an honest and capable kisan. Such a kisan would not know English. The speaker would ask Jawaharlal to be the Kisan's secretary and see the foreign ambassadors on his chief's behalf, and to take pride in such service. Such a kisan Prime Minister would not ask for a palace to live in. He would live in a mud hut, sleep under the sky and work on the land during the day, whenever he was free. Then the whole picture would change immediately. In Panchayati Raj, the man who should count most in India, was naturally the kisan. How to advance him was the question.

Tendulkar, Mahatma, Vol. VIII, p. 247

It is not by some mere theory, however good, that we shall enthuse the masses of our cultivators. The essential approach must be to make them understand and co-operative and develop self-reliance. Hence the importance of giving powers to the village panchayat and the village co-operative. The argument that they might misuse those powers, though it may have some force, has no real validity. The risk has to be taken, as only thus will the people learn through trial and error.

Jawaharlal Nehru, Azad Memorial Lecture, 22 February, 1959

The gram panchayat is at the root of our concept of a new society. It is the root of our Constitution. The panchayat is the synthesis of all the forces of the village and must be kept free from casteism, partiality, factions and divisions, jealousy, recriminations and mutual quarrels. The panchayat is not the handmaiden of the Sarpanch or the Panches but is the expression of the will of the inhabitants of the village. . .They have to be free from difference of caste and religion. They represent the divine power of the people.

U.N. Dhebar, Inauguration of the Panchayat Bhavan, Jotwar<br>Rajasthan, Rashtradoot, Jaipur, 13 November, 1955

Today we are busy in national planning. In fact, we require village planning. People of the village should exercise their own brain to do things. Should somebody err only one village would suffer. But when the stewardship of the whole country is entrusted to four or five persons, the whole country has to suffer the consequences of their one single mistake. But this will not be so when power resides in the village itself. If one village commits a certain blunder, another will not repeat it. Hence, power should be distributed in every village. There must be decentralization of power.

Vinoba Bhave, AICC Economic Review, 24 July, 1954

## PANCHAYATI RAJ AND ITS STRUCTURE

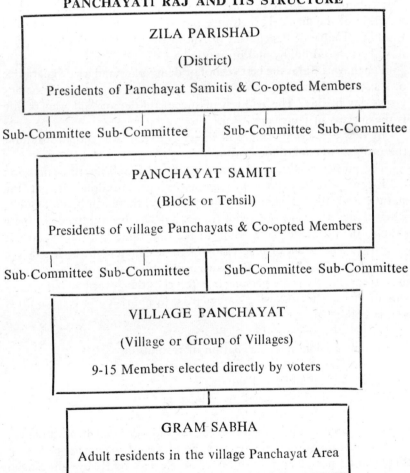

**ZILA PARISHAD**

(District)

Presidents of Panchayat Samitis & Co-opted Members

Sub-Committee  Sub-Committee  |  Sub-Committee  Sub-Committee

**PANCHAYAT SAMITI**

(Block or Tehsil)

Presidents of village Panchayats & Co-opted Members

Sub-Committee  Sub-Committee  Sub-Committee  Sub-Committee

**VILLAGE PANCHAYAT**

(Village or Group of Villages)

9-15 Members elected directly by voters

**GRAM SABHA**

Adult residents in the village Panchayat Area

# PROBLEMS OF PANCHAYATI RAJ

*Vasudeva Rao*

PANCHAYATI RAJ IN Andhra Pradesh is a child of 5 (five) years and it is undergoing those troubles which a child faces when it grows up. One cannot but help remembering Wordsworth nature truth 'child is a father of the man'. This strange paradox is nothing but truth. The toothing trouble of Panchayats in Andhra Pradesh are over as they have been faced boldly and promptly.

Panchayati Raj is the best school of democracy and a safe guarantee of success of democratic growth. It is in this parlours that democracy grows day by day. The acid test of successful democratic way of life is the success of Panchayati Raj.

In view of the importance of Panchayat Raj, we should examine the problems facing these institutions.

The problems which are commonly faced by all the three tiers are:

Extent of supervision—As long as things are done as per the statute and to the standard of expectancy, there can be no trouble, when things are done otherwise than what has been intended, there should be adequate supervision to see that these institutions do not go astray. The extent of supervision of these democractic bodies by the Governmental agency is a much discussed topic and conflicting views are expressed. By some persons it is felt that the governmental agency should have the following safeguards, to nourish and bring up this young child:

(*a*) periodical inspection

(*b*) supervision and cancellation of resolutions

(*c*) Review and revision of programmes

(*d*) periodical audit and surcharge

(*e*) removal of individual office-bearers

(*f*) dissolution and supervision

Under each head detailed procedures and rules may be formulated.

The next question that exercises the minds of some persons is that there should not be any control over an elected body by an official machinery. Hence they think of an independent agency by the District level—A District level Panchayati Raj Commission, with a man of District Judge's rank, an administrative Officer at the District

Collector's rank and a public worker of known ability and character. The proposal involves heavy financial commitment as the Santhanam Committee is siezed of this problem, it is better to await the recommendations.

The control of administrative staff working in the Panchayati Raj bodies is a burning topic. Both the non-officials and officials are equally concerned with this problem. When power has been decentralized, the control of officials who are responsible to educate these things has not been transferred completely to the non-official agencies.

The elected representative feels that the administrative control of the block staff should squarely rest in him as the President is responsible for all developmental activities. On the other hand, the non-official who is not trained for the job and there is no check for his doings except removal and surcharge. It becomes a difficult task to the official to displease his non-official boss.

Maharashtra has done this job of coordination by placing all District Officers under the Chief Executive Officer of the Zilla Parishad whereas Andhra Pradesh has stuck a via media and has made the District Collectors and R.D.Os to coordinate the work of all District Officers and also to bring pressure on the non-officials through the Zilla Parishads. In actual practice no serious trouble has arisen between the officials and non-officials in Andhra Pradesh.

The problem of human frailty is coming topmost in Panchayati Raj while the official has to face the machinery of disciplinary action, no such control is therefore the non-official. So the question of bringing the non-official under a vigilance machinery should be reminded, which may help the machinery of Panchayati Raj to run an oiled wheel.

The extension Officers have their primary responsibility towards the respective departmental bosses and they try to dodge between the B.D.O. and District Officers, causing a slight confusion. The Statement as to who should have control over the Extension Officers and the extent of control has to be solved.

New Blocks are financed from different grants, funds for C.D. come from Panchayati Raj Department, Agriculture Animal Husbandry, Education etc., come from the respective Departments. The departmental heads are showing responsibility to Panchayat Raj bodies and they in their turn show the Departmental heads.

The accounting has become a very big problem, as they are not maintained properly. Audit takes place at a time when persons who spent the amount are no more in that station.

Personal favour and nepotism which has been universally show' their head in Panchayati Raj body. If this gains ground, there is salvation for future progress. It has to be nipped in the bud healthy conventions will have to be developed, as the pangs of law cannot do much.

Coordination with cooperatives and other National building department is still lacking, a sense of cordiality and kingship has to develop.

Of all the problems, the problem of good conduct is the most useful one. Example is better than precept. The functionaries of Panchayati Raj have to set up exemplary codes of public conduct which will make others to behave similarly. If the office-holders do this we need not have any superiority control.

# REASONS FOR DISORGANISATION OF THE GRAM SABHA

IT HAS BEEN the finding of the Team that Gram Sabhas, even where they have been statutorily established, have not been in a functioning order. Given below is a consolidated statement of the reasons, for which the Gram Sabhas, in our opinion, have not been, as yet everywhere, well-attended:

(i) *Lack of Awareness*: The villagers generally are not even aware of the separate existence of the Gram Sabha as an institution as distinguished from the Panchayat. Even where the villagers could recognise that these are two different bodies, seldom have they been aware of their rights and responsibilities at members of the Gram Sabha. However, even when the villagers have been aware of their rights, a sense of lack of effective rights and powers belonging to them as members of the Gram Sabha, has led to the same results.

(ii) *Personal Nature of Village Politics:* A study of dynamics of village politics has made it evident that votes in Panchayat elections are generally cast in favour of, or against personalities. The villagers while exercising their vote, do not take into consideration policies, programmes or ideological concepts. When, therefore, a particular leader is elected to the Panchayat, the villagers who have elected him feel that their duties have ended and that the leader would now act for them. Those members of the community, who might have opposed him and have been supporting an alternative leader—the opposition group; when they see that their alternate leader does not take any interest in the working of the Panchayat, they also find no point in attending Gram Sabha meetings or taking any interest therein.

(iii) *Lack of Common Venue:* Absence of a well recognised common venue for Gram Sabha meeting in each village has also been responsible for disorganisation of the Gram Sabha. A number of villages are often grouped together under a panchayat and the size, thus, being unwieldy, it becomes difficult for people of different mouzas/wards/villages to attend the Gram Sabha meetings at a distant venue.

(iv) *Lack of Time*: The meeting of the Gram Sabha when held at a time when the villagers are not free retards participation. If these meetings are held during the off period or on festival days, the situation would be different.

(*v*) *Lack of Communication:* The usual method to announce date, time, and venue of Gram Sabha meetings has been beating of drum. The Panchayats, however, usually do not take any interest beyond ordering beating of drum; it has been found that the chowkidars sometimes even do not beat drum and even if they do so, it is not done properly and very few people, as a result, become aware of the impending meeting of the Gram Sabha.

(*vi*) *Unwillingness of the Pradhan/members of the Panchayat:* The power structure of the Panchayats is not often keen that the Gram Sabha should meet and more so in view of the fact that the opposition leaders in the Gram Sabha may raise embarrassing questions. The ruling elite of the village, therefore, sometimes even go to the length of ensuring that Gram Sabha meetings are not properly advertised. The members of the opposition group, it has been often found, have taken keen interest to similarly ensure that their followers do not attend Gram Sabha meetings. There is, therefore, in the politically conscious areas, a virtual boycott of the Gram Sabha meetings by the opposition group.

(*vii*) *Apathy of the Villagers:* The villagers are aware of the doubtful value of the Gram Sabha and they find it more useful to be engaged in their own productive venture, or to even enjoy leisure at home, rather than attend the Gram Sabha meeting, which is of no direct interest to them. This apathy, which is also visible in municipal areas, etc., is all the more evident at the Gram Sabha level.

Experiences of the Team from the evidence available to it, thus, made it clear that there were many inherent difficulties in the socio-political climate of the country itself which stood in the way of smooth functioning of Gram Sabha, and that in spite of its importance it would take time for the organisation to grow and gather strength, even if statutory provisions were made to transfer substantial power to it. The Team, therefore, although recognising the importance of the Gram Sabha, realised that the full development of this institution cannot be achieved merely by grant of statutory powers. It appreciated at the same time that tradition, gradual process of growth, and conscious effort for its promotion will have to ultimately determine the exact shape and form the institution will take over years; the Team, therefore primarily engaged itself (i) to define the immediate role that Gram Sabha should play as the lowest base of the Panchayati Raj administration and (ii) to enumerate the steps, which should be initiated to enable the Gram Sabha, through practice, self-education and gradual development to occupy its real place in the scheme of things. If and when the village communities through the institution of Gram Sabha really develop into vital, and functioning bodies, its tremendous

potentialities seem to be obvious. The Team is aware that it is only
when the concept of a participating democracy is fully realised, that
much of the promises which the Panchayati Raj institutions hold out
today, will be adequately realised. The Team, therefore, (in the pages
to follow) has made certain specific recommendations regarding the
role that institution of Gram Sabha should play in the light of its
potentialities. The Team realises that it is only through the practice
of the immediate role assigned to it that the institution would be able
to gather the necessary momentum and grow into an effective organisation of the village people. It may be necessary, when such logical
development in the status of the institution takes place, to endow it
with more powers and functions and a time would come when the
institution developing into a real base of village participation may
demand the same in large measures from the higher tiers, on its own
right.

# CRITICAL STUDY OF DIFFERENT PATTERNS OF PANCHAYATI RAJ

1. Now THAT WE have sufficient experience with the Panchayati Raj, in the various States, it is time for evolving a common pattern at least by the beginning of the IVth Plan for implementation uniformly throughout the country. This uniform pattern, in basic particulars is not only feasible but is also desirable in view of the overall importance of the place of development in the country.

2. Decentralisation of powers and responsibilities to local bodies is desirable, because it has certain advantages over decentralisation or more delegation of powers to subordinate officials. These advantages are: such local bodies will be the training grounds for popular leaders in the art of government, they are more directly responsible and responsive to popular opinion, they are more readily accessible to the general populace, their chance failures will have only local effect, they introduce an element of stability in democracy, they are in a better position to appreciate the "felt needs" of the people, and they can mobilise popular initiative, enthusiasm and resources better. It is not necessary to make these local bodies as governments unto themselves, and to make the Constitution for this purpose.

3. While it is recognized that popular participation is the very crux of a decentralised democracy, the need for popular control is equally, if not more imperative. Democracy cannot be measured only by the extent to which people take part in local affairs, but also by the extent to which such decisions are subject to the influence of public opinion. The role of political parties in Panchayati Raj therefore cannot be ignored, and the existing hard realities of life should be appreciated and recognized.

4. Efficient Technical services are a rare commodity; so is higher administrative personnel. They are also expensive. The best of these could therefore be provided at the district level only for any foreseeable future. Though it is true that bigger the administrative unit, the more impersonal the services. However, the apparently incompatible factors like administrative efficiency and popular accountability could be reconciled by making the district level services subordinate to the elected political head, who is answerable to the electorate.

5. The Village Panchayat could be made viable to function as a self-

governing unit by encouraging them to tap local resources, by way of providing matching contributions from the Government. The Government also should endeavour to provide a minimum of rupee one per capita as an *ad hoc* grant to every village Panchayat.

6. Coordination is an important factor in Panchayati Raj. The district level officers of development department should be brought completely within the scheme of democratic decentralisation. The devolution should be perfect, so that overlapping and duplication of functions are avoided. Duality of control whenever it exists, should be removed, and a single line of coordination and control provided.

7. The primary level at which decentralisation could be most effective seems to be the district in view of the following reasons;

(*a*) Present day planning is so intricate and complicated that the national policy and local desires could be reconciled and correlated only at the district level.

(*b*) If substantial powers and functions are to be delegated, the district has to be the unit of decentralisation since a majority of the schemes require assistance from district level technical officers.

(*c*) Since technical personnel is a scarce commodity it will be available only at the district level for any foreseeable future.

(*d*) The district level heads of departments have to be placed *within* the scheme of decentralisation if they have to be made responsible for the programme and responsive to the local needs. This can be had only if the district level body becomes executive.

(*e*) Where the Panchayat Samiti is an executive body a certain duplication and overlapping functions between State and Panchayat Section is inevitable. This can be reduced to the minimum if the district is the unit of decentralisation where all functions of a development could be entrusted to a single line of coordination.

(*f*) Politics is inseparable where substantial devolution takes place. Political parties will, therefore, play an important role in Panchayati Raj whether one wishes or not. If party alignment has to play a predominant role it is better if higher issues of policy from the basis of such alignment rather than parochial local factors. The district level will be the proper political platform for this.

8. Acceptance of the district as a primary level of decentralisation does not belittle the importance of other tiers. Then village and block level schemes and programmes should be entrusted respectively to the village Panchayat or they Panchayat Samiti. The ensure a balance between popular participation and popular control on one hand and administrative efficiency and financial viability on the other will be ensured.

9. The Zila Parishad should have full and final authority in formulating annual budgets, developmental plans, priorities, taxation, and

should be invested with all developmental functions at the district level. It should be encouraged to raise local resources. Similarly the Panchayat Samitis and Panchayats should have full powers and functions in this respect for their respective levels. Each unit should have an autonomy of its own but it should remember that it forms a part of the organic whole.

10. Regulatory functions (other than municipal or civil) should not be entrusted to the Panchayati Raj bodies because coercion is the very antithesis of Community Development. These bodies will have to devote their full time and energy for the development tasks, and this useful apparatus of decentralisation should not fall into a net of regulatory duties.

11. At the village panchayat level the Sarpanch as well as the Panchas should be directly elected. Since substantial powers of government are to be devolved on the Zila Parishad and Panchayat Samiti direct representation should be provided. All the Presidents of the Samitis should also be the members of Zila Parishad, to have organic links.

12. It is recommended that the legislative should be associated as only non-voting members of the Panchayat Samiti and Zila Parishad. The role of the legislator in Panchayati Raj has to be restrictive in scope, because new leadership has to be developed and also because the legislator's legitimate duties should not suffer.

13. The role of the Collector has to be similar to that of the legislator. He should be an associate non-voting member to fulfil his function of the eyes and ears of government. He should, however, have no control or supervision over the development functions, but should therefore only when maintenance of law and order is involved.

# COMMUNITY DEVELOPMENT—THE WIDER IMPLICATIONS

THE COMMUNITY DEVELOPMENT programme inaugurated in 1952 now covers the entire rural population. Panchayati Raj legislation has been enacted in 13 States. Panchayat Samitis and Zila Parishads have been established in 10 States. Almost the whole of rural India has been covered by Panchayats. The cooperative movement has also been forging ahead. These have vital prerequisites to the evolution of a new equilibrium in the economic and social relationships in Indian society. If democratic socialism is to be realised, its base will have to be the rural sector. Panchayati Raj, Sahakari Samaj and Samuhik Vikas are the pillars on which rural sector has to resuscitate itself.

The scheme of rural development has been limited in scope and there have been deficiencies in implementation. Yet the fact remains that millions of people have been directly involved in increasing production, in creating new community assets and amenities and in seeking new techniques and new ways of life. In every part of the country, however imperfectly, large numbers of extension workers and other personnel are striving to assist the villagers. In some areas in the country, where Community Development has been supported by development in agriculture, irrigation, communications, power and social services, there are signs of self-generating growth. But a large part of the task remains.

Panchayati Raj is vital for broad-basing and stabilising democracy in the country. It is hoped that all the States will establish Panchayati Raj before the end of 1964. Devolution of real power by Government together with resources, assumption of increasing responsibilities by Panchayati Raj institutions and broad-basing of initiative in the people are the major tests of health in Panchayati Raj. Panchayati Raj institutions must assume responsibility for the planning and development of their respective areas. Planning from below within the framework of the national goals and partnership in the building up of new India. A large number of non-official functionaries are participating in democratic processes and in decision-making in Panchayati Raj. Its effectiveness as an instrument of social change will depend on the rapid emergence of new leadership with a sense of social responsibility.

As a result of decade's work, the minimum frame of extension services and social and economic overheads has been brought into existence in rural India. There must be far greater emphasis on intensive work in the selected areas and promotion of special programmes. A beginning has been made with applied nutrition and intensive development of fishery and poultry programmes in selected blocks. Other pre-conditions for a greater impact of Community Development have also been created. Agriculture has been given the first priority and the administrative structure has been streamlined from the State to the village level to achieve a rapid increase in agricultural production. Cooperation is becoming progressively the principal base of organisation in economic life, notably in agriculture, processing, marketing, articles, etc. Unsatisfactory land relationships will have to be tackled through land reforms.

Wider opportunities for the weaker sections of the population are also being created through the rural works and other programmes. But rural poverty cannot be tackled in a fundamental sense unless rural industrialisation becomes an integral part of the entire plan of industrialisation of the country, unless the programme of rural electrification is expanded and there is greater emphasis on the optimum utilisation of rural manpower with responsibility for this squarely cast on Panchayati Raj institutions. Only a firm economic base resulting from a well-articulated policy for the rural areas can provide the needed sustenance to Community Development and Panchayati Raj to achieve the economic and social transformation of the countryside.

# PANCHAYATI RAJ—RURAL LOCAL GOVERNMENT IN INDIA

## Henry Maddick[1]

ANY DESCRIPTION OF local government in India—panchayati raj—
has to recognize that there is not one system of local government but 9
which in the next two years is likely to become 14, possibly 15 different
systems.[2] This article should therefore be recognized as having two
limitations. Firstly the system itself is limited in the main to the rural
area and the municipalities will therefore be excluded from the general
description. Secondly, the description which is given and discussion
which follows can only be on the broad general pattern although
some outstanding deviations from the main trend are mentioned where
they are of considerable significance for future development.

### The pre-independence pattern

The subcontinent has had a long history of village local government through the traditional panchayat or village council which at
certain times and in some places provided excellent government at a
period when social affairs were concerned with communal arrangements for the use of local resources, water, grazing grounds, forests
and the provision of an institutional framework in which the different
sections of these small communities might live together in relative
amity. Nor at that time was there the pressure of population, both

---

[1] Mr. Henry Maddick, M.A. (Oxon) is a lecturer in the Faculty of Commerce
and Social Science at Birmingham University. He was seconded for 12 months
as Ford Foundation Specialist in Public Administration at the Indian National
Institute for Community Development.

[2] At present panchayati raj has been introduced in nine states, namely: Andhra
Pradesh, Assam, Madras, Maharashtra, Mysore, Orissa, Punjab, Rajasthan and
Uttar Pradesh. Legislation has already been passed in the states of Bihar,
Gujarat and Madhya Pradesh and awaits implementation. Kerala, Jammu and
Kashmir, and West Bengal, are currently considering the next step in the deve-
lopment of their system which at the moment consists only of panchayats. No
account is taken in this article of the Union Territories—Andaman and Nicobar
Islands, Laccadive Islands Group, Tripura, Pondicherry and Goa, Delhi,
Himachal Pradesh, Manipur, Nagaland, and North-Eastern Frontier Adminis-
tration.

human and animal, upon food resources which exists today. Whilst the national administrative system, devised first by the Moghuls and later by the British to meet the contemporary demands of revenue gathering, and of law and order, later enlarged to provide protective health measures and a gradual development of resources through roads, railways and irrigation, the village as a unit remained static or languished. In the main the panchayat system failed. To quote Professor Sriniwasan "It is an anomaly that because of the ineffectualness of village councils and their inability to operate, 83 percent of the population has no facilities for obtaining such elementary amenities of life as road, drains, lights, a protected water supply and schools and has no say in what affects them as local communities."[1]

Efforts were made in some states, notably Madras, West Bengal and Bombay, to strengthen the panchayat system and to build an extended system of local government through the creation of district boards. These were given a varying range of functions in the different states, usually including some categories of minor roads, responsibility for education up to secondary level and some responsibility for the provision of rural health services. On the whole, although not in every state, this experiment must be judged a failure. It failed partly for lack of money, partly for lack of sufficient discretionary authority to make the work interesting, partly because before 1920, members of the boards were nominated by the British Authority and therefore suspect and after that date when more were directly elected they became involved in the national struggle for independence, and partly because some members of some boards used their position to secure administrative decisions favourable to themselves and their friends.

Alongside these developments there also took place the strengthening of the district administration so that the functions of government outside the revenue and law and order aspects were not only more diffused but also more effectively performed. Thus specialist technical officers were appointed, particularly for agriculture, to the districts or the wider area of divisions.

Stretching as it did from the capital to the remotest village the administrative machine lent itself to the practices of officialdom and petty tyranny. To the village the patwari was for all save the largest landlords a more powerful figure than the remote collector or the even remoter governor. He was a person to be propitiated and this atmos-

---

[1] Srinivasan, N. "Village Government in India," Far Eastern Quarterly, 15, 1955-56, p. 213.

[2] Lowest rank of revenue collector and keeper of the land register of village or a number of small villages.

phere extended to most minor officers in direct local contact with the people.

## Aftermath of Independence

With Independence, the administrative situation became even more complex. The area of administration and population to be administered was extended by the accession of princely states even though partition to some extent redressed the balance. State reorganization followed, yet even today some states are still handicapped by having had to absorb those areas which often had no modern administrative structure. On top of these complications was one of a far more fundamental character and proportionately far greater, namely, the national urge to develop the whole of the country economically and socially at the maximum possible speed. Thus was added to the previous functions of government the implementation of a policy that eventually overshadowed and embraced most of them, namely, the programme of development.

This programme had many aspects and proceeded on different fronts simultaneously. There was the policy of building up industry, of establishing great hydro-electric projects, steel plants, cement and fertilizer factories and all the other undertakings needed by a nation trying to achieve an economy which would become both self-generating and reasonably self-sufficient. What however, concerns this article more nearly was the multipurpose development programme in the rural areas aimed at increasing agricultural production, developing village industries. and generally raising the standard of production in those areas, so that it would be possible to provide the means for social development, the spread of literacy, the improvement of education, the development of minimum health services, the revision of some care for the destitute and under-privileged, however slender. All these became the accepted national and state targets. To this end, after pilot experiments in Bombay, Madras and Uttar Pradesh, the community development programme was launched ten years ago and this has grown functionally and geographically ever since.

The situation, however, was not regarded with complacency-indeed, far from it. The administrative system ever since 1947 had been subjected to an increasing strain which resulted from the vast increase in the variety and the scope of functions which the government has had to perform. This strain has also been increased by the growth in the number of citizens (some 77 million people over the last decade) for whom the administrative services have to provide. Moreover, as literacy spread, so the number of people who write letters to the authorities which have to be dealt with increases. Poor communica-

tions provide their problems for a government but it is often overlooked that some relief is obtained through the difficulty which the
citizen has in making his wishes and his complaints known! Clearly,
in these circumstances, the case for decentralizing some of the functions relating to rural development was extremely strong.

The Community Development Ministry recognized these factors
by establishing a system of blocks which provided a standard unit
within the district for the purposes of administering the development
programme. These community development blocks on the average
covered a population of 60-80,000 people and through the officers
assigned to them, administered the development programmes for
agriculture, animal husbandry, education, health, social welfare, cooperation and small scale industries. They generally included an
officer responsible for the efficient operation of the village panchayats
in the block area. This particular feature was introduced in an attempt
to secure the people's participation in the development programme,
for without such participation the task of obtaining their acceptance
of changes, social and economic upon which improved agricultural
programmes depended, was insuperable.

In order to enrich the process of official administrative decision-
making a nominated committee was introduced in 1954, the block
advisory committee, which advised the block development officer, the
chief executive of the development block. This later was reconstituted
to include all the chairmen of the village panchayats in the area and
was renamed the block development committee. Yet the Government
from its constant critical self-appraisal and careful evaluation of the
results of these efforts discovered that popular participation in the
development programme was lacking and that the programme itself
was basically an officially inspired and officially driven affair. This
view was supported by the U.N. Community Development Mission
and gave cause for grave concern.[1]

In addition to this the political and social leaders of the country
have been extremely anxious to build up the democratic understanding of the people. Whilst the quinquennial general elections have
produced a voting percentage and an orderly conduct of the election
which only a few countries in the world could rival, it was felt that
this did not represent the true involvement of the people as a whole
in the democratic process, nor was it consonant with the traditional
concept of democracy as practised in the golden age of village government. Thus there came together three compelling trends. The desire

---

[1] Report of a community development evaluation mission in India. United
Nations, New York, TAO/IND/31.17.8.59.

to foster the democratic involvement of the people throughout the country: the urgent need for securing their greater participation in the whole development programme from the village level upwards; and the imperative demands of the overloaded administrative system at every state capital which was forcing a measure of decentralization. The result was the establishment of democratic decentralization in the form of the panchayati raj system.

### The new structure and functions of local government

The seminal report in this situation was that of the Balwant Rai Mehta Committee.[1] This report dealt not only with the administration and working of the community development programme but set the broad pattern of the local government system for India. It recommended the establishment of councils of local representatives called panchayati samitis in every block and these were to be the main functional bodies of the local government system. It also recommended the establishment of the Zila parishad as a district council at the revenue district level. These recommendations have been followed in many states and thus, there has been created a three-tier structure, the zila parishad at the district level, the panchayati samiti at the block level and the already existing panchayat at the village level. In some states, for example Kerala, Jammu and Kashmir and West Bengal, only the panchayats are in existence. In Madras and Mysore the zila parishad is chaired by the collector and bears a strong resemblance to the old district development committees. But broadly the three-tier pattern has been accepted and, as the political situation permits, it is expected that this will be fully implemented by all states.

It is not possible to give any accurate estimates of the size of the units. Thus whilst the all India average population of a village panchayat is 14,000, the extremes range between 260 and 36 000.[2] Proportionately this is the greatest range, but there are quite considerable differences in the size of panchayati samiti arising from the geographical situation and the inherited traditional administrative boundaries. Thus some samitis may be over 150,000 and others less than 15,000 whilst the zila parishads range between 60,000 and three million. In area these latter may cover as much as 10,000 sq. miles but the average size would be about 4,000 sq. miles.

The tiered structure is rooted in the gram sabha—the meeting of all adult members of the village. In the majority of states this has yet

[1] Report of the Team for the Study of Community Projects and National Extension Service. Chapter two, Committee on Plan Projects, New Delhi, November 1957.
[2] In Uttar Pradesh and Kerala respectively.

to be developed as an active and effective institution. In theory it is the meeting of the people who are given by the panches (councillors) of the village an account of their work. This body is to be consulted about the proposed budget and about the drawing up of those plans for development, especially for agricultural production, which will guide the village activities for the next year, or for the next five years in the case of the quinquennial plan. This is the theory. In practice only some states have been able to put it into effect whilst others are wondering how to solve the practical problem of getting villagers together in large numbers and with what powers[1] to endow them.

Whilst a study is currently being made of this section of the structure there is little doubt that the gram sabha will become the means of linking the people with village production plan proposals which in turn will be consolidated by the panchayati samiti and incorporated with their own proposals, and through the repeating of this process at the zila parishad level the district production plan will reflect closely the wishes and priorities of the people themselves. It must be admitted, however, that this description oversimplifies the problems inherent in building plans from the bottom which will at the national level bear a close relationship to the overall needs of the nation. On the other hand, it has often been assumed, far too easily in the past, that plans issued from the top will be adopted automatically by the villages Hard experience has shown this to be far from true, and planned targets have remained figures only.

The linking of the villages with the whole local government system comes about in another basic fashion. Elections to the village panchayats are based on universal adult suffrage and are usually by secret ballot. Those elected themselves elect a representative or a chairman who becomes an ex-officio representative to the panchayati samiti.[2] The members of that body in turn elect a chairman who becomes their representative on the zila parishad. There are variations in this pattern. In the state of Maharashtra for example, some members of the zila parishad and the panchayati samiti are themselves directly elected, and the representation of the panchayats will be through groupings of panchayats whose members themselves elect a representative to the

---

[1] In Bihar the 1947 Panchayat Act empowers this village meeting to recall the chairman of the village council and to approve the budget.

[2] Provision is made to ensure that special sections of the community are represented. In every state, if no women are elected to the councils, two must be co-opted to the panchayati samiti and the zila parishad and in eight states one or two to the panchayats. In a similar way there must be representatives of the scheduled castes in tribes. In five out of the fifteen states the sarpanch is elected at large.

panchayati samiti. There are a number of combinations of mixed direct and indirect election which have the effect of strengthening or weakening the links between the various units in proportion as those units are made more or less directly responsible to the electorate.[1]

Two other links exist between the tiers. The first is the power of the zila parishad to allocate certain portions of the grants available to the system in respect of the panchayati samitis and by these latter bodies in respect of the panchayats. This power which, it should be noted, does not exist in all states, reinforces the general power to discharge the responsibilities laid upon the zila parishad in every instance to co-ordinate and supervise the work of the panchayati samiti. Generally this turns upon the submission of budgets, of detailed development plans and of periodic progress reports.

The second co-ordinating mechanism within the system is that of the administrative framework. The general administrator[2] and the technical officers at the district level are all responsible for ensuring that the officers in the panchayat samitis, both executive and technical are functioning efficiently and carrying through programmes properly.[3] Thus the framework exists through common representatives, co-ordinating powers and the official hierarchy to bring together all three levels in a coherent system of local government and administration.

The functions for which the panchayati raj system is made responsible whether by legal delegation, by administrative order or upon an agency basis vary widely between the states. In some instances, notably Maharashtra, the great bulk of functions formerly discharged by district boards, by the departments directly through district officers, by the development blocks or by the village panchayats themselves, have been transferred to the appropriate levels of the new three-tier system. Thus all aspects of the agricultural programme affecting the farmer directly such as crop protection, distribution of seeds, fertilizers and implements, pilot projects and demonstrations, plant protection appliances, seed multiplication schemes—all these will be in the hands of panchayati raj units. They have been accorded similar responsibilities in the field of animal husbandry, buildings and communications

[1] This does not attempt to describe fully the members of these various bodies for there are arrangements differing from state to state, whereby M.L.A.s. M.L.C.'s Presidents of Municipalities Officers and representatives of the co-operative societies, are ex-officio members, some with and some without voting rights. Maharashtra has included only the final category in the above list.

[2] The collector or deputy commissioner, the senior officer at district level-formerly concerned with revenue collection law and order, now concerned with everything and still regarded by many as 'the eyes and ears' of the government.

[3] An exception to the responsibility of the general administrator is the case of Maharashtra, where he is not thus involved.

education administration including responsibility for secondary education, fisheries, forests, small scale industries, irrigation, medical services, public health, social education and welfare, and for the collection of land revenue. Other states, notably Madras and Rajasthan, have proceeded much more cautiously—for example, in the field of education they have handed over the responsibility for primary education administration and the range of responsibility in every other field is similarly reduced and in some instance virtually non-existent. For the rest states have accorded some functions in most of these fields to the appropriate local unit.

### Staffing and Finance

Staffing and finance are subjects about which it is equally difficult to generalize, for again state variations are considerable. At the base the staffing pattern consists of village level workers responsible for multi-purpose extension functions and the part-time secretary responsible for recording the business of the panchayat. At the panchayati samiti level the chief executive officer is the block development officer who acts as secretary to the panchayat and is its chief officer responsible for ensuring that decisions of the panchayati samiti are carried out, and the work of the various departments within the block area are co-ordinated. This work is in the hands of extension officers and usually there is provided one extension officer each for agriculture, animal husbandry, education, industries, public works, panchayats, co-operatives and social education.[1] In some states the medical officer in charge of the rural health centre and of public health activities would also be included as an extension officer.

Each of these departments would have an officer at district level who reports to the Zila parishad and to the meeting of district officers. Where the zila parishad does not exist the officers form part of the district development board or council which is a nominated organization, sometimes with ex-officio members such as the members of the state assemblies and of the Union Parliament, as well as the chairmen of the municipalities. This body is chaired by the collector, the senior officer in the district. The executive officer, where there is a zila parishad, is both secretary and chief officer of that body. In Maha-

---

[1] The post of social education officer—responsible for the welfare of women and children the development of voluntary associations, the spread of adult literacy and generally for the health growth of social activities within the villages—is being reconsidered. Some states incline to the co-ordination of these activities with those of the education extension officer, and see this work of social development taking place through the village school teachers, especially women teachers.

rashtra he has the rank and standing of a collector, in some other states that of additional collector and yet other of a deputy collector.

The position of the staff vis-a-vis the councils varies. Teachers, village level workers, clerks, accounts personnel and the industrial and manipulative grades are members of the zila parishad service. Extension officers, district technical officers and the samiti and parishad executive officers generally are carried on state or all-India cadres. They are, however, on deputation to the local government unit and subject to it for administrative control and minor disciplinary action. In addition the block development officer is their immediate supervisor of all technical activities and is responsible to the samiti for production and other plans being fulfilled, or for explaining any shortfall. In most states periodic conferences are convened at district headquarters by the collector which discuss progress reports by the block development officers and the comments of the district technical officer. As regards technical policy the extension officers are under the control of the district technical officer. For day-to-day administration the control is by the block development officer, who himself receives his instructions regarding the execution of policy from the chairman of the panchayati samiti or from the chairmen of the functional standing committees as the case may be, or in the form of council or committee resolutions.

The subject of finance is also a complex one. Whilst a wide range of minor taxes is available to the different levels of panchayati raj these, with some notable exceptions, are very little used. The habit of self-taxation is one which has yet to be inculcated for there is on the one hand a strong inclination to deny the existence of any taxable capacity and on the other hand to fear the result of the next election if any councillor has the temerity to vote for the levying of a tax. Madras provides an exception to this and there the habit of adding to the state Governments grants from local taxation is widespread. The major sources available are a surcharge on land revenue for general purpose, and cessing land revenue for a specified service within a particular area; house tax, professions tax (including tax on commercial occupations), a wheel tax and a miscellany of minor fees. There are also the profits from certain undertakings and enterprises such as fairs and markets, ferries, religious festivals, flour mills, pisciculture and similar enterprises. But the greatest portion of local revenue comes from grants. These are recurrent and *ad hoc* and come from both the State and Union Governments. The Union Government is primarily concerned with providing grants for the basic development of blocks in accordance with a schematic development budget spread over a ten year period. There are also grants for certain specified subjects where the Union Government wishes to step up the rate and volume of spend-ing, such as in the field of tribal welfare and the welfare of the depressed classes. For the rest the panchayati raj units look to the State Government and here funds are usually made available for all the activities which have been delegated to the local bodies even though these funds are often woefully inadequate.

## Some Problems and Conclusions

No one would expect a system with such revolutionary content introduced over the area of a subcontinent to be operating without any difficulties. It is typical of India that its leaders should particularly concerned with the way in which the system is working. Yet, un-fortunately, there is a tendency to look for early success before the system has become firmly established and even before the people who are operating it understand what they are trying to do and what sort of change is being wrought by this vast innovation.

There will be in a few years over 210,000 panchayats, 5,000 panchayati samitis and 330 zila parishads. With the system of inter-locking and direct membership varying between states it is impossible to estimate exactly how many elected and co-opted representatives are involved in the system but probably the figure of two million elected would be on the low side.

To the great majority of these the system is a venture into un-known situations. Many have been attracted by the prospect of power with little thought for, or even knowledge of, the responsibili-ties entailed. Few understand the dependence of the non-officials upon the officials if resources are to be deployed economically and services are to be provided efficiently. Again, many are unaware of the way in which business will be conducted and probably some 25 per cent, of the members are illiterate. Consequently, to them the business of the council has to be explained by word of mouth and budgets and progress statements read out so that they may be aware of expenditure, and the way in which programmes and policies are being fulfilled by their own officers.

A further political problem is the pressure of sectional interests upon the non-official. Castes, the immediate village from which he comes, the wide ramifications of family ties, questions of personal gain, village factions and pressures from those political parties who have supported his candidature all tend to make the councillor partial in his approach, to the neglect of the interest of the whole area. In short the knowledge of how to make the council work and the attitude with which the councillor approaches his responsibilities are generally far from satisfactory—a situation found in every country where a new institutional system is introduced.

To meet this situation a very extensive training programme is planned. It is intended to establish a training centre for non-officials in every district by the end of the year 100 centres will have been set up. Some states like the Punjab which have just introduced the panchayati raj system endeavoured to provide some orientation for all members before the system started and probably some 70 per cent. of the non-officials have passed through their training camps and centres. Clearly, when dealing with mainly farming people a long course is out of the question and mostly it is found that seven days is the maximum period to secure any kind of constant attendance. Furthermore, if the centre is far from the home of the representative he will not attend. Some states have used the device of sending around teams to hold training camps lasting about three days within each block and sometimes within sub-sections of a block. It is intended that ultimately the training camps and centres shall be organized and staffed by the voluntary organizations interested in the development of panchayati raj, and not by the Government.

Such a training programme can only achieve limited results and much will depend upon the official element not only in the technical execution of the programmes, but also in guidance and counsel for the non-officials in the discharge of their responsibilities for the benefit of the whole community. But, of course, these officers are themselves sailing on an unchartered sea. None of the familiar landmarks are of much use in the direction which they now have to steer. From being in complete control of the organization[1] and the dominant factor in all situations they now have to assume the role of servants and advisers, and this is a change that comes hard, and has come hard to all those in many countries of the world who have had to undergo it. Training or orientation courses are being given to many of these officers—panchayat secretaries for example are being given brief courses in 100 centres established for them. Block development officers and some technical officers are receiving orientation in ten regional centres. Other special courses are being provided and this whole matter is under the urgent consideration of the Union Government.

The position of the officials is not an easy one. For the first time the great majority of them are dealing with a political situation even if this is on a small scale, without dominating them the officials are having to learn how to influence their councils in order that their knowledge and experience may be taken account of in its deliberations and decisions. All states have kept the executive officers and the

---

[1] "Captain of the team" was the phrase used in the Balvantrai Mehta report (*op. cit.*) to describe the block development officer.

technical officers on state or union cadres whilst deputing the individuals to the authorities to which they are posted. This has provided some measures of independence and security for the officers concerned but many are still subject to very considerable pressure from the chairman, and all have to learn the technique of tactful persuasion and effective intervention in discussions both with and without the council chamber. It will be readily appreciated that tensions and frictions have arisen and some of these have assumed a magnitude which in a less crucial situation would be almost farcical.[1] This relationship is crucial for the healthy growth of the local authority units. Much more needs to be done in the field of training and particularly training and education on the job, than can yet be provided.

In some states over the last decade, community development has been viewed with jealousy and even hostility by other departments with programmes in the field. So long as community development blocks did not cover the whole area, departments were able to concentrate on what they regarded as their own functions as distinct from what they chose to regard as being development activities. These they disregarded even to the extent of not providing normal services within the development blocks.[2] This situation is undergoing rapid changes. By 1963 there will no longer be any areas not covered by the panchayati system and attitudes are steadily being altered. Consequently, most departmental functions in the rural areas other than the very large and specialized activities will depend for their implementation upon panchayati raj units, the non-officials and the officials. This is a radically changed situation and will require a reappraisal of the way in which departmental policies are translated into action programme.

It will no longer be possible for a director of a departmental

---

[1] For example, one of the most widespread and serious difficulties within the panchayati samitis has been the use of the authority's one jeep. This is usually the only vehicle available for the whole of the local authority staff as well as for the chairman in an area where no other vehicle is satisfactory nor any other transport exists. In some cases personal feuds have arisen as to whether the chairman or the executive officer shall have the key of this vehicle and certainly, taking the country as a whole, there would be ample material for a very bulky doctoral thesis to be written on this subject.

[2] This is not so difficult to understand as may appear at first sight. The technical officers at district level were subject to dual control, vertically from their department and horizontally from the officers at the area level responsible for development. The vertical pressure always dominated the officer as it was upwards that he looked for promotion and if his departmental chiefs were more interested in departmental functions than in development functions then he concentrated on departmental functions.

service to rely, as some have deluded themselves into dodging in the past, on directives issued to all officers in the field. He will have to ensure that his district officers and his extension officers can each understand the broad outlines of policy, the dominant conditions and factors which will enable them to guide their local authorities, the essentials which will have to be borne in mind by the councillors so that in their decisions they can match state policy to the particular local conditions. Unless this is done, programmes may peter out somewhere down the chain of command, and yet under tomorrow's changed conditions, there will exist no other programmes which can be implemented by the departments.

Out of many problems which face those responsible for the development of rural India through the new panchayati raj system, two are of crucial significance. The first is how to foster partnership between the officials and non-officials based upon mutual respect for the contribution that each has to make and upon an understanding of the role that each of them has to play. The second problem is to ensure that national and state policies become efficiently executed programmes that cumulatively will provide the advance in economic and social conditions which is the imperative of the present situation. At the same time the methods adopted to secure realization of national and state targets both in the provision of services, and in the volume and type of agricultural production and of rural industrial output, must not be so rigid as to stultify local initiative, enthusiasm and creativity.[1] The balance between these is impossible to define and can only be achieved by a process of trial and error and a sensitivity for the human values involved.

The wider and possible even more fundamental considerations are those affecting the growth of participation and the promotion of a deeper understanding of democracy. Yet these ambitions have to be set against the increased demands of a population which by 1971 may have increased by 117 million.[2] To meet this challenge a reasonable standard of efficiency has to be aimed at and as far as possible provided for. How far is this compatible with the freedom required to promote democratic participation ?

There are many other unanswered questions, for example—what of the municipal areas ? The community development programme concentrated solely upon the rural areas on the basis that their general living conditions and resources were below that of the towns and as

---

[1] Such rigidity in the past has imposed production methods which in some areas were unsuitable and patterns of expenditure, through schematic budgets, with priorities which even today do not meet the real needs of particular localities.

[2] Third Five Year Plan, p. 22 provisional estimates for population figures.

regards the medium and large-sized municipalities this was broadly correct. The panchayati raj system has so far inherited this policy and excludes all places, however small, with the standing of a municipality. As a result, there has been a severance between these towns, often with as few as 5,000 inhabitants, and the rural areas which surround them. This feature is economically and socially unsound, and moreover many of the smaller bazaar towns are no better off in conditions or resources than are the villages of the same size but which, having a rural classification, are aided by the community development funds. This fact has been recognized in the most recent legislation, that of Gujarat State, which is proposing to bring into the panchayati raj system towns of up to 30,000 population. Some other states have co-opted the chairmen of municipalities to the zila parishads for purposes of planning only. But the problem as a whole has yet to be faced implying as it does, a revision of the financial regulations regarding the non-allocation of development funds to municipal areas and the ultimate consolidation of the department of local self-government (dealing with municipalities) with that of panchayati raj. Moreover the government will have to evolve a programme of community development suitable for these urban areas.[1]

The variety of this legislation, although in part accounted for by a developing policy based upon the experience of those states which introduced the system earlier, also shows the extent to which states have exercised their constitutional independence in this field.[2] If the individual governments are prepared to learn from the successes and failures of systems which differ from their own, out of this variety should come considerable strength. One such variation, for example, is the position of the collector vis-a-vis the new system. In some states he is to be found outside the system acting as observer on behalf of the zila parishad, whilst in Andhra Pradesh he is the chairman of the standing committees. Through these sometimes marked and sometimes minute differences in comparisons may be drawn which will give guidance as to the need for this traditional and authoritative representative of government to continue in a system or even to continue to exist at all.

Certainly the whole problem of education, encouragement and supervision has not been squarely faced and the system is confused and in some cases clearly defective. The zila parishads are supposed

[1] Practical experiments in urban community development are being carried out in Delhi.
[2] This subject is reserved in the Constitution to State Governments, although in one case presidential signature to a bill was withheld because of its failure to meet certain fundamental requirements of the system.

to supervise the panchayati samitis, but apart from routine office inspection this is an ill-defined charge. The collector and his staff may be charged with this also, yet this may prove difficult if it is to be encouragement and education rather than direction and suspension of the authority. The former is what is needed, but then the supervisors must be trained and moreover their work-load adjusted to allow for the proper discharge of this time-consuming but very important task. More than anything else, success or failure will depend upon leadership, guidance, encouragement and education.

The objectives of the system require definition in terms which are related to everyday working situations and are not just broad philosophical generalizations which so often confuse the issue in such arguments as 'local government means complete independence of any other authority'. Those who are training, those who are supervising, those who are making or having to make the zila parishads and the panchayati samitis work, those who are responsible for implementing technical programmes through local government units need guidance as to working objectives and the way in which these can be attained. Probably more than anything else they require a greater understanding of personal relations and of ways in which groups can influence— non-officials by officials, officials by those officials who need to realize that there is more in leadership than their superior status, and non-officials who must learn the art of guiding officials in ways which preserve their enthusiasm. India suffers from a grave shortage of those who could supply this training, a deficiency the responsibility for which the departments of political science in most universities cannot be entirely absolved.

To introduce a system so revolutionary in its approach and so important in its potential effects requires great courage and the credit must go to the Union Government in the first place, particularly to the Minister of Community Development, Panchayati Raj and Co-operation, Shri S.K. Dey and to the Prime Minister. Yet each state has had to make their own decisions, and upon their courage has depended the resolution to carry through a change which in its most radical form is bound to affect the power of legislators and ministers alike to intervene in situations which affect their personal position. Local patronage will become a more local matter than formerly; petitioners in the capital will decrease.

Problems there are and will be in plenty but there is also wide determination to resolve them. Much evaluation goes on and the danger in the present situation is that too much may be expected too quickly before the systems have settled down. By that time, say 15 years hence, we shall know whether the system has succeeded. If it does not then the results will be grave indeed for development plans, and with them democratic methods of fulfilment will have been found wanting. Basically, however, the system is sound and the will to make it work is widespread. It should make for a great advance in Indian government and administration and be a world–wide example of democratic decentralization.

# SOME PROBLEMS OF DEVELOPMENT ADMINISTRATION UNDER PANCHAYAT RAJ

## C. N. Bhalerao & I. H. Khan

PANCHAYATI RAJ AIMS at realising two major objectives. Firstly it seeks to arouse the initiative of the people through their participation in democratic and popular bodies at the village, block and district levels. It is assumed that rural development in India would be accelerated if people actively participate in the Panchayat bodies as well as in the execution of development programmes. Secondly, Panchayati Raj aims at establishing a new type of administration of these local self-governing institutions. The scheme of Panchayati Raj, in short seeks to democratise and modernise the rural community of India and in this programme the administration is assigned a significant role. Many programmes in India framed by the Congress Party and the Union Government have proved failure to a considerable extent, firstly because they have not been formulated on the basis of a searching and scientific analysis of the issues, and secondly because they lacked in 'action perspective' and organisation of efforts at the administration level. The problems of Panchayati Raj coming under the former have been discussed at some length by the exponents of Panchayati Raj.[1] In this paper an attempt is made to discuss some of the major problems in the administrative organisation of the Panchayati Raj programme.

## Structure of Administration

The introduction of Panchayati Raj has led to a new administrative structure from the district to the village, in which the earlier district and development administration are intertwined. The Collector is the District Development Officer but his importance as the co-ordinator and base of district administration has suffered considerably. The district is divided into the blocks, each having a Block Development Officer and a team of Extension Officers drawn from various development

---

[1] For a discussion of the theory and basic issues of Panchayati Raj, see the Presidential Address of Shri Jayaprakash Narayan, Seminar on Fundamental Problems of Panchayati Raj, A.I.P.P., New Delhi, 1964.

departments such as Agriculture, Animal Husbandry, Cooperation, Industries, Education, Medical, Engineering, etc. These officers assist the Panchayat Samiti in formulating plans and implementing the developmental programmes. At the village level the development works is being implemented by the Village Level Worker who usually has six to ten villages under his charge. The Village Level Worker guides the Village Panchayat in preparing village development and agriculture plans and is responsible for the implementation of development programme at the village level. In this structure of Panchayati Raj administration the district administration has only a co-ordinating role. The real initiative and powers in the field of administration lie with the Block Administration. Although the role of the district departments is important, it is at the Samiti and Village level that the problems of administration assume importance.

## Politicisation of Administration

In the Panchayati Raj set up, the B.D.O.s, the Extension Officers and the Village Level Workers are emerging as vital functionaries in bringing about changes in the rural society. The introduction of Panchayati Raj has influenced the administration in a number of ways. Firstly, there is a tendency towards the politicisation of administration.[1] The non-officials specially at the Samiti level are becoming conscious of their powers and political parties are becoming increasingly involved in controlling these Samities. There have been cases when the Pramukh and the other members of the Samiti have unduly tried to interfere with the administration. The B.D.O. and the Extension Officers, afraid of their political superiors, try to confirm to the dictates and standards of the non-officials. In this process the independence and neutrality of the administration is likely to be more and more undermined. Secondly, in some Samities there is noticeable a trend towards a bureaucratic control over the Panchayat Samities. This arises mainly as a result of the ignorance of the non-officials and their excessive dependence of the officials. There are, no doubt, some Panchayat Samities where the officials and the non-officials co-operate with each other and recognise their respective roles. But an appearance of cordial relation between the officials and non-officials does not always mean that everything is well with these bodies. Some times such a relation is the result of their joining hands for the mutual sharing of spoils.

[1] See "India's Political Take-Off," Rajni Kothari, The Economic Weekly, Annual Number, Vol. XIV, Feb. 1962.

## Co-ordination:

The panchayati Raj administration raises another basic problem. This refers to co-ordination, both vertical and horizontal. At the Samiti level, the B.D.O. is sometimes unable to achieve proper co-ordination as some of his disgruntled subordinates join hands with some groups of the Samiti. As a result of this, the team spirit and unity of the block staff suffers considerably.[1] Vertical co-ordination, *i.e.*, between the Block and District administration is also considerably frustrated owing mainly to the dual control exercised on the Extension Officers by the B.D.O., and the respective technical heads of the district departments. This set-up envisages active co-ordination of the subject matter specialist with the Block administration. But co-ordination between the Block and the district is more an ideal than a reality. The district officer usually has little time for visits to all the blocks and whenever he visits a block, he generally meets the B.D.O. and has perfunctory discussions with him. Instead of discussing various problems with the Extension Officers in the field, the District Officers call the Extension at the District Headquarters. There are cases where some lethargic or mischievous Extension Officer play the B.D.O.'s against the Extension Officer and the District Officers. As a result of all this, many programmes are held up, files pile up for months, and frustration pervades the Samiti administration. It is, therefore, necessary for securing speedy coordination between the district and block administration.

## Frustrated Bureaucracy

Because of lack of proper incentives and promotion opportunities for the administrative personnel from the B.D.O. to the Village Level Worker, most of the subordinate personnel appeared to be frustrated and do not evince genuine interest in and devotion to work. In doing their work, these officials, emphasise more the statistics and 'targets' rather than the quality of work. The administrative unit of the Block resemble a patchwork of officials drawn from different departments. These officials lack in *esprit de corps*.[2] There is thus a great need to constitute a separate and integrated Panchayati Raj Service for those engaged in Panchayati Raj administration which should also provide for adequate incentives and promotion opportunities on the basis of merit.

1 Unpublished Syndicate Report No. 4, "Administrative Problems in Block Organisation" Central Institute of Training and Research in Panchayati Raj, New Delhi, 1964.
2 See "Some Social, Political and Administrative Consequences of Panchayati Raj," Asian Survey, C.N. Bhalerao, April, 1964.

## Modus Operandi Mechanical

The bureaucracy of Panchayati Raj is undergoing some changes in its outlook as well methods of working. The bureaucracy has become conscious of the need for implementing various programme with the cooperation of the people and to work in collaboration with the representatives of the people. But one does not find the desired basic changes taking place in the bureaucracy. There are several reasons for this. Firstly, the bureaucracy has to operate under the supervision of the representatives of the people in rural areas; the latter are not accustomed to scientific and rational methods of administration. The Result of this interaction between the bureaucracy and the leaders of the traditional rural society is that the methods of working in the administration are assuming new forms, though this introduces a democratic element in the administration. Secondly, the Government does not appear to have given much thought to the qualities and qualifications required of the Panchayati Raj administrators. While recruiting the administrative personnel, such important qualities as initiative, and aptitude for social service and public cooperation are not kept in view. In this connection a strong case can be made out for the recruitment of trained social workers to man important positions in the Panchayati Raj administration. Further, the earlier bureaucratic methods and procedures of administration which still continue need to be re-examined. Generally, Panchayati Raj administration is characterized by delay, excessive formalism and paperwork and concentration of authority; the administration appears to function in a mechanical way, discourages initiative and responsibility and leads to delay, inaction and frustration. These problems have become more complex with the enormous expression of Panchayati Raj administration operating in accordance with both the Parkinson and Gresham Laws. It is clear that the Government will have to devise more appropriate methods of recruitment and improve the existing methods of administration if it is to act as an active force in social change.

The development of Panchayati Raj bureaucracy during the last four years is marked by three features. Firstly, the bureaucracy is becoming politicised and debureaucratised, thereby losing its independence and neutrality. This in itself is not a dangerous trend since democratic administration must be ultimately responsible to the politicians. But the danger here is that the bureaucracy may lose its professional autonomy and may virtually become an arm of the ruling party. Secondly, though the bureaucracy is showing some signs of change, it is basically of the old pattern and, both in term of the quality of the personnel and its working methods, does not seems to be a dynamic force suited to bring about socio-economic changes in the rural society. It is still characterised by rigidity, formalism and a lack of communication between the administration and the society. And finally, the bureaucracy has to function in a traditional society which introduces complex problems for programme implementation and makes it necessary to utilise the existing social forces in achieving the ideals of Panchayati Raj. The utility of the existing bureaucracy to act as an active instrument of Panchayati Raj will depend upon the operative standards followed by the political parties, especially by the Congress Party, the emerging equilibrium between professional autonomy of the bureaucracy and the political control on it, the calibre and quality of lower bureaucracy, the development of more suitable methods of community development work and organisation and the building up of active channels of communication between the administration and the rural society. It is time that the Congress Party and the Planning Commission give thought to wider issues involved in administrative institution-building for Panchayati Raj.

# THE NEW

### William and Charlotte Wiser

A (LATER) MAJOR undertaking on the part of the government, even more far-reaching, has been the establishment of the "Block." Blocks have gone through various phases, but as they have now emerged they form the base of a carefully designed framework which will eventually cover all rural India. The purpose is to provide every village with an opportunity to produce more, to learn more, to earn more, to consume more, and—as a result to enjoy better living. The average number of villages in a block is one hundred. Karimpur is within the Mainpuri block. The word 'block' is now a part of the village vocabulary, heard chiefly among members of the village council. It is the service arm of the government and the officers within it are to render whatever advice or help is needed.

When the villagers first heard of the advent of this new set of officers, they were apprehensive. Their chief contacts with officialdom had been with petty officers, who have a reputation for making their low salaries more than ample at the expense of the villagers. What would these new men expect of them? It took them some time to comprehend that block officers are trained to help them. The old officers are still needed as the new ones do not keep records, nor collect taxes, nor keep law and order. They are here for constructive work that will better the conditions of the villages—an entirely different purpose.

From the point of view of the government, we should start listing the block officers from the chief administrator down, but the villagers start from the ground up. The man whom they meet in their fields or in the lanes, is the *gram sevak* or 'village companion'. Our village companion serves eight villages and any hamlets recorded as attached to them. His chief job is to discover the farmers' special problems and to teach and to demonstrate better methods. He would describe his duties in more impressive terms—to carry the problems of the village to research stations and to bring the results of research to the village with a view of increasing production and raising the standard of living. Village companions are given two years of training, during which time they receive an allowance. They are required to have a high-school education. (Our village companion has completed two years of college). In the beginning, the post of village companion was not popular, but now, with the lively interest in rural development and the larger opportunities, there is strong competition for it. At the Mainpuri training centre for village companions, sixteen hundred young men from the district applied for admission to the most recent course.

They were all high-school graduates pass between the ages of twenty-one and twenty-five. There are three divisions in the final high-school examinations, and they had to be in the first or second. However, those belonging to so-called scheduled castes (below the registered castes) could be in the third or lowest division and eighteen years of age or older. Of all these, eight hundred were selected to take the written examination, which one hundred and eighteen passed. After other tests and a study of merits, the number was reduced first to forty and finally to sixteen. The Mainpuri centre trains men for four districts, with a total admission of fifty each year, selected from all four districts.

The first Karimpur village companion whom we met was brought to visit us in our India Village Service centre several years ago, under the wing of a group of Karimpur farmers. He was young and inexperienced, with little special training and our impression was that he was overawed by these experienced farmers, successful by village standards, while they were apparently exploiting any knowledge he might have for their personal benefit. The present village companions have had longer training, are more self-assured, and are less influenced by the influential.

When the village companion is faced with some particular problem which his training has not covered, he consults one of the Assistant Development Officers, known among villagers as A.D.O.'s each of whom has had training in one special field. There are seven in our block. One has specialized in agriculture, one in animal husbandry, one in cooperatives, and one in rural industries; another, the 'overseer', examines wells for household use and for the cleanliness of the village; still another is sanitary inspector. There was a separate officer to advise the village councils, the panchayats. But last year this was combined with the office of social education. In addition to these there is the A.D.O.W., or woman Assistant Development Officer, who gives help in matters concerning women. There are other members of the block staff—a district medical officer, a compounder, a health visitor, two women village companions, and four midwives, as well as office workers. The B.D.O.—Block Development Officer—is responsible for all work conducted by the block, and in turn, looks for instructions to the D.P.O., or District Planning Officer, who is in charge of the fifteen blocks within the district. Over him is the District Magistrate who has authority over all government services in the district.

Because of his many duties, he delegates most of the block super-vision to a deputy, known as A.D.M.P.—Assistant District Magis-trate for Planning. This is the structure as far as villagers care to reach, and in fact most of them do not go beyond the village com-panion and the specialists who appear from time to time to help them. It is the members of the village council, particularly the president, who must be somewhat familiar with the work of the senior officers.

Of chief concern to the village farmers are the services of the block which are recognized as directly affecting them. Now that I am closer to them than ever before, I have concluded that the heads of families of our village are among the most materialistic of human beings. They are not so from choice. Circumstances have forced upon them a stark materialism—food, or money for food, money for clothing, money to cover wedding expenses, money for emergencies. This has gone on for so long that even those who are now prospering, with a safe margin between them and poverty, cannot seem to break away. Their children may dip into their hoardings for a few comforts and perhaps a touch of man-made beauty in their surroundings. But the present generation wants only that which meets an urgent need or promises greater security. When this much has been acquired, they cling tenaciously to it, unwilling to move further ahead. This limits the possibilities of what block officers can accomplish. One young B.D.O., after three years experience in a comparatively progressive district, exclaimed to me: "This rural development is the damned hardest work in the world!" Perhaps it is. But it need not be discouraging. Rather, it is the most challenging. Certainly, it demands qualities in its officers not called for in the more conventional government services.

There have been two situations here in which a block officer either lacked the necessary qualities or failed to exercise them. On one of my 'house-building' trips to the village I stayed with a friend who showed me a new, screened food cup-board, which most of us accept as an essential piece of kitchen equipment but which village housewives have not yet considered using. It had been brought to the house by a block officer, with the idea that it would serve as a demonstration. This cupboard had two shelves. On the top shelf was a bundle of raw cotton which was waiting to be ginned; this was a convenient place for setting it aside. On the lower shelf was a bowl of milk intended for one of the babies of the family who was ill; the doctor had advised protecting it from flies. The family liked the appearance of the cupboard and appreciated having it for the milk in this emergency, but when I came a few weeks later, it was carefully put away in a store room, where the children could not damage the screen. It was empty, ready for the block officer to call for it.

In another house where I was staying I found to my delight what we call a '*smokeless chula*'. The familiar *chula* is the low horseshoe-shaped cooking fireplace, just large enough to support a griddle or sauce-pan. In our village every *chula* is kept ceremonially clean, with a fresh coating of clay paste each morning. Its chief drawback is that it lacks a chimney and the smoke pours out into the face of the woman doing the cooking. Rural workers have been trying for some time to devise a *chula* which will remove the smoke and still be acceptable. There are several designs now available, all of which have two advantages over the old *chula*. In addition to sending the smoke up the chimney rather than into smarting eyes, they make it possible for one kettle of food to cook slowly or be kept warm at the back of the stove while other food is being cooked over the flame at the front. On the ordinary *chula* only one thing can be cooked at a time. A block officer had constructed this particular *chula* himself and left it ready for use in the home of my friend. But it had not been used. At first the women said that they were waiting until work was less heavy to try it. Later they said that the chimney, which, unfortunately, had been made of tin, had rusted during the rains, so the new *chula* had been rendered useless. They had been told of its advantages, but they expressed no regret at its loss. We had discovered earlier from our own experience and the experience of others that in areas where orthodoxy is strong the women cling to the old smoky *chula* in spite of its disadvantages. They are sure that they can keep it ceremonially clean, but they are doubtful about this aspect of the new one.

The young officer, city-bred, was baffled by both failures—that of the food cupboard and that of the *chula*. The importance of the cupboard screening had been explained by both the block officer and the doctor, but the lesson seemed to have been forgotten after the child's recovery; flies are regarded as a nuisance but not as dangerous, and although the school children bring home books from which they read aloud regarding the diseases carried by flies, the women are too occupied with household chores to listen. Actually, most of the food in the kitchen is either being cooked or kept hot for late eaters, and there is little left over to be stored, except after the evening meal. So flies are less a hazard in the storing of food than in some other ways, such as the flies that sit on the food while it is being eaten, and those that crawl over the baby's eyes and mouth while he tries to sleep. Given repeated opportunities to learn, from many angles, mothers will grasp the relation between flies and their children's suffering and accept their responsibility, in the sequence.

As for the *chula*, the women are willing to go on sacrificing their eyes if this is necessary to safeguard the purity of the food which they prepare for their families. When this problem of ceremonial cleanliness is solved to their satisfaction, the new *chula* will have a better chance of being accepted. In village near Delhi, where city contacts are frequent and where orthodoxy is more relaxed, I have seen a goodly number of smokeless *chulas* obviously being used. Out here in the country we do not move quite so fast. It was not from lack of intelligence that our women rejected the innovation; they were not ready for it. For them there are other improvements that might be suggested which are innocuous and which might help them discover the possibility of change. The idea of change in household equipment is still unfamiliar to them.

On the edge of the village is a farm demonstration, as satisfying in its results as the other attempted innovations were disappointing A young farmer recently took me to see his field near our house, where he and the village companion are testing a new commercial fertilizer. He explained carefully how he had divided the field into four plots. In three of the plots he had applied the new fertilizer, by itself, or combined in different ways with the one he had been using. The fourth plot was left without benefit of fertilizer. The contrast between the fourth plot and the others was most striking, and the gradations of growth in the other three were also impressive. The farmers going to their fields and the men passing by on the way to their own villages have begun to stop to discuss the experiment with their friends. The village companion and the young demonstrator are gratified.

This particular farmer had plodded along cultivating the family fields under his father's supervision. He must have been outstanding in his interest in agriculture because two years ago he was chosen with another farmer in this block and others from neighbouring blocks to go on a conducted tour of North India. He described vividly the places they had visited, including centres where rural development had made exceptional progress and famous places of pilgrimage. He came back eager to move ahead. All that he needed was the encouragement and advice of someone with the training which he lacked. When the village companion outlined the project to him, he undertook it with enthusiasm and is seeing it through. And now, with hot-weather crops being sown, he is asking for a new demonstration.

One of the most important contributions of the government to the life of the village is the development of new leadership. Greater power has been given to the village council, and the members of the council are elected by their fellow villagers. Thirty years ago there was no such election; the elders who made up the council then were men acknowledged by everyone as leaders, who settled disputes and gave advice informally. Their power lay in their personal wisdom and influence; no one was bound to abide by their decisions. They have now willingly stepped aside in favour of younger men. The most outstanding new leaders are sons or nephews of former elders, which is taken for granted in the village as being in accordance with tradition. But they have earned their positions on their own merits as well; and not all have had birth in their favour. Several young leaders are sons of men who were formerly followers, and they too have had to earn their present status.

The twenty-three members of the *gram panchayat*, or village council, are elected every five years. The most recent election was held a year ago and was the third time that the men and women of the village gathered together to vote. After ten years of experience with a council, they realized that it had much greater power than they had supposed at the time of the first election. When the first elections took place, our Indian colleagues in the India Village Service (our experiment in rural development) tried to explain to people the gravity of their choice of council members, but it was too new an idea. Since voting was by show of hands, voters know that the men elected would be able to make it difficult for those who voted against them. So it was politic to vote for the most aggressive men who kept assuring others that they would be chosen. The voting is still by show of hands, which is simpler and much less expensive than voting by secret ballot. But now most men and some of the women who go to the voting spot, usually under a large tree, have talked over the candidates and what they might or might not do for the village. The members of our present council are predominantly young men or men in their forties, As I watch them and listen to them, I wonder if we should not speak of this as a time of Enlightenment rather than of the New. They may not know much of the ways of the central government or even of our province, but through the block officers they are learning about proposals and legislation which concern rural development. They are prepared to co-operate with the block officers in their efforts to introduce improvements, and, best of all, they know the men of their village and what they will or will not adopt.

A village court has also been introduced, known as the *adalati panchayat*. It is composed of men selected from among members of several *gram panchayats*. They are nominated by the district magistrate, with the help of the gram panchayats from which they come. There are eight of these courts in the Mainpuri block. Karimpur has three representatives on the court for our area. Smaller villages have two. Members must be able to read and write Hindi and must be more than thirty years of age. The convener is the *sarpanch*, elected from membership in the presence of the district magistrate or his official representative. This court can decide both civil and criminal cases and can fine defaulters. The civil cases in which it may make decisions are limited to five hundred rupees  And fines may not exceed fifty rupees. Most cases brought before the court have to do with land boundaries. The purpose of the village court is to save farmers' money by enabling them to bring their disputes before this local court rather than  going into the district court where lawyers must be paid and much time lost. However, members of the local court apparently find it possible to get money from both plaintiffs and defendants, and this  has  discounted its influence.

To the villagers, the gram panchayat, which they themselves elect, is more important than the court. The court covers an area  beyond the  limits of the village and therefore seems less concerned with them individually. The council is their own, most  of  the  members  being from  Karimpur  proper, with a few from adjoining hamlets. It is the villagers' working committee, available when they need help with their problems, and it is also their spokesman in any  dealings  with  block development  officers.  The  most  important  post in the village is that of *pradhan*, president of the village council. Thirty years ago,  it  was the *mukhiya*, the man chosen by the government as head of the village, who was most influential and respected.  Now the title of mukhiya is in name only, with little power attached to it. The *pradhan* is elected by secret ballot one week before the open election of council members. His election has become the most bitterly contested election in the village.

People were casual in the beginning, as they  were  in  voting  for council members, but after suffering from the financial demands made by an  early  *pradhan* who abused his office, they have become more cautious. A year ago there were eight candidates, each of whom used a different symbol on the ballot for the benefit of illiterate  voters:  a lotus blossom,  an umbrella, a lamp, a kite, a grain basket, a mortar and pestle, a drum, and a lion. Subedar, Prakash's eldest  son,  was elected,  and  since  then  he  has devoted his time and his strength to the office. I know of other pradhans who  are  less  conscientious, who meet with the council once a month and do the minimum between meetings. The  post  is  honorary, and after observing Subedar's acti- vities these past months, I have concluded that a *pradhan* who is as active  as  he  is  needs not only a family able to support him and his wife and children, but also willing to take over his load of work in the fields. At a meeting of all sixty-one *pradhans* in the Mainpuri block, Subedar was  elected  to  represent them. As their representative, he receives special training which he passes on to the others, and also he may speak on their behalf when attending meetings with block officers.

The pradhan presides at the monthly meetings of the  council  and may call additional meetings. Nine members are needed for a quorum. The council members discuss the collecting and the use of taxes, prepare the budget, check regularly to make sure that they are not exceeding it, and take up any welfare matters which the *pradhan* presents. At the time they are working on plans for fifty new cement-sided compost pits. The council members are trying to keep people from throwing rubbish into the village pond. They are concerned about the wells that are in need of repair, but they have not yet been able to tackle them.

They have talked about the bad state of the lanes and are working on them. Day labourers are hauling in cartloads of *kankar* (earth which has become hard but not to the stage of rock); it is being brought from poor land, under the control of the council, so only the digging and hauling must be paid for. The spreading and pounding down will be done by the men of the village as voluntary labour. This has been the council's biggest undertaking so far.

Almost equal to this task has been the securing of small fish from the Fisheries Department for the village pond. This was proposed years ago, but formerly the pond dried up each year during the hot season. Now the council has the right to use water from the tube well to maintain the water level. The council hopes to earn enough money from the sale of the fish at the end of one year to cover additional or desired improvements.

The council has also put in a request, which has apparently been granted by the District Board, for a new school building. The government will pay half the cost and the village council will be responsible for raising the other half, over a period of several years. The new school will relieve the strain on the old building and make it possible for children to attend school near home through junior high school.

The *pradhan* presents such cases to the council as the request of a poor Christian for a two-acre piece of land on which the soil is so alkaline that no one has tried to cultivate it, and the council votes on these. One of the dreams of council members is street lamps; they are aiming at seven, chiefly to discourage thieves but also to light men on their way home after dark. The council counts on donations for the kerosene oil which will be necessary.

Besides the *pradhan* carries a good deal of responsibility alone. He appoints the village watchman who goes the rounds of the village each night and reports any "bad characters" to the *pradhan*, who decides whether to report them to the police. The watchman also summons all members to council meetings and on occasion acts as errand bearer for the *pradhan*. In an emergency when all village men may be needed, it is the watchman's duty to call them to an appointed spot.

The *pradhan* is responsible for collecting taxes due to the council and keeps a record of all money spent by him or the council.

It is the *pradhan's* duty to report immediately to the B.D.O. if any epidemic such as plague, cholera, or smallpox strikes the village. The B.D.O.'s duty is to send a doctor, and if he does not act quickly the *pradhan* is to inform the District Magistrate, who is ultimately responsible. The pradhan is also supposed to inspect the village school periodically. In addition, he checks the services of the tube well, together with five farmers appointed especially to assist him in controlling the distribution of water.

When a dacoity or a theft in the village comes before the *adalati panchayat* (court), the *pradhan* is supposed to present whatever evidence is available, and usually on the basis of this evidence punishment is determined. When there is a quarrel over land boundaries, he is expected to attempt to solve it on the spot. He is free to call the village land recorder, the man most inaccessible to the ordinary farmer without a generous fee, and the disputants and half the village look on while the land recorder spreads out his map of the fields and measures the two plots. Then they wait while the *pradhan* makes the final decision. He has had some success in such cases, but more often the quarrel has gone too far to be so simply settled. When such a case becomes serious enough to go before the nearest minor judiciary official or to the district court, the pradhan is usually called upon to go with the party. If the men are illiterate they look to him for help, and even those who are literate know that they have a better chance of an early hearing if he is with them. All this was once the *Mukiya's* duty.

The pradhan is expected to attend any block meeting to which pradhans are called, and is usually given an opportunity to present the needs of his village. Not long ago, the District Magistrate summoned all pradhans of the district to two days of meetings in Mainpuri. With the help of block officers, he built up their self-confidence, emphasizing the importance of their position as pradhans, their responsibilities, and their powers. The Magistrate told them how much the government depends on them. He assured them of his desire to support them in their endeavours, and reported that he was leaving immediately after the meetings for the capital of the province to present the requests which had come from them. At the meeting special projects were urged. They were: giving land to the poor and making sure that it is properly registered, increasing grain production, growing more vegetables, keeping better breeds of cows and buffaloes, and working toward better opportunities for children of all groups to attend at least a primary school.

In most efforts to increase production, the *pradhan* works with the village companion, and when necessary they call on the block agricul· tural inspector. Together they promote the use of tested chemical fertilizers. With help from the animal husbandry specialists, the two young men-*pradhan* and village companion-urge farmers to feed and treat their animals better. It is the village companion who must see most of their projects through, but he reports to the pradhan daily when some special project is under way.

In other words, the *pradhan* is an extremely busy man if he does all that is expected of him. Once, when Subedar was looking more exhausted than usual, I asked why he does not delegate some of his duties to members of the council, as he is allowed to do in some instances  His reply made me realize how alone he is: "There is not one member of the panchayat whom I can trust to carry through a job. And where money is involved a man buys inferior material or underpays workmen and puts into his pocket whatever he has not spent. The money entrusted to the panchayat belongs to the govern- ment or to the people of the village. I will not let it be misused." Council members have yet to learn that there are times when the wel- fare of the community must be given priority over family demands.

During the past year, they have learned much about the services of the block officers, of the Seed Store, and the larger cooperative society. They know why better composting is needed, and they know more about the construction of roads. Not all of them are literate, but they realize the advantages of education and desire it for their children. They understand why there must be new village taxes, to which they, like others, have strongly objected in the past. They want the village to make progress. The next step is to accept their share in bringing progress about, even though it may mean the sacrifice of some family interests. As compared with the members of the first elected council eleven years ago, they are decidedly enlightened.

# PUBLIC AUTHORITY AND THE PEOPLE IN COMMUNITY DEVELOPMENT

## Reinhard Bendix

THE PROBLEM IS not only one of resources and administrative organisation, (however). At the level of the village, development officials
have the difficult task of enlisting cooperation with projects of whose
soundness and desirability the villagers must first be convinced. To do
this officials must strike a balance between making suggestions and
listening to demands, taking advantage of modern knowledge but also
adapting it to the local situation. In addition, villagers must exert
themselves with considerable determination if the change in production methods and village amenities is to be an enduring attribute of
village life. The intricacies of this assignment are reflected in a statement by the former Union Minister of Affairs, Govind Ballabh Pant,
entitled "The Right Approach=to the People." A pointed contrast is
made with British rule, which for all its admitted achievements was
alien and authoritarian system. Now, in independent India, an entirely
different spirit should prevail. Pant calls upon the officials to understand their mission in a new sense. No longer are they to work in the
old manner, with an attitude of condescension towards the villagers
as "superstitious men who deserve contempt."[1] Yet, the people have
to be taught how to adopt modern methods of agriculture, develop
amenities and keep the surroundings clean. Above all, they have to be
inspired so that "they may put in their best for their own advancement."[2] Thus the officials must be authoritative but not authoritarian,
knowledgeable but not overbearing.

To serve the villagers, you have to identify yourself with rural life;
to find joy in the air you breathe in and the consciousness of the fact
that you are engaged in the act of building a new society. You have
to see that they move, they move onward and they are pushed onward
artificially. Let them learn the art which enable them to secure for
themselves what we want them to possess. Unless you try to influence
them without imposing something from above, your success will be
shortlived.[3]

---

[1] Kurukshetra, pp. 61-62.   [2] *Ibid.*, p. 60.   [3] *Ibid.*, p. 59.

The whole thing is not a "mercenary undertaking." It depends upon winning the peoples' confidence so that they accept the new ways of working and living.

These appeals clearly call for excellence in a combination of virtues that requires consummate skill in the person who would possess them all. Yet they are addressed to officials who are ordinary men even where they are talented and who work under conditions which militate in some measure against the fulfillment of their many exacting duties. Time and again local officials are told that they must identify with rural life, rather than place before the villagers the "high-sounding theories" they have learned in the agricultural college. "You have to work in the filth and the cowdung and out of it create a clean and wholesome atmosphere.[1] Such a task is difficult for officials who have acquired an "urban orientation" by virtue of the very education which technically qualifies them for the task of promoting rural developments. The following statement characterizes the resulting dilemma.

...I have a feeling that public services in our country are manned primarily by the urban sections of the population, while the Plan that we are trying to put through and the series of Plans which will follow, are directed primarily to making an impact on the rural life of the community. I do not know whether the kind of faith that we would like to see in the public services would be generated among the people who are really not so much at one with the interests of the bulk of the population. It is true, of course, that as education advances there will be greater and greater degree of urbanization and since in the public services you get educated sections, they have to be perhaps more urban in their idea and outlook than the rest of the countrymen. But I always feel that there is this sort of an initial hiatus between the public services and the major section of the population. I do not know how this gap could be reduced, whether the methods of recruitment could be suitably altered in order to see that there is not much emphasis on urbanization, so that there is greater realization of the needs of the rural population among the Services.[2]

In addition, development officials have to overcome the legacies of the freedom movement which discredited not only British rule but inadvertently administration as such, and hence intensifies the personal and social distance between villagers and official representatives of government. Moreover, after independence, rapid expansion of staff militated against the maintenance of standards, and the missionary spirit of development work was difficult to sustain wherever public

[1]  Kurukshetra, p. 60.
[2] Morale in the Public Services (Report of a Conference. January 3-4, 1959, C.D. Deshmukh, Chairman, New Delhi, Indian Institute of Public Administration).

cooperation was not forthcoming.[1] The number and diversity of duties assigned to village workers often exceed what even the most devoted person can accomplish. Pressure for speedy expansion together with the very genuine national need for increased agricultural production have had the unintended consequence of accentuating central control of community development. For all these reasons, the achievement of "visible targets" (like the construction of block headquarters) has been emphasized at the expense of the more time-consuming and intangible task of drawing out the initiative and wholehearted cooperation of the villagers.

[1] See *ibid.*, pp. 75, 127 for comments along these lines by Indians directly associated with rural development work.

# PROBLEMS OF COMMUNITY DEVELOPMENT WORKERS

*Dr. R. S. Shiwalkar*

ATTEMPTS MADE FROM time to time to reorganise efforts of the agencies concerned to remedy unfolded weaknesses and overcome shortcomings are also considered. The changed role of each class of functionary at various levels from the village up to the national level receives equal attention in the training programme. Community Development workers, particularly up to the Block level whom I have had the opportunity of observing and studying closely, not only appreciate the ideas and practices, but they begin to advocate them in their writings, papers, discussions, talks, etc. But, when they go back to the field what do they find? In the follow-up studies that have been conducted from time to time, it has been observed that a year or so after their return from training, a large majority of them begin to complain that there is very little by way of 'on-the-spot guidance' to correct mistakes and wrong methods of working. On the contrary, what is insisted upon is that the job expected should be done any how, and compliance reported. There, thus, appears a very wide gap between "what the programme has to be" and 'what it is in the field'. In this situation, the field worker feels lost and begins to harbour a feeling that all that he had learnt at the Training Centre was only valid in the classroom, and the wide gap between "precept" and "practice," is perhaps one of the most serious factors responsible for shaking their morale.

A question that is often asked at the various Training Centres by C.D. personnel working at various levels is: "What is the use of training us as long as our superiors responsible for guiding, supervising and evaluating our performance and progress do not have a clear understanding of the concept, processes and methods of the Community Development programme and our role, functions, problems, handicaps, etc." Some of the functionaries, particularly those working at the District level and above, feel that the training imparted to them is theoretical. The ultimate result, therefore, is that even the trained Community Development workers find themselves unable to make use of their training in their field work. The problem of problems baffling Community Development workers in this situation appears to be a conflict between implementation of the programme to achieve results through 'universally accepted processes and methods', on one hand, and achieving results 'any how', on the other. As a result the workers find themselves in a dilemma.

# WEEDING OUT OF UNSUITABLE STAFF

IF THE QUALITY of performance of the extension staff as a whole is to be improved, it is necessary to provide a machinery for weeding out those who are, either due to lack of capacity or due to lack of the required temperament, unsuitable for the task. This question has been under consideration for a long time. The need to eliminate incompetent staff, particularly VLWs, was discussed at the fourth Development Commissioners' Conference held at Simla, in 1955. The Nainital Conference of 1956 suggested that a process of weeding out of VLWs, be adopted at the initial stage preferably during the first two months of the training course. The last Annual Conference recommended that the extension staff be rated every year as "outstanding" "very-good", "good", "fair" and "poor". Successive poor entries for three or four years would warrant weeding in the case of temporary personnel and reversion to the parent department in the case of officiating and permanent Governments during the last Annual Plan discussions. It was suggested to them that committees be set up at the State/district level to grade the various categories of extension staff with a view to eliminating unsuitable personnel.

# THE B.D.O.'s ROLE IN PROGRAMME PLANNING

1.  To enable the panchayat samithi chairman and non-official members to understand planning needs and techniques.
2.  To enable the official functionaries to coordinate their efforts towards the common goal.
3.  To involve all democratic institutions as associations in particular and public in general to enlist their faith and cooperation in the plan.
4.  To interpret the state objective and rules and regulations concerning the programme planning to both the officials and non-officials.
5.  To link the schematic budget with the financial aspects of all the programmes.
6.  To harmonize the state objective with that of the objectives set out in the block plan.
7.  To bring out maximum agreement between official and non-official opinion in matters of programme planning.
8.  To take steps to prepare, and finalise programmes well ahead of time to enable speedy execution.
9.  To obtain definite commitments from various Departments through District level officers for supplies and services before taking up the programme planning.
10. To allow various specialist Extension staff to play their full part in programme planning.
11. To effectively supervise the planning process at the village and Panchayat level by himself and through Extension Officers.
12. To process the plans and programme through various statutory committees and get the final approval of the Panchayat Samithies and Zilla Parishad.

Some of the practical difficulties of B.D.O. experienced in programme planning are listed below:

1.  It may not be possible to get the departmental commitments of financial assistance and supplies and services in time and quite likely some of them might be received after the programmes have been finalised.

2.  After the inception of Panchayati Raj, it is quite a difficult task to bring agreement between the opinions of various selected representatives on account of their political character.
3.  Due to the individualistic outlook of various technical departments, difficultya rises in matters of co-ordination not only in allocation of financial resources but also in emphasis and fixing priorities.
4.  The programme planning is a continuous process and needs time to time discussion, review and additions or alterations not as situations vary. It is difficult to visualise and forsee a given set of static circumstances and situations for one year.
5.  It is difficult to make adequate provisions in the plan or programme to contribute to the benefit of weaker sections on account of their inadequate representation in the present system of leadership pattern. This is the reason why there are complaints, not unjustified, that at present the facilities community development movement offers are used only by a limited number of persons who, in many cases, can look after themselves.

# STUDY OF WORK-LOAD OF BLOCK DEVELOPMENT AND PANCHAYAT OFFICER IN PUNJAB STATE

**Reference**

DR. M.S. Randhawa, I.C.S., Special Secretary to the Government of India, Ministry of Food and Agriculture, who paid a visit to this training centre on 22nd April, 1964, desired that the work-load of the Block Development and Panchayat Officer in the Punjab State may be studied with particular reference to his ability to devote his 100% time for increasing agricultural production. This centre therefore undertook a study of the existing workload of the B.D. & P Os in order to find out the factors which stand in their way to devote their cent per cent time to increase agricultural production.

**Methodology**

Interview and group discussions have been employed as the main methods for collecting the data for the study. Observation, as usual, remained the ubiquitous tool for the study. To ensure the reliability of the responses the information gathered through individual interviews was cross-checked with group discussions and vice-versa. The involvement of BD & PO—participants who had come for training have been of great use. Apart from individual discussions about their specific work, they submitted a syndicate report on the problem under study. A few experienced BD & POs who have worked in various Development Blocks were also interviewed. As the participants come from all over the State the observations have been fairly representative.

On the basis of interviews, group discussions, syndicate reports and on the spot observations a preliminary write-up of the report was prepared. To test the validity of responses, to ensure a wider coverage and also to eliminate biases, the write-up was mailed to few highly experienced BD & POs for a critical examination. The final report, thus, has passed through various stages of scrutiny.

A word about the limitations of the study will not be out of place. The time at the disposal was very short and, therefore, the study had to be completed under an incorrigible situation. Moreover, it would have been desirable to take up the study, especially the analysis of work-load of BD & POs vis-a-vis to activities connected with agriculture, a little afterwards.

**The Study**

In order to enable the Block Development and Panchayat Officer to devote his entire time to agriculture, the Punjab Government have recently issued a circular to the effect that while the BD & PO should devote all his time for doubling agricultural production. The non-agricultural activities will be supervised by the Social Education and Panchayat Officer. However, since the BD & PO remains the Head of the Office and also Chief Executive Officer of the Panchayat Samiti, this situation compels him to devote a major part of his time to non-agricultural work. The details of his duties and the time consumed for discharging these responsibilities are given below :—

(I) (*a*) Drawing and Disbursing Officer :

As Drawing and Disbursing Officer the BD & PO has to attend to all payments to be made from the funds placed at the disposal of the Panchayat Samiti. He has to closely scrutinize the procedure involved, sign the bills, verify the treasury memos and initial the cash book entries. In addition, it is also his duty to supervise stores and stocks. The workload varies from day to day, but even at a conservative estimate he is expected to devote atleast half an hour during the day to this type of work. Thus, half a day in a week or 26 days in a year will have to be calculated for this purpose.

(*b*) Supervision of Accounts :

In accounts work the foremost responsibility is in regard to budget. Preparation of budget is a technical job and it needs considerable and exclusive attention, if one intends to do justice to the subject. The budget has many stages. Each stage consumes a considerable part of BD & PO's time and labour. The stages are: preliminary budget, revised budget, appropriations and re-appropriations. With the introduction of Panchayati Raj, this work has further been increased. Previously he dealt with items of expenditure only. He was not required to devote any attention or time to the income side. Now he is also required to get income and expenditure statements compiled monthly, quarterly, half-yearly and then annually. In addition to this Panchayati Raj system has introduced a good number of other books, proformas and statements.

(*c*) Audit and Inspection :

Periodic audit and also inspection by various officials is an essential component of the Block activities. The objections pointed out in such reports are to be answered by the Block Development and Panchayat Officer and replies have to be sent to the person concerned. Additional load has also been cast on the shoulders of BD & POs with the introduction of Panchayati Raj. Now the Examiner, Local Fund Accounts conducts two audits in a year. Occasionally, the District Accounts Committee also comes and inspects the accounts. Furthermore, one annotated copy of every audit note is required to be sent to the Accounts Committee.

Half a day in a month is the minimum period which is to be devoted to all the above-mentioned type of work.

(*d*) The other administrative duties which the BD & PO has to perform are:

(*i*) Verification of all periodical reports and returns.

(*ii*) Verification of loans.

(*iii*) Checking the proper use of immovable properties of the defunct District Board, now attached to Panchayat Samiti.

(*iv*) Flood relief work, such as assessment of damages, distribution of grants, protective measures.

(*v*) Organising vasectomy camps.

(*vi*) Drive for recruitment for Home Guard.

(*vii*) Locust control.

(*viii*) CARE School Feeding Programme.

(II) Executive Officer of Panchayat Samiti:

As Executive Officer of Panchayat Samiti, he has to discharge the following duties:

(*i*) Meetings:

The BD & PO has been declared the Secretary of the Samiti and of the standing committee on Finance and Taxation also. So as such he drafts the agenda for the meetings, ensures its timely service, records down proceedings and then sends their copies within three days to the concerned authorities. He is also required to go through the proceedings of other committees and to give notes and comments thereon with regard to their legality and validity.

(*ii*) Planning and legislation:

Previously the BD & PO was required to formulate the development plans only but now he has to explore the ways and means to augment the income of the Samiti. He is to find out the possibility of the new taxes. In addition to this he is to make the drafts for Bye-laws. For the successful running of the Samiti, Bye-laws on varying subjects have to be drafted, approved and enforced.

(*iii*) Taxation:

The BD & PO in the capacity of the Executive Officer has been declared Assessing Authority, Collecting Authority and the Licensing Authority as well. This itself is quite a time-consuming work. The following are the typical items which fall under this head:

(1) Assessment of Professional Tax.

(2) Hearing of objections.

(3) Attendance of D.C./S.D.O.'s Court in connection with appeals against assessment made by BD & PO.

(4) Collection of taxes on cattle fairs and supervising its management.

(5) Issue of licences to tongas and rairies.

(6) Checking of cycle tokens.

(7) Checking of cattle ponds.

(8) Public Health licences.

(9) Checking of Engine licences.

(10) Realization of Professional Tax as arrears of land revenue.

(11) Checking of leather tanning licences.

(*iv*) Litigation.

Now the Block Development and Panchayat Officer is required to resort to coercive methods also whenever he sees any violation being done of any provision of relevant law, rule or the Bye-law. He is required to launch prosecution against the defaulters.

From the foregoing paragraphs, it will be seen that the Panchayati Raj has added a lot to the workload of the BD & PO. The analysis of the workload, related to Panchayati Raj is as under:

| | |
|---|---|
| (1) Samiti Meetings | 9 days in a year. |
| (2) Standing Committee meetings | 12 days in a year. |
| (3) Preparation of budget and agenda | 6 days in a year. |
| (4) Panchayat Inspection and enquiries per year | 76 days in a year. |

In addition to the above jobs there are a number of miscellaneous duties which the BD & PO has to perform. A few of them are ;

(*a*) Collection of Chulha Tax.

(*b*) Organizing block tournaments and melas.

(*c*) Supervision of Panchayat Election.

(*d*) Duty relating to election of the Panchayat Samiti.

(*e*) Looking after the Revenue earning scheme of the Panchayat Samiti.

(*f*) Management of Panchayats.

(*g*) Work related to Village Volunteer Force.

(*h*) Work related to Rural Forum.

(III) Staff Meetings:

The BD & PO is to conduct two meetings in a month to discuss with the staff their problems regarding implementation of various programmes, availability of technical skill and for taking steps for gearing the executive machinery for the attainment of the objectives, set before the Block team. Thus 24 days are consumed in a year for this purpose only.

As the captain of the Block team, the BD & PO has to attend the monthly meetings of District Coordination Committee and other District Level meetings. His personal presence in such meetings is unavoidable due to the importance of this work and for giving spot replies there about various complaints, programmes, etc.

In brief, his calender of work can be mentioned as under:

| | | |
|---|---|---:|
| (1) | Staff meetings | 24 days |
| (2) | District Meetings | 12 days |
| (3) | Meeting called by the BD & PO and other Departments at District level of BD & PO for discussing, arrears of the pending references, achievement of targets etc. | 12 days |
| (4) | Sub Divisional Level Meetings, meeting for small savings Agriculture and other types | 12 days |
| (5) | Samiti Meetings | 9 days |
| (6) | Standing Committee meetings | 12 days |
| (7) | Panchayat Inspection and enquiries | 76 days |
| (8) | Office Dak, preparation of budget, meeting agenda, work relating to drawing disbursement of funds, checking of stores | 52 days |
| (9) | Audit and Inspection | 10 days |
| (10) | Miscellaneous duties as, attending to the visitors, district and higher officers etc. | 12 days |
| (11) | Organizing camps, drives, campaigns etc., such as vasectomy, flood control, home guards etc. | 8 days |
| (12) | Sundays and other Gazetted holidays | 69 days |
| | | 308 days |

These are the minimum number of days which a BD & PO has to spend on non-agricultural activities. Only 57 days in a year are then left for attending to Agriculture. Usually the frequency of the meetings at District Headquarters is much more than indicated above. He has also to organize the drives for the collection of small savings funds for which the targets are fixed by the Deputy Commissioner and supervise the collection of Red Cross and other similar funds. In actual practice the days available will further dwindle because a considerable period of his time is taken away by the following additional duties:

(a) Hearing and dealing of complaints and objections, relating to professional tax duties.

(b) Attending to public enquiries and complaints.

(c) Distributions of controlled commodities.

Under these circumstances, it will be unrealistic to visualise that with the issue of directives only the BD & PO would be able to devote cent per cent of his time on the Agriculture programme and also that his personal impact on the agriculture production programme will be deep and satisfying.

## Suggestions

Probably a comprehensive and systematic solution may be possible after undertaking a work-study of the functionaries of the whole Block Organization, simplification and streamlining of the office procedure under the expert advice of Organization and Method Division, strengthening the Block organization, wherever necessary. The following suggestions, however, can be put into effect without much financial commitment or deep-seated changes in the existing pattern:

(1) The Head Clerk in the Panchayat Samiti should invariably be deputed from the cadre of Assistants in the ministerial service instead of recruiting him locally. An experienced Assistant with his background and training can relieve the BD & PO from much of the routine office supervision. It is visualised that by providing an efficient supervisor in the office, out of 52 days now being spent for office dak and other allied work atleast half the days will be available for field work.

(2) Both the BD & PO and SE & PO make inspections of the Panchayats. This is to a certain extent duplication. Instructions from the Headquarters should be amended so that only SE & PO could carry out inspection and audit of village Panchayats. In this way a large part of 76 days will be availalbe for the agricultural programme.
A natural corollary to this suggestion will be that more work will be thrown on the shoulders of the SE & PO. This will necessitate that an additional clerk-cum-record keeper be provided in the block staff to assist the SE & PO exclusively.

(3) The standing Committee on Finance and Taxation of which the BD & PO is the Secretary may meet once in two months. Of course if the agenda of the Committee is heavy, it may meet more frequently, but from experience it is felt that its meeting once in two months will meet the needs of the situation in most cases. If this is carried out, 6 more days are available with the BD & PO for agricultural programme.

(4) The BD & PO can be relieved from the duties of the Secretary of the Standing Committee on Education, Social Education, etc. The SE & PO can be equally useful and effective for the responsibilities of the Secretaryship of this Committee.

(5) If the above pattern of work is agreed to, it will be seen that

SE & PO would be intimately in touch with the non-agricultural programmes and activities of the Block. As such at the district level, if he attends the general meetings (excluding agricultural production) there will be no dilution of the effectiveness of such meetings. The District Heads should therefore be issued suitable instructions to that effect. Similarly for discussing the complaints not allied with Agricultural programmes, the District Heads should not insist on BD & PO's personal presence, but rather call the Extension Officer concerned or the SE & PO.

(6) Since the V.L.W. is expected to devote hundred per cent of his time on the agricultural programmes, it may perhaps be of much help if the VLW is made directly answerable to BD & PO in place of the prevalent system of Administrative control of the Panchayat Samiti on VLW. Similar action need be followed for Agricultural Inspector as well. It will not in any way conflict with the basic objectives of the Panchayati Raj institutions, as the BD & PO will still be under the overall control of the Panchayat Samiti. Rather it will assist the overall programme by having a single channel of communication.

(7) The efficiency and calibre of the Panchayat Secretaries be improved. The process of recruitment, conditions of service etc. of Panchayat Secretaries be brought at par with the V.L.W. It will be of great help if the recruitment of all the functionaries in the Block Organization are made through the Subordinate Service Commission Board.

(8) Some short-term courses for the ministerial employees particularly those who were working with erstwhile District Boards be arranged with special reference to requirements in Development work.

(9) With the separation of judiciary from the executive, it is quite likely that the work-load of the S.D.O. will decrease. The enquiries relating to Panchayats, now being conducted by the BD & PO may be entrusted to him or partly to him and partly to District Development and Panchayat Officer. A considerable part of BD & PO's time is consumed by such enquiries. The existing practice is also not in conformity with his role of Executive Officer of Panchayat Samiti. Sometimes the enquiries relate to either the members of Panchayat Samiti or persons close to them. Naturally they manage to exert considerable pressure on BD & PO.

# THE MULTIPURPOSE VILLAGE LEVEL WORKER

## Albert Mayer

IN A MEMORANDUM to Tarlok Singh, then Deputy Secretary of the National Planning Commission, Mayer outlines the crucial, manisided role developed for Village Level Workers in the U.P. Pilot projects, a role projected for them also in the Community Development Projects.

In Etawah and later in all the pilot projects, this new type of worker was created. It may be worthwhile to explain the reasons for devising this instrument, his functions and his limitations, for the use of any who may be contemplating training and use of the multipurpose worker.

### The Conception

At present, various government departments have field workers. Due to budget limitations, the lowest level worker has a large number of villages to cover, in addition to much paper work. This means he rarely gets to any one village, does not become intimately known, and does not get to know the village, its people, or its problems. Also, this kind of departmental worker generally has not been trained in "village approach," in making friends with local people, or in actually being able or willing to do the things he recommends or tells the village people to do.

At the village level, advice and help in agriculture, animal husbandry, and public health are not very technical. It has been found that one worker, backed up by available personnel at a higher technical level, can do agricultural demonstrations (varietal, manurial, and implemental), animal husbandry inoculations and human vaccinations, help with insect control and antimalaria work, and help to organize simple public works by the people, such as lane widening, drainage, and compost pits. Not only can he be trained in this simple work, but his training also includes methods of village approach group meetings, individual discussions, popular songs, and simple dramas—in short, social education. He can use this approach and the friendliness and friendships that flow from it to introduce work and practices not only in one branch, but in several branches of village life and need.

Being "multipurpose," that is, filling many needs at his level, covering the work of several departments, he needs to cover fewer villages. In other words, he visits and works in the villages of his circle frequently enough so that he becomes well known and well recognized and well received. Where this new system has been tried, it has been found that four to six villages per man can be well covered. He can become a close and trusted adviser, helper, energizer, participant.

## Limitations

This system can be worked well, and has worked well. But the temptation must be avoided of overworking it. Here are some limitations to be considered.

Not too many villages.—A careful realistic time-programme should be built, with the Village Level Worker participating, to see how much he really can do and do thoroughly and honestly. In this building up of a timetable, which is really the bedrock, the foundation of any plan of development, wishful thinking must be eliminated. Time must be allowed for the Village Level Worker to go from village to village, to check up on supplies. Time must be allowed for the farmers to gather for a group meeting.

The "multipurpose" idea must not be carried too far. Both the time and the ability of the Village Level Workers are limited. Only certain types of work are suited in any case. And if the work is to be really thorough, really imbedded in village thinking, the idea must not be stretched too far.

Backing up the Village Level Worker.—There are other aspects of limitation on the Village Level Worker: (1) his technical competence is limited; (2) his self-confidence or success is limited; (3) in both aspects, he may get and will get into situations that are beyond him.

He must be closely backed up by technically more competent and more experienced people. This can be accomplished in two ways: first, by frequent visits from the members of the project team to the villages, and second by the fortnightly staff meetings where problems are brought up for discussion and resolved.

# VILLAGE LEVEL WORKER AND THE COOPERATIVE MOVEMENT

*Ram Chandra Tewari*
*Translated by D. R. Goyal*

IN EVERY COMMUNITY development block, there is an Extension Officer for Cooperation just as there are Extension Officers for Agriculture, Animal Husbandry, Panchayats, Rural Engineering, etc. But the most vital role in the Community Development Programme has to be played by the Village Level Worker because he is in intimate contact with the villagers. It is necessary that he is imbued with a sense of service.

In the midst of modern urbanised civilisation, if the country has to be developed, devoted service needs to be rendered in the villages which form the backbone of the country. It requires selfless and constructive workers who should live and work in the villages. In fact, Village Level Worker should be a person of high calibre. First of all, he should be aware of the significance of his work. He should be aware of the objectives and know the ways and means to achieve them. We are progressing towards a society, predominantly agricultural but free from exploitation. Panchayat and Cooperation are the instruments for realising it. Therefore, the Village Level Worker should have full knowledge of these. Besides possessing basic knowledge of agriculture, animal husbandry, village industries, etc., he should be keen to see that the resources are properly employed through mutual help and cooperation.

The Village Level Worker should keep aloof from the internal politics of the village and should have the personality to win the confidence of people holding opposite views in the villages. His constructive sense should be so strong that he should be able to employ all the resources for village uplift. He should have the capacity to understand a situation and suggest solutions of problems. Some understanding of health and hygiene, too, is necessary. In fact, he should be the centre of the entire Community Development activity. Cooperation should be his watchword because without cooperative effort it is impossible to remove the poverty of villages. Unless we remove the suffering and poverty of the village, we cannot convert self-government into good government.

Broadly speaking, the task of the Village Level Worker should be to acquaint the villagers with their problems, to awaken in them the desire for good life and to tell them that their condition can improve by their own efforts. He should help them in assessing and mobilising their resources and also in procuring from Government institutions all the aid necessary for implementation of the programme that they chalk out.

The Village Level Worker should tell the villagers how other villages have improved. The know-all attitude should be avoided and attempt should be made to utilise the experiences of the peasants. He is their friend, philosopher and guide not only in agriculture but also in other spheres.

He should take his work not merely as a job but in the spirit of service. The villagers and peasants, in the present conditions, can make the best use of their available resources through cooperation. In fact, cooperation is the basis of the entire Community Development programme. Its aim of socio-economic uplift can be achieved only through cooperative effort. Community Development can be put on a sound foundation only when there is a network of cooperative farms, service cooperative societies and other cooperatives.

# MUKHYA SEVIKA AS A SUPERVISOR

...The responsibilities of the Mukhya Sevika in a block in relation to the work of the Gram Sevikas are mainly two-fold, *viz.*, (*i*) to guide and supervise the day-to-day work of the Gram Sevikas and (*ii*) to help the Gram Sevikas in overcoming difficulties and inconveniences that they may experience while working in rural areas. She also shares direct responsibilities in starting new activities and in securing community participation.

Guidance and supervision mainly relate to (*a*) helping the Gram Sevikas to know the programme of women and children in the block and its relationship to the overall Community Development programme; (*b*) to understand and know the details of the administrative set up of the block; (*c*) to carry out surveys of a selected number of villages in relation to particular needs of balwadis Mahila Mandal, home visits, etc., and to promote welfare of the child, the mother and the family; (*d*) to solve day-to-day problems arising out of the activities of the Gram Sevika; (*e*) to help.

## Maintain Accounts, Records, etc.

Proper maintenance of accounts, records, as also coordination of work with the other women workers in the block relate to administrative-cum-organisational aspect of the work of the Gram Sevika. The Mukhya Sevika should have adequate understanding of these so as to be able to give the necessary guidance to them. The Mukhya Sevika has also to act as an interpreter. She has to have her hand on the "pulse of the people" all the time and has to convey their needs to the staff under her. Similarly she has to tell the community of the correct role of the field staff so that they get full cooperation in the conduct of their activities and are enabled to live as one among them.

## A Friend in Need

There is another responsibility of the Mukhya Sevika in the personal problems of the Gram Sevika. In our rural areas women generally do not work away from their homes. They are still, by and large, an integral part of the family and look after the major responsibilities of bringing up children, looking after household activities and helping the men in agriculture and other occupation. A woman worker going to another village and working on the basis of payment, is something foreign to the tradition. Gram Sevika in the village is a new experience in the village community. Though the villagers are increasingly accepting the Gram Sevikas, there still remain many problems of adjustment to the village condition. It is quite natural that under the circumstances there will be, at least in the initial stages, some difficulties in securing, say, accommodation for her in the village. The village people may even warn the local women about this girl from the outside. It is in these peculiar circumstances, about which nobody can predict nor can offer a positive solution, the Mukhya Sevika has to be her guide and friend. She has to help and stand by the side of the Gram Sevika in overcoming all these difficulties in the initial stages.

## A Guide and Adviser

A young Gram Sevika may have other problems of relationship with co-workers in the field. The Mukhya Sevika with her proper understanding of the problem of rural life and human relationship, should help the Gram Sevika in adjusting satisfactorily to the new surrounding. This she should be able to do with her mature judgment and proper insight into the problem. The Mukhya Sevika is apt sometimes to rely on her authority, as a supervisor. That may be occasionally necessary but not always the best way of dealing with an erring Gram Sevika. The Mukhya Sevika would do well to build up for herself the position of a 'elderly friend' more by virtue of her worldly wisdom and superior technical competence. The test of this advisory as against supervisory position is to see how often and how intimately the Gram Sevikas turn voluntarily to hear for advice, solace and guidance.

# GRAM SEVIKA'S MULTIPLE ROLE

THE GRAM SEVIKA works as a community organiser. She has to establish contact with individual families of the village and to gain the confidence of the village community as a whole. She has to find out the real problems and the particular needs of women. Not only has she to create a public opinion in resolving the rural problems, she has also to mould the opinion and channelise it for constructive activities. The people have to be given the feeling that they can do it themselves.

A good Gram Sevika should also get as much assistance from the block headquarters to solve some of the villagers' problems. She should not rest content with that. She has to take the follow-up action and see that people's initial enthusiasm in bettering their own future is sustained throughout.

The Gram Sevika is a social welfare worker. She has to revitalise the family through various activities. She has to organise balwadis, children's play centre, etc. She has to gather young and adolescent girls for nation-building activities. She has to organise social education programme for adult women as well.

The Gram Sevika is a teacher and an executive. She teaches in balwadis and conducts adult literacy classes. She conducts craft lessons for the village women. She visits individual homes in the village and advises them on all matters.

The Gram Sevika has to maintain records and registers and carry on some correspondence. She has to keep accounts and maintain liaison with other village functionaries like midwives, etc.

# GRAM SEVIKA—THE USEFUL LINK

THE GRAM SEVIKA is a generalist. She knows something of many a thing. She is not a master in any particular subject, but has elementary knowledge of various aspects of the rural development programme. Her training and background is such that she should not be expected to be a specialist. She is in day-to-day touch with the rural people and, as such, knows them and their problems intimately. She tries to help them in their distress. When it is not possible for her to suggest a solution, she gets the help of the Mukhya Sevak or the Social Education Organiser (men). Sometimes in consultation with them she takes back the problem to the Extension Officers at the Block headquarters. They come to her rescue. For example, she may not be able to give appropriate medicines in case of say, tuberculosis, but she is expected to know the general symptoms of the case so as to ask for help from the doctor at the Block headquarters. She knows, for instance, the damage that the pests do to the crops. When actually there is a visitation, she will seek the help of the specialist at the Block Level in eradicating the same.

# AN APPEAL TO OLD COLLEAGUES

## *Albert Mayer*

AT ONE POINT, convinced of his personal inability to affect seriously what he felt was tendency to general deterioration, Mayer made a personal appeal to some of his old associates, to establish personal fortresses of strength and integrity that would outlast any lowering of standards and drifting with the tide.

New York
September 4, 1955

Dear

This letter is an informal, confidential, and very earnest appeal and recommendation. I am writing it to you and a few other 'old-timers' also.

One of the things that has happened since the early days is that the work in Community and then National Extension Service projects has multiplied manifold, perhaps faster than the quality of men and their training might have made entirely desirable. Another troublesome factor has been that the top supervising organization, which might have helped this situation somewhat, qualified and experienced Assistant Development Commissioners and Deputy Development Commissioners cannot begin to give adequate supervision.

This situation is being partially met by seminar-conferences and, I believe, by visits to certain typical, chosen projects. However, as I see it, what is badly needed is the concentrated multiplication on a small scale of men who are like our early selves, if I may put it that way - people who understand what good work is and who know what thorough preparation and planning are required to accomplish it, who have achieved the personal discipline that will not permit them to do arbitrary things on unproved hunches, or change their minds in the midst of a course of action.

Now due to the big expansion and the dilution of the original system we know that even those who have the right attitudes and training and experience very often cannot apply these as they would like. Let us grant that. Still the only way that final good can emerge is for there to be more of really good people—people who, in addition to the qualities noted above, will keep the flag flying within themselves, will not yield spiritually and intellectually even when they cannot act in altogether the way they know they should. That is the subject of this letter.

I see a way to do it which will not do it on the big scale that would be desirable, but which is the only way that we can command. It is this: for each person to pick one, two or probably at most three people, in whom he recognizes the spark and the will and the internal need, and work with him (or them) on all planes, so that we can definitely multiply men who are strong in faith and in knowledge both. This, it seems to me, is our best assurance of the survival of integrity and effectiveness. Of course, the regular work must continue: seminars, bulletins of instruction, periodic visits, and the improved development is as large a number of people as possible. What I have just tried to describe is beyond that; it means picking dedicated people who must become more dedicated, and who will do because you can concentrate on them and inspire them.

Do think this over carefully, select carefully who the one, two or three people should be, and dedicate yourself to them especially. I know that you are too busy to find this extra time and attention. But somehow you have got to do it.

Sincerely,
ALBERT

# PROBLEMS OF STAFF AND SUPERVISION

## M. J. Coldwell, R. Dumont and M. Read

THE VILLAGE LEVEL worker is both a multi-purpose worker and responsible for disseminating progressive agricultural methods among the farmers, and assisting them in the actual operations. The Mehta Report emphasized that this man had sixty-four different obligations to fulfill in a wide variety of fields. In addition, the scope of his work may cover 2,000 farm families or more, and the Mission observed more than once that a task of this magnitude is virtually impossible of achievement ...

      &times;      &times;      &times;      &times;      &times;

The only way to attract the best types of persons to this career is by giving them reasonable prospects of promotion ...

      &times;      &times;      &times;      &times;      &times;

In addition, the community development programme must give the technical expert his due in modern society, treating him on at least the same footing as the administrator proper. If the status of the agricultural specialist is improved, a better class of agronomists will be recruited and, ultimately, in adequate numbers. If a year of village service as gram sevaks were made compulsory for all students graduating from agricultural colleges, it would provide the community development movement with youthful dynamic and skilled staff, and the prospective agronomist would gain invaluable practical training which, in due course, would make him more valuable than at present. The Community Development movement must aim at inculcating a new spirit, resolutely social in aim in that it affords real protection for the poor, and solidly backed up by an improved technique. In the light of this new spirit, the order of priority of activities and investments would be decided in the interests of the economy as a whole, immediate efficiency and long-term social objectives.

# RELATIONSHIP OF CERTAIN FACTORS TO THE SUCCESS OF VILLAGE LEVEL WORKERS (ABSTRACTS)

## W. B. Rahudkar

THE FUNCTION OF the Village Level Worker has been conceived of as that of a multipurpose extension agent, so that he could harmoniously co-ordinate different types of welfare activities. Though a generalist in conception, his effective functioning demands adequate specialisation in several branches of development activities that he sponsors and guides. His task is, thus, challenging and demands special aptitudes and personality traits. Selection of proper persons for this job, therefore, becomes very important. So, it is necessary to determine the personal traits closely associated with the success of a V.L.W. A study was undertaken to find out the relationship of success of the V.L.W. and various personal traits. 178 V.L.W.s who put in two years of service, selected by stratified randomisation, working in 8 districts of Bombay State were interviewed for this purpose.

On the basis of two tests, 52 V.L.W.s were classified as most effective and 42 as least effective and these two groups were compared to estimate the relationship of the success of V.L.Ws. to various personal characteristics.

The study revealed that rural background plays an important role in making the V.L.Ws. effective. A majority of the most effective V.L.Ws. were born to farmers living in rural areas, had been educated in village schools and had lived in rural areas for more than a year. This is but natural for the promotion of the various welfare activities in the villages requires intimate knowledge of rural people, their habits, customs and culture. It is, therefore, essential that persons having a rural bias are selected for the posts of V.L.W.

The second characteristic which was found to be associated with the effectiveness of V.L.Ws. is educational qualification. Those V.L.Ws. who had completed their high school education were found to be most effective. The greater percentage of the least effective V.L.Ws. was from those who had not attained the high school standard. It was further observed that the college education of a few V.L.Ws. had not increased their effectiveness. This is perhaps due to the fact that college educated candidates desire jobs in urban areas or promotion to higher posts and this stands in the way of their applying themselves wholeheartedly to the job of the V.L.W.

Though the aptitude differences between the most effective and the least effective groups were not wide, it was, however, observed that those who had a higher degree of social participation were slightly more effective than the others.

Other characteristics associated with the success of a V.L.W. were his age, martial status and the nature of his recruitment. The V.L.Ws. who were more than 31 years performed better than those who were below 30. Thus, it appears that the more mature V.L.Ws. had a better grasp of the rural problems.

Married V.L.Ws. were found to be more successful than the unmarried ones.

The V.L.Ws. selected from the Agriculture Department showed better performance than those selected from other Departments and those who were direct recruits. This may be due to the fact that a large measure of the work of the V.L.Ws. is related to agriculture and those who had some practical knowledge of the department could show better performance than those who had other backgrounds of service and those who were fresh recruits.

It was also revealed that the V.L.Ws. who had put in more service proved to be more effective than those who were less experienced.

In order to ensure the success of rural community development, it is necessary that the V.L.Ws. are selected on the basis of these desirable personality traits and aptitudes which have been shown to be having a definite correlation with the effectiveness of their functioning.

# VILLAGE LEVEL WORKERS—THEIR WORK AND RESULT DEMONSRATIONS

## D. C. Dubey, Dr. Willis A. Sutton & Dr. Gladys Gallup

### Some suggested uses of the study

THIS STUDY OF V.L.W's. work and their agriculture result demonstrations covers one of the vital actual action phases of the Community Development Programme. It may therefore be of some use to a number of workers in the programme. A brief suggestion here of a few of its uses to persons at different levels may add to the study's significance.

### Village Level Workers

#### (1) *Increasing One's Efficiency*

To the gramsevaks these case analyses present examples of how they can look back to and analyse their own activities and result demonstrations with a view to increasing their efficiency. To illustrate, after a particular result demonstration is complete the VLW can ask to himself questions such as: How clearly did the demonstrator farmer understood the purpose of the whole operation? How clearly was the "proof" of the demonstrated practice established? What technical support did he get from the block specialist and how much would need in future? Who were the persons influenced by the demonstration? A similar approach should be used for other activities.

#### (2) *Finding One's Own Level*

Such a critical self-analysis of the activities through the process of self evaluation, will lead him to identify his own level in the three groups of VLWs and will indicate what more is required of him to play effectively the expected role of the VLW.

#### (1) *EACH VLW A SEPARATE IDENTITY*

The study questions the block officer's present practice of treating all the VLWs alike. It was reported in each case that the BDO and EOs pay the same number of monthly visits to each VLW and give the same instructions in the same form to all of them. The analysis presented brings into clear focus, the need for block officer's to recognize the all VLWs are not alike in terms of the help they need and in terms of the situations within which they work.

## (2) *CLASSIFYING VLWs.*

In this study the VLW cases have been successfully analysed and classified in three groups on the basis of certain characteristics. This suggests the potentiality of using these characteristics by the block staff to differentiate and classify the VLWs in the block.

## (3) *HELPFUL IN PLANNING SUPERVISION*

Once each VLW is thus characterized helpful supervision and guidance in the light of these characteristics can more easily be developed. Such planning supervision and guidance may increasingly enable the VLWs to play their designated role more fully and ultimately lead to higher achievements of the block.

## (4) *REDUCING CHANCES OF BIASED JUDEMENT*

The studies provide a relatively complete basis for more objective evaluations of VLWs. Chances for misunderstanding and for judging VLWs mainly on "hearsay" are thereby reduced.

# EXPERIENCE OF A VILLAGE WORKER

## Usha Bannerjee

IS ANY LIFE still left in our villages? Are they not dead and absolutely unworthy of living? These are the questions which usually come to the mind of a city dweller, who might have no relation with village or who might have had a difficult experience with village-life. The same questions were asked by Miss Santosh Kumari, a Delhi school teacheress posted in a village, seventeen miles away from Delhi to work as Balwadi worker. She was an average city girl, who was educated in the city but went to unknown village for her livelihood. She was posted as a social worker for which she was given preliminary training. But she being foreign to village life, found that the theoretical knowledge of her work which she had acquired during the training period had no validity in practice. She was lonely soul in the village, trying to bring changes in usual ways. There was no one to help her and nobody to realise her difficulty. She was just like so many other village workers placed under similar conditions.

The village had a population of seventy families, comprising mostly Muslims and Jats. Santosh had to run a Balwadi Centre there for the Delhi State Social Welfare Board.

On her arrival in the village, she found it extremely difficult to find a suitable place for the Centre, not even a proper accommodation for herself where she could put up safely. However, the Pradhan and the Sarpanchas were sympathetic and assured her of their help. But to a city dweller, as Santosh was, the place offered by them did not at all appeal. It was far below the normal level of sanitation and hygiene, though quite safe for a young girl in the village. Thus the problem of accommodation could not be solved, in spite of the fact that the villagers were helpful and sympathetic to her venture. The villagers failed to realise the problem of a girl, born and brought up in the town. Consequently, Santosh decided to waste 50% of her salary and $\frac{1}{3}$ of the day in making trips from Delhi to the village and back. But the problem of accommodation for the Centre still remained to be solved. The caste and communal problem was as acute in the village, as any where else. The Jats would not like to send their children to the Muslim area; nor would the Muslims like to send their children to the Jat area. Therefore, Santosh had to find a place, which was convenient for all. She could only get a thatched roofed room with a dusty courtyard in front. The wooden planks in roofs were infested with white ants and could fall apart at any moment, In short, the entire place was nearly in a shamble.

The children in the Balwadi Centre are supposed to get cleaned and washed up before they start the classes. (The Balwadi class is meant for children in 2-6 years age-group). There was hardly any well nearby, from where the water could be fetched to give the children a wash. Surely, Santosh could engage a Bhishti to carry water from a distance. But the charges were so high that Santosh could not make the authorities to agree. So, she had to remain satisfied by giving them a dry hair brush for the time being.

As the Balwadi Centre started functioning Santosh had to face another problem. The Centre soon turned into a recreational place for the girls in the age-group 6-10 years. One would mistake the nursery for the primary school. These girls came along with their younger brothers or sisters in their arms. But Santosh found it convenient to work with these girls. She had been unsuccessful in getting the young children, as they were too shy and scared of strangers. On the other hand, the centre was an attraction for 6-10 years old girls because the house work and helping mother to bring up the children prevented them from attending the primary school. They found that the nursery rhymes, games, the story-telling and the tit-bits were more interesting than learning arithmetic or rupees and paises in the school. So, Santosh had to cater these girls too.

Santosh presented these problems to the authorities, Balwadi Committee members of the State Social Welfare Board, and asked for their guidance. A date was fixed, when someone from the State Welfare Board, Santosh, the Village Level Worker, Sarpanchas, Pradhans and a visitor working in the village would get together. They discussed all the problems very carefully and with sympathy. Santosh had to go round all these people to get their co-operation. One of the Panchayat members offered the first floor of his pucca building on rent to her for her living in the village. Everyone realised that no village work could be done successfully unless one lived in the village and be a part of its everyday life. But the room suggested by the Panchayat for Santosh's stay did not have the proper drainage facility. However, they decided to dig a big hole in the ground and improvise a satisfactory sanitation arrangement. They also started re-thinking about the sanitation programme for the village as a whole.

Regarding the location of the Centre, the villagers gradually came to realise the need for a proper place for the children to play in. O of the villagers suggested that a newly built room of a villager, which was more in the central position, could be converted into the Balwadi Centre. But Santosh felt, as other members of the Balwadi Committee of the State Board also agreed, that the problems would not be completely solved until she could enthuse the Muslim and Jat members of the village to build up a community Centre for the children, along with a room where she could also live. It had happened in other villages, where the work started earlier. If the worker was tactful and intelligent enough to enlist people's co-operation, she could also get a Balwadi Centre built for the children. She would have to work for this with the help and co-operation of the V.L.W's, and other village workers, working in other fields.

To make the Centre more attractive, Santosh managed to get food for the children from Delhi. The Balwadi Committee helped her to get powdered milk from the Red Cross Association. The result was appreciably better. The number of children in the Centre increased immediately, as they could now get free milk as refreshment. The villagers were also pleased to find their children fed with nutritive food.

Santosh divided the children in the Centre into two groups according to their age. Different types of programme were evolved for the two groups, *e.g.* the clay-modelling, painting and the jig-saw puzzles for the younger ones and the story-telling and singing for the older ones. The youngsters needed all the personal care and attention. So, Santosh herself would remain busy with them. She had to apply her elementary knowledge in child psychology to deal with them. She taught one of the girls from the older group to be the leader and the teacher for them. Sometimes they would help her in managing the smaller children. Santosh tried to repeat the same programme after the interval of ten or fifteen days. Visiting houses helped her to win the hearts of the children. A register was maintained and the roll call system was introduced. If a child failed to attend the class for two or three days, she would visit the mother and the family. She was trying to win the respect of the child through informal chats with the mother. Enquiring into the day-to-day problems of her household work helped to win the hearts of the mother. Once the mother and the family accepted the worker properly the children also started feeling at home in the Centre.

Thus Santosh, once forlorn and troubled with the problems of the village work found herself quite at home in new surroundings. Besides her personal tacts and close contacts with all individual families from time to time, she had constant guidance and supervision from the Delhi Office. She was also encouraged to meet her co-workers working in the near-by villages to share her experiences with them. The members from the Balwadi Committee went to visit her from time to time. This helped to keep up her morale. The worker needs encouragement and guidance at the earlier stage. Later on, she gets used to work and can manage the work herself through the trial and error method. Santosh shared her experiences with other friends, who had started working earlier in other villages and found out that all shared the same type of difficulty in the early days.

Thus Santosh found that life is still flickering in the villages, one has only to light it up to brighten it.

# GARANDA—A COMMENDABLE EXPERIMENT

*A.I. Sahasrabudhe*

I FIND THE instance of Garanda quite notable in this respect. Shri Govind Reddy started work there in the month of January 1956. The village has thirty-one families. Seventeen cultivators had their own land. Fourteen were landless. He concentrated his attention on this village. The first thing to be attempted was to redistribute the land. Bullocks and land were given to fourteen landless families. He could not do much in the first year, to improve the soil or method of cultivation. Some preferred to work as labourers in the field of another and neglected their own land. The Sarvodaya principle of helping the lowest did not succeed in the first attempt. However, the total production of the village increased by about 40 per cent. (but the per capita income did not show an appreciable rise).

Shri Reddy thought about this and started a new plan. He bought a pair of bullocks for the centre, and got prepared some implements. He then began to go to someone's field and work himself there as a labourer for seven or eight hours a day. He would begin work every morning at seven sharp. Even the shirkers were persuaded to follow his example and to work with him. He developed such friendly relations with every family that he would talk to the house-wives and enquire if there was enough in the house to eat. Everyone recognized him as a friend and a guide. He told everyone that no one must go hungry. He went and gave grains to those who had not enough to eat. He began to get the villagers to assemble together at night twice or thrice a week. I must say that he did create a new type of leadership. There is no doubt, that he has succeeded in changing the outlook of the people of the village. The people are becoming fearless and are now conscious of their responsibilities. They are improving their lands and adopting new methods of cultivation. The village council meets regularly. Shri Reddy has now gone to some place in Madhya Pradesh. But the village people still look to him for guidance. He visits Garanda for short periods twice or thrice a year. The villagers had recently sent a batch of young men to him for study. They lived with him for about four months and returned. We have learnt from him that short training courses could be conducted with advantage for the young men from the villages. No doubt, Garanda today is an outstanding village in Koraput.

I feel, that it is worth trying to give the various local works that are conducted under the N.E.S. Blocks, on contract basis to the Gram Sabha in the area. The Sarva Seva Sangh should provide the technical guidance to the Gram Sabha in that case. Some money could be earned by the Gram Sabha this way. It would be earmarked for training camps. Documentary films should be shown for imparting general information. Thus the co-operatives would enlarge the field where earning and learning are combined. A new cadre of workers would then come forth; and it would create a proper climate for developing Gram Swaraj.

In the last three years, we have been holding training camps of two or three days' duration in many places. In the village where land was redistributed Gram Sabha had begun to function. We held special classes for the members of the Gram Sabhas. Various problems of the village life were discussed at these meetings. Gradually the representatives got over their shyness and began taking active part in the discussions. They are men of sound common sense, though steeped in tradition. They have their private responsibilities. They are willing to work for the common good, only up to the point where their personal interest does not suffer. For creating a new spirit in the people, there is need of more imaginative leadership. We shall need to re-educate our workers. If this orientation had to be given to our work. Like Shri Reddy our workers must have the capacity to do physical labour like any other Adivasi. He must be able to do manual work more efficiently. It is only through sharing of common work that a revolutionary spirit can be imparted to the people. Mere repetition of the mantra of Gramdan is not enough. We have to create new outlook and impart scientific knowledge and ability to them, so that they can discharge their day-to-day functions of development. Creating a new leadership on this line in every village and making the Gram Sabha function efficiently is the real need of the hour.

# SOME CONSIDERATIONS IN TRAINING FOR COMMUNITY DEVELOPMENT

THE FOLLOWING GENERAL discussion of training for community development is based on the definition of community development contained in the Twentieth Report of the Administrative Committee on Coordination to the economic and Social Council and on the classification of workers as outlined in that report.[1]

"The personnel to be trained usually fall into one or more of the following categories: (1) political and administrative leaders; (2) professional and technical personnel; (3) specialized auxiliary workers; (4) multipurpose or generalist village level workers; and (5) voluntary community leaders and workers.

"The content of the training of all these categories of personnel includes both special and general elements. The special elements consist of skills, elementary or more advanced, in the various technical subject matters. The general elements relate to mental attitudes and to broad methods and techniques of education and of organization; upon these latter will depend the very effectiveness of the process and of the success in inculcating the technical skills already mentioned."

Of the five categories of personnel mentioned above, the study kit is concerned mainly with the last three, who work directly at the people's level. These three categories of workers are referred to in the study kit as "field workers" or merely as "workers," to distinguish their needs and functions from those of personnel who serve in a supervisory capacity.

The purpose here is to find the common denominators in community development training for all types of field workers. In order to do so, there must be awareness of the interrelationship of various specialized services in community development and a recognition that many different workers can have a share in the process of stimulating growth. It is important that instructors themselves should be in agreement about the way in which different workers can work towards the achievement of common purposes. For this reason a brief review

---

[1] E/2931, annex III, paragraphs 1-6 and 31-32.

of the elements that contribute to community development is given below.

### The need for awareness of forces in community development

The term *development* itself implies a process of change and improvement. This change for the better results from the co-ordinated, continuing and purposive activity of: (*i*) the people; (*ii*) their government; and (*iii*) the appropriate technical and professional services.[1] It is not necessary for these forces to be simultaneously present from the start in order that development may take place. Each has in itself the capacity to produce some change. But when all three are working in combination, the results are more lasting and have a different stamp. Awareness of this by workers at all levels helps to make for better team-work.

### The need for recognition of the human element

The worker must also understand that the effects produced by these forces are complex because all three are basically human forces. In the eyes of the local community, the government is not necessarily a distant and impersonal power; it is made up of familiar individuals, each of whom has some authority from the senior administrative officer in the area right down to the operator of the drill well or other minor government agent on whose goodwill depends some simple but essential service. The individual's idea of the government as being just, indifferent or harsh, may be based on no more than his dealings with a single tax collector or police officer who personifies and exerts authority.

The community itself must be regarded as a human force with complex motivations. The part it plays in community development programmes depends on many intangible factors such as the self-respect and self-confidence of its individual members, their consciousness of common bonds and purposes, their attitudes to their problems and to outsiders who could help them.

All workers need to understand the importance of good human relations and to know how their own behaviour can affect people. To varying degrees they also need to understand the motivations and behaviour of the people with whom they work. This is not easy. Frequently what looks like stubborn and irrational opposition may have a very good basis in the cultural patterns of the community. What appears logical and necessary from the outsider's viewpoint may

---

[1] These services are mentioned separately because they may include non-governmental as well as governmental agencies.

be seriously disturbing to the community if it requires major changes in local traditions or beliefs. It may be quite clear to the worker that if technical improvements are to be sustained the people need to develop certain understandings, attitudes and mental qualities; yet the human mind is not always willing and ready to grow. Certainly the problem of "reaching" people is one that continually challenges the worker's powers of comprehension and adjustment. To succeed, he requires the maximum professional assistance.

### The need for training in practical skills

Establishing good human relations is only one part of the job. A second is to help bring about improvements in living standards and to strengthen, directly or indirectly, the people's economic potential. Even the worker who deals with only a small part of the life of an individual is faced with both these problems simultaneously whenever he is concerned with more than the mechanical performance of a task. The people's confidence and interest must be won in order to make practical improvements fully effective; conversely, the demonstration of practical improvements is part of the process of gaining the people's confidence, relieving tensions or evoking interest.

For most field workers, "reaching" people thus implies more than building friendships, being patient and understanding, or teaching through audio-visual devices; it includes showing in a practical way what can be done to improve levels of living; proving that the worker is not above doing the job with his own hands; and convincing by results rather than merely by persuasive talk. Accordingly, worker nowadays are being trained to use their hands as well as their minds and to do practical tasks well.

From these general observations, one may deduce more specific aims, of which the following paragraphs offer an analysis. However, since workers vary in skill, discernment and capacity to benefit from training, a word of caution is necessary.

Paragraphs (a) to (g) below show the ways in which contributions to community development can be made and are not to be considered as statements of goals attainable by all workers equally. The share of each field worker towards the fulfilment of these broad aims will vary with his functions; *e.g.*, the community educator has more scope than the literacy instructor for contributing to the development process; a health officer concerned with environmental sanitation has more opportunities than a vaccinator. Moreover, some workers have so little formal schooling that to train them in even the basic technical skills is difficult; to hope to teach them even the rudiments of social sciences along with technical skills may seem unrealistic. If training is envisaged in terms of a single course of pre-service or in-service instruction, this difficulty would apply to most workers in community development. Obviously, however, training must be visualized as a long-term process, including a variety of learning experiences; its duration, scope and method must be adjusted to the needs and abilities of particular workers. Clearly the effectiveness of the field worker in community development will depend on the quality and continuity of professional guidance and support that is available to him.

In the following paragraphs an attempt is made to describe in general terms the task of the community development personnel. Who is to carry out the task, how it can be done and what amount of supervision and training is required, are matters best referred to persons in the field.

## Common aims of workers in community development

### (a) *Winning the confidence of the people*

Many workers are recruited and trained to work in their own communities. To some extent they are already acquainted with community values and taboos, which is an advantage in getting themselves accepted by the people.[1]

The worker recruited from outside, however, needs special training in winning the people's confidence. His problem is to make the initial approach, to obtain essential information about the village without arousing suspicion or creating tensions; and to become accepted as a person of goodwill and practical insight.

While not all workers need to enter deeply into the life of the community, they still require the people's goodwill and support if their service, however simple, is to be fully utilised. The arrival of a vaccinator in a village may create anxiety in the community and give rise to superstitious rumours unless the health staff, with their knowledge of local beliefs and ways of life, can prepare the way for him.

Sometimes it takes many months to win the people's trust. The case illustrations in annex A show how the initial response of villagers may vary from complete indifference to threats of violence. These

---

[1] This statement cannot pass, of course, without qualification: not all persons who are born and brought up in a community make acceptable workers, and not all outside workers are necessarily looked upon with suspicion. To some extent the worker's specific function determines the facility with which he or she is integrated in community life. For instance, women home economics extension workers in many countries report that they have little or no difficulty in winning the support of women in the community. The Calioub Home Economics Programme for Rural Women in Egypt provides an illustration. (See case illustration No. 4, annex A.).

illustrations deal with the problem rather than with the process of getting accepted. More analytic study of the process is needed. It is encouraging that some training staff are already compiling simple materials on how to conduct an informal survey, what principles should govern individual interviewing or house-to-house visiting, how to work with local leaders, or in what way demonstrations and mass meetings can serve to establish rapport.

### (b) *Promoting the community spirit*

Besides sympathy between worker and people, there is a need to develop community spirit as a basis for action. A sense of belonging together already exists in many communities. Where it is absent or still very weak, community cohesiveness can be encouraged through activities that are within the scope of many different workers; *e.g.*, a community-wide literacy campaign, a scheme for community water-distribution or impromptu co-operative tasks such as the emergency repair of a bridge or the building of a recreation shed.

For this purpose the worker must be aware of the social forces in the community and the possible integrating or disrupting effects of the particular change with which he is concerned. In some communities, for example, the introduction of sanitary facilities has been regarded as a threat to the sweepers as an occupational group; in other, the pest control campaign has met with resistance due to certain traditional beliefs concerning insect life. In public administration, the use of tribal chiefs or local leaders as counterparts for the purposes of tax collection, book-keeping or the maintenance of law and order has sometimes resulted in a weakening of the traditional role of such leaders as protectors of the community.

Although the field worker must be made aware of these difficulties, he also needs to know how to overcome them, or to contend with them, if progress is to be made. At the very least he must know enough to be able to slow down the pace of improvements or to ask for specialized guidance before a crisis is brought about. The worker may also be able to help individuals or groups to consider their problems objectively and thereby develop a more receptive attitude towards changes that are needed for the common good.

Workers who travel about the village in the course of their normal duties can help to "knit" the community together. They come to know to the view of individuals and are able to bring to their attention the extent of common concern about particular subjects. Use is also made of recreational activities and group discussions to draw the people's attention to their shared needs and collective resources. Devices as simple as a flannelgraph, a chart or a wall-newspaper are used, in informal meetings, to stimulate community self-evaluation.

### (c) Aiding in co-operative action

As the community begins to see itself as a unit, it may feel the urge to do something about its problems but may not know how to begin.

Action by a large number of persons requires good organization and raises many questions. How does one overcome problems of diffidence, personal animosity, feuds or scepticism which hamper people's attempts to work together? If a committee is needed, how is it to be set up? What is the fair way of dividing responsibilities, costs and benefits in a project? Small problems of this type can mar an entire project and create new tensions instead of healthy co-operation.

Co-operative attitudes and habits are strengthened through informal action in many undertakings, whether the need is for draining swamp areas, constructing roads or organizing assistance for the handicapped members of the community. Many workers are, therefore, being given basic training in methods of working with groups. However, even those who do no work primarily with groups need some understanding of how to promote co-operation, e.g., on a person-to-person or family-to-family basis. Thus, the nutrition worker who encourages neighbours to exchange seeds for the kitchen garden is not merely extending the scope of his own services but is helping to build attitudes of mutual aid and mutual respect on which community work can be more firmly based.

### (d) Developing the individual's powers of constructive action

An ultimate aim in community development is the well-being and growth of the individual. In referring to the development of individual ability the term "self-help," is commonly used. However, there is the danger that "self-help," taken literally, may seem to stress the idea of individualism and overlook the concept of mutual help. For that reason there appears to be a need for a term which can be used more flexibly. "Constructive action" can be applied to both self-help and mutual aid. It may be expected that an individual who is positive in his attitudes and habits of thinking will be capable of reconciling his own needs for personal well-being with those of the group. A basic concern in community development must, therefore, be the building of constructive ways of living and thinking.

From the point of view of the field worker, the task of helping the individual to develop his latent powers must be conceived in practical terms such as helping him to think clearly and to apply his own mind to problems; to express or communicate his ideas with confidence;

and to relate more effectively to individuals and groups in his community.

To take, as an example, only one facet of personality: the ability to express oneself clearly and confidently. It is generally conceded that development programmes must take into account the people's expression of "felt needs"; but how can "felt needs" be ascertained? The problems which members of the community bring to the attention of the worker are not always those which they believe to be the most important. Fear of authority, the desire to please, ostentatiousness, or indifference to the programme are among the many reasons why people often state "needs" which are not truly 'felt" by them. Likewise there are many reasons why felt needs are sometimes left unspoken. An individual may prefer not to disclose his opinions out of respect for authority, distrust of the worker, or even his own lack of confidence in the worth of his opinion.[1] Some persons may feel secure in a passive conformity to mass thinking rather than to exert their minds to establish priorities among the problems in their environment.

There is a difference in the degree to which particular workers contribute to the development of the latent powers of the individual. All of them, however, can contribute in two ways: (1) through their own attitude to people, their genuine respect for them, their ability to meet them on an equal level without a false sense of superiority or excessive humility; and (2) through the way they give their service, allowing for maximum participation of the individual, and helping him to understand, to the extent that he is able, the technical basis of the assistance given. This implies that the worker needs to know how to teach new concepts and skills, however simple, in such a way that they are assimilated and not merely initiated by the learner. Sometimes it is not so much a problem of imparting a skill as of creating or producing the conditions that will draw out the skill in the individuals concerned. An informal educational function would thus seem inescapable for most workers in community development, particularly

---

[1] In a survey of social participation in Puerto Rico, a question was asked: "Jose, a neighbour, really wants to do something and feels that he could help to get people together but doesn't dare because he thinks he is just a little man who doesn't count much." This was followed with questions on how frequently this attitude was held and why. Almost 60 percent of the people felt that Jose's attitude was common and understandable for the following reasons: no one would pay any attention to them because they lacked status, were poor or had no schooling and could not express themselves well. Forty percent admitted that they themselves shared Jose's feelings of inadequacy. From Puerto Rico, Department of Education, *Preliminary Findings from a Survey of Social Participation in the Puerto Rican Rural Communities* (Puerto Rico, September 1952). p. 31.

where lack of formal education had stood in the way of full development of the latent powers and resources of the people, (Annex B. describes the educational content of health programmes in Colombia.)

*(e) Interpreting the changing needs of the community*

The remoteness forms the local community of many branches of government, of universities and professional bodies, makes it important that there should be continuity in the interpretation of local needs and resources and of local processes of change, since it is in the light of these that outside agents should plan the timing and nature of their contribution.

In the normal, day-to-day chain of communication between community and government, the vital link upon which both must rely is the worker in the community, who is in the best position to observe and report changes and developments taking place simultaneously on both fronts.

Similarly, the field worker acts as a link between the local people and the professional staff who help the community to translate its needs into a programme of action.

This interpretative function requires, among other things, training in the maintenance of objective records and skill in selecting and analysing current experience of change in the local community.

*( f ) Helping the community to make use of its resources*

Almost every community has unused resources that it does not recognize as such. This applies not only to material assets and technical services but also to human resources within the community itself.

It is often very difficult to bring about recognition of human resources because of local taboos, distrust or prejudice. An example of this is the failure of many communities to develop and use the resources of its women members. Another is resistance to the assimilation of migrant or refugee groups. Similarly the community may fail to recognize the labour potential of its unskilled members for producing commodities commonly imported into the village, merely because it is accustomed to a standard of efficiency comparable to that of more highly developed areas.

In drawing the community's attention to its unused powers, tact and caution are often necessary. If the process is to be both gradual and sustained, there must be common awareness among workers of the resources that need to be developed and some understanding of how interest can be promoted.

## (g) *Helping the community to effect practical improvements*

The improvement of the material side of community life is an important feature of community development, provided a sufficient measure of responsibility for the improvement is assumed by the people themselves. For this reason the worker who hopes to obtain the participation of the people in new practices must be aware that the community may have its own standards for judging what is "practical" and what is an "improvement".

In general, the community expects that the new method or device should produce quick and tangible results, that it should be suitable for use by average persons and that it does not conflict openly with local traditions and values. Although community work cannot always be limited by such standards, it is important that the worker should be sympathetically aware of the reasons underlying the people's responsiveness or unresponsiveness to an improvement, and know how and to what extent he can lead them beyond their accustomed ways of thinking and to appreciate other values.[1]

It is also useful for the worker to understand the economic implications of the proposed improvement. He must know what it will cost, what economic benefits it can bring and whether it is worth the necessary expense of time and energy. The immediate purpose is to protect the people themselves from financial loss and, more positively, to increase their economic gains. A long-term purpose is to associate the enterprises of small communities more and more with the process of national economic development. For this, training in broader economic principles is given to some workers who are capable of assimilating it.

---

[1] There is a clear need for research in simple improvements that meet the standards set by village communities—research that is usually beyond the ability of the field worker and for which training staff can seldom spare the time.

# IN-SERVICE TRAINING ESSENTIAL

ANY GIVEN BLOCK staff assigned the responsibility for assisting the block panchayat samiti and the village panchayat in Community Development programmes can be said to be made up of the best available people at the time of their recruitment, training and assignment to the block. Whether they match their opportunities and grow in competence depends on whether or not all members of the block staff recognize that each new experience is either successful or unsuccessful—that each can in itself be a teaching-learning experience. If the block staff as a team will take his orientation and the block development officer will guide the staff members in learning, from their daily experiences, better ways of meeting similar and new situations, the staff can be said to be in in-service training while it works.

For the block staff to continually consider its working assignment as also a training opportunity requires the highest of leadership from the block development officer. Furthermore, it requires a great deal of give and take from the entire staff. It requires the highest possible dedication from the staff members and an appreciation of the fact that the job entrusted to them is so important to India's future that they must succeed.

In order that the working experience may also be an in-service teaching and learning experience, each block staff meeting must be conducted on a democratic, seminar discussion basis. Each member of the staff must be made to feel at ease, to tell fully and freely of his experiences and to expect other to react on a sympathetic yet critical basis. There can be no place for dogmatic decision which the staff is directed to do things a given way. The gram sevak should feel as to raise issues and express opinions as the block development officer or any of the technical staff of the block.

In addition to the general block staff meetings, the block development officer should invite people from outside the block to sit with the staff from time to time as resource people, when the staff will engage in specialized siminar discussions on such issues as changing village attitudes, searching out and training village leaders, evaluation of staff accomplishments, developing effective panchayats, etc.

The block staff can also provide in-service training opportunities by scheduling occasional staff seminars with the village panchayats, involving give and take discussions with village people on special problems. These village-staff seminars will bring specialized staff members into direct contact with the villager in a way they would otherwise miss.

The gram sevaks can learn much from each other if each is definitely scheduled to spend one day a month with one of his fellow gram sevaks. The block development officer and the entire technical staff of the block should reserve the village nearest to the block headquarters as a continuous in-service training laboratory where they will work together as a team in guiding the village in allround development.

When looking outside the block for in-service training programmes the block development officer should be alert to successful experiences in adjoining blocks. He should arrange for visits to these blocks by various staff members who can personally profit from the experience as well as interpret it to the rest of the block staff upon their return. As a guiding principle the outside study experience should be used to correct the weakness of the staff.

When it comes to State and inter-state in-service training seminars the block development officer should have cross representation from the block staff present. There should in all cases be a block staff seminar following the return of a staff member who has attended an outside in-service training programme. If this process is systematically followed there will be a continuous feed-back of new thinking coming from the outside which will continue to broaden the horizon of the entire staff.

States should organize a wide variety of short courses for in-service training. The objective should be to have all members of the block staff attend at least one refresher in-service training course at least once every five years. This will be in addition to the various steps that the Union Ministry of Community Development & Cooperation is taking for in-service training of the Block Staff under the given special training in Extension Training Centres. The Block Development Officer is also given such training in Orientation and Study Centres. Special seminars are also held when Pradhans and Block Development Officers are brought together to discuss their mutual efforts in solving common problems. At district levels Collectors and Deputy Collectors are sent to the Central Institute of Study and Research in Community Development at Mussoorie for the same purpose.

In conclusion it can be said that in-service training of all kinds must be vigorously planned and carefully directed if the Community Development programmes are to avoid the fate of becoming institutionalized on a low plateau of thinking and working.

For staff members whose normal duty is to attend to one aspect of development programmes, some opportunity should be provided to learn of the nature, though not the techniques, of work done by their colleagues. Not only better comradeship, but mutual assistance would result from this course.

# TRAINING AND EDUCATION

THE TRAINING OF various functionaries, both official and non-official, engaged in the implementation of development programmes has always been recognised as vital to enable them to improve their competence and to understand and respond to the changing problems and needs of the programmes. With the introduction of Panchayati Raj in the majority of States, the need for training at various levels has become all the more urgent. The training programme have, therefore, not only been maintained on a countrywide basis, but further augmented and intensified where necessary.

## National Council of Study and Research in Community Development and Panchayati Raj

The National Council of Study and Research in Community Development and Panchayati Raj, which meets from time to time to review the progress of training programmes, held two meetings in March and December, 1963. Besides reviewing the progress made, it also considered the training schemes to be taken up during the Fourth Plan period. The proposal to convert the National Institute of Community Development into an autonomous registered body was welcomed by the Council.

## National Institute of Community Development

The apex organisation for training, the National Institute of Community Development, continued its programmes of orientation of key personnel, study and research in problems of Community Development and Panchayati Raj and training of Instructors from various Training Centres. In pursuance of the decision taken earlier to move the National Institute to Hyderabad, its Study and Research Wings have already been shifted there, pending construction of the Institute's own buildings which is in progress at Rajendranagar. The first Orientation Course for 1964 will commence at the new venue on the 23rd March, 1964. During 1963 six orientation courses were conducted. In view of the increasing importance of programmes pertaining to Tribal Development Blocks, one of the courses was specially devoted to 'Approaches to Tribal Development'.

Research Projects, both of an applied and of a fundamental nature continued to be promoted by the institute. In collaboration with the Training Centres the Institute completed two all-India studies on 'Perception of National Emergency in Village India' and 'Village Volunteer Force and Defence Labour Bank'. Nine research Projects entrusted to different Universities were in progress (list attached at Annexure VIII). Projects assigned to Training Centres had to be slowed down owing to the Emergency. Four studies were completed during the year and three in progress (Annexure IX). The Institute's Clearing House of information on Community Development brought out two volumes of its quarterly digest and the fifth supplement to the Bibliography on Community Development.

A seminar on Emerging Patterns of Rural Leadership in South East Asia, sponsored jointly by the UNESCO Research Centre, Delhi and the Institute, was held at Mussoorie. Besides participants from India, delegates from Malaya, the Phillippines and Pakistan attended. The Seminar surveyed the present studies on rural leadership in the different countries of the region and examined the significance of such studies for programmes of planned change.

The Instruction Wing of the Institute conducted two courses for Instructors of the Training Centres, one course for District Panchayat Officers and two courses for Sub-Divisional Officers during 1963. The duration of the training course for the Instructors was increased from three to four months and a half. The content of the course was also modified to cover a brief inter-disciplinary instruction in social sciences, besides the theory and practice of training methods. With a view to ensuring an effective follow up this, a team headed by the Honorary Adviser on Training has been constituted.

Particular attention is paid at the Instruction Wing to providing training aids to Instructors from the Training Centres. Apart from regular courses on educational psychology, communication and teaching methods, the Instruction Wing undertakes the compilation of reference material for use by the Instructors. In pursuance of the latter programme a special workshop on 'Dynamics of Human Behaviour' was organised, the report of which has been circulated to the Training Centres. A number of guide books on subjects relating to Community Development were under preparation. The programme for training in the use of audio-visual aids is kept under constant review.

### Orientation & Study Centres

The ten Orientation & Study Centres continued to function during the year. It has been decided to establish one Orientation & Study Centre in each State by the end of the Third Plan period. Accordingly, four more Centres, one each in Maharashtra, Orissa,

Assam and Kerala, will be set up. The Centres for Maharashtra and Orissa are to be set up during the coming year at Poona and Bhubaneswar. The existing Training Centres conducted three series of orientation, job and study courses each during the year. Following the Emergency, the duration of the courses was slightly reduced and the time saved was devoted to field studies of all-India programmes for which the teaching staff was given special training in research methodology at courses conducted by the National Institute.

### Tribal Orientation & Study Centres

As the number of Tribal Development Blocks is fast increasing, it has been found necessary to provide additional facilities for orientation and training in tribal life and culture to various categories of the staff required to work in these Blocks. The Orientation & Study Centre and the Tribal Orientation & Study Centre at Ranchi were amalgamated into one administrative unit with effect from the 1st of April, 1963. Three courses of four months duration were held at the Centre during the year. The Orientation & Study Centre at Jabalpur has been similarly re-organised and is expected to start functioning as a Tribal Orientation & Study Centre from May next It will be followed by the Orientation & Study Centre at Udaipur, which has also been converted into a combined institution for tribal and general training. A Tribal Orientation & Study Centre will be set up at Bhubaneswar during the coming year. Necessary staff for these Tribal Training institutions is being recruited.

### Social Education Organisers Training Centres

Following the assignment of composite roles to Social Education Organisers in some of the States, the last Annual Conference on Community Development laid stress on the need for training in social education to the composite functionaries. Accordingly, special courses were conducted for them at a number of Social Education Organisers Training Centres, in addition to the regular job courses. All the eight Training Centres, however, the duration of their courses was slightly reduced to enable them to take up the field studies during break periods. The Social Education Organisers' Training Centres also organised, as in the previous year, special courses for the orientation of teacher-educators in Community Development. It has since been decided to hold training camps for youth leaders also at these Centres, besides the Gram Sevika Training Centres.

### Mukhya Sevika Training Centres

The ten Mukhya Sevika Training Centres continued to handle job

courses for Mukhya Sevikas. The duration of the courses was reduced from 10½ to 9 months, following the Emergency. These Training Centres have, in addition, been selected as venues for conducting
one month camps for the training of associate women workers.

### Training of Extension Officers (Industries)

The proposal to integrate the separate training programmes for
Extension Officers (Industries), conducted at Khadigram, Udyog
Vidyalayas and Small Industries Service Institutes, was examined in
consultation with the Ministry of Commerce and Industry and the
Khadi & Village Industries Commission. It has been decided to con-
duct integrated training courses, on a pilot basis, at the Khadigram
Udyog Vidayalayas at Nilokheri and Rajendranagar (Hyderabad).
During the year 219 Extension Officers were trained in the existing
separate courses, bringing the number of those trained since the inception of the training programme to 3,159.

### Higher Training of Selected Gramsevaks

The programme for providing opportunities of higher education
to Village Level Workers was continued during the year. 77 scholarships for selected Gramsevaks were offered to State Governments
during the year 1963-64 for diploma courses at Rural Institutes and
another 75 scholarships for graduate courses at Universities. The
number of scholarships awarded under the scheme since 1961 thus
came to 329. Considering the importance of the programme, it has
been decided to double the number of scholarships offered annually,
during the concluding years of the Third-Five-Year Plan.

Following the decision of the National Development Council at
its meeting in November, 1962 that in view of the emergent need for
stepping up agricultural production the Gramsevak should devote all
this time to this work, the syllabus for the training of Gramsevaks
was revised.

### Institutional Training Programme—A Review

(Particulars of training courses and the number of functionaries
trained are given in Annexure X.)

Proper utilisation of the training facilities provided by the Ministry at various training institutions is essential not only for ensuring
that adequately trained personnel is made available for manning
posts at different levels, but also for putting the training capacity to
optimum use. Special efforts continued to be made towards this
end. There was significant improvement in the number of persons
deputed by the State Governments for training during the year, not-

withstanding difficulties created by the Emergency.

Another important factor affecting training programmes relates to the calibre of the teaching staff. Constant effort is made to improve their skills. Besides being trained at regular instruction courses run by the National Institute for all of them, selected Instructors are deputed under a Ford Foundation Scheme, for advanced subject-matter training at various institutions of higher learning in foreign countries. Six members of the staff left for training overseas during the year and arrangments were made for deputing another seven during the coming year. An Assessment Committee periodically reviews the performance of the staff: the deserving are selected for continued retention.

**Five-Village Scheme**

The work done by the Training Centres is related as much to its academic content as, if not more, to its practical orientation to field programmes. With a view to enriching the training programme with field experience on a continuing basis, the staff and trainees at the Training Centres undertake intensive promotion of development activities through extension techniques, in five selected villages in the vicinity. Along with the usual development activities, the Five-Village Scheme aims at covering each of the villages fully under at least one selected programme suitable to the village. The progress of the scheme, as of other training programmes, is reviewed regularly at Conferences of the Principals and Directors of the Training Centres. Two such Conferences were held during the year.

**Field Visits**

Various other steps are also taken as an integral part of the training programme to adapt it to the growing requirements of development in the field. Members of the staff and trainees from the Training Centres are deputed from time to time to blocks and villages to study their programmes in actual working situations. A coordinated programme of study and follow-up tours by Heads and instructors of the Training Centres has been devised to enable them to visit, during off-course periods, not only sister institutions, but also other places where outstanding work may have been done in the execution of development projects and programmes. It has been arranged that the National Institute should, on the conclusion of the tours, organise workshops to pool and exchange experiences gained.

**Training of Foreigners**

The Indian Programme of Community Development has created considerable interest in countries all over the world. During the year

49 administrators and field workers from 26 countries visited India for study and training in various aspects of the programme under the Colombo Plan and schemes sponsored by the United Nations Technical Assistance Board and the United States Agency for Internation Development, etc. The list of countries, together with the number of persons who came for training, is given at Annexure XI.

## Study and Orientation of Non-officials

### *Training of Gram Sahayaks*

The programme of training of Gram Sahayaks (village leaders) taken up in 1957, continued during the year. The number of Gram Sahayaks Training Camps held during the period October 1962 to June 1963 was 13,455. Altogether over six lakhs Gram Sahayaks were trained at these camps, bringing the total number trained from the inception of the programme to about 53 lakhs.

To make the coverage of this programme more broad-based, it is proposed to re-organise the Gram Sahayaks Camps in the coming year. An integrated programme for the Gram Sahayaks, young farmers and selected members of the Village Volunteer Force will be focussed on youth work and agricultural production programme. The duration of these camps will be five days, instead of the present three. Participants will be encouraged to come forward for higher training under more advanced subject-matter training programme.

## Training of Youth Workers and Leaders

The scheme for training of youth workers and leaders initiated in 1961 was slowed down in some States due to the Emergency. It is now being stepped up. The scheme envisages organisation of five training camps at each of the 100 Gram Sevak Training Centres. By the end of June last, 6045 workers had been trained at 226 such camps. In addition, eight days training camps for members of Yuvak Mandals are proposed to be organised in the 222 Applied Nutrition Programme Blocks for giving combined training in Applied Nutrition and Youth Programmes.

Associate Women Workers' Training Camps—25,000 Associate Women Workers will be trained in the country during the remaining years of the current Plan. Owing to the Emergency, only a limited start could be made during the year under review. This programme is also being stepped up.

Study Camp for Legislators—A regional study camp of Members of Parliament and State Legislators from the States of Andhra Pradesh, Kerala, Madras, Maharashtra and Mysore was held at Hyderabad in August, 1963.

Panchayati Raj Training Centres—109 Panchayati Raj Training Centres were sanctioned to various States/Union Territories for the training of elected members and official functionaries of Panchayati Raj institutions. Of these, 80 have already been set up, including 30 started during the year. The State Governments have undertaken to establish another 53 Centres during the coming year. The programme aims, in due course, at providing every district with a Centre of its own.

Model syllabi for the training of members of Nayaya Panchayats and their Secretaries at the Panchayati Raj Training Centres have been communicated to the State Governments.

As recommended by the last Annual Conference on Community Development, the pattern of Central assistance for Panchayati Raj Training Centres has been liberalised by dislinking the payment of establishment charges from the number of trainees attending courses. A sub-committee of the National Council of Study and Research in Community Development and Panchayati Raj also examined the working of these institutions, and made comprehensive recommendations for further strengthening and stabilizing the programme. The recommendations have just been considered by all at All India Seminar on Training in Panchayati Raj held at Nilokheri.

## Central Institute of Training & Research in Panchayati Raj

The Central Institute of Training and Research in Panchayati Raj, run under the auspices of the All-India Panchayati Parishad, organised during the year three courses of three months' duration each for training Principals/Instructors of Panchayati Raj Training Centres. In all 58 Instructors were trained at these courses, bring the total number trained, since the establishment of the Institute, to 200. Members of the Institute's staff also undertook visits to selected Panchayati Raj Training Centres in the States for following up the training imparted.

## Training in Applied Nutrition

An all-India Seminar on Applied Nutrition was held for a week at Bakshi-Ka-Talab, Lucknow for State Nutrition Officers, State Agricultural Officers and Officers in charge of Applied Nutrition, Youth and Women's programmes. Details of the training programmes for various official and non-official functionaries at regional and lower levels in the State have been finalised. The programme down to the village level is expected to be completed by the end of the year.

# TRAINING PROGRAMMES—A SUMMARY

| Sl. No. | Description of the Training Centre (figures in bracket give the number of Training Centres) | Category of person trained | Number trained during the year | Total trained |
|---|---|---|---|---|
| 1 | 2 | 3 | 4 | 5 |
| 1 | National Institute of Community Development (1) | Senior officials and selected non-officials like M.Ps., M.L.As. | 219 | 1178 |
| 2 | National Institute of Community Development (Instruction Wing) (1) | (a) Instructors at Training Centres | 28 | 161 |
| | | (b) District Panchayat Officers/ S.D.Os. | 82 | 315 |
| 3 | Orientation & Study Centres (10) | (a) B.D.Os., E.Os., Non-officials (Orientation Training) | 1481 | 8067 |
| | | (b) B.D.Os., (Job Training) | 551 | 3518 |
| | | (c) B.D.Os., District Officers, non-officials (Study) | 717 | 2582 |
| 4 | Tribal Orientation and Study Centres (1) | B.D.Os., E.Os., (Agri.), S.E.Os. and Mukhya Sevikas | 77 | 103 |
| 5 | Social Education Organisers Training Centres (8) | (a) S.E.Os. (Job Course) | 296 | 4065 |
| | | (b) Principals of Teachers Training Colleges | 342 | 1135 |

| Sl. No. | Description of the Training Centre (*figures in bracket give the number of Training Centres*) | Category of person trained | Number trained during the year | Total trained |
|---|---|---|---|---|
| 1 | 2 | 3 | 4 | 5 |
| | | (c) Teacher - Educators of Training Colleges | 390 | 1276 |
| | | (d) S.E.O-cum-P.E.Os. (From U.P. and Punjab) | 69 | 169 |
| 6 | Mukhya Sevikas Training Centres (10) | Mukhya Sevikas (Job Course) | 301 | 2426 |
| 7 | Small Industries Service Institutes (4) | Extension Officers (Industries) (Job) | 219 | 3159 |
| 8 | Khadi Gramodyog Vidyalayas (5) | | | |
| 9 | Gram Sevak Training Centres (98) | Gram Sevaks | 9147 | 61601 |
| 10 | Gram Sevikas Training Centres (47) | Gram Sevikas | 897 | 5771 |
| 11 | Orientation Training Centres for health personnel (3) | Medical Officers, Sanitary Inspectors and others | 205 | 3314 |
| 12 | Central Institute of Panchayati Raj (1) | Principals/Instructors of P.R.T.Cs. | 58 | 200 |

# TEACHING-LEARNING PROCESS IN INSTITUTIONAL TRAINING OF COMMUNITY DEVELOPMENT WORKERS

## J. S. Mathur

### Community Development

COMMUNITY DEVELOPMENT IN INDIA has assumed vast proportions not only in the programme content but also in the depth of approach to the problem of development of individual villager in the group and community setting. The rural community to-day is in a stage of transition from the old order to the new goals of democratic socialism. It is now given to the task of the elected representatives of the people and other leaders in the community and the entire range of community development personnel employed by the government as well as voluntary organisations to work towards the objectives of community development which may be briefly stated as follows:

Economic goals include higher standards of living for the entire population, specially of the less-privileged sections, equitable distribution of national income and wealth, achieving a high rate of investment of part of the national income, provision of full employment and balanced regional growth making for optimum utilisation of resources in the community.

Political goals include grass roots organisation, building up tiers of political authority, providing for balancing of decentralisation with appropriate centralisation at different levels, promoting consensus participation and delegation of authority in consonance with responsibility entrusted to different tiers. The political structure of the society would balance freedom with discipline and be ultimately linked with the social and cultural norms. In other words the newly created panchayati raj institutions have to develop organic links with the existing community institutions and values.

Social goals include an increease upon class structure providing for vertical mobility, equality of opportunity, and social services such as education, health, housing and social security for the entire community irrespective of income and status differentials. This is not possible without the emergence of a common framework of new social values and rise of the social man based on dignity of the individual personality in the context of social responsibility and a well-developed social conscience.

Cultural goals include development of local arts, literature, folk music and drama, sports and recreational programmes promoting individual participation in a variety of activities and not merely passive observation. These would ultimately make for national integration through cultural diversification and assimilation to be promoted through the basic concept of unity in diversity.

### Training Programme

×         ×         ×         ×         ×

Training of field workers is an essential part of the policy for personnel development, other constituents of the policy being scientific and rational recruitment, induction, salary scales, security of tenure and promotional opportunities. Training centres have to function as centres of intense intellectual and practical activity geared to the dual requirements of linking and integrating the ever-growing theoretical framework of various social sciences with the changing requirements of the actual field conditions.

×         ×         ×         ×         ×

### Five Basic Questions

Teaching-learning process in training, like any other educational situation, relies on the following five basic questions and attempts to translate the import of these questions into practical live learning experiences. These questions are: (*i*) In what areas do we as staff expect changes in the participants to happen during the course? In other works, what are our objectives? (*ii*) How can we ensure that the participants also share the common objectives as perceived by staff of the training centres? In other words, how do we motivate the participants so that a congruence of values and purposes is brought about? (*iii*) What kinds of learning experiences should be provided so that the common objectives are achieved? In other words, what is the exact content of the syllabus and the training programme? (*iv*) How can we be sure that the changes as visualised are actually occurring as a result of the learning experience? In other words, what are the evaluation methods and procedures (*v*) What kinds of administrative support, staff relationships and physical arrangements at the training centre promote the above objectives. In other words, what are the organisational and administrative methods and procedures to ensure attainment of the common objectives?

## Lag between Training and the Field Conditions

It would not be inappropriate at this stage to point out a basic dichotomy in field conditions and training programmes. The objectives of community development being common to both, many times some of the basic principles of community development, for example, reliance on promotional and educational activities, gradual emergence of capacities for growth, get conditioned by the emergent requirements of a developing society with inherent shortages of human and material resources. Productivity is sought to be developed through administrative pressure and manipulation methods. The field personnel view the training centre staff as visionaries and ivory tower observers. While the criticism that the training programme lags behind the field requirements has a grain of truth in it, it is equally true that the field programmes lag behind the basic principles of community development of which the training centres are, more often than not, the true exponents. Several changes in policies and administrative rearrangements in line with the basic entire learning process gets thwarted, may even negatived entirely.

×        ×        ×        ×        ×

## Principles of Teaching-Learning Process

With overall understanding of some of the vital factors affecting teaching, learning process, what follows is an outline of some of the fundamental principles of learning as applied to training centre and drawn from principles of adult learning, extension and social work. These principles can briefly be indicated as follows:

(1) Teaching-learning process is a joint enterprise, responsibility for clarifying objectives, outlining programme content and running the course being shared between staff and participants.

(2) Each individual learner at his own pace and according to his capacity, interest and motivation.

(3) Learner learns as a whole, *i.e.*, the total personality of the earner has to be completely involved in the learning process. Such learning is integral learning and quality of learning experience gets conditioned by response of the individual learner.

(4) Learning has to begin at the existing level of understanding of the learner.

(5) Learning how to learn is more important than merely acquiring specific knowledge content and skills as the participants has to function independently in the field subsequently.

×        ×        ×        ×        ×

**Teaching-Learning Methods**

It would have become clear by now that there are certain basic and fundamental requirements of the institutional training in which teaching-learning process is sought to be promoted through various kinds of learning experiences. Teaching-learning methods have to fit in with the overall requirements of the training programme and are the most suitable links between the dual requirements of syllabus on the one hand and of participants on the other.

The teaching-learning methods give a positive framework and content to the quality of formal and informal relationships between staff and participants. The individual participant relates himself to the staff members individually and as a member of a group. The staff, in turn, also learn to relate to participants in individual and group formal and informal relationships.

The number of methods of training is quite large. It is suggested that in a single course, all need not, or rather should not, be practised together. The participants' objectives of community development are urgently called for so that suitable opportunities and conditions are created for trained personnel to really practise what they learn in training centres. Training centres through direct experience in the field and through appropriate field studies and research programmes can and should be able to effectively contribute to re-shaping of policies and administrative framework of the entire community development programme.

**Participants' Viewpoint**

The task of motivation is more difficult in a training centre than in adult education centre to the compulsory nature of attendance in the former. He comes to the training centre with a smug satisfaction, confidence and self-assurance that the ways of behaviour he has acquired through commonsense, advice and directives from the superior officials are quite alright and he feels that there is no need for him to change. He has a special dislike for bookish knowledge and expects the staff to know and does not have sufficient confidence in capacity of staff to teach him anything worthwhile. On the other hand, finding the existing ways of behaviour as not completely successful, he also wants to learn new things, expects change. He thus exhibits the phenomena of ambivalent attitude towards change *i.e.* resistance to change as well as an inherent desire in favour of change.

The problem of motivation at a training centre lies at the crux of whole training programme and has to be viewed not only from the point of view of the individual personality with its biological, emotional, aesthetic, intellectual and social aspects but also of basic human needs of recognition, status, approval and love. An atmosphere of positive human relations at a training centre provides the incentives for learning and initiates a process of self-actualisation and growth. Human relations and the series of learning experience through various teaching methods provide conditions for extrinsic motivation of the participant and this in turn promotes development of intrinsic motivation which is carried beyond the limited environment of the training centre.

## Human Relations and Training

The entire teaching-learning process is thus conditioned by the quality of human relations that can be viewed from the points of view of intra-staff, inter-staff-participant and intra-participant relationships. The major part of learning takes place within the personalities of individual participants and through the inter-actional process among the participants themselves. The staff can only hope to deal with the learning process as observable in the areas of inter-staff-participant formal and informal relationships. We expect the quality of human relationships at a training centre to be basically conditioned by the quality of human relationships that exist among the staff. A staff riddent with cliques, low morale, authoritarian handling by the head of the institution, favouritism, nepotism, and back-biting can never inspire the participants. They are able to sense the entire situation, strive for personal favours, and themselves divide into cliques. They would otherwise have a sense of bewilderment and get lost in methodology rather than in content and quality of learning experience as a whole.

# OBJECTIVES IN THE TEACHING OF COMMUNITY ORGANIZATION AND COMMUNITY DEVELOPMENT

*(The Working Group was attended by social work educators invited from selected countries in the region in their individual capacity as experts having considerable experience in the development of local teaching materials. They were from Australia, India, Indonesia, Japan, Malaysia, Pakistan, Phillippines & Thailand.)*

THE MAIN OBJECTIVE in teaching community organization and community development in schools of social work is to develop in the student adequate knowledge of the community in which he works and the attitudes and skills required for working the communities. As the role of a social worker in a community setting is that of an agent of change, his training should enable him to appreciate diversity in the culture and value systems of both the rural and urban communities in which he may find himself working. Besides, as an agent of change, though he supports progressive values he should, nevertheless, be prepared to accept resistance by people to change, as well as the limitations of existing patterns of service with which he has to work. He should also accept tension and conflicts as a normal part of group and inter-group relations and social growth.

Some of the other objectives are :

(*i*) to develop in the students the ability to ascertain by study a community's strengths and weaknesses and to discover its needs and problems, as a basis for subsequent action;

(*ii*) to help students to form a professional relationship with the community, to enable them to identify some of its particular problems and to organize it on the basis of its felt needs;

(*iii*) to help students to acquire knowledge of available community resources, both internal and external, and enable them to co-ordinate and mobilize these resources for the benefit of the people;

(*iv*) to help students to locate, identify, develop and involve local leaders in planning and execution of programmes and activities;

(*v*) to help students to overcome dependency on the government or outside voluntary agencies in developing community self-help projects and to inculcate in them faith in democratic methods as a way of solving mass problems faced by communities.

# PROBLEMS OF TRAINING

## B. Mukherji

I HAVE BEEN asked to contribute an article to the special training number of Kurukshetra presumably because I was associate closely and over a fairly long period with the work of training in the Ministry of Community Development. But as I have now been out of touch with the programme for a whole year, I apprehend that some of the things I may say here may not be quite up-to-date. The Community Development programme has been a dynamic programme, fast moving, fast changing and fast growing. To meet its needs the training programme has, therefore, also been changing and growing.

### Magnitude of the Task

The big transformation in the role of the Government administration which the Community Development programmes requires creates the need for training the personnel engaged in the programme. The entire administration, both the generalist and the technical sides of it, has to be geared to the task, for the Community Development programme is an integral part of the Five Year Plans and of the total effort to convert our State into a Welfare Organ. And since Community Development depends equally on a large body of well informed, well meaning and active non-official leaders at all levels and in every branch of the programme, these leaders too need training, as we came to realise before long. The biggest problem of training arises, therefore, from the magnitude of the task, that we have to train not only the personnel directive working on the programme, but everyone in the administration from the village level up to the national level, in every department, generalist or technical, and a vast army of non-official leaders from those functioning in the humble village panchayat and a Panchayat Samiti to those working in the Zila Parishad, in the State Legislatures and in the National Parliament. And we have also to train leaders in the Cooperatives, in the farmers' organisation, and in the women and youth organisations. We have even to train farm leaders and the village school teachers. In fact, the training programme at the village level merges into the programme of Adult Education or education for citizenship, the scope for which is limitless. It can thus

be realised how great is the magnitude of the programme and therefore, the problems that this creates.

We began with the training of three new kinds of functionaries which the programme had introduced *viz.*, the B.D.O., the
V.L.W., and the S.E.O. One by one we had to take up the training of
other classes of personnel, such as, Extension Officers for Agriculture
and Animal Husbandry, Co-operation, Panchayats, Industries, for
Welfare of Women and Children. We soon found that unless some
kind of orientation was given to the officers at the district level, the
block level officers did not get proper guidance and encouragement
from the former, and at times even their work was hampered by lack
of appreciation of the methods and processes of community development on the part of the district level officers. Thus we had to take up
the orientation training of the district level officers. For the same
reason, it became necessary to take care of the training of even higher
level officers functioning at the State and the National levels.

### Training Courses

It was obvious that the same kind of training course could not be
given to all classes of officers. We had to take into account the educational and intellectual level of each kind of personnel to be trained,
the nature of the job performed by them and the measure of their
responsibility. It was also clear that we could not possibly have a very
large variety of training courses to suit every single class of personnel.
We had, therefore, to evolve a pattern of training, having a manageable number of courses of different kinds, as could broadly meet the
requirements of the major categories. The United Nations has divided
the persons needing training into five categories.

(1) political and administrative leaders,
(2) professional and technical personnel,
(3) specialised auxiliary workers,
(4) multipurpose or generalist V.L.W.s and
(5) voluntary community leaders and workers.

This classification takes care of both official and non-official
workers. Those in the first category function largely at the policy level,
those in the second, largely at the supervisory level, those in the third
at the level of field execution, and those in the last two categories at
the village level. Our pattern of training as it has gradually developed
now takes care of all these categories. In our programme the role of
the workers can be broadly divided into three classes—that of the community development worker or catalyst and stimulator, that of the
extension worker and that of the technicians or specialists. These or
some of these roles have been combined in varying degrees in the

duties of different functionaries and our training programme has taken that into account.

## Orientation Training

Before long we were able to evolve what should be the common content of training for community development workers, official and non-official, and this we squeezed into an 'orientation course' of a fairly short duration which I prefer to call the 'basic course in community development'. I am referring to the six weeks orientation training given in the Orientation Training Centres to the B.D.Os. Block Level Extension Officers, and some other officials and non-officials. This orientation course deals with the following aspects:

- (*a*) understanding the village situation—economic, social, cultural, and political;
- (*b*) understanding the Community Development Programme, its philosophy and objectives:
- (*c*) principles, philosophy and techniques of Extension as applied to community development;
- (*d*) the meaning and application of Social Education to community development;
- (*e*) techniques of programme planning;
- (*f*) group mobilisation and community organisation with particular reference to panchayats, co-operatives, etc.;
- (*g*) the administrative pattern and the problems of administration arising from community development; and
- (*h*) evaluating a programme of community development.

The same kind of course is given in the Central Institute for study and Research in Community Development at Mussoorie to higher level officers and members of State Legislatures and of the Parliament.

## Heavy Syllabus

It can be easily imagined how difficult it is to compress all the above subjects into a course of six weeks duration. And this has given rise to one of the big problems of training. The U.N. Evaluation Mission has criticised our training syllabi as excessively heavy. The criticism is valid to some extent. But a very important aspect not generally recognised is that our principal orientation courses have also to serve to some extent the purpose of educational and informational courses. The majority of the administrative personnel suffer from the handicaps of possessing an exclusively urban orientation and little knowledge of the rural people and rural areas. Many may be altogether lacking in the knowledge of the social sciences not having done any of these in college. These deficiencies have to be corrected to the extent possible by the training courses, particularly in the case of political and administrative leaders and professional and technical personnel, and to a lesser extent, in the case of specialised auxiliary workers. The normal administration of which alone most of the trainees have knowledge, and are atuned to work in, functions largely in a routine fashion and on established often stereotyped lines. It does not require much thinking on human problems, the why and how of issues. That a programme of community development cannot be worked well on such a pattern of functioning would need no elaboration. There is need, in my opinion, to throw into our training courses some theory taken from the Social Sciences and to relate these to the principles and practices of community development. I have been always pleading for the creation of an ideological base for our programme of community development, which will build up peoples' faith in it. The basic training must have an inspirational quality. In addition, the training has to pass on information regarding Government policies, schemes etc., so that the workers can see their operational field and responsibilities more clearly. And lastly the workers have to be given some skill in working with people, as individuals, as groups and as communities.

## Education vs. Training

It would be obvious that the syllabus will be heavy what is wrong is not that it is so but that we are covering it into too short a period. The rapid pace set for expansion of the Community Development programmes requiring the training of very large number of officers within a tight time schedule has been responsible for keeping the period of training so short. I have no doubt that as we gain more and more experience in conducting the training courses and the body of knowledge grows through research, case study etc., the content, quality and method of conducting this course will keep on improving. The duration of the course will have to be lengthened. Today, we are not in a position to do so because of the large numbers that have to be trained within a very short period. But when lengthening of the course becomes possible, how long it should be, will have to be very carefully worked out. This problem of devising a good basic course for training in community development, which can be given alike to officials and non-officials, is one of the big problems which the training programme has been facing right from the beginning, and will continue to face until we have acquired enough experience and knowledge in this field to solve it. The basic course should give to the worker, particularly to one working at the higher level, the inquisitiveness to learn more and more on his own from the disciplines that have a bearing on the

Community Development programme, and while he works in the field and grapples with the practical problems he should be able to relate the theories with the practices and vice versa. If the basic training does not achieve this, it fails in an important purpose. We cannot pack into this course all the knowledge that the worker has to have, nor through it help him to acquire all the understanding of the programme and develop all the skill he needs. But it should indicate to him broadly the field of knowledge which he has to make his own, give him the correct approach towards his work and towards the people and thus help him to go on training himself as he does the work. If we attempt to get too much for immediate application to the workers' field of work out of the initial training, we will be making a mistake if we attempt to make the initial training too comprehensive in its educational content. The essential course and a training course has to be maintained and yet in the basic training course of the kind I visualise there will be some features both of an educational and a training course. How to balance these two is a delicate problem.

## Job Training

Distinguishable from the 'orientation' or the 'basic' training is the job training. This aims at giving the special knowledge which different classes of workers need to perform efficiently their respective jobs. It is not a subject-matter training of a professional worker as, for example, in Agriculture, Animal Husbandry, Engineering etc., but the training of a worker engaged in the Community Development programme. The professional workers also need the orientation or basic training which includes the training of an extension officer, but they do not need any job training. Job training is needed by the new classes of functionaries which our programme has brought into being *i.e.* B.D.O., S.E.O., Extension Officer Industries, the Women Extension Officers (Mukhya Sevika), the Gram Sevika and Gram Sevak. One problem of job training arises from the difficulty of formulating clearly the job description of these functionaries. The B.D.O.'s role has been a very difficult one and has been evolving with practice. There has been resistance to his functioning as the captain and coordinator at the block level. But the greatest difficulty has been with regard to the role and job description of the S.E.O. These have undergone some revision which, for limitations of space, I am unable to mention here. I am not certain that the final position has yet been reached. This difficulty has been reflected in the training of the S.E.O. There is still too much theory, taken out of text-books in sociology, figuring in the training of these functionaries. Our difficulty has been that not many of our academicians have had any field experience nor field workers any academic background of the Social Sciences. Only more experience and the method of trial and error will help us to improve this training. There has also been difficulty in giving clarity and practical shape to the functions of the Extension Officer Industries and this also has been reflected in the training. There has been lack of concreteness and effectiveness in the industries programme of the block. How much the Extension Officer Industries must know of the production techniques of the different industries and how much about the business and marketing side is not easy to decide. I am not able to say to what extent the present training is helping the officer to become a successful organiser of village and small-scale industries in his block. Only when the programme stabilises and acquires concreteness, that it lacks today, will we be able to co-relate the job which the Extension Officer is required to do, and which he will be able to do, and the training he has to be given. Some Extension Officers, who after completing their training have worked in the field for some time, have complained that all they are taught was not necessary for them to learn and some things that they were taught, they are not able to practice. To some extent, the training of Mukhya Sevikas has also presented a similar difficulty from lack of effectiveness in the women's programme.

## Training of Gram Sevaks

The training of Gram Sevaks has passed through several phases. Beginning the Extension training of only six months, the Gram Sevak is now given an integrated training in agriculture and other subjects and in Extension for a period of two years. Full advantage has been taken of the recommendations of the Expert Committee set up by the Ministry of Community Development to examine the entire field of training of C.D. personnel, which gave its report in August, 1957, and of recommendations of the Balwantrai Mehta Team. The syllabus now lays adequate emphasis on Agriculture and on Extension. In order that the content of the Agricultural part of the syllabus is suitable for the different regions of the country governed by different climatic, soil and other conditions, expert committees have worked out different syllabi for these different regions. When the initial selection of the Gram Sevaks is good and the staff of the training centres competent, the training is producing fairly good workers. But the two problems that remained unsolved in regard to the training of Gram Sevaks were: (1) about evolving a permanent pattern for the education and training of the Gram Sevak, and (2) about giving him "a foot on the ladder of possible professional advancement" as the U.N. Evaluation Mission has described it. The first issue was considered in the report of the Committee on Rural Education of which I was the

Chairman, and I would reiterate the recommendation of that Committee. A stage has come when the *ad hoc* approach we have followed so far producing Gram Sevaks for the Community Development programme should be abandoned in favour of the long-term approach which the Committee recommended. That approach has to be an integral part of a wider approach required to meet the country's need for a vastly extended agricultural education. In regard to the second problem raised by the U.N. the obvious answer is to arrange that the selected Gram Sevaks should be enabled to join other higher educational courses and complete them in a shorter period than what an ordinary student would need, not having the same background, knowledge and experience as the Gram Sevak.

## Problem of Qualified Instructors

A big problem that the training programme has faced has been the dearth of competent instructors. We have to recognise that the single most important factor which will govern the quality of the training will be the quality of the staff in the training centres. Training in the field of community development being a new field of work in our country, experienced men have not been available. Many who have been good teachers have lacked practical knowledge of development work and have had little understanding of community development methods and process and little acquaintance with village problems and condition and the skill to work with the people have lacked the necessary academic background and the skill to teach. What we could do, therefore, was to pick out the best available material and train them up. Thus was started a Trainers' Training centre at Dehra Dun. The syllabus followed in this centre has also been called a formidable syllabus. It is not intended that the syllabus should be followed mechanically and in a routine fashion. It does indicate broadly the fields in which the trainees coming to the course may need training i.e. education in the ideology and objectives of community development and its processes and techniques, the principles and methods of extension and community organisation, the place of co-operation and local government in our programme of Community Development and teaching methods. I am not shy of advocating that the staff of the training centres must be given good grounding in these fields and that lecture and discussion methods have to be largely followed for this purpose. It should still be possible to develop in the trainees what the U.N. have called 'a likely, alert, sensitive approach to village and rural problems' and 'imagination in handling concepts, originality in thinking about problems, ability to construct a synthesis of apparently diverse approaches, alertness to examine all existing programmes'.

The purpose of this institute is to make the instructors of other training centres better instructors. They can become so only by improving their knowledge of community development and acquiring greater skill as teachers, whatever be the method employed for this purpose. The centre has been deliberately following an experimental approach.

I am not in agreement with the view that there should be a periodical interchange of staff between the training centre and the field. I think that by doing this we are today likely to lose more than we will gain. Good instructors are much more difficult to find than good field workers; and the latter do not always make good instructors. Also in the work we are now doing in the field of training there is scope and need for some specialisation and we should aim at creating in a few years time such a body of specialists by keeping the best men we have in our training centres long enough in the training field.

## Problem of suitable study material

The problem of finding good instructors for the training centres has been aggravated by the lack of adequate text-book material, case studies, and research material which are always needed enrich and strengthen any training programme. We have had not much knowledge in regard to methods of training and have so far used mostly lecture and discussion methods, generally the former more than the latter. Though we have come to recognise the value of discussions as a method of training, the difficulty has been that not all the trainees coming to the training centres have previous experience of the Community Development programme and of their own field of work and, therefore, the discussion method does not add much to their knowledge as it would if they had the necessary background. And when in a batch of trainees some have the background and others do not, then combining the lecture and the discussion methods in the right proportion so as to be most beneficial for the entire class becomes doubly difficult.

## Practical Training

We have been gradually improving upon our training methods by introducing the methods of syndicate studies, guided library work, by organising study circles etc. Greater attention is also now paid to practical work in the villages as a part of the training, as for example, work of surveying a village, conducing village meetings, participating in the training camps of village leaders, in activities of youth clubs etc. Still, the practical training given in our training centres continues to remain weak. The Centres have not been able to work out a good programme of practical training best suited to each class of workers. It has not been easy to fit the practical training into the short duration courses. To arrange the practical work in the neigh-bouring villages on an *ad hoc* basis again and again for successive batches of trainees is also difficult and often annoying to the villagers. Therefore, was conceived the idea that the training centres should operate regular Extension programmes and, I believe, this is now being done. The Trainers' Training Centre has also been concentra-ting its attention on developing a good practical training programme. What the staff of the training centres have to learn, much better than they do at present, is how to use supervised field work as a training method. Opinion now seems to be growing that even with the best practical training given to the different classes of workers, the final answer may be a period of apprenticeship under an experienced worker of the same class, at least for the B.D.O., the S.E.O. and V.L.W.

It is most important that workers are brought for their training after being given some acquaintance with the C.D. programme and its problems. They will profit more from the training. But this requirement coupled with the situation in which very large numbers have to be trained within a short period, has presented another big problem of training. It has not been easy to withdraw large numbers of workers from their posts to undergo the training. Even to plan such a programme has not been easy and so many of our training centres have been running courses after courses without having the full complement of trainees thus involving wastage of training capa-city. The arrangement of putting a worker in his job without any training at all has resulted in his remaining ineffective. We have seen this happen particularly in the case of the B.D.O. The best arrange-ment seems to be to put the workers as extra hands in established and operating blocks for a few months before sending them for the training. But this will mean much additional cost.

## The Central Institute

With the establishment of the Central Institute of Study and Research in Community Development, and its expanding functions, some of the weaknesses of our training programme are likely to be removed. This institution is assuming the role of leader in the training field and this was needed. The training centres functioning at lower levels did need educational guidance and such guidance the Central Institute is beginning to provide. The Central Institute can also take up the preparation of text book material, case studies, and other material needed for the enrichment of our training courses.

In bringing together in one orientation course officials and non-officials falling in the category of political and administrative leaders, the Central Institute has taken a pioneering lead and has helped in smoothening out some of the problems bound to arise from this unique experiment in our country where there has been a back-ground of distrust between the administration and non-official leadership for historical reasons. Yet it will be too optimistic to believe that these problems have been or are soon going to be completely solved. As this system is being gradually extended to the other lower training institutions, the problem will show itself as still existing and in different forms. It will take time and effort to solve it fully.

The U.N. Evaluation Mission have said in their report, "probably no single aspect of community development work in India has received more attention than the need for, and the way to carry out, training schemes Other countries less advanced than India in establishing a community development movement to raise standard of living in rural areas, will find the history and development of training schemes in India, even over the short period since the first projects began, of great value in establishing their own schemes, No small part of the value will lie in examining the criticism and evaluation of training schemes by Indian and foreign experts." The rapid pace of expansion of the C.D. programme has created some of the problems for training. But by attempting to do a great deal, for we had not the option to do less, we have learnt much in the field of training, just as over the entire field of C.D. Improvements must continue to be made and the spirit of enterprise and experimentation, combined with a critical evaluation of the results, must be kept up. The size and diversity which the training programme has come to acquire will prove an advantage, now that we have the Central Institute at Mussoorie to act as the leader and co-ordinator in this field. The research programme now beginning to develop will before long place material in the hands of the training centres to enrich their courses.

# PROBLEMS OF TRAINEES DURING AND AFTER TRAINING

(*a*) THOUGH THERE IS a great deal of contact between trainees and instructors in the daily routine of the training centre, the trainees at the several centres correctly desire to have more opportunities for informal contacts with the staff. Such contacts assist in the building up of right attitudes. The Principal of the Orientation and Study Centre, Bakshi-ka-Talab has gone some way to meet this need by allowing maximum freedom to the trainees to manage their own affairs, holding tournaments and sports competitions in which members of the staff participate and occasionally inviting the trainees in groups to his residence for tea and informal conversation. At Sriniketan trainees are divided into groups and each group allotted to a staff member who meet the groups at regular intervals. It has been the experience that these contacts outside the classroom encourage trainees to come out more frankly with their problems than they normally do even in group discussions. It is understood that in the Administrative Training School, Ranchi, an allowance has been granted to the Principal to meet the expenditure involved in such informal contacts. It is suggested that a sum of Rs. 50 p.m. or a lump sum of Rs. 600 per year be kept at the disposal of the Principal as sumptuary allowance to meet such expenditure.

×        ×        ×        ×        ×

## Teaching Staff

(1) The accepted policy of deputing staff members who have had no field experience or those working continuously as Instructors for more than three years for Block attachment for a period of three months should be implemented. The Principals have been requested to prepare a roster for the purpose and send it to the Ministry for immediate action.

(2) The following recommendations made on page 4 of the report of the Study Group is reiterated the scope and methodology of the studies recommended being finalised in consultation with the Central Institute from time to time :—

"As suggested by the High Level Training Team (para 33(7) the programme for the Principals/Directors of the Orientation and Study Centres, Social Education Organisers' Training Centres to attend Orientation Courses at the Central Institute, Mussoorie, is being drawn up by the Ministry. In addition, in order to ensure continuous contact with field conditions, it is essential that every year, say for a period of three weeks, staff members in small groups of 3 should make an intensive study of 1 or 2 selected blocks in the States attached to the Training Centre. For a similar period, Principals/Directors in a group of three should visit States like Rajasthan, Andhra Pradesh etc. and make an intensive study of the problems of Panchayati Raj. It is further suggested that after the three weeks' tour, the group of Principals/Directors, or some members thereof should participate for a week in the Orientation course at the Central Institute, Mussoorie, if one is in session. Such participation will help to bring them into closer touch with the Central Institute, Myssoorie, giving meaning to the idea of the latter being the apex institution, and provide opportunity for discussion of common problems relating to training and for receiving academic guidance in this regard. Such participation will also assist in better coordination and supervision of the study programme at the several Training Centres."

# IMPORTANCE OF ATMOSPHERE IN TRAINING

NO LESS IMPORTANT than the physical environment is the atmosphere at the Training Centres. Basically, the training has to be self-training; the educational process cannot be achieved unless time is available for study and reflection. Unfortunately except at Sriniketan and Belurmath no training centre was free from the boarding school approach of filling the time of the trainees from early morning to late night and many Principals/Directors proudly displayed the daily programme from 5.00 or 5.30 a.m. to 10.00 p.m. or 10.30 p.m. Three correctives are possible:

(a) The daily programme should be so organised that at least 1 or 2 afternoons in the week are left free for the purpose. The Principal, O. & S.C., Bakshi-ka-Talab is already endeavouring to this end. The experiment of 1 or 2 free afternoons was tried in the IX the course at the Central Institute with good results; on the one hand trainees had more time for pursuing their own projects e.g., intensified study of books or preparation of individual papers on their field problems and on the other, the criticism of regimentation so frequent in the earlier courses completely disappeared.

(b) The trainees should be encouraged, through their own committees to manage their own campus affair mess, lodging, manual work, recreation, seminars, symposium and debates. These activities have been well organised in the Orientation and Study Centres Himayatsagar and Bakshi-ka-Talab.

(c) At Bakshi-ka-Talab, Sriniketan and Belurmath the staff mix freely with the trainees, participate in tournaments and invite the trainees in groups to their residences for informal talks. Such informal exchanges are extremely useful. Ways and means of making this a regular feature in all training centres are discussed in paragraph 32(a).

# TRAINING OF NON-OFFICIALS

*Prof. N. R. Malkani*

SOMETIMES BACK THE Ministry of Community Development published
a pamphlet with rather a pompous title, *viz.*, "From Lok Sabha
to Gram Sabha—A programme of study and orientation," and
straightaway proceeded to mention ten categories of non-officials
which were to be drawn into a vast drive of training, considered
essential for the proper reception of Panchayati Raj. The categories
were imposing for they included members of Parliament and Assemblies as well as Pramukhs of Zila Parishads. But as the categories
proceeded downwards to include members of Block Development
Committee (now elected Panchayat Samitis), Sarpanches, Upsar-
panches, Panches, Presidents and Vice-Presidents of Co-operative
Societies, members of their Managing Committees, etc., the figures
about the number of trainees rose to impressive heights. There are to
be 5,000 Blocks and each Block will have 30 to 40 members, making
a total of 1,50,000 to 2,00,000 members. There are going to be 2 lac
Panchayats, big and small, with 2 lac sarpanches and 2 lac Upasarpanches not considering Nyaya Panchayats. There will be at least nine
Panches to each panchayat, *i.e.*, 18 lac Panches. The members of Cooperative Societies which would not be less than a lac and half, with
comparable figures of Presidents, Vice-Presidents and members of
Managing Committees. As if this was not task enough, the training
programme had youth workers, Gram Lakshmis and even part-time
secretaries of Panchayats and Co-operative Societies thrown in for
this great drive for people's training. The figures have become stag-
gering and the various categories pose problems of approach, content,
method, organisation, let alone finds. In fact the programme becomes
a challenge considering that it requires Instructors not only of some
experience but democratically 'oriented' to acquit themselves of the
task creditably. Such is the size, variety, and urgency of the problem of training for community development work, if not for direct
democracy.

## Past Experience

The Community Development Ministry started the programme of

training long ago, but this was confined to the training of officials—a host of Block Development Officers, with the growing teams of Extension Officers, Social Education Organisers and the broadening base of village level workers, at the rate of ten per Block. This training zeal soon spread to higher echelons of Trainer's Training and District Panchayat Officers training at Rajpura, and the Central Institute of Study and Research at Mussoorie for the training of officials ranging from Collectors to State Secretaries and Development Commissioners. All this training was for officials; by trained officials, in established institutions and according to the syllabi prepared by 'experts' for job, extension and orientation training, whatever that may mean This experience of institutional training of officials provided us with a fund of experience and gave us by a method of trial and error results which are not unsatisfactory. We are thus in a fairly prepared position to launch a bigger drive for the training of non-officials with the difference that this drive is to be for the training of non-officials and by non-official agencies. But we are here on an uncharted sea and out for a great adventure not without risks of failure. It is, therefore, necessary to proceed step by step, slowly first, and then by leaps and jumps.

## Unsatisfactory Training

The first step was taken during 1959-60, when six training camps for the Instructors of members of Block Development Committees were started, which were attended by 208 persons nominated by State Governments. With the help of these trained Instructors, the State Governments have been running about 50 institutions and 15 peripatetic teams for the training of about 20,000 members of Block Development Committees. This experiment was permissible as a first step and I believe has taught us a few lessons that we should not forget. The selection of Instructors was made by State Governments in some cases and by voluntary organisations in other cases. It would perhaps be impertinent to ask whether most of these trained 208 Instructors have been actually working in training programmes. I think the wastage in members alone would be substantial and if we were to look into the quality of Instructors selected there would be 80% to 90% casualties. Most of the Instructors were selected casually without any clear idea about their academic qualifications, leaving aside experience and social service background. The Instructors should be the most important single factor dominating the training programme. But what happened was that they were employed at so many rupees per (weeks') course of training. Government paid Rs. 50 per trainee per week's Course and the trainer's like wage-earners were in turn paid accordingly. Rs. 50 to Rs. 100 per course, as a weekly wage, and then discharged. During a year there would be say 3 to 5 courses of training in each institution. One can well imagine the king of Instructor who would be employed under such a system. He would be either a retired old man or a briefless lawyer or an ordinary social worker or a school teacher. So, 50 training institutions were started on an arbitrary base by 15 to 20 miscellaneous and mostly unknown 'Voluntary' organisations, as selected by State Governments. Almost, all of them had little or no experience of training programmes. They took them up because the Government was paying Rs. 50 per trainee per Course, which was not bad as a job. The number of 50 institutions was also national. The Bharat Sevak Samaj was for example running 7 such training Centres; at present it is running only three; of these only two are fairly satisfactory. Maybe 30 or 40 have survived but less than 20 would be doing some satisfactory work.

### Kind of Trainers and Training Needed

It is therefore absolutely necessary that instructors should be carefully selected and then specially trained for their new job of instructing adults drawn from rural areas. There should be Selection and Appointment Committees consisting of members who understand academic as well as human or social values. Instructors have to be on a quasi-permanent cadre, paid on a decent scale, not as wage-earners paid by job or time, but as professionals of some merit. They must be provided with equipment which is partly formal in terms of libraries and reading-rooms but substantially informal in terms of audio-visual aids, which are not blind and expensive copies of the West but are adapted to rural conditions and to traditional methods of communication. We have to train adults, who are expected to be intelligent men of business with some experience of life but with old attitudes which will not fit in with a new job. The place of instruction must be set in more or less rural surrounding in keeping with the nature of instruction and also its requirements with regard to field demonstrations. A spacious, inexpensive, yet sanitary building should be had preferably on rent, with additions and alterations, if necessary. The syllabus of training would have to be short, simple and of a self-evolving nature. It should be flexible so as to fit in with local and changing requirements. It should be simple but related to field problems and so not made by "experts" who insist on making training comprehensive. More care must be taken with regard to what should not be put in, rather than on what is to be put in. The methodology of training would have to be of a peculiar nature-instructional followed by questions, but mostly by mutual discussions which are problem-centred, and both supported by field demonstrations and audio-visual aids. Where trainees are drawn from ranks of experienced and responsible adults there will always be a few who will know enough to instruct the trainees and even the Instructors and that in a manner of give and take without the differences of trainer and trainee. Instructors should be more like guides and companions to draw out rich and varied experiences in a skilled way so as to illumine difficult and knotty problems of work and life. This type of training and this quality of Instructors cannot be supplied by miscellaneous and local voluntary organisations. It will be essential to bring into the picture a few All India voluntary organisations of position and experience to put in coordinated and directed efforts for a great task. I am of opinion that the Central Ministry of Community Development must involve organisations like the All India Co-operative Union, the Gandhi Samarak Nidhi with its TATTVA Mandirs, the Bharat Sewak Samaj, The All India Panchayat Parishad as well as special educational institutions like the Rural Institutes, the national Vidyapeeths, the various training centres of social service and welfare. These must join hands at the top under the enthusiastic support of the Central Ministry and with constant and continuous assessment of trends and results. A campaign for a big task cannot be left to change arrangement by small and scattered organisations, not knowing each other and not understanding the nature of the job. The C.D. Ministry has now a ready-made instrument at hand for advice on training in the Central Advisory Board of Training and in its three standing committee can easily become a Committee on which not merely members of Parliament but representative of the All India organisations, I have mentioned, can be selected or coopted to carry on the task of non-official training. In fact it should be easy to have corresponding Boards and Committees at the State Level, with close interest in the success of this adventure.

During deliberations by various Boards, Committees, Seminars, it has now been decided that this non-official training should hereafter be carried on in more or less permanent institutions, at the District level and under the auspices of the Zila Parishads, as far as possible. As the funds will be supplied by the Central Ministry, though channelled through the Zila Parishads, I hope the trailer clause of "as far as possible" will become redundant. The recent Seminar of Instructors and members of Block Development Committees held at Hardwar from 25th to 27th October, 1960, discussed all the features and even the detailed programme of district Institutes during each year. The Seminar has framed a generous budget and in place of the provision of Rs. 50 per trainee per course, put in two separate budgets for recurring and non-recurring expenses, the former of about Rs. 50,000 per year and the latter of Rs. 65,000. The last can be reduced to Rs. 50,000 if rented building are used and new ones not built. Provision is made for 3 members on the staff on a scale of Rs. 250 per month, but it is worth-while considering whether one member should not be an official of the status of B.D.O. Institutional training at headquarters for weekly courses will be supplemented by peripatetic training in the village, of 2 to 3 days, for Panches and members of Managing Committees of societies, both following each other according to the course of agricultural seasons. Each District Institute will work for 40 weeks so as to train 1440 persons and its peripatetic item will work for 20 weeks so as to train about 3,000 persons. Thus the work of training will be continuous and intensive to keep the staff fully employed and turn out a large number of trainees. But the remarkable feature of the Institute will be to combine training for Community Development, Panchayati Raj and Co-operative Movement. In fact all these should be organically integrated as essential parts of a new order of society based on community and team work by people's participation. Separate courses or training in different institutions would be basically wrong, and financially unjustifiable. I would however like to raise the period of training from one week to ten days for the reason that Sarpanches (and Upasarpanches) should be jointly trained with members of Panchayat Samitis for one week and separately trained for 3 days. A week's training for responsible persons is in any case inadequate, and more so, if two jobs are combined in the same individual.

One thing remains and that is the poor attendance of Block Development Committee members, in almost all training Centres. To a great extent this is due to the inefficient and inadequate running of Training Institutes. The District Institute under the auspices of the Zila Parishad, as advised by the Seminar, will remove this defect, and more so, if a Training Committee consisting of a few local educationists, representatives of the Zila Parishad and of the voluntary organisations, with the principal as Member-Secretary, is set up as a Managing Committee. A good deal of educational work has yet to be done by officials and non-officials to persuade the Panchayats to consider training as essential. In fact it should in due course be made obligatory. For the rest, both institutional and peripatetic courses should be held in consultation with the Panchayat Samitis to suit the convenience of trainees. But there is one primary need of the District Training Institute which distinguishes it from all other ordinary training Centres. The trainees are to live in the Centre as members of a joint family and the Institute must become a genuine community centre, so as to help change basic attitudes commensurate not only with Panchayati Raj but with a Raj based on community feeling. Of course there will be daily chores of cooking, washing, cleaning, serving meals in which the members will all participate willingly, coming as they do from rural areas. But in the class, in the dormitory, on the playground and the field, the dominant feeling must be of Community life. The C.D. Ministry and its Departments have been putting all the emphasis on development and now on economic development, with some success. Their best friends would not charge them with inculcating the spirit of Community through any of their activities. Here is the chance and the occasion for making it a reality, for without this feeling not only the training but Panchayat Raj would be a body with life but without a soul.

# THE GAP BETWEEN TRAINING AND FIELD CONDITIONS

## B. P. R. Vithal

TRAINING HAS BEEN defined as the imparting of skills, knowledge and attitudes. In any Subject Matter training the proper attitude can be taken for granted because the training is for a person who is already in a particular line, where he would not have been—had he not had the requisite attitude. The imparting of skills and knowledge is also comparatively easy in Subject Matter training because tested and widely accepted skills and knowledge are available in the particular field concerned. All that has to be done in such training is to relate the available body of knowledge and of skills to the particular problems at hand. This again would be easy because the problems in the field in any Subject Matter are likely to be clear-cut and easily defined.

### Special Features of Training

General 'Orientation Training' for the Community Development programme and 'Job Training' for the general administrator in this programme are however extremely difficult because no indisputable and well tested body of knowledge or of skills is available, especially where problems of our own rural communities are concerned. Further the problems themselves are not so easily identifiable; in fact there can be a very wide difference of opinion as to what the problem itself is. And in many cases the problems in the field are such that they are not amenable of solution merely by the process of training.

### Why the Gap

The main reasons therefore for there being a gap between training and field conditions in so far as the training of the general administrator is concerned are three-fold. Firstly, the difficulty in identifying the real problems that exist in the field; secondly, the difficulty in being able to find any body of knowledge or of skills that would be useful in tackling these problems, such as for instance a knowledge of sociology would be in the conditions existing in western countries; and thirdly, many of the problems in the field arise because of basic defects in the programme and its organisation so that no training as such can solve them. When we do not admit this fact and continue to hope that training alone will solve such problems, there is bound to be disappointment and frustration with regard to the efficacy of training.

There is however no doubt that from time to time training programmes get so far out of tune with field conditions that the difference cannot be attributed entirely to the various reasons mentioned above. We seem to be approaching one such phase of complete unreality in our training programme with the introduction of Panchayati Raj in the various States. The present Orientation and Job Training were conceived at a time when the Community Development programme was stated to have Community Development as its aim and Extension as its method, so that it was very largely a comprehensive version of an Extension Programme. The emphasis in the training was therefore on Extension Methods and on the role of the Block Development Officer as the head of the Extension team. He was defined as the programme planner, the programme executor, the co-ordinator and the Extension worker.

### Panchayati Raj widens the Gap

With Panchayati Raj, however, the role of a Block Development Officer has been fundamentally changed. The Orientation Training can be adopted to the conditions of Panchayati Raj by a change in emphasis in the syllabus as it stands, because many of the fundamental, principles of Panchayati Raj are in any case found in the syllabus and what is required is a shift in emphasis from Extension to Panchayati Raj. But the Job Officers has to be completely changed if it is to be in tune with the requirements of Panchayati Raj. The Block Development Officer is now the Chief Executive Officer of a local body. His basic responsibility is to execute the resolutions of the Panchayat Samiti. His major problem is that of co-ordination with non-officials while ensuring that all the rules and regulations are observed. This requires a complete recasting of the existing syllabus for the Job Training of Block Development Officers.

It has also to be considered how far regional training centres can really serve this purpose because Panchayati Raj has by definition to vary from State to State because of the different local conditions. It would be very difficult for one centre to provide adequate Job Training for Block Development Officers from different States hereafter. The basic principles of Panchayati Raj are perhaps the same in all States but these are covered in the Orientation Training. The actual legislation and the rules and regulations pertaining to Panchayati Raj differ widely from State to State and this is what has to be covered in the Job Training. For this centralised training may be neither possible nor very useful. In fact institutional training itself may not be suitable for this kind of training and it may be much better to give apprentice-ship training in the field. Therefore the gap between training and field conditions has widened critically because of the introduction of Panchayati Raj in the field and of not much rethinking being done about the training programme in the light of this.

## Some Gap Inevitable

However even under the best of conditions there is bound to be a gap between training and field conditions just as there is bound to be a gap between theory and practice. This is nothing to be regretted, but in fact to be insisted upon, because this is the gap that constantly urges man to attempt to make the practice approximate more and more closely to the basic propositions and ideals that motivate and inspire the programme. Those therefore that ask for a complete identification of the training programme with field conditions as they exist today miss the entire purpose of the training programme.

A straight line is defined as something which has length but no breadth; a definition which is impossible of achievement. Our practical administrators would therefore look into the note books of school boys and jump to the conclusion that the teaching is unrealistic because in fact straight lines as drawn by school boys have consider-able breadth. They would therefore like to revise the definition in such a way that a reasonable breadth is allowed for the straight line, forgetting that even when the definition allows no breadth at all to the line the school boy manages to give it one. If the definition itself permits some breadth one can imagine what the actual practice would become. The problem of the training programme is very often similar to this.

There are many things in the field conditions which differ from what is stated in the training programme, but for that reason it would not be wise in all cases to conclude that what requires revision is the training programme. It may be that it is the field conditions that have to be further altered to more closely approximate to what is conveyed in the training programmes. The gap between training and field con-ditions is the gap that exists between our profession and our practice. In the very nature of things such a gap will always exist although it should be our constant endeavour to see that this is as narrow as possible. The trouble with our programmes—both the field programme and the training programme—is that this gap is in many cases very wide. The general conclusion drawn from this observation has been that the training programme must more closely approximate to the field conditions. Taking Instructors from the field, posting them periodically back in the field, study and research programme, etc. have been various means by which an attempt is being made to see that the training programme bears closer relationship to field conditions.

## Defect in field conditions

But the fact is forgotten that there may be cases where the defect lies in field conditions and not in the training programme. Man is now said to have reached a new stage of evolution. Hitherto the species had to adapt itself to the environment; today man can adapt the environment to his own needs. Evolution has therefore become a two-way process. The relationship between the field conditions and training programmes is also similar. Unfortunately, we have given very little thought to the question as to whether some of the difficulties of our training programme are not due to difficulties in the field which training alone cannot tackle. The Geeta teaches us the distinction between the Field and Knower of the Field. Similarly, where the problems of our Programme are concerned, there are some which are inherent in the Field and some which arise because of the worker in the Field. Training programmes can help solve only the latter category of problems and not the former. Training can solve problems that arise because of an improper understanding on the part of the personnel; it cannot solve problems that arise because of structural defects in the field organisation.

## Problem of Administrative Co-ordination

Unfortunately we have very often transferred to the training programme problems that rightly belong to the field. One of the most classic examples of this is the problem of administrative co-ordination. Ever since the inception of the Programme one of its problems and of its defects has been the dual control over technical staff at the Block level. We tried to dodge this problem by making a fine distinction between technical control and administrative control. We invented clever concepts, like "Team Spirit" and "Captain of Team," and we expected the training programme to incalculate in the various members of the staff this "Team Spirit". Whenever administrative co-ordination broke down in the field we attributed it to a wrong approach in the part of the staff and generally blamed the training programme for not having been able to impart the right attitude. We have always so far avoided facing the fact that as things stand in our administration today, whether it is in this Programme or outside it, and as our psychology is today, an appeal to any spirit, whether it be the team spirit or the national spirit, may not be a substitute for an appeal to authority.

We have very often preached—and this not in Training Centres alone but also in the field by Executive Officers in charge of the programme—that we could always get more out of the staff by appealing to them than by exercising authority over them. What we forgot in this argument was the fact that an appeal is effective in getting the best response from men only when it comes from a man who has authority. What appeals is not the appeal itself, but the fact that a man who has authority desists from using that authority and chooses to appeal. A man without authority preaching the virtue of appealing seems to most of us to be only making a virtue of necessity. This is one example where the training programme cannot approximate any more to field conditions. Various compromises are arrived at in the field and both the trainer and the trainee are aware of this. If the training programme is to be entirely realistic it will only have to teach these compromises, but it would then have no purpose whatsoever. If, on the other hand, the training is to be true to the principles underlying the programme, it has necessarily to diverge from field conditions nowhere correspond to these principles.

**Conclusion**

The gap between the training programme and the field conditions is therefore the reflection of the gap that exists in the programme itself between its own principles and its practice. It is a gap that exists within each field worker in the programme because he himself is constantly appealing to one set of principles and practising another. It is a gap between what is and what we would wish it to be. The training programme in so far as it diverges from the realities of the field conditions brings this problem out into the open. It is perhaps for this reason that it elicits such violent reactions from field officers. It commits the indiscretion of exposing an inner problem. But to find defects in the training programme alone, without relating these defects to the larger contradictions in the programme itself, would be like the magic ritual of sticking pins into an image hoping thereby to be attacking the original person; a ritual that serves no purpose except that of mental catharsis.

# TRAINING PERSONNEL FOR COMMUNITY DEVELOPMENT

*Carl C. Taylor, Douglas Ensminger,*
*Helen W. Johnson Jean Joyce*

INDIA'S TEN YEARS of experience in training staff for community development now makes it possible to draw a number of generalizations. We shall point out here quite categorically what we regard as the most significant among the many lessons India has learned as the result of this experience. The following appear to us to be worthy of special attention, even at the risk of repetition:

1. As the programme of community development itself changes, either in its approach, areas of emphasis, or methods, there is need for similar updating of the job descriptions of each person on the district and block staffs. Only the policy-makers agree on the job each staff member is to perform can those responsible for training keep it focussed on the function each individual is to perform when he joins the district or block staff.

2. Since the competence of the trainee at the conclusion of his training period will be largely determined by the competence of the instructors, it is impossible to overemphasize the absolute necessity of assuring that only the most competent people available are recruited for teaching assignments in the training centres. They should not, as at present, be assigned by the technical departments of the government. Once selected, steps must be taken to make them fully qualified to teach the subject assigned. Most instructors selected will need special training in the philosophy and objectives of community development, in extension teaching methods, and in relating their specialized subject to an integrated concept of a multipurpose, village-extension worker. Once adequately trained, the instructors should be given some reasonable security of tenure in the training centres. Transfers of instructors out of the centres should be few and exceptional.

3. Since the manpower required to staff community development can now be projected for at least twenty years, and since the

community development programme itself is integral part of the governmental, administrative and technical staff-structure, training centres which are, in the future, to turn out the basic staff should be integrated into established colleges and universities. As we have said above, the centres need a richer intellectual base than can be provided through the present arrangement. It seems reasonable and appropriate, however, for the government itself to direct the centres for orientation and inservice training.

4.  Since all staff members who are to have administrative, supervisory, technical, or extension-educational responsibilities must function as an inter-related team, and since the staff team in turn must be inter-related with village people though their local institutions, one cannot emphasize too strongly the need to orient all staff members in the philosophy, objectives, and methods of community development.

5.  Because community development objectives can be achieved only as the staff becomes effective in helping village people to develop strong panchayats and co-operatives, which in turn must motivate village people to give up their traditional ways of thinking, farming, and living, it is imperative that the training process be carefully balanced between the theoretical side and village practicals. The trainees are at the centres to learn and not to do physical labour as such. It is therefore most important that all work which qualifies for trainee time have a teaching-learning value. Inasmuch as most of the people going into community development have not themselves lived and worked as village cultivators' sons and daughters, it is essential that village practicals be so organised as to assure maximum village involvement, in a planned teaching-learning frame of reference.

6.  India's experience in the community development programme needs to be drawn on realistically in setting new and higher standards of performance as a basis for selection of all categories of personnel for community development posts. If recruitment is vigorously pursued it should be possible in a country of 440 million to find people with the right attitudes and motivations and who, once they are trained, can be counted on to assure the success of community development.

7.  Even with thorough job preparation and careful selection of personnel, it is essential to continue in-service training at frequent intervals for all categories of staff members, if community development is to remain a vital force in helping village

people find new solutions to old problems by applying the ever-growing body of science.

8. While India has taken considerable pains to orient and train a professional staff, this staff has not as yet carried on vigorous, vital, and purposeful educational programmes among village people to make sure that they, who are to benefit from community development, know and understand its philosophy and objectives. It will in the future, with the advent of Panchayati Raj, be especially important that all co-operative and panchayat leaders be trained so that they will know what the village community has a right to expect of them, and so that they, in turn, will know how to carry out their leadership responsibilities.

9. Since community development's past strength has been its willingness, if not eagerness, to be evaluated, and to adjust and change as experience has directed, one must hope that this will also be true of training. India's experience supports the need for training to be continuously evaluated and needed adjustments readily made to meet new needs.

With the new element of Panchayati Raj introduced on the Indian rural scene, training programmes for community development must go beyond even this important series of correctives just discussed. The scope of the efforts to reach and to develop the people who live in India's half-million villages is much greater than it was ten, even five, years ago. Not only must a network of technical personnel be trained to man the 5,000 blocks in India, but the villagers themselves must come alive to initiate and help carry out the programmes they want the VLWs and others to implement. They too, must be taught the techniques and technologies required to improve their agricultural production, get better schools for their children, and raise their levels and standards of living.

In retrospect, we might say that community development is now moving into a new phase, and with it the training programmes to make it effective. The first phase, covering the first two Plan-periods, might be called the foundation-laying stage. During this phase, a whole set of new steps was taken: the structure of the community development agency was built; administration was gradually reoriented from regulatory to developmental; villagers were awakened to their new freedom and its concomitant responsibility for self-help in overcoming poverty, disease, and ignorance; science and technology were introduced into rural India; training institutions for the many and diverse community development personnel opened; and a back long experience in building village institutions was accumulated. At the same time, this phase had another dominant characteristic—the programme was largely created and run by Central and State bureaucracies. The village people, in effect, were invited to participate in village and block programmes dominated by officialdom.

The second phase, now just beginning, will necessarily be different, both in its aims and in its problems. During this phase, there will be an intensification of the development of village institutions such as panchayats, co-operatives, and schools. There will be a growth in understanding between the official bureaucracy and the officers of village, block and district institutions. Planning and development will be based on the interest, initiative, motivation, and leader-ship of the people themselves. The economic base for village development will be strengthened by giving priority attention to increases in agricultural production. And finally, staff competence for educating villagers in institution-building and in utilizing science and technology in their lives will increase.

As this new phase begins, and then develops momentum, its success will depend even more than the last one did on the competence of the staff selected, trained, and assigned to the villages, blocks, and districts. The staff of Community Development will, in fact, be faced with a new set of demands. It was, after all, one thing to begin the programme and to create devices among the people for improvement; it will be quite another to assure successful execution of the high objectives that have been set and to see that these desires are fulfilled. It was necessary to organise panchayats and co-operatives, but it will also be necessary to make them work effectively. It was not easy to introduce improved agricultural practices; it will be even more difficult to motivate the people to accept the findings of science that support them. It was imperative to build schools, but they must be made vital village institutions, with the teacher and important village leader. It was reasonably acceptable for the Village-Level Worker to be philosopher, guide, and friend of the people, but he must also be competent to help village people succeed in solving their problems through village institutions. It was believed essential to put technical extension-specialists in the block organisation; it is equally important for them to understand village problems and the modifications of science that village situations require. It was one thing for the BDO to be the leader of a team of specialists and village workers; it will be quite another for him to enable his staff to help village people develop their own institutions and use their own initiative to solve their problems.

In view of these new goals and problems, India's Community Development programme must again meet the challenge before it, just as it has in the past. It must evolve new concepts of training to satisfy new needs. We have recommended ambitious proposals for advanced education for the various levels of official personnel and for correctives needed in the training programmes. We believe that India can, and will, rise to meet the challenge of the new day ahead.

# PROCESS OF CHANGE

## Programmes in Community Development

*Through these extracts, it is hoped to provide a picture of what is being done in community development through various programmes. They cover a wide range from agriculture to family planning.*

*There is no dearth of material regarding programmes although there is very little in the way of honestly descriptions of "how" these programmes are implemented. Programme is often seen in terms of new goals targets and techniques but if these innovations are to take hold, we need to know a great deal of what exactly goes into the process of acceptance or rejection of new ideas and the role of the worker in this process.*

CONTIBUTORS

1. S. Ramanathan, "Village Agricultural Plan, its preparation and implementation," Kurukshetra, Vol. 12, December 1963, pp. 10-13.

2. V.S. Vasudevaraju, "Rural Industries Programme," Kurukshetra Vol. 13, June, 1965, pp. 13-15.

3. "Aid of Social Education," in Community Development Programme : An Anthology, New Delhi, Ministry of Community Development and Cooperation, Government of India, 1961, pp. 71-77.

4. M.C. Nanavatty, "Social Education as Instrument of Developing Services in Undeveloped Areas, Souvenir of the Seminar on Public Co-operation for Social Welfare with special reference to Third Plan, Chandigarh, 1960, p. 15.

5. M. Chaube, "Developing Rural Youth Leadership," Kurukshetra, Vol. 10, August 1962.

6. "Programme for Women and Children," report on National Conference on Community Development At Mysore City, 1959, Ministry of Community Development and Cooperation, pp. 31-33.

7. M.J. Coldwell, R. Dumont and M. Read, "Women and Village Programmes," report of a Community Development Evaluation Mission in India, Ministry of Community Development and Co-operation, Government of India, 1959, pp. 61-62.

8. "Women in Community Development" Kurukshetra, June 1964.

9. G. Subbalakshmi, "Role of Mahila Samaj—Some Suggestions," Kurukshetra, Vol. 13, July 1965, pp. 16-17.

10. "Village Schools," from A Guide to Community Development, New Delhi, Ministry of Community Development and Cooperation, 1962, p. 74.

11. "The Development of the Village School as a Community Centre," from A Guide to Community Development, New Delhi, Ministry of Community Development and Cooperation, 1962, p. 134.

12. R. Rudramoorth, "People's Movement for Education in Madras State", Summary of a Preliminary Report (cyclostyled), Central Institute of Study and Research in Community Development.

13. Management of Primary Schools under Panchayati Raj, Study Report (Cyclostyled) National Institute of Community Development, Hyderabad.

14. "Jawaharlal Nehru on Co-operation, Ministry of Community Development and Cooperation, Government of India, 1962, pp. 13-15.

15. B.S. Mathur, "De-Officialisation of Cooperative Movement," Kurukshetra, Vol. 15, December 1965.

16. "Cooperative Institutions," from Evaluation Report on Second Year's Working of Community Projects Volume, 1, Planning Commission Programme Evaluation, 1965, pp. 31-35.

17. Horace Belshaw and John B. Grant, "Role of Voluntary Agencies," from A Report of the Mission on Community Organization and Development in South and Southeast Asia, United Nations, 1952, p. 43.

18. "Records and Their Use," from Evaluation Report on Second Year's Working of Community Projects, Volume I, Planning Commission Programme Evaluation Organisation, 1955, pp. 48-51.

19. Nicholas J. Demerath, "Family Planning Plans and Action," Indian Journal of Public Administration, Vol. XI, No. 4, pp. 683-697.

20. "Popular Participation," from Evaluation Report on Second Year's Working of Community Projects Volume I, Planning Commission Programme Evaluation Organisation, 1955, pp. 37-42.

21. "Extracts From Fortnightly Diaries of Gram Sevika and Mukhya Sevika," from A Guide to Gram Sevikas and Mukhya Sevikas, New Delhi, Ministry of Community Development and Cooperation, 1961, pp. 47-51.

22. "Reports by Field Workers."

# VILLAGE AGRICULTURAL PLAN, ITS PREPARATION AND IMPLEMENTATION

## S. Ramanathan

THE QUESTION OF stepping up agricultural production, in a larger context, is linked up with a number of basic issues. These are: strengthening of the administrative machinery of the Agriculture Departments in the States, achieving better coordination between the Union Ministries concerned, active involvement of the Panchayati Raj Institutions in the programme, delegation of adequate powers to officers and Panchayats with a clearer definition of the administrative and technical roles of individuals and institutions, streamlining the supply-line and imparting a sense of direction to the programme. Irrespective of these problems, however, a beginning has to be made at the base *viz*, at the village level to prepare Village or Panchayat agricultural production plans, as the 'only means of involving cultivators in the village in the agricultural efforts and mobilising effectively the resources of the local community to this end."

In the context of the national emergency and the urgent need for increasing agricultural production, it is necessary that the scope of the agricultural production plans should be limited to a few selected items based essentially on the fuller utilisation of local resources. In other words, so far as agricultural production is concerned, the C. D. Programme has to be reorientated with a view to intensify such efforts for increasing agricultural production as are likely to yield quick results.

### Agency for Preparation

The preparation and implementation of such a plan should primarily be the responsibility of the village Panchayats and the Taluk Development Boards/Panchayat Samitis in collaboration with the cooperative society and associate voluntary organisations, and with the full cooperation and assistance of Village Level Workers, Agriculture Extension Officers and others connected with the Agriculture Extension programme. It is expected that associate organisations like Youth Clubs, Mahila Samajs, Farmers' Forums, Village Volunteer Force and Defence Labour Bank should be involved in the process as far as possible. Cooperative are expected to undertake the responsibility for making available the supplies necessary for the implementation of the plan. All these bodies will, of course, be guided and assisted in their efforts by the higher agencies, both official and non-official *viz.*, the Taluk Development Board/Panchayat Samiti, the Taluk Marketing Societies and/or Taluk Cooperative Supervisory Unions, District Central Cooperative Banks, the Assistant Registrar of Cooperative Societies, the District Agricultural Officer, the Collector and the Zila Parishad, etc.

The production plan has necessarily to be a simple plan so that it is understood by all those involved in the programme. It should be unencumbered with complicated and voluminous proforma. Considering the fact that a single Village Level Worker is in-charge of 5 to 6 villages and the other resources available are also limited, it would not be practicable to attempt the preparation of production plans for all farmers in all the villages. Hence, the scope of the plan has to be restricted by involving a selected number of progressive agriculturists in each village within the jurisdiction of the V.L.W. The Plan should also directly emphasise and aim at a positive increase in the production of principal crops in the respective areas, rather than the mere adoption of improved agricultural practices. The plan has to be based on achievements and definite targets for increasing production by a reasonable and agreed quantity. Such targets should then be split up and assigned to individual agriculturists, according to their capacity, enthusiasm and willingness to adopt improved agricultural practices. It is recognised that such an approach to the preparation and execution of the plan would create the psychological atmosphere for its successful working. It would also create among the participants a sense of contributing their mite to the national effort and increasing agricultural production as a second line of defence and would provide a motive force to the individual agriculturists for adopting improved agricultural practices as a means to achieve this goal. It is necessary to relate these plans more explicitly to the Panchayati Raj bodies in order to enable them to play their part in enthusing the village community into action.

## Content of the Plan

In view of this "target-based approach" to the subject the method of preparation and the content of the plan should be as follows:

(1) There should be only one plan for the entire area covered by a Panchayat instead of separate plans for each revenue village. Such a plan should be more conveniently called a 'Panchayat Agricultural Production Plan.'

(2) Such plans should be drawn up by every Panchayat in the State with the assistance of Village Level Workers and in consultation with the village cooperatives. For the immediate present, the plan could be prepared and implemented for at least one major food crop and one major commercial crop having the highest acreage under each in the area of the particular Panchayat. In areas where there are more than one major crop of each category, plans could be prepared for two food crops and two commercial crops. Garden crops need not be included in the Plan.

(3) In respect of each crop, the Panchayat should set definite targets for increasing production in the Panchayat area by a reasonable and agreed level arrived at on the basis of voluntary undertakings given by individual cultivators and institutions in respect of their holdings within the area of the Panchayat.

(4) Targets of increased production can be planned to be achieved through the use of a limited number of recommended practices which will constitute the minimum agricultural programme. More particularly the programme can, for the present, comprise the following items:—

(a) Development of local manureal resources including (i) compost; (ii) farm-yard manure; and (iii) annual and perennial green manure by individuals and institutions.

(b) Use of recommended and improved varieties of seeds and seed treatment;

(c) Adoption of dry farming practices comprising (i) cultivation across the slope i.e. contour bunding; (ii) Strip cropping; (iii) repeated harrowing and frequent inter-cultivation, and (iv) wider spacing and thinner sowing;

(d) Adoption of plant protection measures—both preventive and curative—on a collective basis;

(e) Fuller and better utilisation of available irrigation facilities where water is made available up to the field boundary; and

(f) Double cropping, wherever feasible.

I may mention that the items of the programme listed above are only the 'minimum' which should be fulfilled by every Panchayat and it is left to any Panchayat, in consultation with the cooperative society, to plan for and strive to achieve more than the minimum depending upon their ability and enthusiasm, local conditions, and available external resources such as chemical fertilizers. Similarly, in villages where crops can be grown by the community on Government lands, Panchayat lands, etc., this can also be undertaken.

The increase in production which each of the above practices is expected to contribute against the total targetted yield can be worked out on the basis of standard increased production percentage figures to be furnished by the District Agricultural Officer for the respective practices in the different areas. The District Agricultural Officer should arrange to furnish these figures to all the Blocks within his jurisdiction.

### Calender of Work

Though one would wish that the improved agricultural practices, which are included in the minimum programme, should be adopted at every survey number against which targets have been set in the plan so as to have a combined effect in increasing production, very often this may not be possible since the adoption of practices would depend largely on the conveniences and capacities of individual agriculturists. But, in any case, it is necessary to ensure that the implementation of the adopted practices are in accordance with Departmental recommendations. The preliminary work that will have to be done before the plan is prepared should include the following:—

(a) Collection of statistics by the Village Level Worker.

(b) Preparation of a list of improved agricultural practices and the standard percentage of increase in production expected from each of such practices by the District Agricultural Officer and Communicating the same to the Blocks;

(c) Review of the work of the various non-official, voluntary and statutory bodies in the district to ensure proper functioning and to make alternate arrangements wherever necessary;

(d) Drawing up a draft plan by the Agriculture Committee of the Panchayat on the basis of the available internal resources with the help of the Village Level Worker;

(e) Discussion and acceptance of the plan by the Gram Sabha and assigning individual targets of production for each crop against the total increase targeted for the village Panchayat;

(f) Contacting the participating farmers individually by the Village Level Worker and working out the various improved agricultural practices to be followed by them to achieve their promised increase in production under the plan;

(g) Finalisation and adoption of the detailed plan by the Panchayat at a joint meeting of the village cooperative and indicating the requirements of supplies. Here the detailed calender of operations by the various programmes under the plan both for individuals and institutions can be fixed and responsibilities assigned for follow-up and supervision.

(h) Making arrangements for timely procurement, storage and

distribution of supplies for the plan within the Panchayat area by the cooperative and other agencies.

(*i*) Pre-treatment of seed before sowing with chemicals by the primary societies or other agencies before distribution to individuals.

(*j*) Training of voluntary squads in spraying and dusting operations for plant protection by the District Agricultural Officer and his Plant Protection Assistants and the Block staff at the Block headquarters. For this purpose, the members of the Village Volunteer Force can be trained.

(*k*) Consolidation of Panchayat plans into a Block plan for purposes of effective supervision and follow-up and for arranging supplies and services.

(*l*) Monthly meetings of the Agricultural Production Committee of the Panchayati Raj bodies to review the progress from time to time and to decide upon the future course of action;

(*m*) Evaluation of achievements against targets through extensive enquiries from individual ryots and crop-cutting experiments;

(*n*) Meetings of Gram Sabha for review of the achievements with reference to the plan and consideration of measures to strengthen the organisation and arrangements for the next year's plan.

It is clear from an analysis of the chronological processes mentioned above that the officers and agencies involved in the programme should have a thorough grasp of its mechanism and understand their responsibilities, which should be clearly defined, both in the administrative and technical spheres. However, it will be necessary to safeguard against any compartmentalisation of functions and each agency concerned, whether official or non-official, should take the initiative not only in performing its tasks fully and punctually, but also in assisting others wherever necessary in discharging their specific tasks. In this manner it should be possible to achieve the degree of coordination so necessary for the successful implementation of the plan.

A target set from year to year in these plans should saturate rapidly the entire Panchayat area, at least in so far as the items of the minimum programme are concerned. As an essential and vital part of the programme it is necessary that the Block organisation should, in addition, attend to the programme of laying out demonstration plots and undertake other Extension activities. One of the common complaints against a production plan is that the proformae for the plan are "complicated and voluminous." In the light of the minimum programme outlined above, it is necessary to keep the forms as few and as simple as possible.

## Assignment of Responsibilities

For the programme to succeed, it is essential that the responsibilities of the participants in the formulation and implementation of the plan are clearly defined. Such responsibilities would be both in the administrative and the technical sphere of supervision, guidance, arranging for supplies, etc. Detailed below are the various jobs and the agency which would have specific responsibility in relation to that particular job. It would be necessary for the States to spell out in detail the functions of each of the agencies under a particular job item.

| | |
|---|---|
| 1. Supervision | The District Collector, District Agricultural Officer, Assistant Registrar of Cooperative Societies, Sub-Divisional Officers of Sub-Divisions, Block Development Officer, Agricultural Extension Officer, Cooperative Extension Officer, Village Level Workers. |
| 2. Collection of Statistics | Village Level Worker, Agricultural Extension Officer, Block Development Officer, Sub-Divisional Officer, District Agricultural Officer, the District Collector. |
| 3. Preparation of the list of improve practices and of standard percentage figures of increase in production expected from them. | District Agricultural Officer. |
| 4. Constitution of Agricultural Production Committees of Panchayati Raj bodies in the District. | The District Collector / the Deputy Commissioner / the Chief Executive Officer of the Zila Parishad. |
| 5. Printing Cyclostyling and supply of forms of Agricultural production Plans. | Block Development Officer. |
| 6. Review of working of the voluntary Organisations and Cooperative Societies in the District. | The Assistant Registrar of Cooperative Societies, the District Central Cooperative Bank, Taluk Marketing Society and the Block Development Officer. |
| 7. Meeting of Agricultural Production Committee of the village | Agricultural Production Committee of the Village Panchayat. |

Panchayat for assigning tentative targets.

8. Meeting of the Gram Sabha to draw up a tentative Agricultural Production Plan with targets for individual ryots. — Agricultural Production Committee of the village Panchayat, Village Level Worker.

9. Joint meeting of Panchayats and Cooperatives to adopt the plan. — Village Panchayat, Voluntary Organisations.

10. Indications of requirements of external resources, including short-term finance. — Primary Cooperative Society, Taluk Marketing Society, District Central Bank.

11. Finalisation of alternative sources of supply for Panchayats where cooperatives are not functioning properly or are not organized. — Assistant Registrar of Cooperative Societies.

12. Finalisation of storage arrangement at Taluk and Panchayat levels. — Primary societies, Taluk Marketing Society.

13. Procurement and distribution of supplies, including seed treatment. — Taluk Marketing Society, Primary Society, Village Level Worker.

14. Building up of loan records and disbursement of loans. — Primary Society, the District Central Bank.

15. Training of squads of voluntary organisations or Village Volunteer Force for dusting and spraying operations for plant protection. — The District Agricultural Officer.

16. Consolidation of Panchayat plans into Block plan. — Agricultural Extension Officer, Block Development Officer.

17. (a) Laying out of fields for irrigation where water is made available at the plot head.
(b) Preparatory tillage laying out of nurseries, demonstration plots.
(c) Manuring of fields with green manure.
(d) Preparation of seed beds.
(e) Sowing and incorporation of green manure, drilling or transplanting as the case may be. — Village Level Worker, Agricultural Extension Officer, Block Development Officer and Voluntary organisations like Youth Clubs, Farmers' Clubs, Irrigation Committees etc., Agricultural Production Committee of Panchayati Raj bodies (to meet regularly to review progress, solve difficulties and decide future course of action).

( *f* ) Top dressing.

(*g*)  Plant protection.

(*h*)  Demonstration and field days.

| | |
|---|---|
| 18. Crop cutting experiments and competitions. | Village Level Worker, Agricultural Extension Officer and other Extension Officers also, under the guidance of the Progress Assistant of the Blocks. |
| 19. Storage and preservation of registered seed. | Village Level Worker, Service Cooperative/Panchayat. |
| 20. Assessment of yield/performances and meeting of Gram Sabha for review of the achievements under the plan for the previous seasons and the drawing up of the plan for the succeeding year. | Agricultural Production Committee of the Village Panchayat. |

# RURAL INDUSTRIES PROGRAMME

*V.S. Vasudevaraju*

THE RURAL INDUSTRIES programme is considered to be the weakest link in the Community Development programme. This despite the fact that the need for converting the present purely agricultural economy into an agro-industrial economy has imparted urgency to this programme. No doubt a series of measures have been adopted to put the programme on an even keel, but progress so far has not been commensurate with the efforts put in. The odds are no doubt heavy against rural industrialisation, but the want of a clearcut policy decision at the top level and the paucity of men and material in implementing the programme on the ground are largely responsible for its slow progress. The introduction of Panchayati Raj on a countrywide scale, and the consequent involvement of the people in planning and execution of development programmes have acted as morale boosters and give hope for a bright future in this field. It would be wrong to presume that the programme did not receive due attention in the past. Rather, it was agitating the minds of our planners, shortly after the C. D. Programme was ushered in. The annual conferences on Community Development, between the years 1955 and 1957, deliberated over the problems facing the programme and recommended several measures. The annual conference on Community Development held at Srinagar in 1960 considered the entire programme of rural industrialisation in the light of the experiences gained through the Industrial Pilot Projects, and recommended an integrated programme to be undertaken in the rural areas. The Conference recommended that the integrated programme had to be implemented by pooling the resources of the State Industries Department, All India Boards, the schematic budget of the C. D. Blocks and other agencies responsible for and assisting the development of village and small-scale industries. With the introduction of Panchayati Raj institutions, the Block has become the unit of planning implementation and administration of development programme and is directly responsible for the implementation of rural industries schemes. All these measures have had the desired effect, and rural industrialisation received the much needed impetus. The initiative of Panchayati Raj bodies in the matter lends vitality to the programme and all States in the country have started in right earnest in implementing the programme. Success has come to them in varying degrees. However, it will be too much to assume that the progress achieved in any one State is an indication of the shape of things all over the country. But, one would be justified in presuming that the efforts made in one State in this field represents the all India trend. Judged from this angle it will be worthwhile to examine the implementation of the rural industries programme in Madras State.

Unlike other States, the implementation of the industries programme in the C. D. Blocks in Madras is the responsibility of the State Khadi & Village Industries Board. As a consequence, the services of Extension Officers, who were previously under the Industries Department, were transferred to the Rural Development and Local Administration Department in April 1961. Subsequently, their services were lent to the State Khadi Board for implementing Block programmes.

The task of the Blocks is to prepare artisans as the main participants in the programme form them into cooperative guilds; get the artisans in the village under a common roof: communicate to them new techniques and improved skills; and set up of service cooperatives to provide common worksheds, tools and machines. At present the funds available in the schematic budget can be utilised for (*i*) grants for construction of workshed; (*ii*) stipend for trainees; (*iii*) supply of tools at half the cost; and (*iv*) managerial grant to industrial cooperatives.

An analytical appraisal of the work done in the Blocks can be dealt with under three main heads. Firstly how far the national policy accepted by the States at the annual conferences on Community Development is being actually implemented; secondly, whether there is a correlation between the general approach of the State Khadi Board and the position obtaining in the field; and thirdly, whether the field-workers are doing what is expected of them.

Even a cursory examination of the existing situation reveals that the integrated programme recommended by the Srinagar Conference has been lost sight of an actual implementation. The Industries Department and the State Khadi Board have not broken down the plan for development of rural industries on the basis of Blocks and the funds are not channelised through the Block administration. By administration. By and large, the Block is not being treated as a unit of planning and implementation. Since the State Khadi Board is incharge of the programme, the Industries Department has lost touch with the Block agency. This has created a situation in which the Block is concerned only with the promotion of village industries and the Khadi industry is being looked after by the Department of Khadi, through its own officers. There is, thus, no effort to coordinate the activities of different departments at the Block level.

Another matter that needs to be examined is whether the various Departments concerned are expected to organise and actively participate in rural industries programme, or their role is only to assist, guide and supervise the work done in the Blocks ? In the context of Panchayati Raj, the Hyderabad Conference in 1961 prescribed the 'promotion of rural industries' as one of the ten acid tests for assessing the efficiency of Panchayati Raj bodies in discharging their responsibilities. When all the industrial units are under their control the Panchayat Samitis could show better results in this field. The Departments could render assistance by way of technical guidance and concentrate more on Extension work when they are free from the day-to-day management of industries. The present trend reveals that the Departments are becoming active agents at local levels and blocking the way of local institutions taking the initiative.

The experience of the past four years does not provide evidence to show that even the limited programme undertaken in the Blocks has been implemented with the final objectives in view. The construction of common worksheds for artisans is a popular activity in the Blocks. But, instances are not lacking where the artisans have not been willing to occupy the sheds even months after the completion of construction. Furthermore, insufficient space in the worksheds does not permit all the artisans to enjoy this facility. Local conditions, like the number of artisans, the total space required for all of them in the workshed, the location of the sheds, etc., do not seem to have been properly assessed and the needs and problems of the beneficiaries are not considered in details before undertaking the construction of worksheds. Lack of funds for purchase of site is also one of the causes of inadequate progress. The Block level service cooperatives visualised are yet to be organised. The State Khadi Board has fixed a sum of Rs. 2,000 providing for half the cost of tools for each Block for the five year period. However, even this meagre sum has not been utilised in full in many Blocks. Delay in distributing the tools and the procedure followed are not encouraging the artisans to avail of this facility. The State Khadi Board has prescribed some model schemes. Permission of State Level officers is required even to launch these schemes. It is rather unfortunate that it takes a long time to obtain the sought for permission. Absence of 'vertical decentralisation of power' in such things affects the progress of work in the Blocks.

Training of artisans, creating a cadre of skilled workers to meet the needs of a developing rural economy and financing artisans to set themselves up in their trade are the practical needs of the programme. As a result of development activities, the repairing and servicing of

oil engines, irrigation pump sets, cycles, welding etc. and the manufacture of improved agricultural implements have become new items
of work in the rural areas. The existing skills, therefore, have to be
improved and new skills have to be introduced in the villages. In
order to meet the situation the State Khadi Board has provided
short-term training facilities in some of training centres set up by it
in the villages. The Industries Department is also imparting training
through its Industrial Training Institutes. The Block training centres
have not proved effective in introducing improved practices and the
'response ratio' of the artisans to the training is not impressive. The
Industrial Training Institutes offer good training in about 14 trades.
But, the selection procedure is such that young artisans in the rural
areas find it difficult to get admission. It will be more useful, if one
such institute could cater to the needs of a certain number of elected
Blocks and the Block agency is associated in the selection of trainees.
It is also necessary to increase the stipend given to the trainees.

The annual conference on Community development held at
Hyderabad in 1961 recommended that, in view of the growing needs
of the Block area, at least Rs. 15,000 per Block should be made
available by the State Government for promoting rural industries.
This recommendation has not yet been implemented in Madras State.
The Block is not in a position to give loans to poor artisans and it is
not even associated in the activities of the Industries Department in
this regard. This lacuna needs to be removed.

The Extension Officer (Industries) in the State is involved only in
the limited sphere of activities of the State Khadi Board and conditions have not been created to make him do all the items of work
listed in his job chart. His position in the State confirms the opinion
of the Mathai Committee that "the services of Extension Officers
have not been fully utilised by all the concerned agencies implementing rural industries programme." The consensus of opinion is that
in the present administrative set up they are, so to say, cut off from
the Industries Department, and therefore, cannot be effective in performing the jobs listed in their job chart. Treating them as agents of
the All-India Board at the Block level, placing them under the
control of the Industries Department and routing all assistance and
guidance through the Block agency would make them effective in implementing the rural industries programme. If Industries Standing
Committees, which need to be set up in the Panchayat Samitis in
Madras State could be statutorily constituted with necessary administrative powers for sanctioning schemes on the basis of technical approval by the Extension Officer, without waiting for any further orders
from above it would result in speedier implementation of the schemes.

# COMMUNITY DEVELOPMENT PROGRAMME
## AN ANTHOLOGY

### SOCIAL EDUCATION

#### Aim of Social Education

THE AIM OF social education must, therefore, be to give to the illiterate adult the minimum of knowledge required for a purposeful civic life. It tries to endow their lives with meaning and significance. It recognises the right of every individual to develop the resources of mind and improve upon his heritage.

Social Education, besides promoting literacy, aims at education for citizenship and democracy and the fostering of social solidarity and cultural harmony in the country. It brings the adults an awareness of their rights and duties, develops in them love for a democratic way of life and pride in their cultural heritage.

Social Education also implies training in the basic principles of personal and social hygiene...If people know how diseases are caused and how to fight them, hundreds of valuable lives can be saved. By emphasising sanitation, balanced diet and nutrition, it is possible to build a healthy nation. What is implied in the process of social education is the education of the individual in terms of his personal and social hygiene as a responsibility towards society.

It is equally necessary to satisfy the emotional and aesthetic needs of adult learners. Painting, music, dramatic performances, festivals, exhibitions and melas can be profitably used for the development of aesthetic sensibility in the adults, besides enabling them to demonstrate their creative powers and organisational ability. Group activities and discussions, talks, sport, clubs, education, cultural and historical tours, youth camps, seminars and gardening have also been found valuable for social education.

The opportunity to improve one's economic condition is one of the prime attractions of education. Hence a programme of social education activities should initiate the adult into ways and means of raising his living standard. The social education worker should, therefore, associate him with the organisations which can teach him improved methods of agricultural or new crafts that can add to his earning capacity. The universities and polytechnics should be persuaded to organise part-time technical and professional courses to help him to improve his economic positions.

Finally, social education stands for human brotherhood and universal ethics. It teaches the virtues of peace, and is opposed to narrowness of outlook of any form, such as chauvinism and racialism. It upholds the diginity of man and attempts the elimination of poverty and backwardness.

Children cannot be left out of a programme of social education. As stated earlier, social education is a continuous progress, beginning from birth. The school and play-ground play an important part in promoting social education among children.

Experience shows that participation in groups and organisations by children, youth and adults is the best method of social education. Through group participation individuals find opportunities to work with others, to express their creativeness, to develop their ability and to qualify for leadership, depending on their ability to perform a given function. In addition, group participation promotes a spirit of cooperation and brotherhood.

**Methods and Techniques**

This leads to the methods of organising the programme of social education. As indicated above, the programme is to be promoted through groups and organisations. The group is formed around some common interests......The programme of the group may be recreational, cultural, educational, or economic, or a combination of many of these activities. Efforts are made to expose the members to larger interests and they are helped to relate this multiplicity of activities. The Community Centre in the Community Development Blocks offers the opportunity both of relating one's interest to the interest of the community and of finding self-expression and satisfaction through its recreational, educational and cultural activities.

**Social Education and Community Development**

Social education, as a process of education for life in society, has an extremely vital role to play in community development by relating villagers with their own communities and their social groups. This is in harmony with the current, emphasis on the organisation of three vital institutions, namely the Panchayat, the cooperative and the school. Through the programme of social education, various voluntary organisations such as youth groups, farmers' groups, women's groups, recreation groups and cultural groups act as agencies for relating the villagers with the development programme and providing a base for developing leadership around functions. The programme also concentrates on the training of this leadership through participation in various activities. Therefore the Social Education Organiser, who is a member of the Development Team, tries to promote organisation of the groups described above. He organises community centres and tries to stimulate and develop leadership around various functions. He organises literacy classes, reading rooms and libraries for the spread of education among adults. He utilises various audio-visual aids including films, film strips, radios, posters, etc. The Community Centre, as a multipurpose organisation providing recreational, cultural and educational activities, promoted and organised with the active participation, of the villagers, offers an excellent meeting place for children, youth and adults in the community. The Social Education Organiser, in addition, cooperates with other Extension workers in promoting the programme of Community Development. Every Extension worker is an educator in his own subject, and every social group, including the Panchayat and the Cooperative, offers the opportunity to promote social education among the members of the community. Thus social education becomes an integral part of the total programme of Community Development in rural areas.

(Extracts from the book, *Social Education*)

### School as a Community Centre

The rural school has got a significant role of leadership to play in the community. A school becomes a community school inasmuch as it derives its programmes from the problems of the people whom it serves and draws upon all the available resources in attempts to solve them. It should be an integral part of all community activity. It may be a community centre for the village as a whole. Or it may render assistance in the establishment of adult courses, provide recreation programmes, help in the improvement of health and sanitary conditions and initiate other measures that are likely to inspire the community into efforts for a better living.

It is essential that a village school should primarily be community-faced rather than classroom-faced. Its instruction should be mostly through activity and learning should be closely related to the environment in which the child lives. Sufficient emphasis should be laid on crafts and agriculture. It should be a "People's School," whose curriculum will epitomise their life and whose activity will reflect the characteristic features of the community in their natural setting.

### Cooperatives vis-a-vis Schools

Cooperatives are economic democracies and develop leadership and skill in democratic procedure. They enable the members of the

Community to pool their efforts together for both individual and collective objectives. They have a place in both the cultural and economic aspects of rural life and nothing can be more instructive to the children of the school than to get initiated in proper manner into the activities of these institutions and get a practical first-hand knowledge of their working. The teachers on their part should have a clear grasp of the concept and philosophy of cooperative institutions and be also fairly conversant with their operational procedures. They can introduce in a modest and miniature form, cooperative practices in the school itself.

## School Panchayats

Introduction of self-government in schools as a co-curricular activity is very important. The system of "class ministers," wherever introduced, has developed a sense of initiative and responsibility even among teen-agers. The working of the Panchayats can be demonstrated to the children through these activities.

The school is thus intended to be a vital link in the life of the community. The child should not confine himself to learning of books or some skills but get full scope for expression of his social impulses. He will get training through practical experience to work in cooperation with othersb oth for his personal gain in the service of the group or the community as a whole. The school as a miniature community will receive and impart a healthy impact influence vis-a-vis the community outside. The leaders of the community will take interest and be involved in the programmes of the school, not in a formal manner like the usual type of parent-teacher association which meets once a year on the school foundation or the prize-giving day in a continuous and intimate manner. Thus outside life will flow into the school and *vice versa*.

## School Projects

Each one of the activities mentioned earlier can be brought under a project of school work in which the pupil, the teacher and the village community participate. For example, programmes of cleaning the school, white-washing the school walls, etc., will form a regular feature of school life. Here the parents will join the teacher and student in the work. But instruction of a practical type involving personal cleanliness like cleaning one's teeth, combing one's hair, washing of clothes or using the urinal and latrine can be carried by the children to their homes where it will have a healthy impact upon their parents.

## Social Service by schools

The extension work of a school can be conducted as a school project in the field of social service. For instance, one of the greatest needs of our villages is the planting of trees, and in any programme of this nature the villages themselves will be anxious to participate. If the school gives a lead they are sure to fall in line and the project will be a success. Similarly, collectively, construction of a bund or a drain, cleaning up of a tank or construction of a school wall can be undertaken as school projects.

While the teacher will be closely associated with all these projects, it will be very useful if the extension staff from other technical departments pay visits to such projects and help the children in getting practical knowledge of the various processes involved. Similarly, it will be useful for the teachers and students, especially of the senior classes, to visit demonstration farms which may be available nearly. The students may be asked to adopt, in groups, beds or portions of the farms which they will look after under the guidance of their teacher. It is also possible to maintain small poultry units in the school with the help of children.

(Extracts from a pamphlet *Village Teacher's Role in Community Development*)

**Women's activities under Community Development Programme.**

For the last few years, programme for women had been receiving particular attention under the Community Development programme. The objective, as defined, is to develop "progressive outlook" in women "for intelligently participating in the nation-building activities." The programme is expected to attain this objective by imparting to the rural women "such knowledge and skill (through practical demonstration wherever necessary) as would make them better housewives and mothers, thus adding to the economic and general welfare of the family."

**Coordinated activities**

There is coordination between the Ministry of Community Development and the Central Social Welfare Board for work.

While there had been intense planning to bring about radical changes in women's thinking and activity, it had not yet been possible to engage many workers for the purpose. Only one lady Social Education Organiser, now known as Mukhya Sevika, and two Gram Sevikas are in charge of this programme in a block of about hundred villages. They are, with the help of the team of workers provided by the Central Social Welfare Board and with the assistance of rural women's organisations and the panchayat, supposed to do the following types of work : (1) literacy programme centering round crafts like spinning, weaving embroidery, cutting, sewing of garments, etc.,

(2) improving home through installation of smokeless choola, provision of clean drinking water, protection of foodstuffs, ensuring general cleanliness, introducing nutritious food, laying kitchen gardens or small poultry farms; (3) introduction of cottage industry in each family, keeping in view the aptitude and inclination of the housewife as also her resources; (4) health education including environmental sanitation, care of children, etc., (5) beautification of home; (6) organising women's associations like Mahila Mandals etc., so that eventually they take up these activities and organisation of recreational activities like bhajans, kirtans, etc. These are but a few of the many similar activities to improve the working and living conditions of women in villages. It is not necessary that all of these activities should be started in all the villages. The choice would naturally depend upon the genuine and pressing needs of the local community.

(Extracts from *A Guide to Gram Sevikas and Mukhya Sevikas*)

### A Programme for Children's Welfare

"India's child population under 15 years of age is of the order of 178 million, a majority of which lives in the villages. Inevitably, therefore, child welfare must form an essential part of any community development programme for the rural people. Children's schools, children's centres and maternity and child welfare centres have been set up in villages to promote the welfare of children."

"Children are a highly vulnerable group of the population because they possess low physical vitality. The health of the Indian child in general and of the rural child in particular is far from satisfactory, and in the absence of any kind of medical aid in the villages the infant falls an easy prey to disease. There is considerable mortality among infants due to prematurity and malnutrition. One infant out of every 10 who are born dies. Communicable diseases account for a majority of deaths among children. So the rural child needs regular health supervision, protection against diseases, and nutritious diet."

### Maternity and Child Welfare Centres

"Faced with these facts and in order to meet the basic health requirements of the rural children, the Community Development authorities have, as part of the National Health Programme, opened maternity and child welfare centres in the Community Project areas."

### Primary Health Centres

"Primary Health centres have also been set up at the headquarters of the blocks where proper medical care is given to the ailing child."

## Milk Feeding Programmes

"Milk is the most nutritious diet for children who suffer from under-nutrition and malnutrition. Rural parents are usually too poor to be able to afford milk for their children. Consequently, milk feeding programmes have been started by the Community Development authorities."

## Primary Schools

"Besides the provision of health services to protect rural children against disease, sickness and malnutrition, steps have been taken by the Community Development authorities to promote their intellectual growth. Towards this end, primary schools have been opened in Community Development areas to provide free education."

## Special Programme for Children

"The Community Development authorities have chalked out a special programme of work for children. This programme has been made a part of the overall programme of social education. The target laid down is to provide Bal Sabhas in all villages and a children's park with playing facilities in selected villages. A children's park is located at sufficiently large, enclosed space suitable for playing games and for gardening. The plan is that the villagers should contribute the open space and erect a fencing around it while the Government supplies equipment like swings, see-saws, slides and merry-go-rounds. The cost of this equipment averages about Rs. 250 for a children's park. In addition, trips and excursions are organised and instruction is given in personal hygiene.

(Extracts from pamphlet, *Children's Welfare and Community Development*)

## Rural Arts

Every person is endowed with certain finer emotions which can find expression in various forms of art. India's rural people have natural leanings towards art and aesthetics, which find expression in poetry and music, dance and drama, painting and sculpture, colourful and decorative designs (Rangoli and Alpana), rural jewellery, pottery and toys and embroidery.

## Children and Art

School children in villages can be taught drawing and painting. Children by instinct, are attracted by the shapes and sounds around them, which they express in art if they are given an opportunity to do so.

Children ought to be trained to keep their surroundings neat and clean. Even in their games, teachers should keep an eye on their behaviour. Village children have greater advantages than those in town and cities in enjoying the beauty of nature. It should form part of the duties of village school master, Gram Sevikas and Gram Sevaks to instil in the young a genuine love for flowers, the beauty of the blue sky and the green land. These leave an imprint upon the tender heart and develop the child's aesthetic sense.

## Folk Art

A touch of art on things of everyday use is nothing new. The fine needle work on the Kantha prepared out of waste material, the beautifully printed floral designs on peasant textiles, the village toys and village pottery have drawn appreciation from connoisseurs for ages.

The most popular of village textile patterns are seen on the Kantha which is generally prepared from waste material. Worn-out clothes are stitched together to form designs which have been passed on from generation to generation and thus preserved for centuries. The beautiful floral and spray designs on these Kanthas are in no way inferior to modern designs on saris, shawls or carpets.

## Village Pottery

The village potter, is a born artist. Besides items of everyday use like the pitcher, etc., the village potter produces articles of luxury also. The potters of some villages in Khurja and Jaipur specialize in the art of producing black pottery.

## Village Jewellery

Like the potter, the village jeweller has a keen artistic taste. Unlike his counterpart in the urban areas, the village jeweller fashions the ornaments, engraves them, sets them with stones, and gives the finishing touches all by himself. Floral designs and deities in the form of popular mythological figures are the basic motifs of rural jewellery.

## Village Toys

Indian villagers are quite expert in making toys of wood, clay, cloth and papier-mache. The peach toys of Krishna Nagar in West Bengal, the wooden toys of Banaras, the clay toys of Kondapalle in Andhra and the cloth dolls of Poona are some of the finest specimens of Indian folk art. Indian toys have a market abroad and it can be developed considerably. Given adequate training and facilities, our village people can take to this cottage industry with greater zeal. Therefore, in our programme for the revival of folk art and aesthetic sense proper emphasis should be laid on toy-making.

## Alpana and Rangoli

Village women draw fine Alpanas and Rangolis in the front yard of their huts, and on the walls and doors, particularly during festivals. The Alpana styles are popular in Bengal, Madras, Gujarat and many other parts of the country. In all religious festivals it is a 'must'. During the Lakshmi Puja (in Bengal) and Sarswathi Puja (in Madras) village houses are decorated with many varieties of alpana. In Bengal, both in rural and urban areas, wooden platforms are painted by women folk during marriage ceremonies. It is a treat to watch girls painting lovely hues on wood.

## Folk Dance

That there is a rich variety of folk dances in India is well known. Our Gram Sevaks, Social Education Organizers and other engaged in rural development work are in a position to revive and promote these folk dances. They can organize popular group dances of the locality, particularly in village melas and festivals. It would perhaps be easier to start with regional folk dances. Inter-regional folk dances can come in at a later stage. The songs of the Bratachari Nritya of Bengal inspire young boys and girls to take active part in village reconstruction programmes. Bihu and Khamba Lim, the harvest dances of Assam, Bhangra, the community peasant dance of Punjab, the pastoral dance of Chamba in Himachal Pradesh, Jhora, the community dance of Uttar Pradesh, the Tippanin of Saurashtra, all have a beauty of their own.

## Folk Songs

In the task of reviving the aesthetic sense of the village people the folk songs of the locality should be popularized. Local bards or *charans* compose songs containing anecdotes which give a description of the social condition of the community. Katha or Patha in which the village pundit recites from the Ramayana or the Mahabharata, is very popular in villages and is heard raptly for hours by large audiences. Kavi Durbar or the Assembly of Poets is another popular feature of village life. Poets recite *extempore* poems and, with the participation of others, the whole thing develops into a sort of contest. The harvest songs of different regions can be popularized by Gram Sevaks or Social Education Organizers.

## Rural Stage

Our Gram Sevaks and social workers can improvize suitable plays for the rural stage and use them as an instrument to educate the villagers.

The play can depict some social problems, and centre round the importance of the Community Development Programme or other development projects of the Government.

(Extracts from the pamphlet, *Revival of Rural Arts*)

# SOCIAL EDUCATION AS AN INSTRUMENT OF DEVELOPING SERVICES IN UNDEVELOPED AREAS

*M. C. Nanavatty*

## Social Education as a Process of Promoting Social Values

THE TERM 'SOCIAL Education' connotes education for social life. It is an educational process to promote social values with a view to facilitating adjustment of individuals in a society. The expression "adjustment" is used in a dynamic sense. It covers both education to understand the social customs and social practices prevalent in the community, to abide by them in given circumstances and gradually to try to change some of the social habits and practices which become harmful to the welfare of the members of a community.

A child acquires social values from his parents mainly through imitation and association. These values are supported and stabilised by the caste and the religious group that the family belongs to. As he grows, he comes in contact with other playmates. Later, as a youth he succumbs. Still later, if he has the educational facilities to develop his personality and if he has made use of these opportunities to acquire ability to exert his influence, he can contribute to the changing of some of the prevailing social practices which are harmful to others. During this process of Social Education he is to be helped to understand the problem of the weaker section of the community and to extend his helping hand in overcoming some of their handicaps. The term "weaker section of the community" is not a happy expression. It, however, indicates the group of people in need of care and assistance through social welfare services as explained earlier. This consideration for the "weaker section," should not arise out of pity for the "poor" or the "weak". It should come to every individual as a natural part of his responsibilities and duties to those in need of care, help and assistance. It should be as his obligation and not as a favour. The question thus remains to be answered is, "How does the child acquire these social values and develop considerations for others as an integral part of his personality." Historically speaking, these values are imbedded in religious teachings. If religion is taken as a way of life, various rituals incorporated in the teaching of the religion emphasise the values of "giving" : without the expectation of any return. In all religious teachings the care of the weaker section of the community has been emphasised as an integral part of the responsibility of every individual. The concept of giving, later got associated with the expectation of some privileges after death. It is necessary to reiterate the responsibilities of every individual citizen to look after the welfare of those who cannot utilise the essential services provided by the State on their own. This is specially needed when the joint family system is giving way to the unitary family under the influence of industrialisation. Earlier, the "weaker" members of the family were taken care of by the joint family itself. The child, the handicapped, the aged and the infirm were supported and looked after as a joint responsibility of the family. The caste used to provide orphanages and other welfare services, although to a limited extent. With the change in the situation, the Panchayats, the Municipalities and the State Governments have to extend their responsibilities to the weaker section of the community. In some of the economically advanced countries, with the Government assuming the responsibilities of the full employment, the State provides measures of social security for all including the weaker section of the community. Till this develops, the community and its members have to hold themselves responsible. Even when the State assumes this responsibility, it only acts as an agent for promoting these services on behalf of the people.

This leads us to the duties and responsibilities of every citizen specially in a country wedded to democracy. Democracy bestows both benefits and responsibilities on every citizen; the benefit of law and order, freedom of expression and association and the right to vote; responsibilities of putting in practice the essential tenets of democracy and co-operating with the Government in achieving measures of welfare. Every citizen convinced of the importance of equality, justice and fraternity, has certain responsibilities towards the under-privileged members of the community, who may be handicapped economically, socially, physically and mentally. This he can fulfil in two ways, namely (i) by becoming conscious of one's responsibility to help others in need of care and assistance, and (ii) by creating in the community, with the help of the voluntary organisations and the Government, adequate resources to take suitable steps for the welfare and rehabilitation of the under-privileged. As indicated earlier social values to help—others are to be given during the early stage of growth, Social Education, therefore, should begin in the family, the home and the neighbourhood. Unfortunately, as historically Social Education has been associated with literacy and adult education, this important aspect of promoting social education through the family and the home is not adequately emphasized. The school is the next best source of promoting social education among children. The institution of caste, promoting a feeling of welfare among its own members, suffers from the narrowness of confining this feeling of brotherliness in a narrow circle. This is likely to result in the antagonism for members outside the circle. Casteism is the bane of the institution of caste. The programme of Community Development provides a new opportunity and a challenge to develop a sense of belonging for the whole community and to work for the harmonious promotion of the measures of welfare for all sections of the community. During recent times the attention is focussed to the need of looking after the weaker section of the village community. The Panchayat at the village level and the Panchayat Samiti at the Block Level are being required to provide special measures for the weaker section of the community. It is an effort to draw the attention of the Panchayat to the need of providing resources from its own budget and secure adequate resources from various Service Departments—specially the Directorate of Social Welfare—for meeting the needs of its weaker sections. The Panchayat, with the help of various associate groups, such as youth organisation, the woman's organisation, can contribute considerably in promoting Social Welfare Services, once it has these services in its focus of attention. It is more a question of creating in the Panchayat and the public the necessary consciousness of social responsibilities to the weaker section.

The process of Social Education as an instrument of making people conscious of the need of social welfare services is thus to be promoted through the family, the home, the school, the playground, the youth organisation, the women's organisation and the Panchayat or other civic organisations. It is a question of each social institution and organisation to emphasise in its influence of the process of promoting social values—specially of their responsibilities to the underprivileged. This, if adequately attended to, will plant the roots of social values deeper in the life of every citizen. Although this measure involves all the existing social institutions and organisations and hence can be adopted as a long-term approach, has the value of giving more lasting results. The question of securing public cooperation for promoting social welfare from this point of view is a question of creating consciousness among every citizen and providing the necessary atmosphere of social values, so that both the individual and the institution are made to contribute willingly for social welfare.

# DEVELOPING RURAL YOUTH LEADERSHIP

## M. Chaube

DEVELOPING LEADERSHIP, CHIEFLY rural youth leadership, is not what a layman can attempt. It is a highly technical programme and calls for a highly sustained effort. It requires a long term continuous process of training and developing human elements and puts a rigid ban on seeking tangible results in a year or so.

### New Dimensions in Training

The knowledge we now have about the nature of democratic and functional youth leadership suggests that youth leadership training is not the simple one dimensional undertaking we have traditionally thought it to be. To develop efficient youth leaders we have to work in three dimensions. The first dimension has to do with training in the particular knowledges and skills required for particular jobs. In rural youth clubs this can be achieved by enabling club members to conduct meetings, to lead discussions, to act as presidents and teach particular subjects. The second dimension consists of developing generalized understanding of group behaviour that are applicable to younger age-groups in varying situations. The third dimension consists of training all group members, not just the designated leaders, to be able to perform leadership functions.

### Duties and Functions

In recent years Sociologists, Social workers, Educators, and Extension Workers have given increasing importance to the development of youth leadership. It has been recognized that the voluntary youth leader should be the backbone of youth organisation trying to improve the social, economic and cultural conditions in a developing country. One of the main functions of youth leaders is to develop relationship between groups and individuals so as to enable them to work together and make use of common facilities available for realising their highest values.

Local youth leader often seen the needs of young people and keeps the aims and objectives of the rural youth ahead of the rest. A true youth leader by force of his own example exerts more influence on the group and its activities than does the average members.

To bring about wider and more active participation of some families in action programme through the medium of youth coming from those families, youth leader is the best agent and therefore he should incessantly try to search out new ideas for the group, locate problems and organise collective efforts for their solution. The transmission of research results from the laboratories to the field is best possible through these young agents committed to the task of rural reconstruction.

### Locating Prospective Leaders

Having finally decided that rural youth leaders are to be selected from a broad stratum of people, we should bear the following criteria in mind while locating prospective youth leaders. The first guide to spotting potential youth leaders is the presence of those qualities in them to meet the challenge of the duties to be undertaken. Secondly while selecting youth leaders favouritism should be tabooed unless it were to favour the best man of the job. Thirdly, where more than one leader are to be selected on the basis of their qualifications a system of division of work or rotation can be applied.

### The Steps

Developing youth leadership is a very difficult task and calls for a very cautious and vigilant effort. No definite steps and methods can be laid down for training rural youth leaders; yet the following points, based as they are on field experience, may prove useful :

1. From the very start of the Community Development programme in an area the Extension worker should start keeping a record of the potential youth leaders in the village.

2. A problem census is the first necessity and should include felt problems and felt needs. A list of jobs to be taken up by the youth leaders should also be prepared. The jobs should relate to the needs and problems of the area.

3. Specific opportunities picked up from the fields of Arts, Science, Agriculture, Crafts, Social Service, Music, recreation, etc. should be provided to the potential leaders according to their attitudes and abilities. It would be helpful if interest-finding questionnaires are administered and necessary data collected.

4. In rural youth clubs office-bearers should be trained to conduct meetings in a systematic way. Rudiments of democracy learnt and practised in the club meetings will considerably help them to grow good debaters, Pradhans, Pramukhs, Adhakshas, legislators and parliamentarians in future years. Elections held

for choosing office-bearers of the youth clubs are important training grounds for the rural youth to understand their franchise and exercise their rights. Early training in rightly conducting these elections will eliminate the too cursed system of casting votes on the basis of parochial loyalties.

5. Job training may be provided to the potential leaders who have been evincing keen interest and enthusiasm and who already possess some knowledge about and skill in the project. There may be short training camps organized for a group of young leaders with similar interests or aptitudes. They may also be allowed to work as an under-study to the Extension worker or the adult leader of the village. In rural areas some effort has been made to organize training camps for youth leaders who after their training have taken up the task of forming youth clubs in their villages. But in order to make the youth clubs self-sustaining it is essential to hold project leaders' camps regularly. New ideas, new skills, and new practices taught to the project leaders will result in their steady dissemination among the rural masses. Some of the subjects in which protect leaders should be trained are improved agricultural practices, raising kitchen gardens and orchards, poultry farming and heifer-rearing, bee-keeping, rope and soap manufacture, sericulture, handloom weaving, etc. In building project leaders' care should be taken to avoid the development of one-dimensional leaders who have learnt the skills and information required for a particular job and perhaps some tricks and gadgets also, but who have not acquired the understandings and insights about the group behaviour.

6. There is a great scope for rural youth leadership in the field of social service and recreation. A little responsibility entrusted to the youth club leaders has yielded remarkable results. Projects on social service to the youth are of immense long-range value in so far as they create among them a desire for a common national purpose. These projects should be properly guided and participants suitably incentivised. In the realm of recreation emphasis should not be only on watching and enjoying the programme but on initiating and actively participating also.

7. At the time of inducting newly trained youth leaders into their jobs the most important point to be stressed is that each preceding leader while handing over to his successor should pass on a review of his experience to his successor and should wish him well in his career. The present situation presents a contrary picture and instances abound where preceding leaders have

sabotaged the plans and projects of their successors. This is a very undesirable tendency and it would really be a great day in the annals of rural youth leadership in India when preceding leaders not only start wishing well but also start helping all they can to enable their successors to surpass them and better their own records.

8. Lastly the process of training rural youth leaders has to be continuous. No leader, however tall, should aspire to strut the stage all his life. He should pride in preparing a strong second line and gladly quit the stage as soon as he feels he can be suitably replaced. Even in countries that took an early start in developing rural youth leadership there is a dearth of adequate leaders. In India an organized effort in this direction was initiated in the wake of the Community Development programme. Realizing its value and importance in a developing country any amount of effort and expenditure stands more than justified.

# PROGRAMME FOR WOMEN AND CHILDREN

THE PROGRAMME FOR women and children should be planned and implemented by the village women's organisations such as the Mahila Mandal which are already in existence in the village; if they do not exist they should be developed by the Gram Sevikas and Mukhya Sevikas.

The following are the most important programmes and activities which may be taken up:

1. Educating women regarding mother and child-care and encouraging them to avail themselves of the services offered such as the Primary Health Centre and Family Planning Centre.

2. Helping to spread the knowledge of health and sanitation, including the use of latrines, and inducing village families to observe the laws of health and hygiene and to adopt measures and practices for cure and prevention of communicable diseases.

3. Organising Balwadis in order to :
    (a) Educate and train children of pre-school age in habits and good social practices,
    (b) Enable mothers to be free to join the Mahila Mandal and participate in its programmes and activities.
    (c) enable older girls, who are not able to go to school because they are in charge of their younger brothers and sisters while their parents are at work, to attend school.

4. Organising some economic programme for saving and for supplementing family income or both, such as simple tailoring making of mats and/or baskets, spinning and weaving, etc.

5. Encouraging adult literacy.

6. Educating women in habits of thrift and saving and avoiding extravagance and loans for ceremonial occasions; encouraging Small Savings schemes or any other system of savings.

7. Encouraging improvement of homes by kitchen gardens, improved methods of cooking, labour-saving devices and avoiding wastage of food.

8. Encouraging some of their progressive members to take up the responsibility of giving regular assistance as 'Gram Lakshmis' or associate women workers known by any other name, to Gram Sevikas.

In order to help the Mahila Mandals in carrying out their tasks and responsibilities, and to give due emphasis to the programme, the Panchayat should have a Functional Sub-Committee for this programme.

The principal ways in which the Panchayat can help the Mahila Mandal to grow and function effectively are the following:

1. Creating a favourable climate for the work of the Mahila Mandal.
2. Providing a building and the equipment needed for its activities such as Sewing Machine, Charkha, dholak, Black Board, posters etc.,
3. Providing financial assistance;
4. Helping to launch special drives and campaigns and to organise exhibitions, etc.
5. Helping to select Gram Lakshmis, and particularly helping with their Training Camps (as they do with Gram Sahayaks' Camps),
6. Helping to find suitable accommodation for the Gram Sevika or the Midwife.
7. As recommended by the Mussoorie Conference encouraging the under-privileged class of women to come and join the Mahila Mandals in larger numbers.

The Panchayat Sub-Committee for women and children's programme may include the following as co-opted members in addition to the women members of the Panchayat:

(*a*) The President and the Secretary of the Village Mahila Mandal.
(*b*) Chairman or any other representative of the P.I.C. resident in the village.
(*c*) One or two other progressive village women.
(*d*) Gram Sevika.
(*e*) The Woman Primary Teacher.

It was further recommended that women from the Mahila Mandal should be associated with some of the other functional committees set up by the panchayat, to look after the interest of women and children.

## Co-operative and Industries :

(1) Extension Officers of Cooperatives and Industries should, through Gram Sevikas, help village women (a) to realise the need and importance of co-operation; (b) to establish contacts with the sources from which they can avail themselves of assistance by way of money, instruction, technical guidance, procurement of raw material and marketing of their produce.

(2) The Co-operative Department and particularly the Extension

Officer, should encourage women to become members of co-operatives particularly those supplying; (a) credit, (b) consumer goods required for daily use at home. They should also help in sale of surplus production of women's craft centres.

(3) It should be the duty of the Industries Extension Officers to assist women to choose suitable crafts and industries in the light of (a) availability of resources and raw material. (b) marketing.

# WOMEN AND VILLAGE PROGRAMMES

THE MEHTA REPORT recommended that a single authority in each State be in charge of the administration, planning and supervision of women's programmes. The Mission endorses this recommendation. It seems to be clear, that all states should proceed to establish a women's welfare department wherever it does not already exist. The main advantage in having such a department is that it could be in direct relation with other departments which have an interest in women's programmes, such as community development, health, education and agriculture. According to the Community Development Report 1958-59, three States already have women's welfare departments with a woman director at the head. Seven states have a woman officers incharge of women's programmes, such as at the State level. The position of a chief woman officer without the backing of a department is not fully effective in the general system of Indian administration. In the long run, such a department may work itself out of a job and become as unnecessary as it would now be in many countries where women's needs and interests are more readily acknowledged and integrated in all spheres of national life.

&times;  &times;  &times;  &times;  &times;

The Mehta Report also emphasized the need for a change in the content of women's programmes in the villages. It was a relief to find that certain doubts felt by the Mission about the present programme were confirmed by this report. These were also confirmed by a number of community development officers and other officials who had observed the tardy and patchwork results of women's programmes despite great efforts and expenditure. In one state, a group of younger women sent word to the community development officials that they were tried to knitting and embroidery in women's clubs and wanted to join, or establish their own, Young Farmers' Club and get help and instructions in their own roles in agriculture.

# WOMEN IN COMMUNITY DEVELOPMENT

IT IS IMPORTANT to identify problems in the community in the solution of which women can play a key role. An example is nutrition. Because of limited facilities for food transport and storage in most developing countries, and the limited purchasing power of rural families, programmes must be carried out at the local level in order to increase the quantity and quality of foods available for use within the community. Although the preliminary studies and planning should be done by professionally trained nutritionists and agriculturists in national or regional services, the programme itself must be centred in the community including, in particular, organised groups of local women. Programmes that succeed in reaching influencing families are required if present practices leading to waste and loss of food are to be changed and maximum use made of present and potential food supplies. Programmes for the improvement of nutritive standards illustrate how the efforts of men and women can be utilized in a mutually supporting relationship in community development. For instance, in some projects the men are trained in horticulture, poultry raising and the construction and care of fishponds, while the women are taught improved cooking methods, the making of fuel-saving stoves and methods of vegetable and fruit preservation. Balanced meals prepared by local women's organisations are served in schools. Other technical fields also offer examples of the benefits of coordinating activities among women and men in coordinating activities among women and men in community development, e.g., in the construction and operation of schools, health centres and other facilities.

An important contribution made by women to the economy of the family and of the community is through crafts ond productive home enterprises such as poultry keeping. In community development, activities, are planned in relation to local raw materials, market conditions, and the skills and leisure time of women. Arrangements must be made for their training, for the supply of raw materials, collecting the finished goods, sales preferably through existing co-operatives and ensuring that proceeds get back into the hands of the producers. The extra income, however, small, adds to the domestic budget, contributes greatly to the economic independence of the women and raises her status in society. Training and work centres

can also usefully serve as recreation centres or meeting places for
women, from which movements to improve their social status may
well emerge.

# ROLE OF MAHILA SAMAJ—
## SOME SUGGESTIONS

### G. Subbalakshmi

THE COMMUNITY DEVELOPMENT programme aims at rejuvenating the vast majority of our village population. It concerns itself with planning at the village level for the economic, educational and social advancement of the rural people. Therefore, it is directed towards the welfare of families, as the standard of living of the community depends on the level of living attained by each family. This level is determined by the efficiency with which a woman runs her home, the kind of food she prepares and the degree of knowledge and skill with which she promotes happiness and fulfilment in the home. It is therefore evident that women's education is indispensable and inevitable. Since community development depends on the community efforts, it is essential that more of women's organisations are set up for such collective action.

A Mahila Samaj is a local organisation of women run with the help and support of the Government as well as other welfare agencies. Through the Mahila Samaj the village women are expected to broaden their mental horizon and learn various profitable activities like bee-keeping, spinning with Ambar Charkha, knitting, tailoring, embroidering, etc. Attention must also be focussed on certain key items of the programme like:

1. Elementary health measures including child care.
2. Environmental sanitation.
3. Better nutrition and dietary habits.
4. Beautification of the home by local arts.
5. Cultural activities like bhajans, music, reading daily newspapers, magazine etc.
6. Training in doing the domestic chores in such a manner that require less time and effort than at present.
7. Knowledge about family planning.

It is not necessary that all these items should be taken up at a time. But each C.D. Block should decide on three or four items of work on the basis of the interests and abilities of the women in that particular area and concentrate on them. This would enable the women to learn thoroughly and try to practise the same at home. Though it is a very slow process, we should hope that a time would come when the standard of living of the village community will be better than what it is today.

Successful community development demands a vertical line of administrative coordination from the Block officers down to the village level workers. At present in most of the villages the Mahila Samaj members do not get guidance and help from the Block Officers, the main reason being that the Mukhya Sevika is not able to visit the village as often as she is expected to do. In order to solve these problems efficiently and effectively more women must be trained in this line and the Mukhya Sevikas must be provided with a conveyance so as to enable them to visit all the villages under their jurisdiction in the Block at least once a month. This would keep them in touch with the problems of the members and make it possible for them to give advice and help whenever needed. Gram Sevikas should attend the Mahila Samaj meetings frequently to find out whether it is functioning smoothly. Frequent supervision from top level becomes essential in order to have an overall control of the operational responsibilities of the Extension worker.

Another criticism is that the President and the convenor of the Mahila Samaj hardly participate in any of these activities. The fault here lies with the incapability of the women to elect a responsible person who is one among their own level of living. In most of the villages at present, the President of a Mahila Samaj is either the wife of the Panchayat President or some other important man in the Panchayat. Unfortunately this woman is illiterate and she is not interested in the activities as she is coming from a big family. As a result the Mahila Samaj does not function well. This system of election should be changed if the women's organisations have to achieve the goal. No written constitution is found in any of these women's organisations in Madras State. A written constitution will help the people in learning the mode of election, administration etc.

It is true that more than 95 per cent of the women population in rural areas have not yet come forward to take part in these programmes. The poor response of the village women points out that they have not yet been sufficiently convinced about the merits and advantages of such an organisation. The main reason for their absence may be that they are all wage-earners which means that they are out the whole day and they have to attend to the household activities in the evenings after they return from their work. The only possible way of getting good attendance of these women in a Mahila Samaj is to introduce some permanent profitable activities which would serve as a means of earning their livelihood. The type of activity to be chosen depends upon their own interests and abilities and the extent of demand in the market for that particular commodity. This would keep them engaged in the Mahila Samaj during the day time and at the same time the women can earn a certain amount of money as daily wages which would be equal to or more than what they might be earning by working in the fields or as labourers. The principle employed here is 'learning and earning'.

Another intensely felt need is a common building for conducting the meetings and classes. In some of the villages at present the meetings are held either at the President's or the convenor's house which invariably leads to some misunderstandings. The school which is supposed to be used for this purpose is not electrified. Since the members meet only in the nights, this common building should be electrified and provided with all amenities. The women teachers of the village school who are residing in that particular village should be persuaded to take the lead in rousing greater interest among the women.

Rural folks are generally interested in cultural programmes and are attracted towards the recreational centres like cinemas, theatres in the nights in spite of their tiredness. This would necessitate that the Mahila Samaj meetings and lectures are combined with cultural programmes, like film shows, folk dance, drama and music in which the womenfolk are interested. It has also been observed that some of them would come to attend only that part of the function in which they are interested, and not the rest. It would therefore be advisable to include such common attractive features in the beginning as well as in the last part of the function in order to keep them sitting there throughout. Better attendance could be expected if the members themselves participate in the entertainment programmes.

An exhibition or display of articles prepared by the members may be organised occasionally.

Educational tours to different places will enable the members to acquire awareness of similar activities in other parts of the country and help them to gain more and more knowledge to equip themselves better, for improving their standards of living. Though much emphasis has been laid on these points by the Community Development programme, most of the poverty-stricken, backward villages are lagging behind.

Celebration of National days such as Independence day, Republic day, Gandhi Jayanti day, Children's day and Kasturba day besides the local festivals should be undertaken by the Mahila Samaj. Community feasts and recreational programmes would certainly go a long way in establishing social harmony among the rural women and thereby fulfil the objectives of the local women's organisations.

Education and occupation have been the most predominating factors that affect the membership of these organisations. An intensive plan of social education with a vigorous literacy drive must be included in the programme of women's organisations. As the children are the future citizens of the world, all the children should be compelled to attend school, as that in future they would be able to actively participate in all the civic and political affairs, which means that the standard of living of the village community would be improved in a very short time.

"Every woman is a creator in the ideal of nationhood," said Smt. Sarojini Naidu. So in assessing the progress of the Community Development programme in India, one is tempted to inquire as to how far its impact has been felt by the women in rural India. As a result of this, the present appalling situation in most of the villages indicate that Block authorities should take much more interest and give greater attention to Mahila Samaj in order to create a "new village culture".

# VILLAGE SCHOOLS

LACK OF VILLAGE schools poorly trained and inadequately paid teachers, a school programme unrelated to village life and development, and high illiteracy among teen-age youth and adults, constitute major educational problems of the villages of India.

Some of the more important things which have Contributed, and still do contribute, to the educational problems of the villages are listed as follows:

1. Because of the economic pressures on the village families to earn and produce the bare essentials for survival, children have, of necessity had to remain out of school and go to work.

2. Much as they value education for their children, the villagers look at their past experience and conclude, with some at least of the actual facts on their side, that the youth who have gone to school have become dissatisfied with the village life and have moved on to the larger towns and cities.

3. The village school, the village teacher, and the school programme are not effectively related to village life and to the training of youth to live harmoniously within the village and to earn an effective living either as a cultivator, artisan, or village schools.

4. Many villages are without schools.

5. Many villages are without teachers.

6. Because the villages of India pay such low salaries to teachers and have such limited facilities for their effective living, including meagre recreation and health services, the better trained teachers who have other opportunities avoid going to the villages where they are so sorely needed.

7. Until we gained independence and new opportunities those for all to contribute to the nation's development and to their own personal economic and social advancement, being literate held no particular attraction for the masses of village people, for it could not be convincingly demonstrated that to be literate would result in their advancement.

8. Now that it can be demonstrated that being literate is essential if all are to fully profit from independence and are to make their maximum contribution to the building of New India, there are limited facilities and too few teachers trained in the

modern techniques of literacy education.

9. There is a great scarcity, of good reading material, readily available at a reasonable price for the neo-literate.

One has only to exercise his mind to understand that, in building of New India through the process of re-building each of our 558,000 villages as significant cultural units, effective education for all is essential. The study of world history and of the rise and fall of great civilizations supports the conclusion that a nation's greatness is dependent upon the importance the nation places on education, and upon the effectiveness of the educational institutions in training people with creative, reflective minds capable of guiding the nation's growth and sustaining a great and significant culture. It is, therefore, of great importance that the Panchayat Samithi and village panchayats accept the challenge which is theirs to help all villages in the Community Development blocks tackle the village educational problems, bring to this task the forthright leadership the people deserve and must receive if India is to again grow into a great nation.

Action Steps for Improving the Status, Services and Facilities of Education in the Villages;

1. Through various education media, demonstrate to the people the importance of all being literate in order to take advantage of the benefits of science and technology and all children having an opportunity to attend a school taught by a competent, well-trained teacher adequately paid.

2. As the village grows in its interest in having a village school, help the village organize itself to contribute its labour and as much material as possible toward the construction of a school.

3. Assist the village in organizing literacy classes. Whenever literate local people are available, they should be trained and assisted conducting the literacy classes. When local literacy instructors are not available plans should be worked out for outside instructions systematically to visit the village to conduct the literacy classes.

4. To assist in the socio-economic upgrading of the village teacher and thus in enabling the village to secure and keep a competent teacher, the panchayats, should be encouraged to see the importance of the village providing the teacher with a house and an adequate vegetable garden. Panchayats should also be encouraged to develop plans for self-taxation to contribute towards increasing the salary of the village teacher.

5. So that the village school can increasingly become an effective village institution and the teacher can play a more prominent role in village development, the Panchayat Samiti should in the

first instance organize a ten-day training camp for all the village teachers in the block. The purpose of this training should be to train the village teacher to serve as a village leader, assisting in stimulating the entire village to be interested in all-round development. Following the first camp yearly refresher camps of a week should be organized.

6. Continue to emphasize to the village people that, while in the past they have survived with limited or no education, in the future education will become more and more important for success as a cultivator, artisan or industrialist, and for participation in village and state affairs. Point out that, whereas in the past survival was based on familiarity with traditional methods, the future will require familiarity with an understanding of the application of science.

# THE DEVELOPMENT OF THE VILLAGE SCHOOL AS A COMMUNITY CENTRE

IF THE COMMUNITY Development programmes are to succeed in the development of all village people to become responsible and responsive citizens capable of applying science and technology, and making wise decisions and contributing to the maximum in the building of new India, the school as a village institution must become a focal point for village education and service. The future pattern for village development must be to elevate the village school to a position of prominence making it a vital centre of community education. That the village school today is not capable of performing this broader role of guiding the village in its total educational growth is one of the village problems which only the Community Development programme is capable of solving.

Looking at the village school problem from the point of view of education one finds the village teacher is poorly trained, poorly paid, poorly housed and looked upon as a second-class citizen in the village. The conclusion is immediately obvious. If the village school is to become an effective village institution capable of playing a significant role in balanced village development, the village teacher must immediately be better trained, better paid, better housed, and elevated to the position of a self-respecting citizen in the village.

# PEOPLE'S MOVEMENT FOR EDUCATION IN MADRAS STATE*

## Introduction

THE PEOPLE'S MOVEMENT for Education in Madras State has evoked considerable interest in the country. Started on a modest scale in 1957 by the people themselves in a few villages, it has now spread almost to the entire State.

The beginnings of the movement were humble. Back in the later part of 1956, some villages made arrangements for the supply of free mid-day meals to the needy children. These efforts were entirely voluntary and could be regarded as self-initiated. As the movement spread from village to village, the Department of Public Instruction, Madras State took it upon itself to consolidate its organisational base and carry its message to the rural communities in the whole State. Gradually the people in hundreds of villages were inspired to organise similar efforts to feed their needy children in the schools. Later, supported by the recognition and financial assistance of the government, this scheme spread to most of the villages in Madras State. This movement is no longer confined to the mid-day meals schemes alone. It covers the wider area of school improvement.

The present study was confined to Development Blocks in Chengulpet district where initially the School Improvement Conferences were started. The three Development Blocks selected for the purpose of this study were:

1. Poondi ;
2. Trivellor; and
3. Kadambattor.

Some of the elementary schools in these Blocks were visited, and discussions were held with the members of the mid-day meals committees, teachers of the schools, and Panchayat Board Members. The problems connected with the movement were also discussed with the Director Public Instruction, Special Officer (Text Books), and other responsible officers in the Education and Rural Development departments.

* Summary of a preliminary report by Shri B. Rudramoorthy.

**Mid-day Meal Scheme :**

The People's Movement for Education is actually a twin movement comprising the mid-day meals schemes and the school improvement conference the latter being an offshoot of the first.

It was being increasingly realized that under-nourishment and malnutrition of school-going children was coming in the way of their education. In a gathering of teachers and general public in Tuticorin in February 1956 the slogan of "Anna-dan" to famished school children was raised. Village leaders and the common people present at the meeting responded to the call and resolved that everyone owing a plot of cultivable land will contribute a specific quantity of foodgrains at the time of harvest. Encouraged by this, the Director of Public Instruction, Madras, gave further fillip to this movement. The movement was officially launched later in 1956.

The Government is now providing contribution at the rate of 0'06 Paise per student per day for the mid-day meal scheme. This has to be matched by a local contribution of at least 0.40 Paise per student per day. There is a Mid-day Meal Committee in every school/village in which one of the non-officials serves as the President and the Headmaster of School as Secretary.

**Role of the Panchayat :**

The recent decision of the Madras Government entrusting the administration of the primary education to the Panchayat Union Council has further encouraged this movement. The school administration has now come within the purview of Panchayat Union Councils. The Panchayat Union Council Commissioner and the Extension Officer (Education) have been placed incharge of the administration of elementary schools and teachers. As a result of the Panchayats taking over school administration a direct relationship has been established between the Panchayat Board and the teacher. This has in certain ways ameliorated the lot of the teachers and they are in a mood to cooperate with the Panchayat Boards whole-heartedly. The interest of the teachers has contributed significantly to the success of this movement.

The number of students served with mid-day meals in the school depends on the contribution received by the school towards providing food to its students. The impression gathered during this survey in the course of discussions with teachers and village leaders was that most of the students who really needed food were being served; other children generally went back to their homes for food.

The practical arrangements covering the mid-day meal scheme vary from village to village according to local conditions. Ordinarily food is cooked by one of the members of the Mid-day Meal Committee and sent to the school. In a few places, teachers have taken upon themselves the responsibility of cooking the food either at their home or at the schools. Sometimes, old women are engaged on a salary of Rs. 5.00 to Rs. 10.00 per month for cooking and serving the food.

The Government contribution, immediately after it is received and cashed, is kept in a Savings Bank Account in the name of the President of the Committee. The contribution from the villagers is collected either in kind or in cash. The grains thus collected are stored in the house of the President. The cash goes to the account. The school teacher and the President are responsible for the accounts.

**Factors which contributed to the success of the mid-day meals schemes:**

The following factors appear to have contributed to the success of the mid-day meal scheme :

1. Systematic harnessing of local initiative, willingness to raise voluntary efforts in the cause of education, and mobilising the resources of the people howsoever meagre they may be.
2. The role played by the Department of Public Instruction both at the Headquarters and the districts.
3. Transfer of administration of primary education to Panchay Union Councils.
4. The interest of teachers in the Mid-day Meal Scheme and the School Improvement Conferences.
5. Timely receipt of government contribution towards the mid-day meal schemes.
6. Constitution of Mid-day Meals Committees in every school/village so that the local interest is not only providing the mid-day meals but also in managing the mid-day meals scheme is sustained.
7. School Improvement Conferences which have helped to evoke public interest in schools and have helped in providing the schools with necessary equipment and teaching aids.

**Benefits from the Mid-day Meals Scheme**

1. Increased and regular attendance at the schools.
2. Better attention of children to studies.
3. Improvement in the health of the children.
4. Cultivation of social habits. Irrespective of their caste and social status the children sit together to take their mid-day meals. This has helped the children to feel as though they are all one notwithstanding the differences in their caste and social status.

5. Fostering community's interest in education.

**Results achieved so far:**

This voluntary movement gained momentum as a result of government support. Today, out of 26281 elementary schools not less than 25294 are providing free mid-day meals to poor children. The number of pupils who benefit from this scheme is as large as 9,11,820 in addition to these as many as 13,319 students reading in 506 high schools are also receiving free meals entirely out of people's contribution without any subsidy from the government.

**School Improvement Conferences:**

The functioning of the Midday Meal Scheme in thousands of village of Madras State gradually provided the stimulus for the associated "School Improvement Conferences" movement. These Conferences are being held at Block, Taluq and District levels. Through them the teachers and the people assess the requirements of their school and devise ways and means to meet them locally through their own effort. Priorities are not dictated to them; in fact compulsion in any form is avoided.

**Stages in the School Improvement Conferences:**
1. A comprehensive survey of the conditions of each school in the area, keeping in view the normal requirements of an elementary school in regard to accommodation, furniture, equipment, teaching aids, library, sanitary arrangements and space for sports and gardening;
2. Fixing of priorities out of these requirements;
3. Teachers approaching the villagers with the lists of requirements and accepting gifts in any shape readily forthcoming from them; and
4. Organizing school improvement conferences at the Block headquarters and then at the District headquarters inviting Headmasters of the schools, Presidents of the Panchayat Boards and Mid-day Meals Committees and all others generally interested in the educational movement.

In such conferences, the donors have taken upon themselves a variety of responsibilities towards their respective schools; such as:
1. Construction of school buildings; their repair and white-washing;
2. Donation of land for school buildings;
3. Electrification of school buildings;
4. Construction of latrines and quarters for teachers;
5. Fencing of school compound;

6. Donation of furniture;
7. Supply of small library; and
8. Provision of pure drinking water.

So far 140 School Improvement Conferences have been held and donations worth more than five and a half crore of rupees have been received. The School Improvement Conferences are still in full swing. The way they are being organized and the enthusiasm with which the people are responding to them are of sufficient significance to indicate an awakening of interest among the rural people to the cause of education.

**Future of the Movement:**

A few factors deserve consideration in the interest of the future of these two inter-related movements. It is a matter for speculation if the enthusiasm and interest generated by these movements can be sustained over a long period of time. The people have in some measure started toying with the idea of resting on the oars. Villagers think that the magnitude of their contribution towards their schools has reached a point of saturation and that it is now for the government to come forward with a greater measure of assistance to help sustain the tempo of movement. Therefore, it is now a question of institutionalizing this movement through various decentralized organisations which are coming into being in the wake of Panchayati Raj. The Panchayat Board Sub-committee for Education needs to be entrusted with the task of maintaining the school and its standards and a definite plan for continued contribution or assured income has to be thought of. There appears to be a trend of thinking among some of the local leaders that this movement from this stage onwards should be linked to some definite production programme in the village agricultural production plans of industrial production plans. The cooperative societies have to be brought in more directly into the picture with reference to the financial assistance for the educational movement. Already in a few villages people have donated lands to the schools to ensure regular income to finance the Mid-day Meals Scheme and maintenance of school. This aspect has to be emphasised much more.

# MANAGEMENT OF PRIMARY SCHOOLS UNDER PANCHAYATI RAJ

**Objective :**

THE MANAGEMENT AND working of Primary Schools under Panchayati Raj has, of late, been subjected to bitter criticism in the State of Rajasthan. Primary School teachers all over the State have shown their disapproval of the new set-up in one way or the other. It was, therefore, thought desirable that an objective study of the management and working of the primary schools under panchayat Raj should be made with a view to testing the validity made in this regard.

**Scope and Coverage :**

This interim study is a part of the bigger research project on working of Panchayati Raj now in progress in 3 Panchayati Samitis of Dedu, Jhotwara and Sikri in the Jaipur District.

**Methodology :**

The study attempts a qualitative appraisal of the management of Primary Schools. Before a full scale enquiry was launched, a Pilot study was made with a view to determining specific problem areas, by having detailed discussion with officials and non-officials at Zila Parishad, Panchayat Samiti and Panchayat levels and also with a good number of teachers of Primary Schools. Thus a number of problems emerged for assessment. These problems have formed the basis of field investigation. The actual investigation was two-fold, first, study of official records, reports and statistics; second, intensive interviews with officials, non-officials of Panchayats, Panchayat Samities and Zila Parishads. There were also detailed discussion on the problems pertaining to the primary schools in the Panch Sammelan and the Headmaster's Conference at Dehu and Sikri.

**The New Set-up :**

The relation behind the transfer of Primary Education to the Panchayati Raj Institutions is that local institutions are better equipped to manage educational institutions in their area because of their local insight, experience and influence. Besides this, the Government was also motivated by the following considerations in effecting the transfer:

(*i*) Centralised administration from a far off place under the old pattern resulted in abuse and indiscipline on the part of the teachers and did not fit in squarely with the ideals of free and compulsory education which the Government is pledged to introduce.

(*ii*) Transfer would be in the interest of sound school community relations.

(*iii*) Transfer would enthuse the Panchayati Raj institutions to raise local resources for the extension of primary education in rural areas.

**The Statutory Pattern :**

The Rajasthan Panchayat Samiti and Zilla Parishad Act of 1959, handed over the management/primary schools to the Panchayat Samiti. The Panchayat Samitis share the responsibility of management with Panchayats not merely because the latter form the executive arm of the former, but because the Rajasthan Panchayat Act of 1958 as amended by the Act of 1960 has specifically made the Panchayats responsible for spread of education and culture. Thus the services of primary school teachers have been placed under the control of Panchayat Samiti and Zilla Parishad. Consequent upon this the Panchayat Samitis determine the vacancies, appoint teachers, confirm their appointment, transfer and promote them.

**The actual management pattern—the dual control :**

The administrative control of primary schools rests with the Panchayat Samiti, while the technical and financial control is entrusted to the State Education Department. The Samiti can only put forward the budget demand to the Education Department which is free to accept or slash it in any way. The Samitis are not competent to make rules and regulations to regulate the conduct of school teachers. The Education Extension Officer who serves in the Panchayat Samiti on deputation from the Education Department is under the technical control of Education Department. The Director of Primary Education and the whole host of officials under him have also the right to advise and inspect the schools. The B.D.O. has a double role to play in the management of Primary School—he has to implement the resolutions of Panchayat Samiti and its Standing Committee on Education and at the same time to carry out the directives from the State Department of Education.

However, a wide area of administration is left in the hands of

Samiti with regard to (1) Distribution of Salary of teachers; (2) recommending the establishment of new schools; (3) taking steps to increase attendance in schools; (4) purchase of stationery and furniture; (5) preparation of budget demand and (6) on-the-spot control and supervision of schools including confirmation transfer and promotion of teachers.

The new system has been in existence for just over two years. This is too short a period to attempt any critical evaluation of its working. The system has only thrown up certain tendencies—both good and bad, which are analysed below:

(*i*)     *INCREASE IN NUMBER OF SCHOOLS:* The number of schools has increased since this transfer, not only in 3 Samitis under the study but also in the whole of Jaipur District or for that matter in the whole of the State. The increase over a period of four years has been 100 per cent in some cases. It is to be noted that the increase is a part of Government policy to provide free and compulsory education and would have come about even if management had not been transferred to Panchayati Raj Institutions. What is worth noting, however, is that Panchayat Samitis and Panchayats have pressed for opening of schools. This is a wholesome trend.

(*ii*)     *GROWING NUMBER OF STUDENTS:* There has been a steady increase in the number of school-going children thanks to the interest and initiative evinced by Panchayats. The Go-To-School movement and award of prizes to the best Panchayat Samiti doing this work obviously have resulted in creating consciousness among parents to send their children to schools. At times Pradhans and Sarpanches have also used their good offices in persuading parents in this regard. The trend of increase is especially encouraging in respect of girl students.

(*iii*)     *THE STAFF:* Panchayat Samitis have shown reluctance to increase number of teachers beyond the strength sanctioned by Education Department, as that would call for raising additional resources on the part of the Panchayats. That is why of late the teacher-student ratio has been fixed at 1:60 which has come in for carping criticism by the Smitis. Even with regard to filling up of the sanctioned posts there has been a shortage of teachers in general and lady teachers in particular.

(*iv*)     *EQUIPMENT AND FACILITY TO TEACHERS:* Though the number of schools has increased and the strength of students has gone up, the standard of Primary Education has not improved from the point of view of teaching facility provided to teachers. In many cases classes are held either in temples, community houses or under trees. A situation of this kind needs to be rectified urgently. In many cases the Panchayati Raj bodies which are very much alive to the situation, have not been able to improve it appreciably because of lack of funds.

(v) *RAISING OF LOCAL RESOURCES:* By and large, people's participation regarding construction of school building has been very niggardly. Whatever contribution is collected for availing the benefit of matching grants from Education Department of the State Government, is only shown on paper. Panchayats have always shown great reluctance in imposing and collecting a special cess for education as they are afraid of annoying the voting population. Secondly Go-To-School drive organised by the Panchayats seems inconsistent with imposition of an education cess. Thirdly, education cess is likely to lessen the enthusiasm of the parents at the initial stage. Lastly people in general object to the imposition of cess in the name of the ideal of free and compulsory education to which the Government is committed.

(vi) *ON-THE-SPOT SUPERVISION AND CONTROL:* It is worthwhile to note that the management of primary schools under the Panchayat Samiti has been advantageous in positive terms as far as supervision and control is concerned. A number of shortcomings can, however, be noted:

1. There has been too much of supervision and inspection from Samiti as well as Panchayat Level authorities. The teacher naturally feels harassed as he has to face a multiplicity of "bosses".

2. Technical Inspections by the S.D.I. (popularly called Education Extension Officer) are few and far between and are not upto the mark. In a few cases where the inspection report of the S.D.I. required to be very firmly acted upon, political backing of the teachers came in the way.

(vii) *POLITICAL FACTORS AT WORK:* The weakest spot in the management of primary schools under Panchayati Raj is the association of politics with administration. Almost every Panchayat Samiti and Panchayat has been split up into groups and factions. This division has aggravated after general elections with the coming in of the political parties into the arena of Panchayati Raj more actively. The management of primary schools could not escape the impact of this development and consequently the following harmful trends are discernible:

1. Teachers, sometimes on their own and sometimes under pressure, become political camp followers of their new

bosses and serve them as errand-boys and personal assignments to the utter neglect of their own teaching duty. These among them who are conscientious and refuse to toe the line are victimised.

2. Political considerations have heavily weighed against the merits of the situation, in the location of primary schools, recommendation for upgrading them to Middle School and distribution of grants.

(*viii*) *ADMINISTRATIVE ASPECTS:*

### 1. Dyarchical management—Apathy of the Education Department:

This dyarchical control, the administrative control being vested in the Panchayat Samiti and technical-cum-financial control being vested in the State Department of Education has been the bane of the new system. Delay in the transfer of money to the Samiti for payment to teachers, lack of interest in Samiti meetings, refusal to consider the cases of primary school teachers for promotion, are some of the manifest examples of apathy of the Education Department. On the other hand as in the case of teachers, the Pradhans and Sarpanches have brought to bear political pressure on the Education Extension Officers and have utilized their services for personal aggrandisement. The cause of the Primary Education has suffered much in an intriguing situation like this.

### 2. Service Conditions of Teachers:

1. Almost all teachers appreciate that they do get their salary more regularly and conveniently than before.

2. Also, their grievances are mostly readily looked into and redressed than previously when they had to run to the headquarters for even small things.

3. But all the teachers appear to have a sense of uncertainty about their service conditions as they fear that they would not get the same privileges as they had under Government. They are in doubt about their seniority, prospects of promotion, pension and medical relief.

4. Teachers have been ordered to run Adult Education Centres with no extra emolument. They viewed it as a sort of forced labour and have not performed this task with any sense of devotion. The position would be considerably improved if a district cadre of primary school teacher is created. At present there is a service cadre only at the Panchayat Samiti Level. Since this is a small pool, chances of promotion are very limited. If they happen to incur the displeasure of politicians victimisa-

tion is not ruled out. A district cadre would minimise harassment of this kind and open up larger avenues of promotion.

**Summary:**

The management of primary schools under Panchayati Raj despite its many abuses, is definitely an improvement over the earlier situation. The demand that the State Government should treat from this position to the old one, does not carry much force. The transfer of management of primary schools to Panchayati Raj has meant:

1. Mobilisation of local leadership in support of the cause of free and compulsory primary education;
2. Organisation of a better system of on-the-spot supervision and control; and
3. Facilities to teachers in terms of regular payment of salary, better access to authority and quicker redress of grievances.

The transfer, therefore, has been well conceived in principle and must be strengthened. What is necessary is to find out ways and means to implement it in the possible way. Suggestions in this regard are :

1. To safeguard the management of Primary Schools against the baneful effects of politics, an autonomous school board will go a long way in solving related problem.
2. To provide for adequate number of teachers and teaching facilities so that while Primary Education spreads on a mass scale, the quality is not sacrificed. Panchayats may create a Primary Education Fund to raise more resources for this.
3. To achieve better coordination between the Education Department at the district level and Panchayat Samiti level special efforts should be made.
4. To better the service conditions of the school teachers all possible measures should be taken.

# COOPERATION

*Jawaharlal Nehru*

**I Have Faith in Village People**:

IF YOU WANT progress and the introduction of modern techniques, then these infinite number of small farms should be worked co-operatively, so that they get the benefits of modern techniques.

When I say "work co-operatively," it means a cooperation of many kinds. We think the first step should be cooperatives, not merely for credit—that is there of course—but for all kinds of services, for buying and selling things, seeds, fertilizers and the like. The next step is gradual removal of the middle man. Then comes the next stage, which may be called joint cultivation, though property rights remain. That is the approach, so that the problem of ceiling is more and more tied up with the question of cooperatives; otherwise there is the danger of production going down. It is a complicated problem and it is being considered.

May I say, when I talk about a cooperative, I mean a village co-operative and nothing bigger; at the most two or three villages if they are nearby. All our thinking now is based on the panchayat and the village cooperative and giving them power and authority to take decisions, and also to make mistakes, as they might. We take the risk. It is better to do that than to hedge their authority and make them feel helpless. Speaking for myself, I have a good deal of faith in the innate good sense of the village people. They will no doubt make mistakes. It does not matter. All of us make mistakes. But if you give them that feeling, they gain self-confidence; they gain initiative and they do things and not wait for officials to do them.

I repeat that the cooperative we conceive of is a small one so that there is intimacy among its members, knowledge of one another. It is not an impersonal thing. If the members of a cooperative know who is bad and who is good in their village, there is probably a greater chance of its success than through some complicated processes of the law or some superior officers who know nothing about local conditions.

Normally speaking, there is not much party politics in village panchayats or cooperatives, and I do not think it should be encouraged. They stand on a separate footing. In corporations and municipalities in big cities, party politics comes in. But the problems of the panchayat almost entirely cut across party barriers.

There are only two ways of increasing production: through the efficient big landlord or through efficient peasants working in cooperatives. The former is, relatively speaking, oppressive to the peasantry. Therefore, we are driven to the second alternative. We have to consider not only food production but human advancement. You cannot, in raising food production, forget the *human factor*. Indeed, if you forget the human factor, ultimately food production comes down. That is why in every country, including capitalist countries, the landlord has been more or less eliminated, as in Japan. The U.S. Government encouraged the Japanese to put an end to the landlord system. Nobody can describe the United States Government as socialist. I am afraid some of our people have not quite understood this modern approach.

×     ×     ×     ×     ×

**Basic Considerations**

At the last meeting of the National Development Council, the question of cooperative policy was agreed to broadly. On every important factor there was complete agreement, the basic thing being that each cooperative should bring about a certain intimate relationship among the members. That is the idea of coordination. It should not be just a kind of bank, merely a credit cooperative. It was also accepted that, essentially, there should be small cooperatives. They should be homogeneous and not have official interference, although officials would, of course, help. All these basic things were accepted by everyone.

Then certain other points were raised. First of all we had to separate the tribal areas. That is to say, we could not force some uniform and rigid rules on the tribal areas. We have to deal with them differently. The cooperatives there have to be run on different lines. In other words, our policy will be flexible, although certain basic things which have been accepted will naturally apply.

One of the points discussed was whether there should be large cooperatives or small. In actual practice there is really not much difference, because the really large ones are ruled out altogether. In some other places it might be desirable to have slightly bigger ones than village cooperative. Of course where there are very small village, two or three villages might be grouped together and it is ultimately left to the discretion of the State Government. If it feels it to be necessary to go up to five or six villages, it would be done, though we would like to avoid that as far as possible.

Another point that was much discussed was whether the Government should take shares in the cooperatives. Some of us were of the opinion that it should not. We admit that help is necessary for the cooperatives. That help should be given in schemes of production, rather than in money. These minor points are being discussed by a committee we appointed yesterday but, as I said, we cannot lay down too rigid rules.

# DE-OFFICIALISATION OF COOPERATIVE MOVEMENT

## Dr. B. S. Mathus

THE COOPERATIVE MOVEMENT has been in existence in the country for about sixty years and yet the movement has not lived up to the expectations of its founders. Numerous causes which need hardly any repetition have been reported by various committees, commissions, economists and research scholars for the failure of this socio-economic movement. The non-official cooperators have, however, always contended that the movement has largely failed on account of the rigid official control. The soul of this movement according to them has been 'suffocated' by the stifling interference of the officials.

Of late, a vigorous campaign for 'de-officialisation' of the movement has been launched in the country by the non-official cooperators. These cooperators now do not consider the Registrar of the Cooperative Societies as a friend, philosopher and guide' but look at him as 'Inspector General of Cooperative Police' in charge of erring and suspect bands of non-official cooperators. The Fourth Indian Cooperative Congress which met in New Delhi in 1963 stoutly stated that official control was impairing the growth of cooperative leadership and urged that it should be done away without delay. The late Prime Minister also desired that cooperative movement should be free from Governmental control and deprecated the dependence of the cooperative movement on officialdom.

In this connection a pertinent and heart-searching question that confronts a serious student is whether the slow and inadequate growth of the cooperative movement has been due to official control or other factors which appear to have been conveniently glossed over by the non-official cooperators. It would be worthwhile here to quote the views of Dr. (Miss) Eleanor M. Hough who made a special study of the cooperative movement in India, she writes:

"It is hardly debatable that there have been fewer failures of cooperative societies in India due to over-direction than have been due to too slack a guiding rein for new societies or those with a low credit rating."

Specifically she might mention the inadequacy of the education of officers and members of societies in cooperative principles; failure to insist on practices in conformity with these; incompetent or slack supervision ; too infrequent audit and lack of follow-up on audit findings ; the ineptitude of members ; the inadequacy of credit available; failure to detect in time malpractices of committee members of misappropriation or misuse of funds ; and the want of expert guidance for societies of other types than credit. This long chargesheet seems to the writer quite to overbalance the over-strictness now held up to reprobation.

The Cooperative Planning Committee, it may be re-called, attributed the main cause of the failure of the Cooperative movement to the laissez-faire policy of the State and not to the acts of commission on the part of the officials of the State.

The Cooperative movement, as is well-known, is based on the concept of mutual help and self-help. Nobody should, therefore, ordinarily dispute the claims of the non-official cooperators that the Cooperative movement is a people's movement and managed by the people themselves. But the paradox is : who is there to prevent the spontaneous growth of the un-official character of this people's movement ? The State and the officials come to the scene only because the movement was not developing on its own initiative. It is a well-known fact that ever since the passing of the Cooperative Credit Societies Act of 1904, the movement had the moral, material and financial support of the Government. Excessive bureaucratic control is to be deprecated but to allege that all the ills of the movement are due to excessive control over it, is far from the truth. Without the State support and patronage there would probably have been no trace of the movement worth the name. Even if this State support was to go today, the movement in many parts of the country would collapse like a house of cards.

The difficulty with our non-official cooperators, however, is that they want governmental assistance liberally and at the same time desire that it should not be a condition for interference, directly or indirectly in the affairs of the society. This theory of the non-official cooperators cannot be easily digested as it is repugnant to sound canon of business. Risk taking and some control should always walk side by side and one cannot be without dire consequence, dis-associated with the other. It has to be made clear that where Government finance comes in it would be naturally followed by some official control to keep a vigilant eye on the use of those funds. This is necessitated not because of the distrust of people but because the general tax-payer should be in a position to see that the societies are run properly and efficiently and that funds are not misused.

The need for official supervision and control was never greater than today when Government is providing large-scale financial assistance not only in the form of loans and share capital but also in the form of grants and subsidies. The lure of these large-scale subsidies and loans together with other concessions in matters of sales tax, stamp duty, income tax and registrations fee is tantalising to greedy and unscrupulous opportunists to form societies which are nothing but pseudo-cooperatives. The ease with which facile credit can be obtained under the guise of Sahakarita has been one of the most important factors giving birth to many sham cooperative societies. In this way these cooperatives are getting reduced to the level of what a former Registrar dubbed as 'subsidy consuming devices'.

It is rather unfair and ununderstandable that the public servant should have nothing to do with cooperative accounts or with the general functioning of these societies even though the bulk of their working capital is provided by the Government or Reserve Bank of India.

It is rather distressing that people at the helm of affairs do not know or care to know as to in whose hands the leadership of the co-operative movement is drifting in many a State. These well-wishers at the top who are anxious to develop a 'cooperative sector' to be a balancing force between the public sector and the private sector, should know that there is a high gravitation of vested interest in the movement. The leadership of cooperative movement in one of the States, of which the writer has made a special study is predominantly in the hands of rival class blocks consisting of ex-jagirdar politicians as well as militant farmers. The way these pseudo-politicians and other vested interests have been moulding the movement to serve their respective class interests ought to be a matter of serious concern to the champions of de-officialisation.

How deep-rooted and how powerful the vested interest is entrenched in the cooperative sector can be illustrated by a practical example. An estimate made by the Cooperative Department in one of the States put the figures of spurious and sham societies at 265-about 2 per cent of the total societies in the State. These were formed according to the Department for taking advantage of facilities offered by the Government, by contractors, middlemen and other vested interests. The Registrar of the Cooperative Societies, therefore, very rightly issued orders asking the Assistant Registrars to cancel the registration of these 'bogus' societies. They were also enjoined upon for taking strong and prompt action to prosecute those persons who have been found guilty of embezzlement of money of the societies. However, even after 14 months of this order the Assistant Registrars could neither cancel registration of even one society nor take action against any culprit. The Registrar, thereupon asked the Deputy Registrars to prepare a list of these societies and asked them to cancel the registration of all these societies within 3 months. It is surprising to note that registration of not even one society could be cancelled even after six months of issuance of this order. An enquiry into this matter revealed that the officials were helpless on account of political pressure of the vested interests.

Warning against the exploitation of the Cooperative movement by politicians and other vested interests has been voiced by such an eminent personality as Prof. D.R. Gadgil very recently. Even in 1957 Sir Malcolm Darling, in his report on certain aspects of cooperative movement in India stated that while ant of politics was eating its way into the movement. Shri S.K. Dey Union Minister for Community Development and Cooperation has written :

"The Cooperative movement, with notable exceptions, had grown to be the preserve of many vested interests. All types of people from saint to the villain had rushed into cooperative movement. Control in cooperative organisation from the ground to the national level continues to be vested with notable exceptions, in a narrow circle which cannot be dislodged, however hard one may try. There are outstanding examples of services. But alas, the instances of exploitation are far too many in comparison. What is worse; the needy rarely get the help meant for them."

In view of this deplorable position would it be expedient to do away with official supervision? In the past, many parts of India were indeed fortunate in having the services of selfless and zealous non-officials who devoted every ounce of their energy to propagate the mission of cooperation without caring for honours or honoraria. Had all the States been gifted with such eminent souls, who were moved by philanthropic notions of service there would have been hardly any occasion for official interference. It is a lamentable yet true fact that the Cooperative movement has largely failed to attract men of integrity and missionary zeal to catch the imagination of people. To get the service of persons who are prepared to dedicate themselves of the cause of this socio-economic movement is a real problem in many parts of the country. So long as there is a dearth of such selfless non-officials, there is no escape from reliance on official control and supervision.

The wisdom of those who want to pack the official, bag and baggage, is doubted by a student of cooperation. It appears that there is a positive co-relationship in India between the orgies of de-officialisation and corruption. Shri S.K. Dey shares this view and he also admits : "Cries against Government interference is growing loudest because corruption is becoming most rampant."

The impact of this unwarranted and unjust criticism of the officials of the cooperative movement has been having a serious repercussion. The official has become subservient to the non-official cooperators who are mostly politicians. He is hardly in a position to give his free and frank opinion on matters of policy. These officials in one of the States were reported to be under pressure from meddlesome politicians interested in getting certain things done by hook or by crook. The Cooperative Department in the State (under study) appears to have become a complete handmaid of a militant coterie of politicians. As a result, the shrewder among the officials and the more intelligent ones do not usually inspect or interfere with the working of societies where the interest of such politicians and their satellites are manifest. These powerful politicans hardly heed for the request and even warning of the officials.

In the opinion of this writer the greatest danger to the Cooperative movement in many a State comes not from bureaucracy but from 'super-imposed' non-official leadership which mainly consists of politicians and other vested interests. Let the leadership of the Cooperative Movement grow spontaneously, let it evolve from the base rather than be imposed from the top.

The primary task before the non-officials if they sincerely desire to get rid of the officials control, is to bring within its fold more and more efficient, capable and honest cooperators. Once the movement succeeds in commanding the unflinching allegiance of honest and upright cooperators, it would be practical politics to talk of de-officialisation of the movement.

The solution to the ills of the Cooperative movement in most of the States lies not in the hasty de-officialisation as has been made out by some non-official cooperators but in simplifying the rules and procedures, avoiding red-tapism, inefficiency and slackness on the one hand and eliminating unfair dealings and vested interests on the other.

# COOPERATIVE INSTITUTIONS

THE SPIRIT OF self-help and corporate action which is intended to be developed by the Community and extension schemes is properly institutionalized in cooperative societies. Hence as a pointer to real progress experience about cooperatives has a special significance. During the second year good progress was made in some States. Bombay, Andhra, and Uttar Pradesh, among the older, and Saurashtra and Madhya Bharat among the newer States showed evident signs of a determined policy of associating cooperatives with project efforts. Kolhapur, in Bombay, which was already a cooperatively developed area, succeeded in drawing cooperatives into its production as well as social programme. In the sphere of credit the societies followed a policy of extending credit on the basis of production needs, thus serving a large number of medium and small-sized farmers than was possible under the older ideas about credit-worthiness. Women were encouraged to join cooperatives. Some progress continued to be made in the other States as well.

While progress in quantitative terms cannot be said to have been striking in any area the lines of progress and the variety to tasks attempted to cooperatives are such as should strengthen a feeling of confidence. The multipurpose type of village society is gaining ground, though there is need to make it clear once again that a 'Multipurpose' society is a credit and allied purposes society. It is not intended to be an all-purposes society. That way lies danger. Making societies responsible for things which would strain their resources, interests, capacities and loyalties beyond a reasonable limit is plainly inviting discomfiture. What a multipurpose society is normally expected to do is to supply credit, in cash and kind, according to estimated productiveness of the borrower, keep a watchful eye on the proper use of these loans; and help in marketing the produce on an agency basis, advancing reasonable payments against stock on sale. Anything that engages the general resources of the society in trading, production or construction has to be avoided. It is true, and in fact it is an encouraging sign, that the spirit of cooperative endeavour fostered by one kind of activity is helpful in guiding that endeavour into other kinds as well. But it will do none of these activities any good to mix up either financial or operational responsibilities.

The responsibility of indenting for distribution of seed, fertilizers, implements and other aids to improved agriculture is being more regularly placed on cooperatives, and the societies are discharging these functions quite satisfactorily. Marketing, however, must be treated as an important activity by itself, and in small and large Mandi centres suitable cooperative organisations, equipped with the requisite storage, transport and credit facilities must be set up. The draft outline of the community projects programme had provided for some of these developments, but except in States where already some progress had been made in the field of cooperative marketing there is no planned activity to promote new cooperative marketing societies. As the whole of this subject of developing of rural credit facilities and allied cooperative services is now attracting wide attention, it is worthwhile recording that in the absence of adequate service for credit and marketing the success of the technical or production aspects of national extension is seriously hampered. Only a small section of the people can take advantage of them, and even they would do so much more enthusiastically and steadily if better marketing and credit facilities are made available.

There are two other types of agricultural cooperatives which have a close bearing on extension programmes. The prospects of assured and continuous water-supply are obviously very vital to successful farming. The putting up and maintaining of bunds often needs investment which exceeds what one person or a handful of people can put together. Even if the investment is found by a few well-to-do people, it is desirable that smaller holders also are enabled to participate in an advantage, which is really a natural asset. The installation of power-lifts and their service and maintenance are further stages of lift irrigation schemes in which unless institutional action is channelized through cooperatives, there will either be no progress, or the progress will be limited to a few well-to-do people. In States like Andhra, having good prospects of lift irrigation cooperatives have been deliberately chosen as instruments of extension effort in that field. The adoption of intensive methods of cultivation and greater employment in agriculture have been promoted in this way.

Another type of cooperative society in respect of which the community and extension programmes could have been expected to do something is the cooperative farming society. The general case for cooperative farming with a view to increase the unit of cultivation to its optimum size under prevailing conditions of tillage is now well known. It is also well-known that the Planning Commission attached great importance to undertake experiments in cooperative farming and land-management. Although in two or three States some beginning in co-operative farming has been made, there is hardly any development block or project in which co-operative farming figures as an important item of the programme. Neither the executive nor the technical officers seem to have attached much importance to this aspect of agricultural progress. While too rapid an advance in such a developed form of cooperation as is represented by farming cannot be either expected or desired, it is reasonable to expect that in so far as augmentation of the size of a cultivating unit beyond the actual size of holding is considered to be economically advantageous steps at establishing an appropriate form to joint farming should be regularly encouraged. It is only out of demonstrable experience gathered through such experiments that the future place of cooperative farming in any extension programme can be specifically determined.

It would perhaps be best to refer to another type of cooperative about which much is said but not so much is done, *viz.*, industrial or artisans' cooperatives. The whole area of village industries is really an unoccupied area so far as community projects and national extension are concerned. This is so far no fault of those who are responsible for either shaping or guiding these programmes. Whereas, in the case of agriculture, health or education there is some proved programme which the developmental and extension organisation can adopt, in the field of industry, except perhaps in the case of Khadi, there is no proved programme. Unless on the basis of an assigned sector of estimated total demand production of village industries is fitted into the overall national programme of employment, investment and production, conditions, cannot be said to be ripe either for industrial extension or for cooperation. When this stage is reached industrial cooperatives will be a suitable agency for a gradual transformation and improvement of the non-agricultural sector of village economy.

It is a depressing though that in by far the larger number of States little should have been done in promoting cooperation even in the more familiar channels of rural credit. It is surprising how even now in some of the best administered states two departments of state activity can go in almost complete in difference, if not hostility to one another's objectives. While the old 'take it or leave it attitude of the developmental departments of the state was the order of the day, it was natural that cooperatives, acted as select clubs, even more so than joint-stock companies whose shares could be freely traded in. It was also natural that howsoever assessed the amount of loans actually made should be based on the real or personal disposable security offered by the borrower. But when a high-powered, multipronged and nation-wide effort at bringing the desire and knowledge of improved practices to all the villagers was launched through a special organisation, that many of the cooperatives should still function as privileged and subsidized associations of the better-to-do was astounding. Many societies in cooperatively developed areas were too exclusive to touch the medium and small men. In the cooperatively underdeveloped areas there were few cooperatives and few members. Thus the extent of the social as well as physical success of the extension programme has been unnecessarily restricted by the fact that principles and practice of cooperation were not brought into line with planning and extension which were adopted as national policy. As is well-known a new outlook on these issues is now being popularized and perhaps a more assured place for cooperative efforts may be found in later years. In a few exceptional cases, as that of Bombay noted above first steps to move in the new direction have already been taken.

On account of excessive selectiveness and narrow and individualist interpretation of the nature of credit, societies did not admit many members. Naturally the financing agencies also had not much to do for a long time. Gradually, they had lost vigour and fallen in public esteem. It is, therefore, by no means rare to find in development areas and blocks, that there are no societies, what few there are have not many members, what members there are cannot get adequate funds, because the financing agencies are working with very meagre resources. Unless an overall strengthening of the institutional structure of credit and allied activities is urgently undertaken extension activity will not reach below the upper layers of social and economic influence in villages.

In the vacuum created by the absence of a widespread and well-endowed cooperative system direct State assistance in the shape of tagai loans has filled the need to some extent. This is a valuable service which the Union and State Government have rendered. Its favourable influence on the success of the extension effort was proved when tagai was distributed in the form of fertilizer loans. Such loans must continue as an accompaniment to extension and they should be made available to as large a section of the people as possible. In fact they should be disbursed by preference to persons of limited means. But for obvious reasons the state cannot indefinitely continue to lend moneys through its executive departments. For a proper choice of borrowers, assessment of needs, supervision of use, follow up by sale of produce and timely recovery, an appropriate public institution must be utilized for this purpose. The unsuitability of departmental agency for operating a regular issue and recovery of loans on a wide scale is already being revealed in the form of large arrears. The cooperatives offering their services to all, who are ready to participate in the development programmes, and acting in harmony with social policy are obviously the appropriate type of institutions to figure in schemes of development and extension.

# ROLE OF VOLUNTARY AGENCIES

**Preliminary Considerations**:

IN THIS CHAPTER we discuss the role of voluntary or non-governmental agencies other than village organisations. Such agencies have their limitations in promoting rural betterment on a national programmes. We discuss both the limitations of voluntary agencies, we are anxious not to be misunderstood. A major theme running through this report is the importance of self-help activities. The positive contributions of voluntary organisations to this end, which we discuss below, may be very real. However, in emphasizing the characteristics of projects if they are to be economically and administratively viables, we are not advocating static uniformity. Voluntary organisations may provide important elements of flexibility and variety, and thereby contribute to progress by exploration of new approaches.

It is not often that the stimulus of self-organisation for formulating and giving effect to a continuing programme of village betterment will emerge naturally within the village. The bonds of tradition are usually too strong and the technical and material resources too small for this to be likely. Stimulus, guidance and technical and material help must usually come from outside the village.

Voluntary agencies may assist in this task in several ways. They may operate programmes in a village or group of villages, or undertake particular activities on a wider scale; such as training, organizing and working with village women, encouraging cottage industries or promoting and assisting cooperatives; or they may promote voluntary cooperation in governmental programmes or formulate and propagate philosophy which inspires and gives direction to community programmes.

The contribution of voluntary agencies may be judged in terms of a number of criteria among which the following are important;

1. (a) their ability in planning the content of programmes and formulating methods and techniques ; and the effectiveness of the methods and techniques in bringing about all-round improvement in village life in the area of operation, with special emphasis on self-help.
2. The extent to which villages in the area surrounding the area

of operation have been stimulated and proved able to undertake similar activities to improve their condition.

3. Economy in the use of personnel and resources as affected by
   the scale of operations, ability to draw on the necessary technical services, and administrative feasibility.

4. The extent to which the methods and techniques have been
   adopted by governments or by other voluntary-agencies.

5. The extent to which they have contributed or trained personnel
   for participation in other programmes, especially government
   programmes.

6. Their influence in stimulating national consciousness of importance of, or national interest in, community programmes and
   giving direction to thought and action in planning and executing programmes.

# RECORDS AND THEIR USE

As THE EXTENSION programme is a part of the scheme of planned development of the country its implementation and progress should be capable of quantitative measurement at fairly frequent stages. To make this possible quantitative records have to be maintained. In most cases these are in the nature of noting down the implications of the activities of the extension staff itself. What is needed here is only an appreciation of the importance of quantitative record and the regularity of habit to maintain it. The feeling that maintenance of records is an unnecessary bother imposed by unimaginative theorists on practical men is gradually yielding place to a readiness to maintain what are conceded to be essential records. A series of relevant forms and registers have accordingly been approved by the Developmental authorities and these are awaiting actual adoption in selected areas. The sooner this step is taken and the more the basic records are relied on for all quantitative reporting the better will it be for the planners and administrators themselves.

Where the action of the extension staff affect the fortunes of village people the maintenance of records becomes more difficult, but on that account not less necessary. For instance, in almost every item of the developmental programme great reliance is placed on the method of demonstration on the cultivator's own farm or premises. Unless full records of these demonstrations are maintained they cannot be utilized for all they are worth. A new method often affects both the expenses and proceeds—the inputs and outputs—of an operation. Unless full detail about these are available the extension staff will not be able to determine in a specific way the net advantages of an improvement. In several cases as for instance the use of a particular form of fertilizer, what is available is only the quantitative issued to the farmer and the instructions about its use. Whether the fertilizer has actually been used in the manner in which its use was recommended has to be watched if the 'demonstration' value of an experiment is to be retained. This, of course, is done in most cases, but there is no uniform insistence on it.

What is aimed at in most demonstrations is the broad visual effect —e.g., relative heights or look of two ways of raising a crop. This effect is good enough as a beginning but no more. The net advantage

of an improvement cannot be assessed unless all the incidental disadvantages and advantages are carefully recorded and compared.
Moreover the comparison has to be carried on from year to year, as
many effects are cumulative in character. It is true that the primary
responsibility for such accounts keeping should be with the farmer
himself and in future while making a selection of persons on whose
farms demonstrations are held their capacity and readiness to co-
operate in maintenance of records should be an important consideration. People are becoming more factual and quantitative minded
themselves, and it will not be very difficult to get persons who are
otherwise suitable and are also in a position to afford the service of
record-keeping. Even the yield figures are not always very carefully
collected, and the expenses figures —cash, kind and labour—are maintained only in exceptional cases. In Uttar Pradesh so long as Special
Assistant Project Officer was put in charge of Statistics and Rural
Survey this part was better attended to. Similar arrangements need
to be continued in U.P. and they should be introduced where they do
not obtain at present.

Quantitative reporting, when it is resorted to, often tends to be
very inexact. Thus while any work for which full or partial payment
has to be made is normally measured and checked by technically
qualified personnel, there are several degrees of inaccuracy in some of
the reported items. Thus the number of participants in voluntary
labour is more a cumulative calculation of man days, without too
much insistence on the length of the working day or the quality of
work. Even when work is measured by the piece some departures
from approved methods, are resorted to which vitiate the calculation
of work done. Sometimes work is inferred from a standard table of
items, like say a well, and their equivalent in hours of labour. Or
instead of measuring earthwork from the size of the pit an estimate
of quantity spread or used is made. Whatever the method used may
be some clear directions for use of the method should be given and
its operation should be checked. Progressively more standardised
methods of measurement should be adopted. Without such data the
planning and organisation of works based on voluntary labour cannot
proceed a long way.

Several items of programme normally reported on have ceased to
have any significance at all. The compost pits are an extreme example,
especially in their description as 'newly dug and remodelled'. Almost
as a general experience these particular figures are not checked, nor
is there any systematic follow-up to ascertain the extent and causes
of disuse. The production value of this improvement is very real,
and if the degree of disuse had been recognised in time a further

probe into its causes followed by an appropriate educative campaign would have been undertaken. Even now rather than treating this programme as one of the lighter sides of the extension movement, efforts should be made to educate the villager in its ultimate advantage and to offer constructive suggestions to meet all the valid objections which the villager may have to raise.

A more important case is that of reclamation and irrigation. The ultimate advantage of both these reforms is that they add to the quantitative and qualitative resources of agricultural production. The estimate of area benefited by these should therefore, be based on the firm prospect of use for cultivation. Actually, estimates range, all the way from what is termed 'command area', that is, area physically capable of receiving water from the source, to a mere 'guess-estimate'. There are really very few projects for reclamation, and hence inaccurate reporting does not affect the progress reports very much. While there is no harm in any of these estimates so long as their basis and nature are made plain, it is desirable to have a reasonable common measure to be verified by a technical scrutiny. For irrigation, both command and served area giving details of crops, and for reclamation, area and crop would appear to be necessary. It should also be specifically stated that the reclamation consisted in the transformation of hitherto uncultivated land, into cultivated land, and not merely in a rotational recultivation of land which was temporarily fallow.

A more appreciative and constructive approach towards quantitative records is necessary we would then not take so much liberty with them. We would also use them more positively both in our plan making and in our extension. More and more the enlightened farmers will want to know about costing, prices, employment etc. Extension is a continuous and steadily improving process. Records, quantitative and others, are an indispensable aid to guiding the extension planning at all stages. A more appreciative approach to maintenance of records, and a readiness to welcome special staff as was represented by the Assistant Project Officer, Statistics and Village Surveys, in Uttar Pradesh are needed.

# POPULAR PARTICIPATION

The CONCEPT OF public participation tends to have different meanings. Initially participation was intended to imply popular initiative and sharing in the whole process of development of a rural community. As, however, the governmental organisation became the most noticeable outward expression of the developmental effort, and as proformas of schemes intended to be illustrative came to be put to people as suggestions, plans took the character of state or governmental rather than community or local plans. This development, which in most cases happened naturally and imperceptibly rather than as the result of any deliberate intent on the part of officers, gave to public participation the restricted meaning of contributing to the execution of a state plan approved by the people of a village. The shift of emphasis from popular to state activization is sought to be corrected by constant admonitions from the top-level leaders of the community movement. In several places this insistence was already practised and in other it is being re-emphasized. But the relative balance between the two concepts, viz., popular plans carried out with state participation, and state plans carried out with popular participation has not yet been completely corrected in favour of the former.

Even in its restricted application participation has come to mean different things for different people, and hence either qualitative or quantitative measurement and comparison in the aggregate is ruled out. Thus, in some places the expenditure that an individual villager incurs on his own land or house by way of constructing a well or a soak-pit according to a programme of reform advocated or assisted by the State is counted as public participation. In one or two places the proceeds of a labour tax levied by the panchayat is counted as public participation. Where schemes of compulsory land consolidation are in progress, and as a part of them some fraction of each holding is claimed for collective use in a suitable area the process has been described as public participation. Subscriptions collected in one place, an urban centre, for assisting developmental projects in another place a village, have also come under public participation. Contributions to works of social amenity received from panchayats, cooperative societies and other bodies have also been added to the account.

All these methods are legitimate ways of mobilizing the resources of the community for utilization in planned development. By and large, not only do the people react favourably to their stimulus, but they have a fairly clear perception of both the individual and collective aspects of benefit and burden. In view, however, of the extreme importance of encouraging the augmentation of available resources for democratic planning the central idea of public participation deserves to be clarified. Obviously participation has to be voluntary, it is to be something more than a tax in cash or kind which would normally go into an estimate of available public resources. Secondly, the contribution even when voluntary must be in addition to resources already available for a purpose. Thus if the Panchayat whose duty it is to make a road or a tank contributes out of its balances some amount to an *ad hoc* body to get the work done more cheaply than through normal channels, it is not the panchayat's contribution which constitutes public participation, but it is the margin of sacrifice which the participants in the *ad hoc* effort have suffered that is entitled to be counted as public participation.

Even a voluntary additional effort if made for one's own individual betterment, howsoever, enlightened and socially beneficent such an act may be, should not count as public participation, with sharing of benefits. The other aspects of participation are by no means unimportant and deserve every encouragement. But when descriptive or quantitative assessments are made the nature of the participation should be clear. In this context the relative emphasis placed on local labour and resources, as distinguished from that on skilled labour and better material which have to be imported from other places within and without the country varies from place to place. In some areas great importance is attached to this distinction between a policy of making the best use of all local resources of material, talent and personnel on the one hand, and that of raising local financial resources to promote works which mostly utilize materials and skills imported into rural areas on the other. Whenever the former policy is actively promoted popular contribution to a real augmentation of resources is very significant. The balancing considerations of satisfactory quality and the extent of development have also to be kept in view. If only the risk of a dominant local group or official sweeping people off their balance is kept out such variations in concept and design would be seen to be natural and on the whole beneficent.

A point often discussed with regard to popular participation refers to the part played by officers in initiating and organizing the same. It is wrong to treat every act of official initiative, encouragement and organization as a coercive act. The development officers have been specifically exhorted to assume leadership in a programme which is designed to bring forth popular leadership. In suggesting an idea and in backing it by their influence the developmental authorities do but their duty. It is only when influence attains the substance of coercion, which is pressure with a sanction, that the risk of a higher value, that of promoting the democratic progress of the people, being sacrificed to a lower one, that of obtaining a merely material result, clearly arises. Sanctions may range all the way from a refusal of a normal benefit like a taccavi or a forest permit to some arbitrary action in regard to revenue demand or property rights. It is so difficult for one and the same person to forget his disappointment as a development officer while administering his discretionary authority as a revenue or a magisterial officer that it is better to rely more and more on the influence of officers whose main responsibility is that of development.

Within their own proper sphere of action development officers who can easily and normally fit into the natural prestige scale of a village community, can play an important part in inducing progressive action on the part of hesitant elements. Sometimes these elements need to be reassured as to the merits of a proposal; they are occasionally more responsive to a detached source rather than one which may have got mixed up in the local tangel of prejudices. Moreover to be doing something which the government, that is now the popular leaders on high, have indicated as a desirable line in behaviour is a legitimate source of civic satisfaction. Considering all these things it must be admitted that official leadership and participation in the process of evoking and organizing public support to community causes ought not to be ruled out. On the other hand, the wholesome principle enshrined in a service rule to the effect that no government servant should collect contributions for private purposes must not be lost sight of. The most reliance is placed on development officers, and the more local bodies are themselves drawn in to initiate and organise an effort the legitimate nature and extent of official participation in a predomi- nantly popular effort will be more satisfactorily ensured.

For works like construction or repair of a road or of a tank of drinking water which obviously serves a common purpose spontaneous public support is generally forthcoming. For much of other work there is need to get together money contributions and then make pay- ments out of the funds for material as well as services and labour. In relative shares of different classes of the village community in money contributions the principles of progression, *i.e.* of the better-to-do contributing at higher rates than the less well-to-do, is receiving broad acceptance. The poorer sections who contribute by way of labour are in many cases remunerated at less than standard rates, thus providing for a sacrifice margin which is measure of their contribution. As the standard rates adopted for purposes of estimates and calculation are the P.W.D. rates for labour to be hired and employed by a contractor, the employment offered by community work is at a fair rate, especially in the off season. If the purpose is such that it would normally find a place in the developmental programme of the nation these methods of execution must be considered to have both an educative and economic advantage.

Labour, mostly unskilled labour, land and material, are all contributed by people. The proportion of these varies from work to work and block to block. In the sample of one of the blocks the relative magnitude of these contributions was; labour, Rs. 12,000; land and materials, 6,000; and cash, Rs. 3,000. In areas where people are on the whole well-to-do and better employed, as for instance in the irrigated areas of East Godavari District (Andhra) the people as a rule prefer to make a cash contribution. Sometime in well-developed areas there is resistance to the whole idea of voluntary contribution as it is felt that even for local works the resources of local bodies like panchayats and local boards to which people make contributions should be considered as adequate. It is here that the utility of *ad hoc* bodies formed for planning and executing particular work is the greatest. The process has to start from converting the people to the special need and suitability of a project. Thus a special organisation of the people themselves can do better than any official or semi-official organisation.

There can be no doubt that the people of all classes are realizing the importance of turning to productive use what is called the hidden wealth of the unemployed, and under-employed manpower of the country. The works done hitherto have served an educative purpose not only in bringing home this truth to all, but also in emphasizing the conditions in which it will be possible to organise a major project based on voluntary unremunerated or partially remunerated, labour. Distance is no doubt an important determinant. Psychologically the conditions in the country as a whole cannot be said to be ripe for inducing large numbers of people to be far away from their normal habitations for a long period to go to work on a national project. The extension of the boundary of the village say to a district seems to be within the limits of practical possibility. Inquiries made in areas where schemes of voluntary labour have shown a good response would lend support to this hope.

On the district level the principal difficulty would be firstly to select a project which has suitability to the employment and benefit of the people of an area. For roads having local and regional benefit which pass through a number of villages, and for bunds and channels which benefit more than one village a joint organisation of voluntary labour has already been used in several places. It can be improved in scope where circumstances permit. The benefit to the participants must be clearly stated that and to the extent to which the benefit is indirectly some material compensation will have to be offered to the less well-to-do and the poor. The idea of a 'famine of employment' is easily understood by villagers, so also the need to bring about economic progress for the country as a whole. If confidence is inspired in a plan, if the non-exploitational character of the project is made clear, and if the executive organisation can be trusted to be efficient it appears that fairly large works on something like a district or regional level can be organised as voluntary labour works in almost all parts of the country.

# EXTRACTS FROM FORTNIGHTLY DIARIES OF GRAM SEVIKA AND MUKHYA SEVIKA

## (a) GRAM SEVIKA :

### 1st to 15th March, 1957 :

IT IS NEARLY a month since I joined duty in this village. This is my first fortnightly report.

Within a radius of $1\frac{1}{2}$ miles there are 3 hamlets. My work, therefore, will have to take into account all the 4 villages. Altogether it is likely that there are nearly 600 families.

These are fresh villages in the sense that work for women and children has to be started for the first time. Because of this and also because I have come straight from the training centres, the Mukhya Sevika has been good enough to pay me 4 visits since my joining duty here. With her help a quick study has been made and I have now some idea of the different type of people, their occupation and their needs. A rough plan of work has been prepared and shown to the Mukhya Sevika. Of course, this will have to be revised as my knowledge of the village increases. I do not think I can start with any centre for the adult women. They appear to be very conservative. They have to be won over. A creche also will not work now, though I find there is a need for this; but unless they have confidence in me, they will not entrust their infants. A Balwadi, on the other hand, will work well and necessary arrangements have been made to start a Balwadi school in the coming week. Nearly 20 children are bound to come.

Some of the older girls, who had left the school, have become friendly with me and I am confident that a youth's (girls) club can be started. This club can work well and, I think I will make use of the girls, and draw out the adult women for starting either a community centre or a mahila mandal.

I have established good contacts with my co-workers, the Gram Sevak as well as some of the important men and women here. Also with the S.E.O. and Agriculture and Industries Extension Officers on the two occasions they have visited this village. Thanks to the local leaders, I have been shown good accommodation. This will greatly help my work.

**16th to 30th June, 1957 :**

The Balwadi is showing good results. At present there are 40 children on the roll with an average attendance of about 30. Not only do the children come of their own, but, in some cases, the mothers also accompany them and, in some other cases, the older sisters bring their children. Also they are much neater, cleaner and can narrate a few stories and sing a few songs together. Incidentally, I am making them help me in running the Balwadi, and thus enabling them to take some interest in this programme. It is very interesting to see the mothers themselves looking after one group and the older girls joining with the little ones when action songs are being taught.

About 7 girls who had discontinued their studies have been re-admitted into the girls' school.

Of the 3 neighbouring villages I could start only one Balwadi in village X. Even in this it will be difficult to conduct it satisfactorily until I secure a Gram Lakshmi to assist me. For the time being one of the girls from this village, who is very much interested in the work is accompanying me, whenever I visit the village.

As expected the Youth (girls) Club is full of life. They are only 14 girls, at present but they are very much interested. I think about 5 more will be joining this club. The Secretary is very enthusiastic and she gave an interesting talk on the importance of such youth clubs at the last club meeting, to which some of the adult women were also invited.

As suggested by the Gram Sevak I followed up the demonstration of compost pits. This demonstration has aroused some interest and in one or two places it is coming up. The Gram Sevak suggests that, next month, we might collect the women on the occasion of the visit of the Agriculture Extension Officer who could speak to them about different types of manures.

Yes, the women are now coming to me with their problems. They appreciate the advice given. The parents of P who has been ill-treated by her husband and driven out of the home, have approached me to get her sent to a good home. Again R, aged 10, is now declared totally blind by the doctor to whom I took him. He has to be admitted in a good school for the blind. I trust I will succeed in my effort to get them admitted as this will help the villagers to have more confidence in me. I have discussed this with the Mukhya Sevika and have also written to the Social Welfare Board.

**1st to 15th February, 1958 :**

The Republic Day celebrations were very successful. I was myself happy since this is my first attempt to organise such a function independently. All joined in the common celebration in the morning but in the evening special entertaining was got up by the young girls and the women. One thing about this is that the women of other three villages also participated. The exhibition was quite good and attracted attention. Some of the charts were educative. The children's items were appreciated. The items by the youths (girls) were the best of all. The Secretary's (Youth Club) welcome speech was appreciated by everyone. I only hope that this does not turn her head as such things can well create certain complications.

At the last meeting of the Youth's Club the members decided:

(*i*) to take turns and help the Balwadi and the creche;

(*ii*) to start a Bal Mandal or Children's Club;

(*iii*) to approach the elders for a Children's Park and a Youth Club, Bal Mandal and Mahila Mandal ;

(*iv*) to attend the same regularly in future.

We have been arranging meetings for the women once and sometimes twice a month. Attendance had been good when films were shown. They linked the one on Saving Campaign and one on Youth Clubs, also the one on Family Planning. They have now promised to come regularly. I trust that with the help of the Youth Club, the Mahila Mandal will be a success.

I have informally discussed the idea of having a sanitation campaign and a "clean house" competition sometime later on.

It is almost a year since I came to this village. On the whole I feel that the results have been encouraging. Sometimes, no doubt, it is very tiring particularly the house visits, but I must say the response has been satisfactory.

## (*b*) MUKHYA SEVIKA :
### 3rd to 18th June, 1958 :

My predecessor whose place I have taken is very well spoken of in this block. She has left a good name and I must try to keep it up.

I have now acquainted myself with all the members of the Team. I had a long talk with the B.D.O. who gave me an insight into one of the problems. I have also met the leading members of the place as well as the members of the Project Implementing Committee. The Chairman is out of station.

The previous Mukhya Sevika has made arrangements to start a Mahila Mandal in this village. My first task will be to complete this and see that the Mahila Mandal functions properly. There is good scope for this. There is also a good scope for Youth Club (girls). Many of the girls after their schooling are idling away their time. I find them full of energy and they can be brought into this. There is a great need for a creche but this will have to come later on.

Studying the records in the office, I have an idea of the area, the people and the work done so far. I also paid a quick visit to three of the nearby centres. One Gram Sevika is untrained but she is mature and experienced. The other two trained workers have to pick up much; they are still new. I am not satisfied with the way in which they are maintaining their records and doing their house visits.

I have to visit and see the other Gram Sevikas soon in course of the next fortnight. After this I will get some idea of the block and the various activities and can then plan my programme for the entire block. The three Gram Sevikas whom I have already met, I find, they have no idea of what planning the programme means. I have to help them to plan for their respective villages.

I visited the local school. Attendance is fairly good. I have suggested that it would be a good idea to start a Parent-Teachers Association.

### 16th to 30th April, 1958 :

This fortnight is important in these that I had my first staff conference with all the Gram Sevikas. After my visits to all the centre I find that understanding of certain common procedures and techniques are necessary. The B.D.O. and District Welfare Officer (Women) also agreed that this was necessary.

The main things discussed were:

(*i*) how to maintain registers properly;

(*ii*) how to make visits effective so that they are able to carry conviction to the women (home visits were actually done by way of demonstration);

(*iii*) how to go about the work, so that women do not expect the Gram Sevikas to do everything for them. For instance in some places, I find the Gram Sevikas were expected to attend all the children's requirements, in another they are expected to assist them in house work while others, especially the well-to-do, expect them to go to their houses and teach their grown-up daughters.

District Welfare Officer, B.D.O. and the Chairman of the P.I.C. also participated in the discussions. Altogether these were very helpful.

We also discussed about the steps to be taken in regard to the training of the Gram Lakshmies. It was agreed to have one in June. The detail will have to be worked out.

### 10th to 25th July, 1958 :

Touring in the monsoon is an ordeal. I have been visiting villages X.Y.Z. The activities here have, more or less, come to a close. This means that women and children have to be gathered all over again. It is quite a set-back. The staff has to be encouraged to keep going with each of the Gram Sevika I myself visited some of the houses. I have suggested to them that we may all join together to celebrate the coming local festivals. They liked the idea and the Gram Sevikas must follow it up. I have given them necessary instructions as to how they should plan. In village Y the Balwadi is not successful. I understand that the primary school is also not drawing sufficient number of children because older ones are kept to look after the little ones while the mothers are away in the field. We have to think of starting a creche and, if possible, see that the creche and the Balwadi are not far away from the school. Children up to the age of 6 can be taken care of in the creche and Balwadi while the older girls can go to the primary school close by. During intervals they can go and see the children.

I find it somewhat difficult to maintain regular supply of the material and equipment to the centres. There are administrative and financial difficulties in procuring and sending them to the Gram Sevikas in good time. Sometimes this does leading to embarrassing situation after having enthused the group to avail itself of certain services. If there is a slackening on our part it recoils on us very badly. I have to discuss this at the next P.I.C. meeting.

In the centre at X the craft class is popular. But the difficulty is they want to try all the crafts without completing any one in particular. The Gram Sevika must be very tactful in convincing them of the need to concentrate on one craft at a time and going through the whole course methodically.

In most of the centres some of the local women have shown some keen interest in the activities. We have now to think of arranging a short camp for them on the lines of Gram Sahayakas. It may be possible to have it in August or September. About 21 women are ready to join and they will prove useful to their community when they go back. They will also help the work of the Mahila Mandals.

# FAMILY PLANNING : PLANS AND ACTION

## *Nicholas J. Demerath*

So GREAT IS India's population pressure, and so crucially her efforts at population control, the detached analysis is difficult; exhortation and criticism are easy. Lest the reader draw negative inferences hastily from the account which follows, consider the context. India is a new and heterogenous nation with democratic institutions and a federal system in which the States are very strong. The bureaucracy is slowly struggling out of a law and order past into a developmental and problem oriented future. And leaders are driven socially and psychologically in a current of change from personal to universal standards and stratagems. However great their value in some respects, these characteristics are obstacles to a family planning programme; obstacles that are especially formidable because national family planning, unlike other development programmes, has no model of success to go by. Thus, "the case of India" is understandable: efforts at fertility control here are not new but the organization and management resources pre-requisite to any significant programme impact have yet to be mobilized.

In the Nineteen thirties voluntary societies and birth control clinics were established in several cities. In 1951, the Planning Commission appointed a committee on population growth and family planning. In 1952, with the Second Five Year Plan, the Central Ministry of Health got a family planning unit and a first annual appropriation of about Rs. 6,500,000. This was increased to more than Rs. 50,000,000 annually in the Third Five Year Plan (1966-70). Most of these funds are intended as grants-in-aid to States, cities and voluntary organizations, on the basis of 75 or 100 per cent of costs.

However modest all these Central Government appropriations, not one has been fully expended. The first year (1952) the Central Government had funds for family planning only about Rs. 3,000,000 of Rs. 6,500,000 was utilized. Twelve years later, the percentage of expenditure to budget provision was not much higher: it averaged 58 per cent for the 10 States where data are available.[1] Numerous explanations are offered, all of which spell lack of instrumental performance capacity. This hiatus between plan and instrumental capacity is not peculiar to family planning or to India. It will come as no surprise to sociologists: they expect this in societies like India whose structures of social behaviour continue to emphasize affiliation needs, traditional thinking, particularism, and functional diffuseness. Economists will recognize in this inability to mobilize the human input a characteristic of the pre-take off stage of development. And several public administrators have already pointed to Indian difficulties of development administration, given the Indian Administrative Service with its British colonial past; given the constitutional autonomy of the 15 Indian States to a degree resembling U.S. States rights before the Civil War; and given insufficient management skills among the public health physicians who have been in command of the family planning programme.

The plan and instrumental gap, then, is to be expected on the basis of various general considerations. But what have been the particulars? What needs to be done and how in respect to India's family planning programme? To get at these questions I will use two concepts from the sociology of managed organizations: (1) the organization as blueprint (2) the organization as action. Though I will not trace the scholarly pedigrees of these ideas, the reader will likely recall the attributes and concepts described by Roethlisberger and Dickson. Barnard, Mannheim, Weber, W. Moore, A. Gouldner, G. Friedmann, and others.

| Organization as Blueprint | Organization As Action |
|---|---|
| Status prescriptions and expectations | Members compliance or deviance |
| Plans | Workable programmes |
| Authority | Communication |
| Formal and official | Informal and unofficial |
| Functional rationality | Substantive rationality |
| Rational model | Natural system model |
| Papers, charts, boxes | Personalities, groups processes. |

Let us apply these concepts to the Indian family planning scene as described in government documents. Chronologically, three stages of effort are discernible and I have used them as major categories following :

[1] India, Programme Evaluation Organization, Evaluation of the Family Planning Programme in India, Report of the Panel of Consultants, Planning Commission, Government of India, 1965, p. 27.

## STAGE ONE (1956-61)

**Blueprint One**

The Second Five Year Plan period (1956-60) saw the first official planning groups and blueprints for family planning on a national scale. Numerous plan and policy boards were created. In 1956 there appeared a Central Family Planning Board, chaired by the Minister of Health, and by 1959 there were State boards in 14 of the 15 States. Top officials were named and by 1959 there were 10 States with Family Planning Officers and, at the Centre, a Director of Family Planning responsible to the Director General of Health Services. All of the latter officials and the Health Minister, since 1962, had medical and public health backgrounds. To plan or to "chalk out" became an ever-greater activity. Two other preliminaries to programme action also came to be emphasized, understandably enough: training and research.

There was training in demography, training in family planning methods, and training courses for public health and other community workers. Demographic institutes, medical colleges, schools of nursing, health education agencies were involved in these instructional activities. In addition, special family planning training centres were established at several points, some under the Centre and others under the States. Then, travelling teams of trainers were formed, including usually a physician and health educator, or physician and social worker. These teams worked with "camps" (*i.e.* meetings) of local leaders in the community development blocks or other areas. The camps assembled for one or two days to learn about the population problem, the Family Planning Programme, and methods of contraception as well as to consider the most appropriate procedures locally.

Research activities increased. There were demographic studies in government funded centres at Delhi, Calcutta, Trivandrum and Bombay. At medical centres physiological researches were conducted, including investigations of reproduction and of contraceptive techniques and materials. Problems of motivation and communications began to be studied in several small pilot projects.

**Action One :**

Though planning, training, and research were given the principal attention during the first stage, there was also a measure of programme accomplishment in rural clinics and in lesser ratio, in a few towns and cities. By 1961, 1500 were reported in operation. They provided contraceptives (condoms, diaphragms, jellies, foam tablets) and advisory services either free or at minimum cost, depending on ability to pay. About five million couples were said to have been contacted of whom one fifth were given appliances, materials, or contraceptive advice. In a few States sterilization was promoted and hospitals were being utilized for the operations. Also several mobile surgical teams were doing the operations, several score a day, at sterilization camps. This method was being promoted by mass advertising and small subsidies were being given to the sterilizees as compensation, presumably for time lost from work and for costs of transportation. As of July 1961, about 130,000 sterilizations had been reported, with a slight preponderance of males over females.[1]

That this action was insufficient, was the central finding of the high level Health Survey and Planning Committee (the Mudaliar Committee) whose report was published in 1961.[2] The Committee wanted to see the national family planning programme become both a broad scale and an intensive "mass movement". This was prerequisite to success, though the Committee thought Government alone could not launch the movement. They urged efforts to enlist more interest and help of voluntary organisations, like the Indian Family Planning Association, with the Central Government providing financial aid. High priority should be given for procurement of large supplies of contraceptive materials, either by Indian production or import. Expansion of informational efforts was strongly recommended, and family planning education efforts should be co-ordinated with the education work of other national programmes, such as community development and social welfare. The Mudaliar Committee sought an expanded sterilization effort, but with careful study of the social and demographic effects. The Committee, of course, had done its work four years before the IUCD, (Intra-Uterine Contraceptive Device), or loop, was to be emphasized.

Of particular interest is a supplement to this 1961 report. There, a minority of the Mudaliar Committee went on to urge that quite bold and different steps be taken, if by 1966, Indian population growth rate had not clearly turned downward. In effect, they urged that India take up population planning and control—a more comprehensive stratagem than family planning. The minority proposed: 1. graded tax penalties (lesser advantages) beginning with the fourth birth; 2. removal of income tax disadvantages for single persons; 3. no maternity benefits for those who refuse to limit their progeny; 4. limiting Government services, like free education, to no more than

---

1 Government of India, Ministry of Health, Report of the Health Survey and Planning Committee. Madras, Government of India, 1961, V.I., p. 399.
2 *Ibid.*

three children in a family; 5. enlisting the help of all Government employees in promoting family planning; and 6. permitting abortion when justified for socio-economic reasons.[1] There seems to have been little serious consideration given subsequently to many of these ideas. Although in 1965 the Minister of Finance did announce certain income tax inducements for smaller families, the income tax payer and the highly fertile masses are by no means synonymous.

STAGE TWO (1962-64)

**Blueprint Two:**

In April 1963, the Director of Family Planning, as if he were responding to the Mudaliar Committee Report, presented a detailed blueprint for what was termed "the reorganised or extended family planning programme." He explained that careful observations by many observers had led to conclude "the overall progress of the programme must be admitted to be remarkable, considering the scope of the programme."[2] The progress was documented by tables showing that Centre allocations to State Governments had risen 200 fold in five years, almost 11 million pieces of "educational materials" had been produced, there were 8,441 service centres. A total 22,631 persons in four categories had been trained and were reported to be on the job. Figures were presented which showed increasing sale of various types of contraceptive supplies between 1956 and 1963.

"To make still further improvements in the programme," the Director reported 25 pages of criticism and then spelled out his re-organisation scheme. Heretofore, the key service unit had been mainly a clinic set-up to which women came for rather elaborate medical examination and prescription of contraceptives. Now, a re-organisation was needed in the direction of an "extension" approach designed to reach the masses rapidly. Accordingly, the re-organised scheme would emphasize extension education, greater availability of contraceptive supplies, and less dependence on the traditional clinic approach. In addition, there were to be better statistics and evaluation, and a much stronger 'ladder" of organization and supervision.

The main programme goal was said to be reduction of the nation's birth-rate from more than 40 to 25 per 1,000 population, possibly by 1973. For this purpose, "operational goals" were defined as achieving for 90 per cent of the married adult population of India three basic pre-conditions of family planning namely: (1) Group acceptance of

---

[1] *Ibid.*, pp. 406-410.
[2] Lieut. Col. B.L. Raina, Family Planning Programme : Report for 1962-63. New Delhi, Ministry of Health (no date).

## PROPOSED STATE FAMILY PLANNING ORGANIZATION

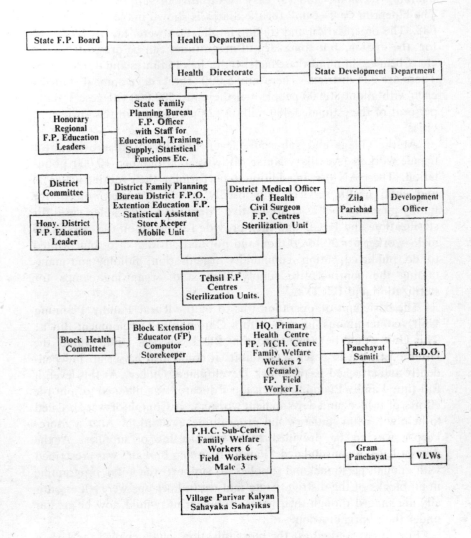

At village level, committees under village leadership will plan for education and action in their own groups. The village programme will be assisted by Contraceptive Depot Holders, and by Gram Kalyan Sahayaks and Sahayikas.

the smaller family size norm, (2) personal knowledge about family planning methods, and (3) easy availability of supplies and services. The blueprint or "set-up" for the States is shown in the chart on page 688. The organisation and staffing implication were not spelled out for the nation, but some idea of magnitudes can be drawn from the chart bearing in mind these facts: India has 15 States and 4 territories. There are 324 districts. There are 5,000 rural development blocks, each with about 80,000 people and there are 500,000 villages. Twenty per cent of the estimated 480 million population are in the towns and cities.

At the village and sub-centre level, the blueprint provided for female workers (Auxiliary Nurse Midwives), at one per 10,000 population. These ANM's, in addition to performing their routine maternal and child health services, supposedly would educate women for family planning, act as contraceptive "depot holders," refer cases for sterilization and IUCD and then provide follow-up on the cases. One male worker per 20 to 30 thousand population was also blueprinted to do public education, community organisation, building and main-taining the contraceptive supply lines, and organising camps for sterilization and IUCD's.

The basic unit of operation was to be the Rural Family Planning Unit, conterminous in area with a Community Development Block. This Unit would be attached to the Block Health Unit, where the latter exists; but in absence of a unit, it could also be set up independently and attached to the Block Development Officer. At this level, a full-time Family Planning Extension Educator was planned to join the efforts of leaders and development workers. A Computor was specified to help with vital statistics and programme evaluation. Also a Store-keeper was to be provided to ensure the flow of supplies. At the district level, a consolidated "Family Planning Bureau" was prescribed with enough personnel and supplies to support the total programme in all blocks of the district. State and central set-ups were felt essenti-ally unchanged though their loads, in blueprint, would now be greater under the re-organisation.

For towns and cities, the reorganisation scheme called for Urban Family Planning Units (rather than centres or clinics). Presumably, emphasis would go to a mass programme to reach all the people in each urban area of 50,000 population. But there was no provision for supporting and co-ordinating these urban units.

The Government of India (the Centre) accepted the blueprint for the re-organised family planning programme. In October 1963 there was issued to all State Governments a 45 page circular letter with three enclosures. This document states the basis and line item budget for financial assistance to the States; specified job qualifications and duties at all levels, tables of organization, administrative relations, community relations, training requirements and even specified the bicycle allowances for three positions.[1]

**Action Two :**

The author of the 1962-63 Annual Report and "Blue-print Two" wrote:

"Even such a sympathetic observer as the demographer Kingsley Davis, only 12 years ago, wrote that he doubted whether an official programme could be launched in the foreseeable future. Not only it is launched but India's Third Five Year Plan states that the Family Planning programme is at the very centre of planned development."[2]

Just how national was the programme's coverage, how effective its implementation, how real its accomplishment were to become matters of mounting concern over the next two years.

Inaugurating the seventeenth meeting of the Central Family Planning Board in July 1965, Asoka Mehta, Deputy Chairman of the Planning Commission (The Prime Minister is the Chairman), spoke as follows and in a manner accurately described in the reports of the occasion as "Vehement," "raising his voice,"[3] He said:

"We should not waste our time on petty worries of scales and salaries and status. These are undoubtedly important. I do not deny them. But I want to know if there is a famine somewhere and we are fighting it, will be insisting upon saying what are the patterns of assistance, what are the scales of pay you will give us or what are going to be our service conditions before we can fight the famine? Do we, specially those of us who are actually engaged in this task, not realise that this is a life and death struggle for us"?[4]

Shri Mehta, a development minded man personally as well as by virtue of his office, clearly thought all was not going well "at the very centre of planned development."

That this was the case,—despite the larger figures on people trained, materials printed, units manners—was revealed clearly in reports of the evaluation of the family planning programme by the Planning Commission's Programme Evaluation Organisation. The evaluators had visited the States in 1964 and early 1965; with reports

[1] *Ibid.,* pp. 86-131.
[2] *Ibid.,* p. 63.
[3] India, Family Planning News, Ministry of Health, August 1965, p. 3.
[4] *Ibid.,* pp. 2-3.

and implementation beginning in the 1965 summer.

The Evaluation Group had not attempted a full-fledged evaluation of the programme's impact. Instead, as they pointed out, they studied "the current and emerging problems in the implementation of the "Reorganized" family planning programme".[1] They observed what I am calling here the gap between plans and instrumental capacity. And the critical importance of the gap was now the greater in view of the clinical and administrative advantages of the IUCD or loop which the Indian Council on Medical Research in early 1965 had endorsed for mass utilization.

The findings of the evaluation report[2] provide facts on the 1964 action outcome of "the reorganised and extended" blueprint. At block and district levels, 3,195 family planning service units were reported. Over 80 per cent of these were managed by State Governments. Local government bodies (towns and cities) were still under-represented, with less than 2.6 of the total. The average population per unit varied from 48,000 in one State (Kerala) to 715,000 in another (Bihar). Staffing of the units was quite deficient; averaging only 1.1 workers full-time equivalent per unit.

In the service units, workers did not know what they were supposed to do, and with whom they were to do it; job descriptions and supervisory methods had not been spelled out. Local leaders had not been trained in the ways to promote family planning in their areas; indeed, training of all kinds was weak.

At block and district levels also, there were not enough supervisors, either positions or people. There was a tendency to economize on supervisory posts. Support from district family planning committees was not what it should be, though this could not generally be expected until full-time district staff were available to inform, stimulate and guide the district committees. Recruitment of the full district staffs, including district family planning medical officers and family planning extension educators, had not been given a very high priority. Family planning workers were not getting the maximum level of salary, allowances, and service benefits which other staff with similar qualifications received. As the evaluation team put it, the "shortages" of staff often were really shortages in appealing conditions of work.

The States lacked assurances of long-term financial support for family planning. That Blueprint Two, "the reorganised and extended" programme, had been launched in the middle of the Third plan period,

---

1 Evaluation of the family planning programme: Reports of Assessment Teams and the Panel of Consultants. *op. cit.*, p. 64. (This is the basic document, in addition, there have been two condensations).

2 *Ibid.*

had compounded the financial uncertainties. The State financial authorities had no assurance that subsidies from the Centre would be continued or increased in the Fourth Plan, starting in 1966. Therefore, they hesitated to create new positions and to think of expansion. There was widespread caution, delay, and inaction.

In the State family planning bureaus, presently sanctioned positions were inadequate to carry out required leadership functions. The State Family Planning Officer was commonly an Assistant Director when, to get the necessary resources and collaboration from other officials for his programme, he needed the rank of Deputy Director of Health Services, plus imagination and drive. He would then be aided by helpers at the Assistant Director level to supervise the key aspects of the programme. It was noted that State Family Planning boards were not always very effective, and the State Family Planning Officers needed help in activating these bodies.

Another set of findings on "Action Two" came out of my own travels and observations. During the summer of 1965 I observe family planning work in eight States and five of the largest cities. At the same time I observed and participated in various developments at the Centre in New Delhi. My findings pertain mainly to promotion and accomplishment by means of the IUCD or loop, the method that was emphasized in 1965. There had been real accomplishment in a few States, some of it quite impressive. But as the table shows, the all-India picture was very spotty indeed. Five States accounted for about 82 per cent of the 166,768 insertions by the end of September: Gujarat, Maharashtra, Mysore, Punjab, West Bengal. The same five States, at the end of November, had inserted a total of about 78 per cent of the 271,386 which the Ministry of Health reported for the national IUCD effort. These five states show good accomplishment, but the cumulative total is barely a beginning toward the figure required for any noticeable effect on the birthrate—5,000,000 and upward in each of several years. My other findings so closely parallel those already discussed, no detail is warranted.

## STAGE THREE (1966–)

**Blueprint Three :**

The Planning Commission's evaluation[1] concluded with several recommendations that, in effect, constitute a third blueprint, with a quite different Centre set up and changes in Centre-State relationships. The States should get more technical help from the Centre as

---

[1] Evaluation of the Family Planning Programme: Reports of Assessment Teams and the Panel of Consultants, *op. cit.*

well as from other states. Such assistance is needed not only where progress is slow, but also where some extra help might move a State programme "over the edge" to success. A "State Consultant Panel" was urged, to include outstanding State workers with experience in special aspects of the programme who could be called upon by other States for limited periods to help with specific tasks.

## LOOPS INSERTED: MAY 1 to NOVEMBER 30, 1965.

| S. No. | Name of State or Territory. | Cumulative Totals as of | | | |
|---|---|---|---|---|---|
| | | *July 31* | *Aug. 31* | *Sep. 30* | *Nov. 30* |
| 1. | Andhra Pradesh | — | 1,500 | 1,500 | 4,500 |
| 2. | Assam | 1,731 | 3,812 | 5,455 | 8,881 |
| 3. | Bihar | 2 | 86 | 1,014 | 2,331 |
| 4. | Gujarat | 20,431 | 22,192 | 38,868 | 51,316 |
| 5. | Jammu & Kashmir | — | — | 285 | 733 |
| 6. | Kerala | 575 | 900 | 5,013 | 12,428 |
| 7. | Madhya Pradesh | 145 | 120 | 1,324 | 2,170 |
| 8. | Madras | 338 | 358 | 428 | 960 |
| 9. | Maharashtra | 13,257 | 15,282 | 21,216 | 31,450 |
| 10. | Mysore | 3,238 | 6,192 | 10,541 | 21,246 |
| 11. | Orissa | 187 | 701 | 1,301 | 1,961 |
| 12. | Punjab | 7,343 | 16,404 | 24,570 | 39,239 |
| 13. | Rajasthan | 3,986 | 2,494 | 4,549 | 6,245 |
| 14. | Uttar Pradesh | 1,135 | 1,658 | 2,668 | 8,788 |
| 15. | West Bengal | 16,233 | 27,539 | 40,524 | 68,270 |
| 16. | Delhi | 2,000 | 7,000 | 7,000 | 10,000 |
| 17. | Himachal Pradesh | — | 27 | 472 | 801 |
| 18. | Manipur | — | — | — | 67 |
| | Total | 70,601 | 106,265 | 166,768 | 271,386 |

Source : Central Family Planning Directorate.

There should be decentralization of certain powers to the States, particularly powers of grant allocation to local voluntary organisation and other bodies. The Centre would make the general policies and guidelines for such grants.

In respect to finance, the evaluators recommended: (1) Each State should have a "master-plan for building up all the component parts of its total family planning programme," and the plan should underlay a schematic budget that would assure any unit, once started, of specified budgetary resources for the next ten years, irrespective of the Five Year Plan period. (2) For better use of funds and greater flexibility of operation, the family planning programme should hereafter be handled not as a "centrally sponsored scheme out as one of the State plan schemes and thus enjoy a specified pattern of Central assistance covering the planned and budgetary operations as above. (3) The proportion of Central assistance should be kept at least at 75 per cent of cost, and possibly raised to 100 per cent.

At the Centre, the evaluators emphasized the need for much more administrative and financial authority, and a greatly strengthened headquarters staff with sections of planning, contraceptive supplies, administration, training and education, and—of key importance—field operations with six regional officers. (The Director of Family Planning had only two or three professional assistants in his office). The evaluators urged a "Central Family Planning Organization" be established as a Directorate General of Family Planning in the Health Ministry. The Director General of Family Planning should be called "Commissioner of Family Planning" and be ranked an ex-officio Additional Secretary to Government. This would imply also conferring corresponding secretarial status to the Director General of Health Services.

A five-member Family Planning Executive Board should be set up as a semi-autonomous body composed of: (1) Secretary to Government, Ministry of Health; (2) Director General of Health Services; (3) Joint Secretary and Financial Advisor (Health), Ministry of Finance; (4) Joint Secretary and Establishment Officer, Ministry of Home Affairs; and (5) Director General of Family Planning as Member-Secretary. The Board should be able to exercise full powers of financial sanction and administrative action, including appointment of staff, within the annual budget allocation for the programme. The Panel noted that an alternative would be to establish a ministerial level board, but they preferred the secretarial board because secretaries could be convened more readily than could ministers, and could still take action.

### Action Three :

The Planning Commission's blueprint, outlined above, was paralleled in all essentials by the recommendations of two other expert groups; the terms sent to India in 1965 by the World Bank and by the United Nations (Technical Assistance). These groups also called for a reorganisation and strengthening of programme administration. At the new year, 1966, the visitors' reports had still not been released, but there had been confidential readings by Indian officials. Directors were changed in August, 1965, and the new man is called "Commissioner of Family Planning". Five months after taking office, however, the staff recommended for the Commissioner had not been sanctioned—much less, appointed. When it came to giving the ex-officio of Additional Secretary to the Commissioner, the Indian Administrative Service is presumed to have opposed successfully the physicians in the bureaucracy: the new Commissioner is only ranked An Additional Director General of Health Services. As for the Family Planning Directorate, it remains under the Health Minister instead of becoming the "semi-autonomous" arm of a "semi-autonomous Executive Board." Indeed, there is no Executive Board—only the same Cabinet Committee for Family Planning composed of the ministers of health, finance, information and broadcasting, food and agriculture, labour and employment, member of the planning commission, plus three advisers—all health officials. The name of the national advisory body to the programme was changed from Board to Council, but the Minister of Health continues on as Chairman.

## INTERPRETATION

I have described the persistent gap between the plans of family planning and the instrumental capacity to carry them out. This I have done by comparing blueprints and action over the last 13 years, drawing on government documents and my own observations. One may say of family planning what one observer has said of India's Community Development Programme, "the emphasis has been on expansion of schematic pattern at a pace faster than the implementing personnel could organize."[1] The massiveness of India's family planning challenge unquestionably calls for big plans. The population is now estimated at about 480 million growing at a rate of about 2.5 per cent or 10 to 12 million annually, whereas growth of national product is barely ahead.[2] But the plans must become action if there is to be accomplishment and if India is to attain her development objectives in food, agriculture, industrial employment, etc. What is the likelihood of closing the plan and instrumental capacity gap ?

There are several favourable factors in the present situation. The Planning Commission's recommendations growing out of their 1964-65 evaluation, gives emphasis to management problems and solutions. The availability and administrative simplicity of the loop combined with its evident appeal in a ready market requiring only in-

---

[1] Mrs. Durga Deshmuk, Kurukshetra, Jan. 26, 1965, p. 17.

[2] Gross national product increase, 1952 to 1963, was at an annual rate of 3.3%. Among 12 Asian countries, only Indonesia was lesser (2.8); Japan (10) and Thailand (6.0) the leaders. India's agricultural product increase is the same as her population growth rate 2.5%. Economic Commission for Asia and the Far East Survey, as reported in the Economic Times, Bombay, Oct. 6., 1965.

formation and service centre to begin with, is clearly an asset. And the loop as the method for emphasis does not conflict with the alternatives of condom and sterilization of males. Among staff and consultants, more thought is being given to setting operational goals or targets as a first step in workable programming; and this process may be facilitated by such techniques as critical path analysis and performance budgeting. Most favourable, is the first evidence of consensus in the Cabinet and in the Congress party that national family planning is not just another health programme to be promoted co-equally with tuberculosis control, small-pox eradication, leprosy control and the like. Instead it is beginning to get number one priority along-side food production and defence, though the politicians probably must have more confidence in the programme's capacity before they will commit themselves fully: they need "a winter" in India as elsewhere. Finally, on the favourable side, there are examples now of family planning accomplishment in five States (see table page 693).

Of the factors unfavourable to manage action, the most basic are high illiteracy and self-seeking peasant familism. Eight per cent of Indians live in the country, and millions of city residents remain villagers psychologically. These and other institutional factors may frustrate purposive population control. But if the control effort is to have a chance, other more nearly manageable factors must be reckoned with. Of these, one of the most pervasive is the penchany for symbols; plans and paper, meetings and assemblies, talk and print. The problem is often thought corrected once the law is passed. The goal is commonly considered won if everyone on a committee assents, if the funds have been appropriated, if the employees have been posted. Numbers of games are often substituted for more threatening assessments; numbers of bodies in place, numbers of rupees earmarked, numbers of anything assembled or processed. Also, co-operative action on the job comes hard, for caste-like practices persist regardless of statutory prohibitions.

Every man is an island: each man to his function, his private contract with God. This is the realization of the Gita's selfless action. This is caste. In the beginning no doubt a useful division of labour in a rural society, it has now divorced function from social obligation, position from duties. It has led to the Indian passion for speech-making for gestures and for symbolic action.[1]

[1] V.S. Naipaul, *An Area of Darkness*, London, Andre Deutsch, 1964, p. 83. For accounts of the caste factor in contemporary India, see M.N. Srinivas, *Caste in Modern India and Other Essays*, Bombay, Asia Publishing House, 1962 ; Vikas Mishra, *Hinduism and Economic Growth*, New York, Oxford University Press,
(*Continued on next page*)

As observers both Indian and Western frequently note, organizational behaviour generally is characterized by difference to age and seniority, to rank and authority and, more subtly, to caste and to colour. It is easier to distrust than to trust. The power to make decisions, even the smallest decisions, is usually held zealously at the top by means of tight review, and by endless noting up and down the parallel hierarchies of administrative generalists and of experts. Organisational goals are set at the top and too seldom translated or broken down for the involvement or understanding of subordinates.

Leaders who inspire and who catalyze group action and co-operation, as well as many competent managers are called for. While it is true that India possesses a large number of intellectuals and professionals than most other societies in transition, their per cent of the population is low and the ratio of managers and organisational leaders is even lower probably. Thus shortages of personnel qualified to manage and staff and a national family planning is a negative factor alongside the difficulties of communication and cooperation in pursuit of common goals.

Already apparent is an overloading of the family planning elite—overloaded by communications, overloaded by matters for decision.[1] This elite in the States, the regional offices, and Centre needs a very large enhancement of its leadership and management capabilities. This could be done by adding experienced managers from business or government, orienting them to family planning problems, and giving them expert social science assistance.

Brief, practical management training and development courses for present health professionals in supervisory positions could also be helpful. Whether the family planning programme will develop strong executive leadership, whether and when a sizable management input will be made one cannot say, though this is now the most critical factor in India's family planning accomplishment.

(*Continued from previous page*)

1962; Selig Harrison, *India : The Most Dangerous Decades*, New York, Oxford University Press, 1960.

[1] Karl W. Deutsch and Amitai Etzioni write on the communication capability of an elite as a factor in the process of inter-nation political unification. It is also important in the management or administration of national development programme. Etzioni defines "overloading" of the elite as "presenting it with more communication than it is able to digest (and) requiring more decisions per time than it is able to make". Amitai Etzioni, "*The Epigenesis af Political Unification*", in a book he edited, Social Change, New York, Basic Books, 1964, p. 487.

(Reprinted from the Indian Journal of Public Administration Vol. XI, No.4, pp. 683-697).

# REPORTS BY FIELD WORKERS

*In 1958, the Ministry of Community Development of the Government of India Instituted a system of national awards to outstanding village level workers who have shown marked excellence in their work.*

*The selection in the first instance took place at the state level. At the national level, the adjudication committee consisting of official and non-official representatives (with some members of parliament included) made the final selections.*

*From 1958-59 to 1963-64, six men and two women workers were awarded these prizes at the national level. Besides these workers, eight workers from centrally administered area were also given prizes.*

*It proved to be a difficult task to obtain correct addresses of these sixteen workers because of transfers, change and termination of jobs. Detailed letters were addressed to these workers and their block development offices, explaining our project and requesting extracts from their field experiences. We are enclosing only five reports from the material we have received from these field workers.*

## AN EXTRACT OF FIELD DIARY—I

THIYAM KONJIN IS a village on the eastern side of the Waithou lake. It is fortified on the north and west by the hills. The first crying need of the village is land for cultivation. The vast and ever-growing population of the village against the meagre land available for cultivation has been being a problem to the village, and on account of this, some people of the said village, has migrated to some other villages.

The matter has been taken up for the first time when I have been posted in the circle which comprises the said village also. There is no land available for reclamation nor is there scope of Jhuming. But there is only one scope the Swallow part of the Waithou lake may be converted into cultivated land by making a bund across the lake and separate the northern narrow and swallow part from the main body. If the scheme is successfully implemented some 100 acres of cultivable land will be available. However it is not an easy scheme for implementation. A bund ½ mile in length 20 ft. in depth has to be constructed in order to successfully implement the proposed scheme. The time also is very limited. It must be all over during the winter before the advent of the Monsoon. Many times the meeting of the village Development Committee has been held, many a discussion have been held but to no effect. Last of all, it has been decided that one Farming Cooperative Society should be set up and the society should be held responsible for the construction of the said bund. With this view in the mind one Farming Society has been established in 1958, with a total membership of 50 seats. The society has started taking initiative for the construction of the bund in the very year. Every member with the society donates 2 man-days every day. Within 6 months one third of the total estimated work has been completed.

The Imphal East Block has examined the bright and dark side of the scheme, and after an enquiry of the progress of work undertaken on the spot of a contribution amount to Rs. 5000.00 has been earmarked in next year's budget programme. By now some external people from the society has strongly objected to the bund's being constructed. There was a quarrel between the two parties. The work remain suspended for one year. At length it was again agreed upon that every house must be represented in the society, resulting that the society becomes almost identical with the village. This completion of construction of the bund has been made in 1960-61 and 100 acres of new cultivable land which was formerly and partly marshy has been brought under agriculture.

## AN EXTRACT OF FIELD DIARY—II

ARAPTI IS A village on the Imphal river. It is not so poor in food materials. What attracts my attention most in the village is bowl of 40/50 acres in the north. This portion remains submerged under water every year and in the dry season, a part of it may be used as grazing ground. If a sluice gate is inserted to connect it with the river, it may be converted into a large fishery pond. In order to examine the feasibility of the scheme, a general meeting of the village has been called and after a loud weary discussion it is decided that one Fishery Cooperative Society will be established and the society will be held responsible for the successful implementation of the proposed scheme. It has also been calculated that a sum of Rs. 3000.00 may be required for it. At the infantile stage each house will contribute Rs. 5.00 and preliminary work will start. Simultaneously it has also been resolved that the Imphal East Development Block will be requested for some feasible grant. But when the preliminary work is started some people, of the village has strongly objected to the idea that the bowl should be converted into a fishery pond. They say that no grazing ground will be available if the scheme is implemented, many times the village

Development Committee meets in order to make them understand that it will be a source of income of the village. But they never yield to it consequently, the scheme has become a cry in the wild air.

## MY EXPERIENCE IN SOCIAL WELFARE PROJECT

THE FOREMOST qualities which every individual, devoting himself to the task of social welfare, should possess and cherish are, "Patience, a cheerful and smiling countenance and the tendency to listen kindly to the queries of others".

Each Gram Sewak must consider it as one of his duties to be conversant with every aspect of social welfare to a certain extent, as far as possible. For instance, while speaking to a group of farmers and agriculturists, we must analyse, understand and assimilate the subject before starting to elucidate the same to them. My experience has taught me the above view. This service has given me presence of mind to pursue of my object with perseverence, sincerity and ceaseless effort, in spite of repeated failures.

I have formed a habit of doing anything after analysing the subject and planning in a systematic way. Such a habit has, in many of my deeds, brought me besides success in enterprise, enthusiasm and efficiency in my work. Many farmers consider that they would require seeds just a week before the time of plantation. If we are unable to supply the particular seeds they ask for at that time, they would feel disgruntled and this may lead to a feeling of dissatisfaction at our service. Here I wish to point out that, without giving any room to such queries, by enquiring in advance from the farmers of the village where I serve, the particulars as to what kind of crops they would plant, at which season, the seed they want etc., and by making the necessary arrangements to supply the seeds they require, at the proper time, I have won the confidence and goodwill.

The secret of my success in my enterprise is the effort that I make in understanding the difficulties of each farmer individually and in solving their problems. In my opinion, it is the small group discussions, seminars, especially those like the Village Leaders' Camp etc., that give the opportunity to mingle socially with all classes of people and to have intimate contacts with them and to appreciate their grievances. Above all, what I consider as most important is to understand well the viewpoint of those who participate in the camp and the development work which they have volunteered to perform and to render them the required assistance besides providing them the initiative and enthusiasm in their work.

A Village Leaders' Camp was organised in my area, in which man farmers participated. In the camp, many engineering and technical workers, officers and persons experienced in agriculture spoke about some new methods of organisation. The farmers who were present, exchanged views and got clarified their doubts. Various demonstrations of methods were done. Arrangement was also made for an exhibition. The peasants requisitioned different varieties of seeds etc., from the Camp thus organised. One farmer asked for procurement of agricultural implements another wanted supply of apparatus for sprinkling insecticides on plants; yet another requested for supply of beehive so that he may start "bee-keeping" thus almost eachone of the trainees of the camp voluntarily chose some activity. I noted the names of all of them in a register and started paying individual attention to the progress made at each of the farms etc., right from the day they started. I met them all occasionally to study the extent of satisfaction and contentment that they derive by their choice, and also succeeded in inducing them to take part in other activities also.

In this way, by gathering all the youths of the village and by organizing meetings and camps, and thus kindling their enthusiastic service by forming associations like "Youth Farmers' Club" etc., project work started gaining momentum themselves. Each member of the Youth Farmers' Club started building his own poultry farms; kitchen gardens; Bee-hives etc.

A few took up two or three such hobbies individually. Such young enthusiasts besides being themselves active, also attracted other who did not take part in such activities, by explaining them about the advantages of such a practice. Therefore, I consider that the root-cause of my success is the establishment of the Village Leaders' Camps and the persistent follow-up work by the people engaged in such activity.

In this way, in a village called 'Renanguppam' in my area, the old cocks were slowly neglected and gradually a superior breed of cocks called 'white leghorn' were brought in and about 80 cocks were supplied into village. Thus the superior breed cocks are being brought up and are increasing in number not only in that particular village but also at the neighbourhood. It is also significant to note that practical demonstrations, camps etc., in the development and extended use of fertilisers and manures are also bringing rapid changes. I would venture to say that there is no peasant in my locality who does not have a 'manure cub' for collecting compost manures.

We must permanently have a separate register in which the names of the peasants whom we meet everyday, their needs and requirements, and other miscellaneous particulars etc., should be entered in detail. Occasionally, at least once in a month we have to turn the pages of the register and see whether the needs of the farmers have been fulfilled, and whether any arrangement to that effect has been made. In my opinion, such a system, if applied, would be of immense use in performing our work. I also follow the above system. I feel that meetings, exhibitions etc., should be regularly conducted in the villages, which will help promoting understanding and amity between us and the villagers. Moreover, this paves the way to create gradually a better understanding of our projects and plans in them. Some people are, by nature, endowed with a cooperative attitude, and by approaching such agriculturists time and again, I could succeed in attracting many others also.

There is another important aspect of this matter to be kept in view—viz , the psychology of the people. If we were to go on explaining about our projects whenever we meet farmers, it is but natural that they may turn a deaf ear to us or scorn us. We have to chose the opportune moment after studying their mood, before commencing our topic of discussion. We must cultivate the habit of doing a thing at the appointed time. Such a practice, besides adding to our success, would also create a feeling of confidence and faith, in them.

Success can be achieved by creating an interest in them on our project work and attempt to complete the same with their cooperation and coordination endeavour.

In my area, I exhibited detailed advertisements, playcards, cement boards etc., about the work performed in my section, the work yet to be performed, and the work to be completed by the villagers etc. In addition to this, I also exhibited the opinions of "Gandhiji, the Father of the Nation" and also that of Pandit Jawaharlal Nehru, the Light of Asia," about such social welfare projects, to make the enterprise a success.

Ultimately, I should say that it is in the initiative and enthusiasm which the Block Development Officers and other development officers provided and also in the unstinted cooperation of the villagers, that the success of a gramsevak is founded upon.

## CASE HISTORY—I

### General Condition of the Village:

HAJI RAFIPUR IS a goan sabha having two small villages—Hajipur and Rafipur. The Goan Sabha contains 350 acres of land and 74 families of cultivators. The cultivators generally belong to poor or average class of men. Most of the old cultivators are too much conservative, but in young persons are comparatively flexible. They can be moulded to adopt new techniques in their profession. Formerly the source of irrigation included the masonry wells and kachcha tanks; but now a sub-branch of canal passes through the village, and provides water to the fields of the villagers. My case relates to the period when the canal did not supply water.

*Case* :— Rabi campaign was going on. It was the month of September and October when I began to call the general meetings of the cultivators in all the villages of my circle in connection with the Rabi crops sowing programmes. In the same continuation I reached the village Rafipur, called a meeting of the cultivators. Various programmes were told to the audience, in connection with the Rabi campaign. One of these programmes was the popularizing of the *"dibbling system of wheat and barley sowing."* How dibbling system is very common in U.P. It is a technique of wheat and barley sowing specially. A Wooden or iron implement having 24 to 27 teeth is used in sowing. Each teeth dibbles a hole in the ready field and one or two seeds of wheat or barley are sown into each hole. This system requires less quantity of seeds, generally six to eight seers per acre. The technique is specially adopted for seed-multiplication, though the field is also considerably high in consequence of the technique and proper care of the crop.

In that meeting I asked the cultivators to prepare their fields to apply the technique of dibbling in the sowing of coming Rabi crops. They told it expensive and bothersome and none of them agreed.

After a fortnight again I called there a meeting of the same pattern. This time also the condition was same. No one agreed.

It was a problem before me. How to popularize the technique was a puzzling matter. In the end I talked to a twentysix-year old man named Mohd. Muzanimil. I told him the economics and advantages of the system in many ways. He was anyhow convinced and agreed to adopt the technique for sowing a plot of half an acre. He selected the plot which was near a well and applied there $1\frac{1}{2}$ bags of mixture No. 1, chemical fertilizer, besides compost (manure) which had already been applied in that plot.

On 28th of October the wheat No. P. 710 was sown in that plot, with the help of a wooden dibbler. After a week in field bore a very few plants in line and less seed was sown. The villagers saw it and laughed saying that where, there was no plant, there is no grain; as there are a few plants, there would be less produce. The master of the plot Sri Mohammed Muzammil met me and made a complaint against the few number of plants in the field. He was totally puzzled as the other cultivators made ironical remarks against him. I asked him not to be dissatisfied as the few plants would spread into heavy tillering and would cover the whole plot although it seemed then blank. Anyhow he was satisfied.

He irrigated the plot after 21 days of sowing; again top dressed it with 10 seers of urea (a kind of chemical fertilizer). Inter-culture operations were properly done in the plot. After one month the crop was worth seeing. It began to attract the whole village as well as the neighbouring villages. Timely watering, required top-dressing and proper sowing brought a considerable development in the crop.

When the crop was ready, it was reaped timely. It was the real time of test—yield and comparison. The total yield of the plot was measured in shape of grain. It was 19 maunds in half an acre—just double of the common yield of the village.

The result was praiseworthy. It attracted a lot of cultivators. People talked very high of the technique.

Next year when I went there again with the same programme, I found a great change among the cultivators. Most of them praised the dibbling system and told me that they would sow their fields with the help of the dibbler. I told them proper watering and manuring are very essential in this technique. They agreed. This year 23 cultivators who had resources adopted the system.

In this way the technique was popularized by *individual approach*.

## CASE HISTORY—II

### Place:—**Parakamal and Aryanagar Kalan**

**General Situation:**

ARYANAGAR KALAN HAVING 1500 of population, is a big village on a pucca road leading from Jampur to Shahganj. It is a town like village with a small market on the roadside. Parakamal is rather an interior village, two miles eastward from Aryanagar kalan. It is bigger than Aryanagar. An ordinary route goes from Parakamal to Aryanagar pucca road.

*Case:*—The month of January came. This month is specially notable for Shramadan works in community development set up. I had already got a plan in my mind to build a good road either kachcha or pucca from Parakamal to Aryanagar kalan. In the same reference I called a meeting of the villagers in Parakamal, and proposed my scheme before the audience. I told them clearly that they had to work on the existing ordinary route from Parakamal to Aryanagar kalan and the work would be done on Shramdan basis (without any wage). First there was a great discussion among the villagers themselves, again they concluded that the route can be built as a road by Shramdan. But it was their condition that they would do the Shramdan upto the area which comes under the boundary of their village, beyond it the people of Aryanagar would do as it is under their jurisdiction. The condition was right to some extent, but it was the fact that the route was generally used by the inhabitants of Parakamal because they had often to come to Aryanagar market or to go somewhere else through the same village or that pucca road.

Even then I agreed upon their condition as it was justified to an extent. Next day I reached Aryanagar and set at the house of the Sarpanch, Sri Ram Raj. A special meeting was called for consultation of the programme. I told them the scheme that they had to work on the road as Shramdan. They discussed the matter for a long time. At last they told me the decision that as the road would be used by the inhabitants of Parakamal, they should build it, I told them that as it comes under the jurisdiction of Aryanagar Kalan, the work should be done by them. But they did not think it reasonable.

Next day a general meeting of the whole village was called on the same subject. The people gathered in the night. I proposed the scheme. But the plan was rejected on the basis of the reasons as mentioned above.

It was a very critical problem before me. Its failure was the failure of a good scheme which was very badly needed. I found no way to solve the problem, and to get agreed the people of Aryanagar. Leaders of the village were village-minded and did not agree to work for the sake of another village.

Soon after my mind sought a way. I thought that sometimes the topmost social workers like Gandhiji and Vinoba Bhave had to go through hunger strikes. They had the community agreed through various moral measures. I proclaimed in the meeting that I was not happy with that negative answer of the people of Aryanagar; it showed me though I always thought and did for their betterment. This proclaim compelled them to think over my last services to them and to their village, soon after quarrelsome discussions were heard at three or four places of the crowd. After a few minutes the voice of the Sarpanch came to my ears, "From tomorrow we shall start the shramdan work." It was youth leader said, "Be happy we shall do the work." It was nothing but my past services to the villagers and a cheerful treatment to them, which compelled them to follow my scheme.

Thus the people of both the villages began to work and the road was built within a few days.

*Note:* Here the word, "route" has been used for a "path" or an ordinary, "way".

## THE FARM PRODUCTION PLAN

WE WERE ASKED to prepare Agriculture Production Plan of 100 cultivators from each VLW circle. For preparation of the farm Production Plan we were given necessary instruction and booklet. Accordingly I started my work. I persuaded the cultivators and experienced the following difficulties:

1. The time given for completion of the production plan was inadequate (*i.e.*, 7 days).
2. The cultivators do not give the correct figures and many times they also submit fictitious figures. They are afraid that perhaps these data are being collected for putting more taxes. While collecting data sitting in group some cultivators in order to keep their prestige submit exaggerated figures.
3. Mostly we have to collect that data from the Patwarees but they do not cooperate to give information and were absent from the duty.
4. At times the party politics of the village also prove a great hindrance in the work.
5. We are heavily loaded with various work of urgent type so the real work is not done properly.

**How the difficulties were not met by the worker:**

1. Due to shortage of time, the cultivators were interviewed in short time.
2. In order to get the correct figure, other agencies such as Patwari record, cooperative society records, Panchayat records were also taken for judging the figures of the cultivators and accordingly questions were put up and tried my best to get the correct figures.
3. In order to remove these difficulties individual interviews were taken wherein the cultivators was free to talk of his problem.
4. Whenever the party fraction is existing question put up to them were so balanced that no such item of conflict comes out of the question. In such villages I am very particular to remain away from the politics and party.
5. This problem can only be overcome if the division of labour is properly done.

**Demonstration Plots:**

1. Advance Programme of laying out D. Plots are not given but always received the programme at the eleventh hour.
2. Supply of seed and fertilizer is not met accordingly to the need

and time of the cultivators, so the cultivators are hesitant.

3. Site selection of D. Plots: When we got a good cultivator we do not get a good site and when we got a good site then we do not get a good cultivator many a times this happens.

4. Flood and Rain Water: Due to rains many patches of Alipur Block were water-logged. Every year flood control measures were not taken to bring control over Jamuna river flood

**How these difficulties were met:**

1. I myself chalk out the advance programme for D. Plots and keep in mind to do the necessary arrangement for laying out D. Plots.

2. This is being experienced since long however steps are being taken by I.A.D.F. (Package) scheme to overcome the difficulties.

3. However, to overcome these difficulties we tried to find out the way in between.

4. Due to floods D. Plots showing better results were destroyed. To overcome this difficulty we tried to select the site which is not effected by the floods in the previous year.

When I stepped into this job nine years back I had my own apprehensions whether I would succeed well in my tasks depending as they were mostly on the mental transformation and response of the people I had to move with and work out the programmes. This part of our country is rather very backward, especially the women-folk, in the field of education. It has been a tough job breaking through their orthodox customs and traditions to get at the women-folk and help them to social awakening. The pleasant welcome they gave to the visitor namely the social workers as eclipsed with some sort of reserve and suspicion with one could feel well in spite of all their friendly gestures. This was rather embarrassing in the beginning. But with hope in mind and faith at heart the problem was not such a Gordian knot for the preserving social worker. Once their confidence is gained and our sincerity is established it is a smooth and pleasant job to help these simple-minded illiterate rural folk to help themselves. It is then only a case of harnessing the good elements in them and polishing them out of the crude encrustrations and we get the pure gem of pristine glory in its natural surroundings a good and useful citizen.

My first and major problem was to convince the illiterate parents about the benefits of literacy and make them send their children to school. This involved shaking them out of their deep-rooted convictions of bringing up the children along the traditional family occupations. They curse their poverty and illiteracy but at the same time accept it as their legacy nonchallengingly. A labourer wants his sons to be a good labourer. But he could not envisage that besides being a good labourer he could also be a better man. It is duty of the social worker to extend this knowledge to the parent and point out to him or her that social education is as much important as basic education in individual as well as national development. During the village visits which I undertake during the afternoons I used to call upon the parents frequently, have friendly chats with them and slowly prevail upon them on the benefits of literacy, about elementary civics etc. I would inform them about the various Governmental plans and schemes drawn up and implemented for the growth of the people socially, economically, and educationally, and discuss with them why their children should not be allowed to avail of these privileges and amenities and improve upon their lives. In solving this problem of disinterestedness on the part of the illiterate parents to educate their children there were some practical difficulties too. For example in a family where the child is of school-going age he may be the eldest and on his tiny shoulders falls the onerous responsibility of looking after the younger ones when both the parents are away at their work. In places where there is creche nearby this is not a big problem but where there is no creche this poses quite a problem. In our balwadies we can admit only children of the age-group of 3-6. What we have been doing if we get these children below three years also to our centre who are the proteges of our little balwadi children, seat them separately and leave them in charge of a part time, 'ayah who is maintained out of donation accounts of the Project. When our donation accounts is on the bane this extra activity of ours suffers but somehow we have been struggling through successfully with this activity in Thirunallar, since 1961. In this context, I must say that the free-midday meals programme is inevitable for dealing successfully with this activity in Thirunallar since 1961. In this context, I must say that the free midday meals pro-gramme is inevitable for the success of a Balwadi, for most of the children are poor and of working mothers. This free supply of food acts as an incentive as well as practical solution and for whatever reason it is, it benefits and practical enterprises our Balwadi is a success.

The second major task to which I had to set myself was adult education. This I aimed to achieve through organising mather sangams and working out the twin-programmes of social education and adult literacy classes. Here again in the organisation of mather sangams caste creeps in. The caste women would not join hands with the non-caste women. So what we do is to organise separate mather sangams for them at the first instance, bring them together to meet during celebrations and functions and slowly bring about their fusion. We have succeeded to a great extent in this endeavour and our social education programme are well responded to and successful through these mather sangams. But in the matter of literacy-spreading, I must say that still a long way is to be made. Social Education programmes can be worked out at the occasional, periodical meetings of the literacy classes there are some practical difficulties too. For one thing it is difficult to gather the grown-up girls, in one place in this orthodox area where the system prohibits grown-up girls from stepping out of their homes. It is not possible for the social worker either to go to each house and teach as desired by these girls. Such problem does not arise much in the case of non-caste women but they have another problem. Whole day long they work in the fields and when they come back they have their household duties to attend to. But still I find that they are interested in learning even late in the night. But this poses a refracted problem for the social worker. It would be too much to expect these tired working women to walk all the distance to the centre and back after the day's hard labour and household duties for these literacy classes. It would be better to hold the classes in their hamlets. But this would be exposing the social worker to the danger of visiting hamlets late in the night, and back to the centre a women worker as she is. Moreover, she cannot be reaching all the hamlets under her jurisdiction and covering up the literacy classes this way. Thus the literacy adult programme important as it is, is problematic too. I think the difficulties experienced in the field can well be solved to a great extent by opening as many adult schools (night schools) in the villages and hamlets as possible instead of leaving the entire programme to a single social worker—the Gramasevika—who is a multipurpose worker.

# EVALUATION

*The extracts in this section are included not so much because they are good examples of evaluation reports but because they throw much light on the mechanics involved in the task of evaluation.*

*The value of evaluation in an activity like community development is now widely recognized. While evaluation is of course closely related to goals and objectives of a given programme and is seen as providing objective assessment of the successes and pictures, evaluation may also be seen as a helping process.*

*The extracts in this section include parts of some evaluation reports besides those that describe the criteria of evaluation and the techniques of evaluation. Needless to add, there is a great need for more and more material dealing with the techniques as well as problems of evaluation as applied to what is still a nebulous programme like community development.*

## CONTRIBUTORS

1. Samuel P. Hayes, "Extract from Measuring the Results of Development Projects," (A Manual for the use of field workers), Prepare for Unesco, Published by the United Nations, September 1961.

2. Douglas Ensminger, "Assessing Progress in Community Development" Kurukshetra, Jan. 1965, pp. 6-7.

3. "Extract from Programme Evaluation Organisation Structure, Functions and Activities, New Delhi, Planning Commission, Government of India, 1964.

4. J.P. Bhattacharjee, "Approach to the Formulation of Criteria in Evaluation" (Cyclostyled).

5. C. Chandrasekaran, and Moye W. Freyman, "Extract from Evaluating Community Family Planning Programme," (Presented at Symposium on Research Issues in Population Change, at University of Pittsburgh School of Public Health, June 3, 1964) (Cyclostyled).

6. "Summary Recommendations" from Report of the Working Group on Evaluation in The States, Planning Commission, Government of India, 1964, p. 38.

7. "Some Aspects of Social Change," from Evaluation Report on Working of Community Projects and N.E.S. Blocks Vol. I, Planning Commission, Programme Evaluation Organisation, April 1957, pp. 53-69.

8. R.K. Patil, "Community Development, Achievements & Failures," Kurukshetra, Jan. 1965, pp. 5-6.

# MEASURING THE RESULTS OF DEVELOPING PROJECT

*Samuel P. Hayes, Jr.*

## A MANUAL FOR THE USE OF FIELD WORKERS

### Introduction

MOST NATIONS OF the world today give high priority to projects and programmes intended to advance economic and social development. Governments have accepted greater responsibilities and are using greater resources than ever before to aid development. Intergovernmental organizations and their agencies are increasingly concerned with development activities. Private organizations, both business and non-profit making, are more and more adopting economic and social development at home and abroad among their major goals.

In this atmosphere of broadened and intensified concern for economic and social development, it is not surprising that demand is growing for better information about the results being obtained in development projects. The more objective and the more quantitative the information is, the better. And the more directly it can be related to actual project operations, the more convincing its testimony. The art of inducing and guiding social and economic change is not yet highly developed. Data that show how things are going can be immensely helpful in improving projects operations in mid-stream. And what can be learned about the results of completed projects can be most valuable in planning subsequent projects.

Obtaining such information on project results is not in itself 'evaluation'. But it is essential for evaluation. Those who are primarily interested in evaluation may wish to consider the types of information described below when they plan their own evaluations. Both those interested primarily in measurement and those interested in evaluation will find very useful the practical examples of data collection reported in the International Social Science Bulletin, 1955, Vol. VII, No. 3, on 'Evaluation Techniques'.

## CHANGES SIGNIFICANT FOR DEVELOPMENT

Economic and social development result from change. Certain kinds of change are of strategic importance in transforming a traditional social system into one characterized by a self-sustaining process of technological advance.[1] Those strategic kinds of changes are highly interrelated but may be grouped under three major headings, as they affect primarily individuals, social relationships and social overhead capital.

Changes in individuals. (Their Information, Skills, Attitudes).

1. Increasing literacy, scientific knowledge, scientific and technological training and a scientific or engineering approach to problems.
2. Increasing dissatisfaction with traditional levels of living, traditional status relationships, traditional economic activities.
3. Increasing belief that economic and social advancement can be obtained through new techniques and new economic activities.
4. Increasing belief that economic and social advancement can be obtained through individual competence and effort (rather than through preference based on bribery, political favour, kinship, caste or social status, national origin, race, religion or sex).
5. Increasingly specific definition of economic privileges expected from society, and economic obligations to society (rather than the vague, open-ended security often expected from the village or family, and the indefinite but broad economic obligations often felt towards the village or family).
6. Increasing respect for honesty in business and government and for the use of contracts in economic relationships.

### Changes in Social Relationships and Institutions

1. Increasing interpersonal communication (through adoption of common language, growth of literacy, increased media of communication, social mobility, travel, etc.).
2. Increasing economic opportunity (through decreased monopoly, increased availability of credit and greater occupational mobility).
3. Increasing rewards for economic activity (through land reform, tax changes, governmental aid of various kinds).
4. Increasing power of groups participating in these changes, and diminishing power of groups resisting change.
5. Increasing governmental activity in public service and in economic and social development.

[1] See particularly the significant article by Professor Everett E. Hagen. 'The Process of Economic Development', in: Economic Development and Cultural Change, 1957, Vol. 5. pp. 193-215, from which the scheme given here was largely taken.

**Changes in Social Overhead Capital**

1. Increasing investment in education, public health and sanitation, water supply.
2. Increasing investment in transportation, communications, power, irrigation.
3. Increasing competence (likely to involve investment) in public administration, civil police, and the military establishment.

In appraising economic development, attention has often been focussed on superficial changes in production, consumption or saving, perhaps because they are relatively easy to measure. For example, fertilizer may be provided (at a subsidized price) and the increased harvest may be looked upon as the primary measure of accomplishment. A more fundamental measure is the change in the willingness of the farmers to buy fertilizer at commercial prices in subsequent years. Still more fundamental is the change in their interest in trying out other improved agricultural techniques. Most fundamental is the change (if any) in their willingness to support, or to co-operate in, the development of new agricultural techniques. It is possible to obtain data to indicate the extent of all these kinds of changes. Methods of collecting such data are discussed under 'Step One' below.

## PROGRAMME RESULTS AND PROJECT RESULTS

Attention is given below to the results of development projects and of the individual operations comprising those projects. Results of development programmes are not discussed.

Development programmes usually comprise a wide variety of important activities, in different regions, over different time periods. Measuring the results of development programmes is, of course, very important. Governments cannot determine their policies, allocate their funds or administer their agencies without information about the results obtained. To measure these results, they call upon the whole statistical paraphernalia of censuses, records of production and trade, index numbers, input-output analyses, national income accounting, etc.

Uncovering the results of individual projects is simpler and less costly and can often be carried on by the persons directly involved in the project. Moreover, project results show up most clearly at the 'level' where a particular group of individuals comes directly in contact with particular project operations. The fewer the complicating factors present, the clearer will be the link between cause and effect. As governments improve their methods of collecting data for use in evaluating their development programmes, however, a valuable by-product may be the increased availability of data useful in indicating the results of particular development projects.

## STEPS IN INDICATING THE RESULTS OF A PROJECT

The logical process of identifying (and measuring) changes and attributing them to a development project may be outlined as follows:

*Step One.* Describing the development project and specifying its goals.

*Step Two.* Deciding what data to use to indicate project results.

*Step Three.* Collecting the data—before, during and after.

*Step Four.* Analysing and interpreting the findings, and reviewing these with interested groups.

All the steps but the third are simple ones-dictated by logic and demanding only the time and effort to think them through and reach agreement. These steps are little different in small, inexpensive projects from what they are in large, elaborate ones. They can be carried out without requiring additional staff or funds.

'Step Three' can be done simply, without additional staff or funds. On the other hand, if the project is of such size or significance as to warrant it, this step can be developed in as great depth and detail as desired. The Bibliography lists references for use in carrying out such more intensive studies, together with reports of a number of field studies carried out in Asia and Latin America. It may be that a centre for social research exists in a local university or in some government department and can be called upon to carry out a detailed, scientific study of the changes induced by a project.[1] Here it is assumed that little if any additional staff or funds are available to obtain and analyse data about project results.

---

[1] An illustration of the excellent social research that such centres may be willing to carry out is contained in A.F.A. Husain's Human and Social Impact of Technological Change in Pakistan (Two volumes), Dacca. Oxford University Press, 1956.

# ASSESSING PROGRESS IN COMMUNITY DEVELOPMENT

*Dr. Douglas Ensminger*

INDIA'S COMMUNITY DEVELOPMENT programme is a powerful innovative force working in manifold ways to aid the growth of the nation. In this venture, India has blazed a trail for many new nations to follow, in social revitalization through new attitudes, new practices, and new ways of thinking.

As in any educational process, Community Development widens and deepens with the passage of time. Indeed, its planned growth in size and effectiveness, still lies in large measure in the years and generation of the future. However, the current workings of the programme must be kept under continuous scrutiny, both for assessment of its progress and for tracing up its courses of action. This need exists at all levels—national, State and local.

Local scrutiny and assessment of local operations are the beginning point of realistic measurement. The people most intimately involved with the implementation of Community Development—the Block and Village Level Workers—have the basic task here. They need to make periodic detailed appraisals of the advances and difficulties of the programme in their localities. Their assessment is uniquely valuable, for in their daily work they are the real index of village development as well as most conscious of lags in performance and the further gains required. Practical local appraisals, regularly made, can do much to assure better programme effectiveness at the village level. Also, they provide an essential guide for programme actions and policies at the district, State and national levels.

Realistic measurement of any programme must be in terms of its aims and objectives. This applies at all levels. At the local level each Block and village worker would do well to "rate" the Community Development programme in his own areas at frequent intervals, in terms of the objectives stated at the inception of the programme. This rating test should be done seriously and in detail; each objective might appropriately be scored in terms of identifiable and satisfactory progress toward its achievement.

Broadly speaking, the objectives of Community Development are:

A. To develop the people's capacity to rely on themselves for meeting their local needs, instead of on the Government. Block and village development personnel have close-up knowledge of many examples of individual and community initiative in tackling common local problems, doing what they can with their own resources, and obtaining added outside help, if necessary. Purely local actions to repair village lanes and approach roads are frequently observed by those on the scene, though such actions do not stir up headlines. Similarly, Panchayat-led improvement of village wells and drains and village attempts to make homes and schools cleaner are other important indications of a spirit of self-help. Local efforts to improve village and Block libraries and information literacy, and to expand sanitation measures, are also important, along with the characteristically unchronicled steps of cultivators to improve crop practices. Though basic in the development picture, these things are seldom known to distant observers. For knowledge of their reality and importance, dependence must be placed on the field workers who see them in daily action. Their assessment of such self-help changes can be knowledgeable and meaningful in terms of real-life achievement.

B. To develop the people's competence to make wise decisions based on known alternatives. At times, it has happened that improvements have been brought to villages from the outside and instituted without the villagers having any real understanding or appreciation of them—with the result that the gains have soon disappeared. The real test is the villagers' (or urbanites') voluntary actions. Do some villagers now seek out credit to buy new production supplies, such as fertilizer or on improved variety of seed, to increase their yields? Or use new tools? Or decide to send children to school in order to increase the families' opportunities for a better life? Or adopt other changes? Block and village level workers can provide many examples of innovations introduced, debated, and finally adopted on the basis of a rational choice, first by a few people and then perhaps by many.

C. To increase the people's awareness of modern technology and their willingness to look to science and technology, rather than the traditions and habits of the past, for answers to their problems. In assessing progress in this area, the development worker has to consider changes in health and sanitation practices, the increases made in the use of fertilizer and pesticides, better choice of seed, better tillage of the soil, new attitudes toward education, adoption of modern practices of animal care and breeding, etc.

D. To develop vital and effective village institutions and to promote increased reliance on these institutions for leadership and services in meeting village needs. Here local Community Development workers are in a good position to recognise progress in the three most important village institutions—the school, the Panchayat, and the Cooperative. Some relevant questions might be: What percentage of village children now attend school and how many years of school do they complete? What is the nature of their studies and the quality of the teaching? How do the village children use their education after they leave school? Does the village contribute to the costs of the school? Have there been any changes in attitudes towards the Panchayat? Are Panchayat elections more democratic? Is there an increasing tendency to view the Panchayat as a people's forum for expressing their common desires and for planning how to obtain them? In turn, is there evidence that the Panchayat functions with an increasing sense of responsibility to the village community? Is the co-operative society being used more and more as a source of needed agricultural supplies and credit? And, equally important, is there evidence that all these institutions are regarded as belonging to the village, reflecting and serving the needs of the people?

E. To strengthen the economic base of the village community through agricultural development and industrialization. Are agricultural practices changing in line with modern knowledge? Is production per acre on the up-grade? Are new demonstrations under way? Are villages doing more supplementary industrial work at nearby centres, to obtain increased income to pay for the new and additional things they want (better health services, better schools, better housing, etc.)?

A useful rating device, geared to objectives of the programme might be set up about like this:

| | | Progress | | |
|---|---|---|---|---|
| 1 | 2 | 3 | 4 | 5 |

Objectives
A
B
C
D
E

On such a rating scale, progress is meeting each objective would be deemed excellent at the 5-level, medium at the 3-level and poor at the 1-level. A total score of more than 15 points for the five objectives would represent above-average progress for the undertaking as a whole. And any objective whose advancement is rated much below that of the other four would call for added work on it as soon as possible.

This approach to continuous rating of Community Development progress should be especially helpful in the field, as a guide for Block and Village Level Workers. First, the field worker may well be surprised and heartened at the relatively high progress rating he finds his area deserves. Also, the scoring will help him concentrate his effort on work which is most in need of attention. And the continual reminder of programme objectives that is entitled in such scoring will help him move forward in all phases of his work.

This approach seeks an objective appraisal of progress, rather than mere identification of deficiencies. It is oriented to measuring success in terms of the programme's goals, as well as to identifying strong points and weaker points as a continuous guide to further efforts. Since progress is the goal, objective by objective, progress is the thing requiring measurement. Deficiencies always exit in any large programme and it requires little effort or thought to point a finger at them. In development seeking programmes, it is advance being made that counts and which requires studious and detailed evaluation. Goal-oriented assessment is a true development tool, aiding all workers in carrying out their on-the-ground tasks. Local workers, especially, will find it helpful to their morale and working effectiveness.

# PROGRAMME EVALUATION ORGANISATION STRUCTURE, FUNCTIONS & ACTIVITIES

## Objects and Scope of Evaluation

EVALUATION HAS BEEN conceived in India as an essential aspect of the formulation and execution of development plans and programmes. It was in the context of administrative reforms envisaged in the First Five Year Plan that evaluation was thought of as a method of continually improving the execution of development programmes. At that stage, it seems to have been linked generally with the administrative organisation and arrangements for plan projects and programmes. It was stated that "With every important programme provision should always be made for assessment of results.....Systematic evaluation should become a normal administrative practice in all branches of public activity." The emphasis in evaluation work at this time was on regular assessment of results through a system of periodical reporting and arrangements for analysis and follow-up of the reports.

The approach to evaluation in the Second Plan was in some respects different from that in the First. It was more specifically linked to the field of rural development, though its need in other fields was not overlooked. The Second Five Year Plan states that "with the progress of land reform, co-operation, village and small industries and with the rapid pace of urban and industrial development, fundamental changes are already taking place in the country-side. These are likely to be accelerated during the second plan. It is of utmost importance that social and economic changes should be analysed objectively as they occur and the impact of economic development on different sections of the rural population observed, at first hand. The need for evaluation exists in all fields of development and more especially in those in which new or expanded activities are being undertaken. In all planned development many unknown factors have to be reckoned with. Understanding of the interaction of different elements that enter into programmes which bear closely on the life of the people can be of material help in enhancing their contribution to the welfare of the community. Evaluation has, therefore, to be increasingly oriented towards studies of a selective and intensive type motivated by and leading to purposive action."

In short, evaluation was assigned in the Second Plan the role not only of helping programme administration and execution, but also—perhaps more so—of aiding planning and policy formulation. The importance of evaluation has been further emphasised in the Third Plan in the context of the need for follow-up of the implementation of the Plan programmes.

### Functions of the P.E.O.

When the P.E.O. was set up in 1952, its work was defined by the Planning Commission as including the following :

(*i*) keeping all concerned apprised currently of the progress being made towards accomplishing the programme (community development programme) objectives;

(*ii*) pointing up those extension methods which are proving effective and those which are not;

(*iii*) helping explain why some recommended practices are adopted while others are rejected by the villagers; and

(*iv*) furnishing the insight into the impact of the community development programme upon the economy and culture of India.

In its report on the Second Five Year Plan and in the Resolution in December, 1956, setting up the Programme Evaluation Board, the Planning Commission envisaged a wider scope for evaluation studies. It was stated that "During the second five year plan, the organisation of the national extension service will spread over the entire country. Evaluation will therefore encompass the entire field of rural development and the bulk of the activities which are comprised in the district plan."

The actual functions of the P.E.O., as these have developed over the years may, probably be re-stated, with reference to the entire field of rural development programmes, as :

(*i*) to study the progress of a programme and to measure its impact on the socio-economic life of the rural people;

(*ii*) to ascertain the reasons for the success or failure in respect of different items of the programme; and

(*iii*) to indicate the directions in which improvements may be sought.

It should be noted that the P.E.O. has not been expected to take up normal checking and inspection work which generally falls within the sphere of day-to-day administration, but to undertake studies with a view to providing an independent and detached assessment of a programme by a body not concerned with its implementation.

### Organisation and Staff

In deciding upon the initial size and structure of the Organisation in 1952, primary consideration was given to the size of the Community Projects Scheme at that time. A total strength of 33 technical staff was sanctioned. During the years 1953 and 1954, some additional posts were created, bringing the total strength to 81.

Since then the responsibilities of the Organisation increased greatly due to (a) increase of blocks under the Community Development and National Extension Service Programme and (b) the development of the programme itself. But the size of the Evaluation Organisation remained unchanged till 1956-57. The need for strengthening the Organisation was then keenly felt.

In May 1962, an evaluation Advisory Board was constituted by the Planning Commission to provide advice and guidance to the Programme Evaluation Organisation in selecting problems for investigation, planning and designing evaluation studies and presentation of their results. The Government of India (Planning Commission) Resolution No. F. 13(38)/62-Adm. I dated 7.5.1962, setting up the Evaluation Advisory Board appears at Annexure II.

### Structure

Besides mobile Units at the Headquarters, the Organisation has at present 39 field evaluation units located in various places; (called Pro ject Evaluation Offices). These field units are under the supervision of five regional offices. The headquarters of the Organisation are in New Delhi. An Organisation Chart showing the structure of the P.E.O. is given as Appendix III.

Each field unit is under a Project Evaluation Officer (PEO) who is assisted by suitable number (one or two) of Economic Investigators. The Project Evaluation Officer is mainly responsible for reporting on the working and progress of the development programmes in his area and for conducting, with the help of Investigators, the socio-economic surveys and evaluation enquiries taken up for study in the field. Until 1959, the normal jurisdiction of a Project Evaluation Officer used to be the block in which his office was located, though of course, for certain special enquiries he was expected to cover other blocks in the district. From 1959, however, the Project Evaluation Offices began to be shifted from their old locations to district Headquarters. The relocation of the Project Evaluation Offices has been done keeping in view the desirability of securing a reasonable representation of different regions within each State. Within the region that is allocated to each Project Evaluation Office, the staff there are expected to cover any area selected on a sampling or other basis for the purpose of field investigation for approved studies.

**Functioning of the P.E.O.**

It will appear from the account given above that the principal activity of the P.E.O. is to undertake evaluation surveys and studies and bring out the results of these in the form of reports for consideration by concerned ministries and departments of the Government. A brief account may be given here of the way in which the P.E.O. selects problems for study, plans and designs the survey and field investigation to be carried out and presents the results thereof.

The procedure for selection of problems for study starts with the formulation of proposals by the Programme Evaluation Organisation every year. The P.E.O. takes into account the suggestions and recommendations of the Central Ministries concerned, before formulating the final set of proposals. The selection of problems for study is made on basis of the relative importance of different aspects of the programme at the time, in consultation with the Evaluation Advisory Board. The proposal is submitted to the Planning Commission; and after the topics have been approved by them, a plan of study is prepared. An attempt is made in the design of the study to deal with the programme comprehensively from the stage of planning through administrative implementation to its ultimate execution in the field.

Thereafter, a seminar of the officers is held to discuss the plan of each study and its methodology in detail. The available data and material bearing on the field of each study are collected from the concerned Ministry of the Central Government and Departments of the State Government. Technical consultations and discussions are also arranged with the specialists at this time. The draft schedules or the relevant parts of these are then pre-tested by the Project Evaluation Officers. From 1961, another link has been added to this chain, namely, regional seminars of the field staff to discuss the schedules, etc. finally drawn up.

The State Governments are informed at this stage of the sampling design and other broad aspects of each study. The views of the departmental heads are always ascertained and taken into account before finalizing the selection of areas for each study. The field inquiry is then started. The data are collected by interview method; the views of the people are ascertained; the functioning of institutions observed and discussed; and relevant information collected at different levels of operation of programmes, *viz.*, household, village, block, district and State. Suitably structured schedules, questionnaires and guide points are used for eliciting information from appropriate sources. The available data in official and other records are also collected and studied.

The results of the field survey are representative of the restricted universe from which the sample is drawn for each study. The findings of case studies naturally hold for the limited areas from which cases are selected. The larger surveys, however, are currently designed to yield results representative of a restricted universe of either blocks and/or districts. The technique now being used is to purposively select in each State a few districts (The number being determined by the resources of the Organisation) from the categories of good, average and poor, or from the single category of average in respect of the programme under study. For the selection of units at the next stages, a scientific statistical procedure is usually followed.

The data collected through the field units under the supervision and checking by the Regional Offices are scrutinized, processed, tabulated and analysed at the Headquarters. From 1960-61, with the switch-over of the field of evaluation to plan programmes like irrigation, improved seed, soil conservation and rural electrification, the need was felt for giving added attention to the technical aspects of the programmes under study. Consultation and discussion have been arranged for this purpose with specialists in each field. The most recent development in this direction is the appointment of specialists as part-time consultants and technical associates for each programme taken up for study. Their services and help are sought to be utilized both for checking the technical soundness of the assessments made at the field level and for interpreting the technical inferences drawn on the basis of the analysis of data at the Headquarters.

**Presentation of Results**

The results of each study are written up at the Headquarters and presented in the form of a report which is considered by the Planning Commission before its release. A convention has grown over the years of making the annual reports of the P.E.O. one of the items on the agenda of the Annual Conference on Community Development. This practice has tended to ensure an adequate consideration of the reports not only by the concerned Ministries at the Centre but also by the different departments of the State Governments, which are usually represented at this Conference. Besides, the reports of the P.E.O. are also sent in the normal course to members of Parliament. It is through these arrangements that the results of evaluation of rural development programmes have tended to receive adequate recognition and follow up by the executive and the legislative departments of the Government.

It should be recorded here that since 1961 the findings and suggestions given in the evaluation studies have received a warm and vigorous follow-up. The Ministries of Food and Agriculture, and of Community Development as well as the Planning Commission have drawn the attention of the State Governments to these and in some cases, organized Regional seminars and Conferences for consideration of these.

**Studies conducted**

Most of the studies conducted by the P.E.O. are issued as its publications which are distributed free to official and non-official agencies and institutions interested in these. These studies have always been based on current data collected and analysed within a year. In fact, the Organization can justifiably take pride in the fact that it has every year issued its reports before the deadline of the Annual Conference on Community Development. It has so far issued 43 publications in its own series. It has also conducted a number of other studies, often at the special request of other bodies. Only a few of such reports have, however, been published. A list of the P.E.O. publications is to be found in Appendix IV.

Prior to 1960-61, the Evaluation Reports as well as other studies conducted by the Organization dealt more or less exclusively with one or more aspects of the Community Development programme. These reports display an interesting pattern in their evolution. The early years of the community development programme were characterised, quite naturally, by a preoccupation with the administrative and organisational problems. The first three annual reports of the Programme Evaluation Organisation bear testimony to this phase, dealing as they did with the achievements and shortfalls in creating the social overheads and the infra-structure for this programme, sounding caution against rapid administrative expansion and issuing danger signals about pitfalls in organisational structure. It was during this phase that the P.E.O. had also been harping on the desirability for periodical reporting of progress and collection of intelligence data through the administrative channels. This need was soon recognised fully by the administrative departments and ministries. Eventually, the present system of monthly, quarterly and annual reporting on progress through the administrative channels of the community development programme was evolved. A number of special studies was also conducted during this period with a view to obtaining an insight into social aspects of extension methods. Rural group dynamics and structure, training of village leaders, extension of cotton, were some of the topics studied.

The P.E.O. studies can be classified on the basis of their approach and contents into five broad groups. One group comprises reports of a "current evaluation" nature based on continuous observation and discussion in blocks, and collection of data from the field. Such reports have covered the community development programmes and more recently, the rural works projects. Detailed surveys and studies of agricultural or rural development programmes or special aspects of these come under the second group, as has been mentioned in the last paragraph. The third category may be said to include studies including case studies of the organization and functioning of institutions like panchayats and cooperatives. The fourth group covers studies and assessment of area development through methods like bench-mark and repeat surveys. The remaining studies may be grouped under the omnibus category of extension and social change, ranging as these do over areas like leadership, group dynamics, acceptance and diffusion of new practices, etc.

The approach to evaluation has, by and large, been to find out the extent to which the selected rural development programmes or any aspects of these are achieving their objective, the measure in which they are reaching the different sections of the rural community, specially the weaker sections, the people's reactions and attitudes, and the nature and magnitude of the various difficulties and hindrances. Attempts have been made not only to analyse the data and derive factual conclusions, but also to draw inferences regarding the strength and weakness of the programmes and give broad suggestions about directions in which improvements may be effected and corrective action initiated. The policy on which the programmes are based has not, generally, been the subject of evaluation by the P.E.O. except to the extent that an assessment is implicit in analysis of the data collected and studied.

### Evaluation of the Impact of Planned Development

In connection with the preparation of their Fourth Plan by the State Governments, the need has been felt for a comprehensive assessment of the stage of development attained in different parts of each State and the distribution of the benefits of development. A study of the impact of planned development on different regions and socio-economic groups has accordingly been sponsored by the Planning Commission and initiated in each State. The objective of the study is to attempt evaluative analysis of differences in levels of consumption and living, improvements in agriculture and similar fields among the regions in each State and, as far as possible, to bring out changes that have taken place in the recent past.

In view of the diversity in the approach to evaluation in the States, and the need for strengthening the evaluation arrangements in the Fourth Plan, a Working Group on Evaluation in States was set up in November, 1953, under the chairmanship of Prof. V.K.R.V. Rao, Member, Planning Commission, with the following terms of reference:

(*i*) to examine the current orientation and approach to evaluation in the States and review the nature, progress and follow-up of evaluation studies they have conducted during the Third Plan period;

(*ii*) to broadly formulate, in the light of current thinking on the subject and foreseeable trends in the near future, the scope, content and method of evaluation to be adopted in the States from the beginning of the Fourth Plan, if not earlier;

(*iii*) to critically examine in the light of (*ii*) above, the adequacy of the existing arrangements for evaluation, specially in respect of the organizational set-up, independence in work, the quality and strength of staff;

(*iv*) to roughly estimate the financial resources likely to be required for properly setting up and/or strengthening the evaluation machinery in the States; and

(*v*) in general, to suggest ways and means of coordinating the evaluation activities in different States with those at the Centre and making arrangements for the training of evaluation personnel.

The Group is submitting its report to the Planning Commission shortly.

### Training in Evaluation

There has been in recent years a growing demand for facilities for training in evaluation. The P.E.O. has been receiving requests from official and non-official agencies both in India and abroad for providing training to personnel interested or engaged in evaluation work. With the facilities available to the P.E.O., these requests could be accommodated only in a limited way. While training or orientation in evaluation methods and techniques has been provided to a few persons from abroad, sponsored by the U.N. agencies, the facilities provided by the P.E.O. are geared more to the needs of State Government personnel. Such orientation and training have been extended to the personnel of the evaluation organization in a few States.

### P.E.O. and Universities

The Programme Evaluation Organisation has also tried to sponsor a few schemes of evaluation studies through Universities and Research agencies. The following two schemes were sanctioned under this arrangement:

(*i*) Health and level of living in Kolhapur Community Project—(University of Poona).

(*ii*) Cultural change in Dudhi Development Block for 1958-59 (University of Lucknow).

Arrangements have been made with the Universities concerned for the publication of the reports on these studies. They have since been printed under the following titles:

1. University of Poona, "The Report on Health and Level of Living in Kolhapur Community Project."
2. Prof. D.N. Mazumdar, "A Village on the Fringe," Asia Publishing House, Bombay.
3. Prof. D.N. Mazumdar, "Chhor Ka Ek Gaon," Hindi Version Asia Publishing House, Bombay.

# APPROACH TO THE FORMULATION OF CRITERIA IN EVALUATION

*J. P. Bhattacharjee*

PRAGMATISM AND LOGICAL positivism have exercised considerable influence on the development of the scientific approach to social sciences, at least during the last few decades. The influence of these schools on economics has directly or indirectly been so strong that economists have been systematically warned of the dangers of subjective value judgement and advised to stay away from such ventures. Findings and conclusions of an enquiry are required to be 'objective'. Yet judgement is the basic core or evaluation; and to distinguish it from value judgement requires some exercise in semantic acro-bations. The dictionary meaning always stands in the way.

As a type of study, evaluation can hardly be distinguished or differentiated from social science research in most respects. While a distinction can *somehow* be made out in respect of the nature of some of the problems that may be included under 'evaluation', no such difference can validly be established in the operational aspects of methodology. In general, evaluation may be said to be a special field of social science research. It is most commonly related to a programme or a project or a scheme *in operation*. Its purpose is not usually to do a post mortem examination, but to perform a check-up of a live activity and a clinical analysis of its weak or diseased aspects.

Evaluation may include study of problems and issues involving judgements about the goals and approach in the formulation of a programme—conceived on right lines or not—, the justifiability of the machinery set up, the satisfactoriness of its working, the desirability and effectiveness of the organizations created, the adequacy and appropriateness of the efforts vis-a-vis the difficulties and impediments, and the adequacy, depth and desirability of the results achieved. In most of these cases, a judgement in terms of a scale of values or norms is implied.

There is one way of, at least, partially by passing the problems of value judgement. The basic assumptions and expectations behind a programme may be accepted without questioning. The evaluator tries to steer clear of any attempt at projecting these. Judgements like good or bad, desirable or undesirable, proper or improper can thus be avoided. For example, in an evaluation of the community development programme one need not question the desirability of the relative emphasis that may have been allocated, say,—as between the agricultural production and the social education activities.

The problems do not, however, end there, because there will still remain the specific task of finding out and inferring from the course of a programme in implementation and the nature of its impact, whether it has been proceeding on right lines, and its effects are in the desired directions and fulfilling the expectations. These tasks have to be accepted and the problems squarely faced. One way to tackle is to translate the objectives into quantifiable variables, the quantification being either cardinal or ordinal. Another way—the easiest way—is to go by the targets fixed, if any. The nature of the judgement that results in such efforts is best illustrated by expressions like adequate or inadequate, sufficient or insufficient, high or low, large or small, significant or insignificant. In actual practice, the finding may run in terms of combinations of these, as derived from assessments on a number of scales. In case of combinations of conflicting findings, a rating or ranking procedure may have to be adopted, though here again the subjective factor may enter and has to be guarded against.

The Methodology followed in evaluation studies is bound to be the same as in socio-economic investigations. The first stage is the well known one of formulating hypothesis. This can very well be done in terms of the state objectives of the programme, both intermediate and final. As long as these statements are clear and specific, the hypotheses are easy to formulate. More often than not, however, the opposite is the case in the early stages of development, particularly in countries like India. The planners and administrators of the programme cannot be blamed for this vagueness, since it is almost unavoidable in the initial stages. With the growth of a programme and the accumulation of experience in developmental and administrative effort, the intermediate as well as the final objectives of a programme begin to be more clearly visualized and specified. In any case, hypotheses have to be formulated by an evaluator whether there is complete information or not. This is a necessary task always left to an evaluator to tackle to the best of his ability.

The importance of the hypothetical framework for a study needs no special emphasis. The so-called criteria of evaluation depend on and are derived from these. For example, in an evaluation of a programme like seed multiplication and distribution, the hypotheses that may be formulated relate to the basic approach adopted for this programme. The hypotheses may, for example, be that every state, every district and every village have to be self-sufficient in the production of improved seed and that the most efficient method of distribution of improved seed is through cooperatives at the village level. What is to be noted is that this hypothesis does not question the tenability or desirability of this approach but takes it as a datum. This helps to narrow down the study to investigation of a few variables like degree of self-sufficiency in seed plans at different levels etc. Let us take another illustration. In an evaluation of Panchayati Raj, say, in respect of its effect on people's participation, the hypothesis may be that the Gram Panchayats and Panchayat Samities promote the growth of people's participation in developmental activities. Data may be collected to throw light on the opportunity created by these bodies and availed of by the people for participation in the planning process, in the implementation of the development programmes and in making labour and cash contributions. Supposing the data do not bear out the hypothesis, attempts may be made to find out reasons for this state of affairs. But it will not be justified to infer from the data the unsuitability of democratic bodies at the block and/or village levels for this purpose, or the undesirability of democratic decentralization.

In short, it is in the formulation of the hypothesis that objectiveness should be aimed at so that evaluation can be saved from too much of arbitrary judgement in terms of value scales which may or may not be subscribed to by differeut people.

The other aspects of the methodology of evaluation like sampling design, organization and methods of collection of data, their processing and analysis are the same as for any research in the field of social sciences.

The analysis in evaluation studies may be either in terms of indicators of progress in different respects as measured in value of relevant variables, or of "qualitative" information about the programme. It is necessary to be clear about the so-called "qualitative" data. Most often they represent observations or incompletely quantified variables. To the extent this is the case, the use of this term is understandable. But when it is extended to mean data of an unsystematic type or those collected by a non-statistical process, it is really used as a protection or shield from possible criticisms.

Finally, the end-product of any evaluation is with the help of the indicators and observations to throw light on the operation of a programme, its impact, the difficulties and hindrances experienced in the course of implementation and the possible lines of its improvement, to the extent such suggestions flow from the data and can be derived from their analysis.

# EVALUATING COMMUNITY FAMILY PLANNING PROGRAMMES*

*C. Chandrasekaran*

## Evaluation Concepts

GENERAL PRINCIPLES OF evaluation of community action programmes are applicable in the field of family planning as in other fields. These include (*i*) defining the objectives of the programme, (*ii*) selecting the criteria by which achievement can be judged, (*iii*) deciding on the design of the evaluation, (*iv*) collecting and analysing the data, and (*v*) providing interpretations of the findings to the programme administrators. This paper will identify and discuss some of the special problems to be met when applying this evaluative process to family planning programmes, with illustrations from experience in India.

Evaluations might be roughly categorised as relating to long-term or short-term efforts. A long-term approach might, for example, be used to answer a question about the overall effects of the Indian Family Planning programmes since its beginnings some 12 years ago. Such questions imply that the overall "programme" may encompass many activities undertaken at various periods, inspired directly or indirectly by the government policy to popularise family planning. It is assumed that the activities need not be very precisely defined, and that rather gross measurements may be involved.

Short-term evaluations are the main focus of the present paper. Ideally, this type of evaluation is built into a programme from its outset; its main purpose is to improve a programme, through identifying gaps in planning and execution and suggesting appropriate modifications. The evaluative effort may also have important promotional uses, to educate the evaluator and the evaluatee and to maintain official support for the programme. This aspect may be particularly important in family planning programmes, where the ultimate objectives only after a considerable time. In addition, the evaluation process is likely to identify fresh problems requiring further research and may enable the use of action situation to test basic research hypotheses.

* Presented at Symposium on Research Issues in Population Change, at University of Pittsburgh School of Public Health, June 3, 1964.

The theoretical basis for programme evaluations has been strengthened in the last few years by the concept developed by Knutson and James that an action programme can be analysed in terms of a "hierarchy of objectives 1, 2". A programme is conceived as having an ultimate objective, from which is derived a descending and branching series of subsidiary objectives. Each of sub-objectives is a means of achieving the objective at the next higher level, and is the goal of an objective (or set of objectives) at the next lower level. Each objective is formulated on the basis of certain assumptions about the best means of achieving the objective above. The ultimate success of a programme would depend upon two major factors: the extent to which the objectives in the programme net-work are met, and the validity of the assumptions upon which the various objectives are based.

When this form of analysis is applied to a community action programme, the higher-level objectives usually refer to changes which are expected to occur within a target population, as part of the programme. These may be termed the *programme impact objectives*. They may be sub-divided for convenience, into *ultimate impact objectives* most directly related to the programme goal, and *intermediate impact objectives* of a lower order.

At still lower levels are the *programme execution objectives*, referring to development of activities and resources needed to achieve the impact objectives. Programme execution objectives may be sub-divided, for convenience, into *performance objectives*, referring to activities which should be carried out, and at a lower level, *efforts objectives*, referring to the mobilisation of the personnel, funds, or materials required to perform the activities.

The dimensions of time and area must then be added to this analysis, especially when dealing with a new programme. On the basis of certain assumptions, an optimal order of progression of the programme elements over time, and from area to area, plus the possible need for concentration of resources at certain points, can be proposed. These aspects may be described as a set of *phasing objectives 3*.

This type of conceptualization makes the programme evaluation process more orderly and sensitive. A programme is first analysed in terms of its programme impact, execution, and phasing objectives, and their underlying assumptions are identified. Appropriate methods for assessing the achievement of each of the objectives can then be developed and applied, depending upon such factors as the resources and time available and special problems of measurement. Usually the assessment of lower-level, programme effort objectives can be done relatively quickly. Among the higher-order objectives the measurement problems often increases, unfortunately, along with the value of such measures for judging the ultimate success of the programme.

Quantitative measures of achievement must be accompanied, insofar as possible, by observations on the possible factors influencing the degree of achievement. As a strategy to facilitate this diagnostic process, target groups where there has been differential achievement of an objective may be identified and studied for related differences in the characteristics of the groups or in the nature of the activities which reach them.

Obviously, the shape of the set of objectives for a given programme will be influenced by the type of ultimate goal, the population and the available resources. The extent of detailed primary analysis of groups of objectives, as well as the attention given to overcoming measurement problems, would also be influenced by judgements about which aspects of the programme are most in need of study. In order to consider the application of evaluation concepts to current family planning programmes, therefore, we must pause for a moment to note some of the special features of such programmes which may influence their evaluation.

# RECOMMENDATIONS OF THE WORKING GROUP ON EVALUATION IN THE STATES*

IN PURSUANCE OF a recommendation of the last meeting of the State Planning Secretaries, the Planning Commission constituted the Working Group on Evaluation in the States with Member (ES&IT) as Chairman Secretary, Planning Commission and representatives (mostly planning Secretaries) of five State Governments as members, and Director PEO as Convenor. On the basis of visits and discussions in five states, and data and information obtained from all the State Governments, the group have examined the objective, orientation, scope and content of evaluation work undertaken so far in the States and assessed the organisation and arrangements of evaluation set up by some of them. In the light of this assessment, the Group have offered recommendations on the technical and administrative issues involved in extending the scheme of evaluation in the States, and assisting and coordinating it from the Centre. The financial estimates for the Fourth Plan, and the advance action needed during the last year of the current plan have been formulated on this basis.

## Background

The State Government are attaching increasing importance to evaluation—an essential aid to their efforts for improving the formulation and implementation of programmes. Whereas prior to 1960, there was a full-fledged evaluation organisation in only one State and arrangements for undertaking organisation limited evaluation work in three other States, since 1960 as many as nine State Governments have set up a separate machinery (directorate, wing or cell) for evaluational and nearly all the other State Governments have either formulated plans for setting up a unit or indicated their desire to do so. While this is the general trend, the actual position in respect of activity and organisation varies from State to State, depending on the administrative set-up, the availability of resources and the specialisation as well as systematisation achieved in planning, progress analysis and evaluation work. The Group have noted a wide diversity among the State Governments in their approach to, and interpretation of the

* Summary.

role and function of evaluation and in the administrative arrangements made or envisaged for undertaking this work. The Group have emphasised that since evaluation is a potent instrument, it should be used positively, satisfactorily and effectively. There should be in all State Governments a common measure of understanding of the objective, orientation, scope and method of evaluation, An adequate and competent organisation should be built up on the basis of such understanding and enabled to function within the appropriate administrative framework and with the needed cooperation and support from all the implementing departments and agencies.

**Objectives and orientation of evaluation in the States**

Broadly speaking the objectives of evaluation at the Centre include purposive assessment of progress and impact of a programme, finding out areas of success and failure at different states of administration and execution, analysing the reasons for success or failure, examining the extension methods and people's reactions thereto, and deriving lessons for improvement in the formulation and implementation of programmes. Evaluation in this sense is distinct and separate from progress analysis and review on the one hand, and inspection checking and scrutiny of schemes and works on the other. Most often, it means problems oriented type or case studies of programmes under implementation and schemes under execution and should as such be clearly distinguished from large-scale statistical surveys for estimation purposes.

The case for two separate types of evaluation with different objectives has been recognised by the Group. One type has been described as 'internal evaluation', which is oriented to the current operational problems that the implementing agency is facing. The objective of such evaluation is to help the administrative and executive personnel decide on the course of strategy and action in problem situations by providing them with an understanding of the nature and implications of the problems and alternative methods of solving them, Arrangements for such evaluation should be built into the programmes, especially the more important ones, and made a part of the programme set-up. Cells for internal evaluation could also be created in the major spending departments like the P.W.D.; Irrigation and Electricity, in every State. Expenditure on such evaluation should be included in the programme outlay or departmental budget, as the case may be.

The second type of evaluation—and this is the one with which the Group have been concerned in their reports—is "independent" assessment by an agency not charged with the responsibility for administering programmes. For this type of evaluation, the following areas have been mentioned as requiring special emphasis in the States:

(a) In the States, performances, problems and achievements will have to be related to the given system of administration in its working in different regions and as a whole. This implies the need for special emphasis on the study of methods, efficiency and economy in the operation of the given system.

(b) The functioning of statutory and other institutions. Panchayati Raj, Boards, Cooperatives etc., requires regular observation and assessment, in view of their crucial role in planning and implementation.

(c) The area approach to the assessment of development programmes is of special concern to the State Governments and, as such, study of inter-regional differences and inter-group disparities becomes an important objective of evaluation.

(d) Extension methods and recommendations in relation to the special needs and problems of local areas.

(e) People's participation, public cooperation and voluntary organisations

The following points bearing on the approach and orientation in evaluation have been emphasised:

(a) Evaluation should be based on an objective approach to the study of problems; subjective or impressionistic elements should not be allowed to enter in the findings.

(b) Evaluation should be in the nature of positive service designed not only to find out shortcomings, failures and weaknesses but also to suggest methods of improvement and corrective and remedial measures.

(c) Evaluation has also an educative function, as its findings can create a better and enlightened understanding of the implementation and achievement of different programmes and schemes, and, in general, of the progress towards the goals underlying the plan. The results of evaluation should be made available not only to organs of the Government, but also the people, except in special cases or for special reasons.

(d) Evaluation should be forward-looking, not merely a post-mortem of the past in a static framework. Such an ex ante orientation would help the Government in using evaluation findings for understanding the future course and prospect of achievement.

## Scope Content and Method of Evaluation:

The Scope of evaluation in the States in the Fourth Plan has been envisaged as follows:

(*a*) Evaluation should extend to most of the sectors of the State Plan, the possible exceptions being sectors like power (barring rural electrification), manufacturing and mining industries.

(*b*) However, the importance of different sectors from the point of view of need for evaluation should vary from State to State, depending on the structure of the State Plans.

(*c*) It would be desirable for each State Government to work out, as early as possible, a tentative three-year programme of evaluation studies keeping in view the need to cover over the period of the Fourth Plan, a cross-section of the sectoral programmes not only for agriculture, C.D., irrigation, rural industries and electrification, but also for the social and welfare services sectors, the emphasis being larger on the former group.

(*d*) Among the implementation sectors, the performance in the Panchayati Raj and cooperative sectors should receive special attention in the States.

Selection of Problems. For the selection of programmes and schemes, the following guide lines and criteria have been suggested;

(*a*) all projects and programmes of a pilot nature;

(*b*) programmes showing persistent shortfalls, lags and problems and difficulties in implementation;

(*c*) impact programmes of a 'crash' nature like the intensive cultivation schemes;

(*d*) Programmes and schemes involving large outlays and relying for their success on the cooperation and participation of the people and institutions; and

(*e*) special programmes for the benefit of backward areas or weaker sections.

prior knowledge based on progress analysis helps in selecting problems for evaluation and narrowing down the areas of study.

The evaluation agency in each State should have one of two important programmes and/or institutions for current evaluation or a regular nature, an annual report on each of which should be a feature of the evaluation organisation. Special emphasis may be given in selecting such topics of pilot projects, agricultural extension and Panchayati Raj institutions.

*Content and Method*: The content and method of evaluation should have their basis in the methodology of social science research. The need for a manual on evaluation is recognised, and it has been recommended that the P.E.O. should address itself to this task.

Evaluation studies are different from statistical estimational surveys;

they are problems-oriented diagnostic studies yielding therapeutic results. The diagnosis has to be done in relevant type situations and cases in such a way that remedies or correctives can be derived from the finding and results. Within this framework, the place of type studies, case studies, and bench-mark surveys in evaluation has been indicated in the report. Broad guidelines for formulation of problems, hypothesis and criteria and the working out of the design of the field investigation have been suggested on the basis of the methodological work done in the P.E.O.

### Review of Evaluation Arrangements and Activities in the State:

In reviewing the present organisation and functions of evaluation in the States, the Group have also analysed, however briefly, the existing arrangements for planning and progress analysis. It has been mentioned that in a majority of the States, planning has not yet been organized as a separate department with adequate status and free from any other administrative responsibilities. In a number of States, the Planning machinery does not also appear to be technically well organized and adequately staffed. In a few States, it is also having difficulties in making use of the services of the Statistics Bureau for progress reporting and analysis.

Arrangements for progress analysis and implementation review display a wide diversity among the States. It is only the Community Development sector, *i.e.*, the programmes and activities executed by the block agency, that a systematised pattern of reporting and review has been laid down and is being followed in all States. Many of the programmes in other sectors have not been subjected to the same degree of systematisation in respect of administrative intelligence for planning purposes. In fact, there appears to be a good case and scope too for introducing a planning orientation in the types of data reported for these and the processing made of these at different levels. There is room for qualitative improvement in progress reporting and analysis in a number of plan sectors like irrigation and power, cooperation, education and health.

In a number of States, there is scope for the systematisation and streamlining of the existing arrangements for reporting, *e.g.*, coordinating and the routing and analysis of such data at higher levels. In most States, the Bureau of Economics and Statistics and its district organisation could be involved more effectively than at present in the systematic reporting and analysis of planning-oriented progress data at least for sectors like rural industries, education, health and welfare of the backward classes. It has been suggested that the Planning Commission might give due attention to this matter and consider referring these problems to a Study Team or Committee.

A distinct organisation for evaluation work, whether as a cell or as a wing or as a unit, exists in ten States, while in another evaluation studies are being conducted, though no separate machinery has been set up. In three other States, there is a proposal to establish an evaluation unit. The Governments, of Himachal Pradesh, Manipur and Tripura have also reported proposals for setting up evaluation machinery of their own. Four broad patterns of State evaluation set-up have been distinguished. One isolated pattern is represented by the Planning Research and Action Institute in U.P., one section of which is engaged in evaluation studies of pilot projects in rural areas. The other three patterns are represented by the respective organisations in Andhra, Maharashtra and Rajasthan. These form part of the planning department in these States. Details of evaluation set-up like Committee arrangements, staff and administrative structure, budget and expenditure, the evaluation studies conducted and the follow-up of their finding have been reviewed in the report. The survey reveals varied patterns, sizes and effectiveness of the evaluation arrangements in the States. The evaluation studies so far conducted by the State units relate mainly to programmes in the field of agriculture, community development and Panchayati Raj, though of late there has been a tendency to go into fields like rural industry, educational and welfare of backward classes.

**Proposals for Evaluation in the States in the Fourth Plan:**

Noting the importance attached to evaluation by the State Governments and their keenness to build up a suitable organization for this purpose, the Group have taken the stand that the State Governments need to be helped and assisted in their efforts to develop evaluation organisation and activity. They have recommended that evaluation should be included among the Plan programmes and the resources needed for carrying on evaluation work should be adequately provided for in the Plan outlay on this programme.

Every State Government should have an evaluation organisation as an integral part of their planning machinery. This organisation should function either as a wing or division of the Planning Department or as a directorate attached to it. It should not be under the administrative control of any other department. Nor should it be located in the Bureau of Statistics either as a wing or a division.

There should be evaluation committee in each State with Chief Secretary as Chairman, planning Secretary as convenor and Secretaries in charge of Finance and a couple of other departments as members. This committee will be responsible for selection of problems for evaluation, securing coordination and cooperation and taking follow-up action. It should be the responsibility of the Planning Secretary to initiate follow-up action. The arrangements made in Andhra for follow-up action have been considered effective and commended to other State Governments.

The State evaluation organization, as conceived by the Group, will have a headquarters unit and a field organisation. The field organisation will include a nucleus task force unit to be located at the headquarters and 3 to 6 field units according to the size of the State, the intention being to locate at least one unit in each of the major regions of each State. There is no need for a field unit in every district. The headquarters strength would include Director, 2 Deputy Directors, 1 Assistant Director, 3 Research Assistants, 6 Investigators and 6 computors, along with supporting clerical and other staff, as shown in the Statement. The headquarters organisation will have four subject matter divisions—economics, statistics, administration and sociology.

The likely expenditure on State evaluation organisations of this size and composition has been worked out in the statements on the basis of scales of pay obtaining in some States. For an average-sized State, the anticipated expenditure per year on an evaluation Director of this size would come to about Rs. 1,86000. This works out to a total of Rs. 9,30,00 for five years. The approximate total expenditure to be incurred on the evaluation organisation in the 15 States will thus work out to a sum of Rs. 1,40,00000 for the Fourth Plan. There will also be a non-recurring expenditure on the purchase of calculators and typewriters of the order of Rs. 13,200 per State or a total of Rs. 2,00,000 for the 15 States. For Union Territories, a provision of Rs. 8 lakhs has been suggested. On this basis, it has been recommended that in the Fourth Plan, provision be made for a sum of Rs. 150 lakhs for evaluation schemes of States and Union Territories.

Most of the State Governments desire Central assistance of a higher order for financing evaluation arrangements and activities. The Group have recognised the need for central assistance to the State Governments in respect of schemes for evaluation organisation, but considered in premature at this stage to suggest any proportion or pattern.

**Advance Action**

In view of the shortage of qualified and experienced personnel the group have suggested that the State Governments should try from now on to formulate a policy regarding recruitment and service of personnel in the field of economics, statistics and other social sciences. It has also been suggested that the State Governments might approach the

Central Government with a request for deputation of officers from the Indian Economic and Statistical Services for manning these posts, along with an advance indication of the number of such officers required in different years and on different scales.

Advance action during 1965-66 should also include the setting up or strengthening of the core unit at the headquarters of the evaluation organisation, creating the recommended set-up and providing for funds in the budget. In States where the basic organisation exists, the expansion of the headquarters organisation may be included in the plan for 1965-66.

The Group recommended that the outlay needed for such advance action in 1965-66 should be treated as additional outlay to be met with 100 per cent central assistance; and such assistance should be provided over and above the annual plan ceiling.

**Coordination of Evaluation Work at the Centre and Role of the P.E.O.**

The envisaged expansion in the evaluation set-up and activities in the States will impose additional responsibilities on the evaluation machinery at the Centre, especially in respect of coordination and administration of plan schemes, extension of technical advice and information, and training of personnel. The Group have recommended that the P.E.O. should adequately strengthened so that it can assume this added burden of duties. It has been envisaged that P.E.O. will have two wings. One wing will include the organisation as it exists now with the addition of two more regional offices. This wing, apart from conducting studies on its own will also be responsible for extending technical advice and guidance on evaluation to the State Governments and other agencies. The other wing will deal with the following functions:

(a) Administration, processing and coordination of the evaluation schemes in the Plan.

(b) Operating a regular and round-the-year training programme in evaluation (of suitable duration) for personnel of the State Governments and other agencies.

(c) Running a clearing house and documentation centre for evaluation literature and information.

The additional minimum staff needed for strengthening the P.E.O. has been estimated as I joint Director with the supporting technical and administrative staff, and new Regional Evaluation Units on the present scale of staffing. The staff expenditure for the Fourth Plan period has been estimated at Rs. 10 lakhs.

In addition to this expansion in the strength of the P.E.O. there is also the need for suitable all-India forum which can impart to evaluation a higher technical and administrative status. With this end in view, the Group have recommended that there should be a Central Advisory Council on Evaluation on which the State Governments, the Planning Commission, the Central Ministries and the P.E.O. should be represented. It should meet, at least once a year to review progress of studies, discuss problems, methods and techniques of evaluation, and advise the Central and the State evaluation agencies on the programmes of study, and coordination of the activities of the different agencies. The composition and terms of reference of this Council may be similar to those of the Central Advisory Council on Statistics.

With such an evaluation set-up extending from the States to the Centre, it will be possible to bring out an annual evaluation review of the whole plan. The Group envisage this as one of the basic annual documents to be placed before the Nation. The document will be discussed at the Central Council on Evaluation before it is finalised and will incorporate the evaluation experience during the year of the Central and the State organisations.

# SOME ASPECTS OF SOCIAL CHANGE

## Introduction

The present enquiry is the first attempt to undertake a study more specifically related to assessment of social change. Such an assessment is a difficult task, partly because of paucity of basic statistical data, and also because the concepts and methods in this field are not well developed. The present study by the Evaluation Officers represents only a preliminary attempt and it is hoped that it will be possible to follow it up with a more detailed enquiry. This study is connected with the other PEO studies, especially the Bench-Mark Survey and the Acceptance of Practices Survey because it has been conducted in three out of the six villages selected for the latter enquiries. In building up a picture of the changing economic and social life of these villages, therefore, the data of this study are complementary to the quantitative data collected through these two latter surveys.

This study was conducted by the Project Evaluation Officers between September and December 1956, in 17 evaluation centres (listed in Appendix I). The method of the study consisted of the Evaluation Officers' stay in each of the three selected villages for a period of one week, in which he was engaged in observations of village life and interviews with respondents belonging to different social and economic groups. It may be mentioned that the Evaluation Officers have known these villages over a period of more than three years because they conducted the Bench-Mark Survey, the Acceptance of Practices Survey and other enquiries there and have also kept themselves in touch with developments in these. Therefore, besides one week stay for the specific purpose of this study, the Evaluation Officer's acquaintance with these villagers for this entire period has gone into his observations.

Besides stay and interview in the selected villages, each P.E.O. had discussions with project and departmental officials and selected non-officials on various questions included in the study. These discussions were particularly important for the portions dealing with the attitude of the officials towards the people and cooperation between officials and non-officials. But here also the P.E.O.'s continuous touch with officials and non-officials in the area and his knowledge of the working of the projects/blocks of about 3-4 years has gone into his observations.

*Criteria for Social Change* : In a study of this kind the most important factor in the design of the enquiry is the selection of the criteria for measurement of change. Keeping in view the objectives, and the content of the programme, the following 6 criteria were selected for this study:

(1) Awareness among the rural people of possibilities of improvement through adoption of scientific methods in various fields of activity—agriculture, animal husbandry, health and sanitation, cottage industries etc ;

(2) Confidence in their own ability to adopt these practices;

(3) Realization of advantages of cooperative action;

(4) Community life;

(5) Understanding and cooperation between the officials and non-officials;

(6) Awareness of possibilities of economic and social improvement through the development programmes and a feeling of participation in these, among the under-privileged groups.

It will be seen that in these criteria the emphasis is on *changes in attitudes and ways of thinking among the people.* These changes in attitude have inevitably to be expressed in concrete terms—adoption or rejection of a particular practice; success or failure of a cooperative venture or of an effort in community action; the working of an institution in which officials and non-officials come together etc., etc. These concrete situations and the reactions of the people towards them are the main materials on which the judgements of the Evaluation Officers are made. The individual project reports are full of references of this kind ; this has enabled the P.E.O.s to guard against any tendency on their part to generalise merely on the basis of their own pre-conceptions. As these reports are being included in Vol. II of the Report, it also enables the reader to form his own judgement on the rate and direction of change in respect of different criteria.

Although the criteria of social change were designed keeping in view the objectives of the community development and national extension service programme, the changes revealed reflect the impact of all development programmes, project and non-project in the area, as also the effects of the general process of social and economic change in the country-side. It is almost impossible to separate the three influences in a preliminary enquiry of this nature, one is such a separation considered necessary because the primary function of the national extension service and community development programme is to serve as a spear-head for the general process of social and economic advance.

*Results of the Survey*: The data of survey is presented in two parts. The individual reports from the Evaluation Centres appear in Volume II of this report. The main findings of the study are presented in the following pages. Discussion on criterion 3 is not included in this part because, a separate chapter entitled 'growth of Cooperative Endeavour' in which the results of this study are also incorporated, appears earlier, in this volume.

*States in Social Change*: From the experience of this study, it appears possible and useful to distinguish several stages in the process of change. These stages are most clearly distinguished in case of an item of technological change *e.g.*, adoption of an improved agricultural practice; but are equally relevant for the other criteria also. The following five stages are suggested:

(*a*) awareness of the existence of an improvement or facility;

(*b*) passive acceptance by availing of the facility or improvement offered without any particular effort;

(*c*) preparedness to put in some effort, for availing of the facility or improvement;

(*d*) active acceptance *i.e.*, preparedness to make the efforts needed for continuation of the improvement in facility;

(*e*) getting into an attitude of progress *e.g.*, trying new practices, making adaptation from recommended practices on own initiative.

This classification admittedly a rough one and is meant only to illustrate the different kinds of situations which have been observed in different projects in the course of this survey. With future work, it should be possible to devise a more adequate and refined classification. But, the value of a classification of this kind consists in providing a tool for measuring the strength of the change that has occurred in a particular field. For example, the mere fact that an improved practice like an improved variety of seed has spread in a project area does not given an adequate indication of whether this change is going to be lasting or not; as it turns on the question whether acceptance of the practice is dependent only upon continuation of the existing facilities, or the people are prepared to continue with the practice even if these facilities are reduced or withdrawn. But, if we can successfully make a classification of this nature and further though quantitative enquiries indicate the proportions of people who can be considered to be in the different stages of change, we have a much more precise indication of the strength of the change. The value of such knowledge as a guide for future policy cannot be over-emphasised.

The process of social change involves changes in the mental attitudes of the people, in the values, the cultural patterns and the economic organisation of the communities. Progress from one stage to the next involves successful overcoming of these resistances to change. In any given community nt any time different individuals are in different stages of changes. In stagnant communities, the bulk of the population has obviously not even reached stage one. But frequently it would be found that even in such communities there are some people who are eager to change and might even have made some experiments on their own. In general, however, as the process of change proceeds, the proportion of people in successively advanced stages increases. The increase in the last two stages is particularly important. Until a sufficiently large proportion of the population reaches these stages, the process of change cannot be considered to have attained self pro-pelling proportions, where the communities are themselves willing and anxious to try new things and make improvements of their own.

We now proceed to review the results of this study.

## CRITERIA (1) AND (2)

These two criteria deal mainly with technological change, as these are concerned with adoption of improvements by villagers in agriculture, animal husbandry, prevention or cure of disease and other fields of development activity. As already stated, the primary aim of the study is to assess whether the improvements have been grasped and accepted and not merely recorded physical fact of adoption.

The first criterion deals with awareness of improvements, the second with the confidence of the villagers in their capacity to adopt these arising from successful adoption of at least some of them. The first obviously represents the first stage in social change, the second a considerable advance in the form of acceptance. Since it is felt that it would be more useful to analyse the progress in respect of both these criteria by fields of endeavour, the two criteria are considered together for each field.

### Agriculture:

In the field of agricultural practices, the main improvements pro-pagated by projects are the use of improved seed, use of chemical fertilizers and organic manures, compositing, green manuring, improv-ed methods of cultivation particularly the Japanese method of paddy cultivation and line sowing of crops, use of improved implements; plant protection measures, crop-rotations; growing of fruits and vege-tables etc. etc.

The extent to which each individual improvement has been tried, accepted or rejected in different centres; is brought out in individual project reports. A few illustrations have been given here to draw attention to the more important points. Reference may here be made first to one noteworthy fact. It has been observed in all centres that among the large number of improvements which are carried on the list of the Grama Sevaks in every project, only a very few, seldom more than half a dozen and frequently not more than 2 or 3 have been found acceptable on any significant scale. The rest are either rejected or their acceptance is so small as not to be of any great importance. In view of this record of experience in almost all the centres, there is need for more careful and rigorous selection of the items to be propagated by the project staff. Only a few items should be selected keeping in view their feasibility and the economic importance of their widespread acceptance. Efforts of the project staff should be concentrated on making these truly and widely accepted instead of being distributed over a large number of items. All the snags in the widespread acceptance of these improvements should be progressively removed so that after a certain period of effort, the improvement is on the way to becoming an integral part of production methods in the area. Such concentration of effort on a few really important improvements would give better results both from the point of view of economic advancement of the area and the psychological impact upon the people. Wide-spread acceptance of a few practices, will generate a psychology of progress and the cultivators themselves will be moved to further improvements. It has been observed that in the majority of the progressive areas of the country, it is only wide-spread adoption of a few practices, generally improved seed or chemical fertilizers which gives these areas an air of progress and which leads the cultivators to be more receptive to new improvements as these come along.

*Improved Seed*: Propagation of improved seed is one of the oldest programmes in the field of agriculture and in many centres improved varieties were extensively used, at least for commercial crops and the cultivators were well aware of the advantages of the improved seed, even before the project started.

With the coming of the projects, efforts in propagation of improved seed were greatly increased. Supplies of seed already in use were considerably increased and improved seed of other crops were introduced. As a result of these efforts, there has been a considerable increase in the use of improved seed in most centres. The following few examples have been selected to illustrate a few kinds of acceptance situation observed.

Bhadrak (Orissa) and Silchar (Assam) are examples of comparatively less advanced agriculture areas. In Bhadrak, improved seed and other improved practices had begun to be adopted only with the

coming of the project, the progress was slow and even at the end of
the project period only a few cultivators in each village were
seen using improved seed or fertilizers. In Silchar, on the other
hand, although improved seed has been distributed in some
quantities during the project period, consciousness of its value is
still in an elementary stage. When asked a cultivator would say
that improved seed is good; but he does not value it enough to keep
the unimproved and improved variety separately to be able to
distinguish between the two. This kind of situation is undoubtedly
found in other areas also and part of the reason is the indifferent
quality of the 'improved' seed supplied to a large percentage of
cultivators. Improved seed is still seed in these areas and is taken
by the cultivators because it is available, anything else available at the
time of sowing would do also. Another illustration which is of interest
is that of Bha-that-U.P. Here improved seed has been extensively pro-
pagated for both paddy and the rabi crops, and has been accepted
widely in the case of the latter. However, it was reported that non-
members of cooperative societies who were given seed in the first year
on the understanding that they would become members in due course
did not show any great inclination to do so even at the risk of losing
the facility of having improved seed from the cooperative stores. This
may be considered a typical case of passive acceptance (stage 'b'
above) *i.e.*, if an improvement is easily available, there is acceptance,
but any effort needed to effect the improvement is not welcome. It is
doubtless that such acceptance would end in reversion to the old
practice at the first sign of a difficulty. Manavadar—Bombay illustrates progress to an advanced stage of change within a few years. In
this area, after successful acceptance of one improved variety of cotton,
the cultivators are changing to the use of still another which was not
accepted over before. Awareness has gone to the stage where the
cultivator is not only convinced of the use of improved seed as such
but is prepared to try different types to maximise his advantage.
Kolhapur presents an interesting case. In this area, the advantages of
improved seed, use of fertilizers and other improved seed, use of fertilizers and other improved practices were widespread even before the
project came. An improved variety of paddy was introduced but after
four years of trial it has not been found widely acceptable. In spite
of the fact that the cultivators were aware of the advantages of an
improved practice, and were prepared to made the efforts to adopt it,
this did not lead to extensive adoption because the practice did not
meet with the local requirements. The experience with the Japanese
method in this area is also interesting as it gives a very good indication
of the level of consciousness of the cultivators. In the first year (1953),

the majority of the cultivators to be progressively convinced of the merits of the method so that the area under it had increased nearly to 7,000 acres (out of 50,000 acres) under paddy in 1956. But the cultivators have accepted only those elements in the method which they considered most useful—regularly spaced sowing, lower seed rate, dibbling and use of chemical fertilizers. It is noteworthy, however, that they have had the initiative to apply the principles of regular sowing and less seed rate to another local grain crop—Nachna. Here we see the beginning of the last stage of change (stage 'e' referred to above), where the cultivators are themselves prepared to make adaptations on their own. A self-generating process of improvement can be seen to be beginning in this area.

*Japanese Method*: The experience with the Japanese method of paddy cultivation is of considerable interest as will be seen from the individual project reports. In this case, a process of pick and choose from the large number of elements which comprise the method, and adaptation of the few suited to local conditions has been going on extensively. The result is that the term 'Japanese Method' means very different things in different areas. All the recommendations are rarely, if ever, followed; one or more found acceptable by the cultivators are in vogue. As mentioned above, it is spaced sowing, dibbling and lower seed rate in Kolhapur and the principle has been extended to other corps. In a number of other centres, the method means only use of chemicals, fertilizers or sowing in lines. In a few centres, the method has not found acceptance because of alleged excessive requirements of labour as compared with the increase in yields that it gives (Manavadar —Bombay and Mohd. Bazar—West Bengal).

*Plant Protection Measures*: Plant protection measures particularly use of pesticides have made considerable progress in several areas (*e.g.* Chalakudy—Kerala and Pusa—Bihar). But it is interesting to note that the value of pesticides is appreciated for curing plant diseases and not for preventing their occurrence with the result that sometimes use of pesticides is started only after the disease is in an advanced stage. In Bhathat—U.P. Plant protection measures were accepted as along as these were being provided free by the project. This has been stopped in the post-intensive phase and there is no active demand from the cultivators even for its revival. This is an illustration of passive acceptance of the type mentioned as stage 'b' above. In Pusa—Bihar, on the other hand, partly because of greater need for spraying in this fruit growing area, there is greater awareness of the value of plant protection methods and people are prepared to undergo considerable effort to buy pesticides, and obtain sprayers in order to adopt these practices (stage 'd').

*Improved Implements*: Use of improved implements is most advanced in commercial crop growing areas like Sonepat, Batala, Kolhapur and Pusa where, besides cultivation implements, such implements as cane crushers and furnaces for making gur have also been in use for a long time. Advance in the adoption of improved cultivation implements has been very slow in most project areas; there is greater progress in adoption of such mechanical appliances as pumps for irrigation. An example of increase in awareness and acceptance of the possibilities with use of mechanical methods offered at particular points in the agricultural activity is afforded by Bodhan—Andhra, where there is reported to be such a great demand for tractor ploughing that the Agricultural Engineer feels that the number of tractors at his disposal is too small to meet it.

### Animal Husbandry:

In this field, the distinction between veterinary aid and measures to improve quality of livestock is of primary importance. The former viz., veterinary facilities have been in existence for a considerable long time, and also because of the imminent danger of losses of cattle resulting from sickness, there is much greater sense of urgency about availing of them. Facilities to improve the quality of livestock have been comparatively recent introduction and as the effects of the improvements are visible over a longer period, the acceptance of these practices can well be expected to be a much slower process.

Veterinary Aid—Veterinary facilities have been increased as a part of the project programmes in most areas, and the cultivators who were already familiar with their advantages have availed of the new facilities as these have become available. In some less advanced areas, like Bhadrak—Orissa, where such facilities were not available before, their availability and acceptance by cultivators represent a change in attitude i e., acceptance of modern medicines in place of the traditional methods of cure. But it is significant that in only a few cases e.g., Sonepat—Punjab and Erode—Madras has there been an active demand for more veterinary facilities, indicating that acceptance even in spite of long familiarity has been largely passive in most other areas (between stages 'b' and 'c'). In the Erode area, the cultivators made available buildings for housing the dispensaries and the demand was so keen that instead of three dispensaries originally planned four had to be opened during the first two years of the project.

In regard to inoculation and vaccination against cattle epidemics also, there is ready acceptance whenever these are offered. However, it is notable that in one North Indian project an outbreak of cattle disease was not even reported to project staff indicating that in this case there is not yet any awareness of the advantage of these measures and the prevailing attitude is only one of not resisting a facility, if it is offered.

While the veterinary measures are readily accepted and there is increasing readiness on the part of cultivators to take somewhat greater trouble to avail of them, e.g. bringing cattle to dispensaries from longer distances, the experience of a few centres where disease prevention measures requiring some effort on the part of the villagers have been tried is not very happy. Thus in one project where veterinary measures were quite popular, foot-baths kept by the veterinary staff in the villages as a preventive against cattle disease were reported to be not in use. The effort involved in this case was only one of using the facility, and its proper maintenance. But acceptance had not yet advanced to the stage were people would make even this degree of effort.

*Animal Husbandry Measures*: The main activities in this field are: natural breeding with improved bulls artificial insemination and castration. In case of natural breeding, there are no difficulties of acceptance and most cultivators readily recognise its advantages. Wherever facilities of breeding with improved bulls are made available these are utilized, but frequently resort to breeding with unimproved bulls also (e.g. Mohd. Bazar—West Bengal, Bhathat—U.P.). In Kolhapur, the value of superior quality livestock is realised by the cultivators to such an extent that they are willing to pay very high prices for good quality animals and it is reported that this is an important channel in which the increased incomes of the cultivators go. But there is not the same eagerness to make sustained efforts to improve livestock in most other areas. It is only in a few areas notably the Punjab project of Sonepat where there is an established tradition of good husbandry that the value of breeding with improved bulls is widely appreciated.

The case of artificial insemination is on a different footing. It is a new practice which seems to the villagers to depart from the natural law, so that there is considerable initial prejudice against its acceptance. The difficulty of making the facility widely available by operating sub-centres within convenient reach of the villages is another handicap. In some areas (e.g. Bhadrak—Orissa), mistakes by staff in applying the methods in the initial stages due to lack of experience gave a set-back. In another area (Kolhapur), the impression got round that artificial insemination is meant only for sterile cows. These difficulties are being progressively overcome and the practice is gaining wider acceptance in a number of project areas. But a set-back is reported from some areas where the sub centres have been closed, just as the method had begun to be popular. The best example of progressive acceptance comes from Chalakudy—Kerala where the initial prejudices have been considerably overcome and there is demand for opening of new sub-centres and extension of facilities over wider areas.

*Poultry Keeping*: A major difficulty in the development of poultry as a subsidiary activity for the cultivators is the prejudice against keeping poultry or use of eggs or chicken. This prejudice is very widespread among the upper castes in all parts of the country. However, there is evidence from a number of centres that the prejudice is slowly breaking down. Contact with the towns especially of the younger generation is an important factor in the weakening of the prejuice. Poultry keeping as a side activity by the farmers, particularly those near towns, is becoming popular in a large number of centres. The programmes for improvement of poultry have consisted of breeding; inoculation and other disease prevention measures and distribution of eggs, and birds of improved breeds. In Chalakudy-Kerala again, inoculation is so popular that there is considerable demand for an expansion of the facility. As regards the supply of birds of improved breed, there are two main comments:

(*i*) the birds are often not found resistant enough to the local conditions and (*ii*) better guidance is needed in feeding and rearing practices.

## HEALTH AND SANITATION

The observations made above while bringing out the differences in acceptance between veterinary and animal husbandry measures apply, perhaps with greater force, to the difference between acceptance of health measures on the one hand, and on the sanitation measures on the other. Also, this is a field in which the different stages of change, mentioned in the Introduction are very clearly illustrated. Knowledge of efficacy of modern medicine is spreading rapidly in the rural areas and local village methods of treatment are giving way to this phenomenon, an entering side-light on which is provided by Kolhapur where there is reported to be craze for injections. Whatever medical facilities have been provided under project or other programmes are being avidly grasped, and there is an increasing demand for more. The primary health centres opened during the project period have been very popular. There is a large programme of opening of rural health centres in the Second Five Year Plan. In some States, notably West Bengal, the State Governments are thinking in terms of establishing a chain of rural health centres, one for every 10 villages which will bring medical assistance within effective reach of every village.

Even in case of maternity facilities, although there is greater resistance, there is a notable advance everywhere. An interesting fact has been reported in this connection. In two projects—Pusa Bihar and Mohd. Bazar—West Bengal it is reported that the higher castes have a disinclination to send their women to the maternity centres as the facilities are free and available to all, but the lower castes having no such consideration are using the facilities more readily. In spite of the ready and growing acceptance of medical facilities, it is noteworthy that the experiment of providing medicine boxes to the penchayats which was tried in some areas has not been successful. There are two reasons for it:

(1) the difficulties in running a programme of this nature; and
(2) the fact that the communities even though appreciating modern medicine, cannot bring forth the resources or rather the organisational effort necessary to make this facility available to themselves.

Sanitation—In this case, progress is much less than in that of use of medical aid. In fact it appears that one of the most difficult areas of attack by extension workers will be this one of sanitation, because besides improvement in habits of personal hygiene which necessarily takes a long period of education, improvements in environmental hygiene often require considerable investment *e.g.*, on drainage. Lack of awareness of the importance of sanitation or its role in preventing disease is perhaps best illustrated in case of the programme of drinking water supply. In all projects, programmes for improvement of water supply have been among the most important. New wells have been constructed, old wells have been renovated and sanitary constructions like parapets have been constructed on wells to avoid contamination. Water being a prime necessity, people's participation has been generally available for these works. Participation of Harijans also has been widely and enthusiastically available. Disinfection of wells has also been carried out extensively in the project areas. As a result of these measures, water supply facilities have been considerably improved in most project areas and in some of them *e.g.* Mohd. Bazar, a decline in the incidence of waterborne diseases has been reported. However, consciousness of the need for safe drinking water as distinct from adequate drinking water is yet to come. In Bhathat—U.P. where a large number of wells have been improved, new wells constructed and hand pumps installed, it is reported that there are few wells which remain sanitary. Keeping a well from getting contaminated is a function of usage which in turn depends mainly upon the consciousness about safe drinking water supply which has been created in the community. Obviously such consciousness and the resulting collective effort which may keep wells from being contaminated are yet to come.

In case of latrines, even the first stage, that of acceptance of the merit of the practice, has not been reached in most projects. This is due in part to the faulty designs of the latrines which do not meet all the requirements of the villagers, with the result that in many cases even the latrines which have been constructed at considerable cost are not being used. It is interesting however, that in some projects (Kolhapur and Sonepat) awareness is coming to the extent that people feel that it is not desirable to allow children to defecate on the streets. This is undoubtedly the first step which has to be followed by numerous others before a change in practice can be accomplished in this sphere.

Difficulties of a somewhat different type are being encountered in connection with programmes of pavement of lanes and construction of drains. These programmes were taken up in some projects and involved considerable contributions from people. Their maintenance *i.e.* keeping them clean and in good repair is in the nature of a municipal function which has to be carried out by the panchayats. But even where panchayats exist, the lanes and drains are generally not being well-maintained, for a variety of reasons. This is an illustration of the tendency which affects every field of development activity (and has been commented upon in another context in the chapter on Social Education); that it is comparatively easy to obtain participation of people in development activities under a way of enthusiasm, but to bring together the sustained efforts and the organisation required for the continuation of the activity is much more difficult.

## CRITERION 4: COMMUNITY LIFE

Community life in the rural areas has been subject to a succession of important changes in the wake of Independence. Among these universal suffrage, abolition of Zamindars and other privileged groups in some areas and expansions of the village panchayats are perhaps the most important. Under the impact of these influences as also of the general process of economic change, the patterns of influence, of leadership, and of social and economic relationships within the community have been undergoing a rapid change.

The coming of the community projects accelerated the process and also introduced significant new elements. In assessing the impact of the programme upon community life, the experience with the works and amenities programmes is of particular interest, because the reactions of the village community to this programme furnish a good illustration of the processes of change. Under this programme, financial and technical assistance became available for improvement of community facilities on a scale hitherto unknown. Most villages have availed of the assistance for one or more activity and a quantitative idea of the proportions of villages benefiting from different types of activities is obtainable from the date of the coverage study in the following chapter.

*Extent of participation*: The first thing which needs emphasis in this connection is the great variation in the character of participation by the communities in this programme. In some areas like the Chala-kudy project in Kerala, where the works were entrusted to contractors and people's participation consisted merely of the difference between the scheduled rates and the payments actually made by the project, there was little opportunity for participation by the community. The effect was largely similar where the funds of large multi-village pan-chayats or such bodies as Cane Development Unions were utilized for making up people's participation. At the other extreme, in some pro-jects (*e.g.* Batala—Punjab) where contributions of voluntary labour had to be given by every family, there was a vivid sense of participation in programmes of benefit to the whole community. In general, it can be said that the possibilities which the resources available under the community projects offered for the mobilisation of village communities and creating in them a sense of self-help and collective action, were nowhere adequately utilized. In the earlier stages, there was some emphasis on preparing villages to undertake programmes of collective benefit and the Grama Sevaks did some work in community mobilisa-tion. But, as the emphasis on targets and expenditures increased, these community development methods were given less and less emphasis even in those projects where they had been adopted earlier.

To the extent that possibilities of participation were available to the communities, these presented both a challenge and an opportunity to the existing leadership and institutions. In the majority of the social change villages, the traditional leaders were themselves receptive to the new opportunities. They participated in the programme and helped in mobilising the requisite effort. Although there are many instances of difference, it is noteworthy that there is none of hostility. This is due mainly to the fact that the facilities which were being offered under this programme satisfied the most basic necessities, about the desir-ability of having which there could be no question of difference of opinion. Emergence of new leadership, especially of young leaders has been noticed in a number of villages. The young men have been parti-cularly active in assuming institution leadership positions *e.g.*, in panchayats. Other examples of new kinds of leaders are encountered in some of the former Zamindary villages where persons with education or new ideas have replaced the Zamindars and have taken initiative in community development activities. Instances of young or new leadership emerging and existing side by side with the older leadership have also been reported in a few areas.

The works have also provided opportunities of testing the qualities of leaders especially their honesty, their willingness to take initiative and to work for the common good. It is reported by a number of P.E.O.s that, as a result of experience in connection with project works, people in many social change villages have a better knowledge of the qualities and limitations of their leaders. The differential progress of development activities in different villages of a project is reported by the Evaluation Officers to depend more upon the character of local leadership than any other single factor. And, with increasing opportunities of undertaking collective works, which the projects afforded the scarcity of leaders with the requisites qualities of initiative, public spirit and integrity and having the confidence of the people has been increasingly felt. Here obviously is a field where some positive and helpful action is required on the part of the project authorities.

Instances of deterioration in the existing relations within the community *e.g.* of increasing tension between rival factions have also been reported in a few villages. In most of these cases, the project staff, instead of waiting to bring together the rival groups and then initiating a development activity, have resorted to the quicker (but often harmful) way of taking the assistance of the group or faction which was co-operative, with the result that the rival group has been left feeling even more hostile and dissatisfied than before.

Village institutions especially panchayats have also been affected by this programme. As is well-known, most of the project activities are included among the functions of the panchayats which however, are not able to undertake these because of very inadequate resources, organisational deficiencies or such other difficulties as existence of factions. The availability of project funds enabled many panchayats to participate in these programmes and to fulfil some of their own obligations. Panchayats have rendered considerable assistance in collection of contributions and organising people's participation in many projects. Largely because of this, there is an increasing realisation of the importance of panchayats in many areas. It is reported by one P.E.O. that the people now realise the importance of the panchayats better and feel that they should be more careful in electing panchayat members in future. In another project, where the panchayats have been particularly successful in mobilizing labour contribution, it is reported that the mukhyias of the panchayats are assuming positions of leadership, their advice is sought even in social matters and given greater weight than even that of the traditional caste leaders. Such realization of the value of institutions and institutional leadership is a most hopeful sign. As it grows, it will strike at one of the major factors responsible for inactivity or failure of the panchayats, *viz.*, the lack of awareness among the people as also among the panchayats themselves of the roles and functions of these institutions. Secondly, the beginning of such feelings indicates that it may progressively become possible to organise community life around such institutions. In a situation where the traditional bonds of social relationship are becoming weaker, the emergence of institutionalised relationship is of crucial importance. To the extent that such relationships grow, the foundations for a democratic social life will be laid in the villages.

Besides offering new opportunities for purposive action, the projects have helped to enrich community life by making available such facilities as the radio, the newspaper, the recreation centre, the youth club. These facilities opened up new possibilities of participation in social events which have been availed of in varying degrees in different project areas.

The strengthening of community life should not, however, be over-estimated. The communities have, by and large, participated only when given the opportunities and actively encouraged by the project staff to do so. Participation, moreover, has been dependent on a continuation of efforts by the project staff and is motivated in most cases by the desire to avail of financial assistance offered by the project. There are a few instances of villagers organising themselves for even traditional community activities like festivals more frequently or more enthusiastically, of organising recreational, literacy or development activity on their own initiative or of doing some collective activity on their own which they had not done before. Even maintenance of most facilities created by the project is found difficult as has been mentioned in a number of chapters in this report. Whatever advance is visible is dependent upon the external stimuli given by the project staff and project funds, and continuing advance is still dependent upon a continuation of these. It cannot be said that community life has acquired a greater vigour of its own. All that can be said is that the coming of the project programmes has offered it new avenues of expression which have been utilised. But such expression will have to be continually supported for a considerable time before it can reach the self-generating stage.

*Youth*—A systematic and comprehensive programme for rural youth has yet to be evolved. The most common activity so far has been organisation of youth clubs which are in reality sports or recreation clubs in most cases. In some villages members of youth clubs have also taken interest in development activities. These youth clubs are dependent largely upon project grants and with their cessation many of these have already closed. Only in one project (Kolhapur-Bombay), where the efforts of the project staff lead to a revival of the *traditional akhadas* which is an institution of considerable vitality in Maharashtra villages, the efforts have had more lasting results. In general, the youth have not shown any greater propensity for the successful working of collective institutions than their elders.

In a few projects there are instances of youth acquiring experience of leadership positions. Here, two kinds of situations were met. In one village of the Mandya block of Mysore, the elders themselves have encouraged youth to take up leadership positions particularly in the panchayats because education and knowledge of procedure, which the selected youngmen had, were considered to be an advantage for such positions. In this case, the association of youngmen with positions of responsibility led to the more successful functioning of the panchayat and was also a factor making for progress in the village. The same was the case in another village in the Ashta block in Madhya Pradesh. On the other hand, in another village youth have tried to acquire positions in opposition to the established village leaders. The experience has not been successful in their attempt and there is increased tension in the village.

With the progressive spread of education, there can be seen emerging in many of the project villages, a new class of educated youth, many of whose members are unemployed, not fully occupied or just not fit for absorption into village life. The young matriculate or middle standard son of the medium cultivator illustrates the situation. The youngmen are prepared to take up white-collar jobs in towns. They would prefer not to undertake cultivation, partly because their talents would not be fully utilized in it, and partly because there is no real need for more man-power on the family holding. They are also looking increasingly to jobs of Grama Sevaks, villages school teachers, Panchayat secretaries, patwaris, sanitation staff, etc. In view of the vast expansion of such services in rural areas, the emergence of a class like this is an advantage, but the difficulties that it creates during the transition period should also be fully recognised. The problems will be particularly serious in the case of Harijan youth because in their case the kind of absorption which is possible in the families of middle or large cultivators will not be possible because their families do not have the resources to support them through periods of virtual idleness and there are no such things as supervisory duties on the family holding to keep the semblance of being engaged. This question of what the educated rural youth and particularly those belonging to the handicapped classes will do, will become of increasing importance in the coming years with the spread of education in rural areas.

## CRITERION 5: UNDERSTANDING AND COOPERATION BETWEEN THE OFFICIALS AND NON-OFFICIALS

The advent of the community development and national extension service programme with its accent on the educational approach, stimulating of cooperative effort and building up a healthier and richer community life marked a significant point in the process of richer community life marked a significant point of change of outlook among the officials towards the people. These attitudes had been changing rapidly in the wake of Independence and with the growth of democracy in the country. But with the coming of the projects, this process was greatly accelerated, as there was a conscious attempt by the project staff to make a marked departure from the existing methods of work and of approach to the people.

The crucial test of improvement of relations between the officials and the people is in the working of panchayats, advisory commitees, planning committees and other institutions in which the officials and non-officials leadership come in together. The working of the advisory committees has been commented upon in the earlier Evaluation Reports and although there is considerable improvement in their functioning in many areas mainly because of better organisational arrangements, it must be admitted that the advisory committee has not fulfilled the role envisaged for it—that of an active body aiding planning for development in its areas, whose members help in formulating policy, preparing public opinion for development programme and assisting in carrying out these programmes in their respective areas. In most areas, the major role of the BACs or the Planning Committees for that matter is of according formal sanction to the proposals put up to them. The difficulties of cooperation between the officials and non-officials are well known among the non-officials rivalry, political or personal, and lack of interest in development programmes; among the officials distrust of the non-officials and fear about present inadvisibility of giving greater power to non-officials in development programmes. In a number of cases it is evident, therefore, that the changes in attitudes of the officials towards the people and the vice versa although very marked have not yet established themselves in institutionalised stable patterns of working relationship or behaviour. This is necessarily a slow process but actually the process of change in this sphere cannot be considered to have established itself.

## CRITERION 6: AWARENESS AMONG THE
## UNDERPRIVILEGED GROUPS

It has been generally recognised that the project programmes did not provide adequately for improvement of the economic and social conditions of the under-privileged groups. This deficiency is sought to be corrected to a large extent by the increasing emphasis on programmes of cottage industries, by measures specially designed to make facilities of the cooperative movement available to the small cultivators and the artisans and by such programmes as housing for Harijans. Changes have, however been taking place in the economic and social conditions of these groups under the impact of the project and other development programmes, some of which are of considerable interest.

*Better Employment Opportunities* : There has been some increase in employment arising both from operation of development programmes, project and non-project, and from measures of land improvement notably extension of irrigations facilities and increase in agricultural production which have followed as a result of the development activities. In some areas, notably Manavadar—Bombay it is reported that as a result of greater employment opportunities and increases in production, wage levels have also shown a significant rise. In this increase in employment opportunities the main beneficiaries have been the labouring classes, Harijans and others. On the other hand, agrarian legislation is reported to have resulted in ejectment of tenants and resumption of holdings by the owner themselves in one Project—Pusa (Bihar).

Among the project programmes which have been of direct benefit to the under-privileged groups, provision of drinking water wells for Harijans is perhaps the most important. The wells have satisfied a genuine felt need and the Harijans have shown themselves to be ready to contribute their share in their construction. The experience with production-cum-training centres for artisans has not been particularly happy, however. These centres have not succeeded in their primary objective of initiating a process of improvement in techniques in village crafts and industries. In all the social change villages surveyed by the P.E.O.s., there are hardly any instances of trainees going back to villages and improving techniques of existing industries. A noteworthy programme in West Bengal has been granting of small loans to help provide equipment and capital to artisans. Assistance to *Harijans* has been an important programme in a few centres e.g. Erode (Madras) and Bodhan (Andhra).

The under-privileged groups have also shared in the benefits from the rising standards of welfare services and facilities provided during the project period. As regards use of school facilities by Harijans two opposing trends are reported. In most areas, the Harijans feel that the young boys are needed for work on or around the house or to supplement the family income and are therefore reluctant to send them to school. But in a few cases notably Bhadrak (Orissa) and Pusa (Bihar) it has been reported that the Harijans are quite anxious to send their children to school because they see in education, an opportunity of change (or escape) from their village life.

Instances of improvement in the social status of Harijans have come to notice in a few centres. As a result of universal suffrage and the specific representation given to the panchayats, the voice of the Harijans is now heard more carefully and with greater consideration. This is the general report. Indications of reduction in the rigours of untouchability are also reported from a few centres e g. Bhathat (U.P.), Pusa (Bihar), Bhardrak (Orissa). In these areas, the social distance between the caste Hindus and the Harijans was never as great as elsewhere. In Bhathat for instance the Harijans draw water from the same wells as the caste Hindus and there is no prejudice about it. In this connection, a report from Pusa (Bihar) which illustrates how the taboos are being progressively weakened is of interest. On the outskirts of a village near the railway station, a small market has grown up. In the tea shop, Harijans and caste Hindus eat together. In cities such distinctions have always tended to break down, it is the extension of the modes of the city into the village which is apparently having the same effect in them.

# COMMUNITY DEVELOPMENT
# ACHIEVEMENTS AND FAILURES

THE COMMUNITY DEVELOPMENT programme completed 12 years of its existence last October. The programme has drawn the nation's attention to the developmental needs of the rural areas, in an era where development was apt to be equated with big projects financed with foreign aid and collaboration. The villagers' expectations have also been aroused. A development agency has been created which aims at reaching every village, though not every family residing therein. Representative institutions have been erected, at the village, Block and District levels through which the programme is operating. A network of cooperative organisations now exist or is being rapidly created to provide the necessary supplies to the villages. Largely through a price-incentive mechanism, which provides a higher price paid through a cooperative purchasing organisation, pure seed is finding its way into the villages. Fertilizers are being slowly absorbed, and their in-take is on the increase. The pressing need for increasing agricultural production seems to have been realised, and there appears to be less stress on developing amenities than what was noticed in the initial stages.

## Debit Side

On the debit side, the programme has failed to create a genuine spirit of cooperative and community endeavour amongst the people. It is self-centered. This is inevitable in a rural setting where agriculture is individually operated. But better results could be achieved if these could be backed up by a broad-based cooperative endeavour directed to providing supplies, technical assistance and guidance to self-working cultivators.

Secondly the development agency has yet to become in every sense an Extension agency. Today if it is that, it is so only in name. Thirdly, unless supplies of all types can be made to reach the self-working cultivators, the present criticism that only a few rich take advantage of the programme would continue to be there. Fourthly, a programme of agricultural extension must be supported by a "rural works" programme which will provide productive work to needy people according to their need. A programme providing rural employment on a large-scale is a necessary complementary to a programme of agricultural development. But no concrete programme has yet been evolved to tackle the problem of rural unemployment.

The result is that while we concentrate on targets the net results of our labours elude assessment. Bulls are provided without provision for their feeding; in due course they are neglected, and relapse into early disuse. New Bulls are provided without any assessment of the services rendered by old bulls, and their present condition. A particular breed of bulls is insisted upon, though the local area has a fancy for another breed. Targets of fertilizer distribution are counted towards increased production though there is considerable evidence to show that it is resold or diverted to particular crops. Above all the Extension agency has unfortunately not been established at all, and it is so only in name. It is in effect an administrative agency. The result is that it has succeeded in popularising pure seeds, fertilizers, etc., but not intensive agriculture, which is a combination of all agricultural practices based on scientific knowledge and practical experience. Unfortunately, it has neither the knowledge, nor the training or capacity to function as a genuine Extension agency.

### Panchayati Raj:

The introduction of democratic decentralisation in a national atmosphere where the tendency to seek individual advantages dominates over public good is also having its inevitable consequences. The three institutions of Panchayat, Panchayat Samiti and Zilla Parishad, were intended to transfer real power and authority to units of local Government. For various reasons, they have succeeded only in association representatives of the people with development programmes. And these programmes are yet to be devised and operated from above. They have not yet become the programmes of these bodies. This is one reason for their comparative failure. The other is that these institutions are not yet able to discharge the services expected of them because the desire to secure public good is frequently subordinated to the desire to secure individual advantages at the cost of public welfare.

### Remedies:

What can be done to overcome these drawbacks? The remedies lie in various fields, and there is no short-cut to raising the people's consciousness and instilling in them new ideas and habits. Some suggestions in this respect can, however, be made. Even today the first necessity is to make the development programme a "people's" programme. It is still very much a Government programme. This is the chief reason for the comparatively poor results achieved from the Community Development programme in spite of huge expenditures incurred on it. The various schemes are still Government schemes, not the people's schemes. And they cannot become the people's schemes, in the absence of a genuine Extension agency. The present agency is far from being such. At best it is an administrative agency. And now that the Village Level Worker has been made the Secretary of the Panchayat as well as the village Patwari, as in Maharashtra whatever little possibility of his doing Extension work existed has also vanished. But perhaps the old idea of the village Level Worker working as an Extension Worker needs revision. He could only function as a help to an Extension Worker. He cannot be a substitute for him. He has not enough knowledge, training capacity and experience to enable him to make any impression on the self-working experienced cultivators of the village. Therefore the alternative is to increase the number of agricultural graduates and reduce the area of their charge. The Mandi centre idea developed in the Wardha plan as an intermediate centre between the Block and the Village Panchayat deserves consideration. The test of successful extension is that the people ask for the schemes extended and make them their own. Genuine extension must aim at developing intensive agriculture rather than the distribution of seeds fertilizers.

The generation of initiative and a sense of self-reliance amongst the people is dependent on a change in the attitude of the Government as well as the village leadership. Such an attitute cannot be generated while the Government considers itself responsible for increasing production. Government's initiative becomes inconsistent with the development of the people's initiative and vice versa. While the Government's anxiety to speed up economic development through increased production is understandable, it must be reflected in the voluntary efforts of the people to improve their condition by drawing up schemes and efforts which they need and understand. It is necessary therefore for the people's institutions thrown up by democratic decentralisation to draw up plans, and for the Community Development Ministry to finance them after proper scrutiny. Then alone can there be a welcome change in the present situation.

**Party System:**

How can the representatives of the people be enabled to work for genuine public good transcending all consideration of personal and party advantage is the most fundamental problem before our infant democracy. Here the remedies lie elsewhere than in the policies and precepts of the Ministry of Community Development. The main purpose of democratic decentralisation is being thwarted by the introduction of the worst evils of the party system; groupism and faction-

# BIBLIOGRAPHY

Agarwalla, S.N., *Social Dynamics of Family Planning*. Delhi, American Women's Club, 1965.

Apthorpe, Raymond, *ed.*, *Social Research and Community Development*. Lusaka, Rhodes, Livingstone Institute for Social Research, 1961.

Balten, T.R., *Communities and their Development ; an Introductory Study with Special Reference to the Tropics*. London, Oxford University Press, 1957.

Bhattacharijee, J.P., *Refresher Course for the Field Staff*. Delhi Municipal Corporation, 1963.

Bhattacharya, S.N., *They Showed the Way, new stories from old Indian villages*. Calcutta, Thackers, 1961.

Bose, S.K., *Some Aspects of Indian Economic Development; a Study of the Leading Problems of Indian Economics*, 2 vols. Delhi, Ranjit Publishers, 1962.

Bowles, Chester, *The Makings of a Just Society; What the Post-war Years Have Taught us About National Development*. Delhi, University of Delhi, 1963.

Carstairs, G. Morris., *The Twice-born; a study of a Community of high-caste Hindus*. London, Hogarth, 1957.

Central Institute for Training and Research in Panchayati Raj, Delhi. *Role of Voluntary Associate Organisation in Panchayati Raj and Community Development*. Delhi, Author, 1964.

Coldwell, M.J. *et al.*, *Report of a Community Development Evaluation Mission*, November 23, 1958—April 3, 1959; prepared for the Government of India by M. J. Coldwell, R. Dumont and M. Read, appointed under the U. N. Programme of Technical Assistance. Delhi, Government Press, 1959.

Dayal, Rajeshwar, *Community Development Programme in India*. Allahabad, Kitab Mahal, 1960.

——, *Community Development, Panchayati Raj and Sahkari Samaj*. Delhi, Metropolitan Book Co., 1965.

Delhi Municipal Corporation. Deptt. of Urban Community Development. *A Report on the Training Programme for Mohalla Committee Workers*. Delhi, Author, 1961.

——, *A Review, September 1958—March 1962*. Delhi, Author, 1962.

——, *Selected Case Studies*. Delhi, Author, 1961.

Delhi Municipal Corporation. Deptt. of Urban Community Development. *A Study of Women's Attitude and Practices and Working of the Mahila Samitis.* Delhi, Author, 1963.

——, *Training Mohalla Committee Workers*, Delhi, Author, 1961.

Dey, S. K., *Community Development*, 2 vols., Allahabad, Kitab Mahal, 1960.

——, *Community Development Through Panchayati Raj.* Delhi, Govt. Press. 1961.

——, *Nilokheri.* Bombay, Asia, 1962.

Dhekne, B. R., *Hubli City; a Study in Urban Economic Life.* Dharwar, Karnatak University, 1959.

Du Sautoy, Peter, *Community Development in Ghana.* London, Oxford University Press, 1958.

Dube, D. C. *et al., Village Level Workers; Their Work and Result Demonstration.* Delhi, Government Press, 1962.

Dube, S.C., *India's Changing Villages; Human Factors in Community Development.* London, Roultedge and Kegan Paul, 1958.

——, *Perspectives on the National Emergency.* Mussorie, National Institute of Community Development, 1963.

Einsiedel, Luz A., *Success and Failure in Selected Community Development Projects in Batangas.* Quezon City, University of Philippines, Community Development Research Council, 1959.

Gangarade, K. D., *A School is Built.* Delhi, Delhi School of Social Work, 1964.

Gore, M. S., *The Beggar Problem in Metropolitan Delhi.* Delhi, Delhi School of Social Work, 1959.

Gupte, Ranjit, *Community Development, Cooperation and Panchayati Raj in Alipore; a Pilot Survey.* Delhi, Indian Cooperative Union, 1964.

Hoslitz, Bert F. ed., *The Progress of Underdeveloped Areas.* Chicago, University of Chicago Press, 1952.

Inamdar, N. R., *Report of the Survey of the Administration of the Community Development Block Haveli.* Poona, Poona University, 1962.

India. Ministry of Community Development and Cooperation. *Annual Conference (on) Community Development.* Mount Abu, May 20-24, 1958. Delhi, Govt. Press, 1958.

——, *A Chronicle, 1954-1961.* Delhi, Govt. Press, 1962.

——, *Community Development at a Glance.* Delhi, Govt. Press, 1962.

——, *Evolution of Community Development Programme in India.* Delhi, Govt. Press, 1963.

——, *A Guide for Secretaries of Service Cooperatives.* Delhi, Govt. Press, 1963.

India. Community Development and Cooperation, *Guide to Community Development*, 2nd rev. ed. Delhi, Govt. Press, 1959.

——, *A Guide to Gram Sevikas and Mukhya Sevikas.* Delhi, Govt. Press, 1961.

——, *Leaders in the Making.* Delhi, Govt. Press, 1965.

——, *Manual for Village Level Workers*, Delhi. Delhi Govt. Press, 1956.

——, *Manual of Agriculture and Animal Husbandry Development Work in Community Projects.* Delhi, Govt. Press, 1962.

——, *National Conference on Community Development, Mysore, July 23-28, 1959.* Delhi, Govt. Press, 1959.

——, *People in the Plan.* Delhi, Author, 1959.

——, *Report of the Study Team on the Position of Gram Sabha in Panchayati Raj Movement.* Delhi, Govt. Press, 1963.

——, *Report of the Working Group on Panchayats and Cooperatives.* Delhi, Govt. Press, 1962.

——, *A Report on the Annual Conference on Community Development and Panchayati Raj*, New Delhi, July 1964. Delhi, Govt. Press, 1964.

——, *Report on Training Centres Visited by the High-level Team on Training.* Delhi, Govt. Press, 1961.

——, *The Scope of Extension in Community Development.* Delhi, Govt. Press, 1961.

——, *Study, Research and Training for the Community Development Personnel.* Delhi, Govt. Press, 1960.

——, *Village Volunteer Force.* Delhi, Govt. Press, 1961.

——, *Manual on Village Road Construction.* Delhi, Govt. Press, 1961.

India. Ministry of Information and Broadcasting. Publications Division. *Problems in Plan Implementation.* Delhi, Govt. Press, 1964

India. Planning Commission. Programme Evaluation Organisation. *Draft Manual of Village Level Workers' Records.* Delhi, Govt. Press, 1956.

——, *Programme Evaluation Organisation: Structure, Functions and Activities.* Delhi, Govt. Press, 1964.

——, *Research Programme Committee.* Research for Planning Delhi, Govt. Press, 1954.

India International Centre, New Delhi. *Proceedings of the Seminar on Social Administration in Developing Countries.* Delhi, March 16-21, 1964; organised by India International Centre in collaboration with Indian Institute of Public Administration and Association of Schools of Social Work in India. Delhi, Author, 1964.

Karve, Irawati and Yashwant Bhaskar Damle. *Group Relation in Village.* Poona, Deccan College, 1963.

Kreitlow, B. W. *et al.*, *Leadership for Action in Rural Communities.* Danville (Ill.), Inter-state Printers and Publishers, 1960.

Krishnamachari, V. T., *Community Development in India.* Delhi, Govt. Press, 1962.

Kumarappa, J. C., *Overall Plan for Rural Development*, 4th ed. Varanasi, Akhil Bharat Sarva Seva Sangh, 1960.

Lal, Ramavatara, *Community Development, Principles, Practice and Problems; with Special Reference to the State of Bihar.* Calcutta, Bookland, 1963.

Lalvani, K. C., *Community Development and Extention Service.* Calcutta, Arth Vanjya, 1963.

Lewis, Oscar., *Village Life in Northern India*, Urbana, University of Illinois, 1958.

Madras School of Social Work, Madras. *Report on the Beggar Survey in Madras City.* Madras, Author, 1956.

Majumdar, D.N., *Social Contours of an Industrial City; Social Survey of Kanpur, 1954-56*, by D.N. Majumdar, N.S. Reddy, S. Bahadur and a field team. Bombay, Asia, 1960.

Malhotra, P.C., *Socio-economic Survey of Bhopal City and Bhairagarh.* Bombay, Asia, 1964.

Marriott, McKim, *Village India; Studies in the Little Community.* Bombay, Asia, 1961.

Mayer, Albert, *et al.*, *Pilot Project India; the Story of Rural Development of Etawah, Uttar Pradesh*, Berkley, University of California, 1958.

Mezirow, Jack D., *Dynamics of Community Development.* New York, Scarecrow, 1963.

Mishra, J.N., *Small Scale Cottage Industries in Saugar District.* Sagar, University of Saugar, 1963.

Misra, B.R. *ed.*, *Report on Socio-economic Survey of Jamshedpur City.* Patna, Patna University, 1959.

Mittal, O.P., *Study of Etawah Rural Development Pilot Project.* (Thesis: M.A. Social Work, Delhi University, Unpublished.

Mukerje, B., *Community Development in India.* Bombay, Orient Longmans, 1961.

Mukerjee, Radha Kamal *and* Baljit Singh, *Social Profiles of a Metropolis; Social and Economic Structure of Lucknow, Capital of U.P., 1954-56.* Bombay, Asia, 1961.

Nagpal, P., *Programme for Women and Children.* Delhi, Municipal Corporation, Deptt. of Urban Community Development, 1961.

Nair, Kusum., *Blossoms in the Dust; the Human Element in Indian Development.* London, Gerald Duckworth, 1961.

Nandjundappa, D.M., *Community Development and Employment.* Dharwar, Karnatak University, 1963.

National Council of Applied Economic Research, New Delhi. *Attitudes Towards and Motivations for Saving.* Delhi. Author, 1964.

——, *Development of Dandukoranya.* Delhi, Author, 1963.

——, *Socio-economic Conditions of Primitive Tribes in Madhya Pradesh.* Delhi, Author, 1963.

——, *Techno-economic Survey of Gujrat,* Delhi, Author, 1963.

Nayar, Sushila., *Family Planning.* Delhi, Govt. Press, 1963.

Nehru, Jawaharlal, *On Community Development and Panchayati Raj.* Delhi, Govt. Press, 1963.

Pareek, Udai *and* R.P. Lynton, *First Course in Personnel Organisational Development.* Hyderabad, Small Industries Extension Institute, 1964.

Planning Research and Action Institute, Lucknow. *Action, Research and its Importance in an Underdeveloped Economy.* Lucknow, Planning Deptt., 1963.

——, *Agro-industrial Pilot Project in Uttar Pradesh.* Lucknow, Govt. Press, 1964.

——, *A Case Study of Panchayati Elections.* Lucknow, Planning Deptt. 1963.

——, *Guide to Rural Youth Organisation Based on a Pilot Project,* rev. ed. Lucknow, Govt. Press, 1963.

——, *Uttar Pradesh Gobar gas and Potential for its Utilisation.* Lucknow, Govt. Press, 1963.

——, *Youth Club and Sericultural Programme.* Lucknow, Govt. Press, 1963.

Raman, K.S.V. *Problems of Community Development in India.* Patna, Lakhmi, 1965.

——, *What is Community Development ?* Delhi, Govt. Press, 1963.

Ross, Murray G., *Case Histories in Community Organisation.* New York, Harper Bros., 1963.

——, *Community Organisation; Theory and Principles.* New York, Harper Bros., 1955.

Ruopp, Phillips, *ed. Approaches to Community Development.* New York, Lounz, 1953.

Samuel, Thomas, *People's Programme, Community Development in Cartoons,* rev. and enl. ed. Delhi, Govt. Press, 1965.

Sanders, Irwin T., *The Community; an Introduction to a Social System,* New York, Ronald, 1958.

Sanders, Irwin T., *Making Good Communities Better.* Lexington, University of Kentucky, 1953.

Sarvesheswara Rao, B., *The Economic and Social Effects of Zamindari Abolition in Andhra.* Delhi, Govt. Press, 1963.

Schltz, Theodre W., *The Economic Test in Latin America.* Ithaca, N.Y. State School of Industrial and Labour Relations, Cornell University, 1956.

Sehgal, A.N., *Visual Aids in Community Development.* Delhi, Govt. Press, 1960.

Sen, S.N., *The City of Calcutta; a Socio-economic Survey, 1954-55 to 1957-58.* Calcutta, Bookland, 1960.

Shah, P.C., *Tribal Life in Gujarat.* Bombay, Gujrat Research Society, 1964.

Shah, Vimal, *Perspective Village Planning.* Bombay, Khadi and Village Industries Commission, 1960.

Srinivas, M.N. *ed., India's Village,* 2nd ed. Bombay, Asia, 1960.

Sussman, Marvin B., *Community Structure and Analysis.* New York, Thomas Y. Crowell, 1959.

Taylor, Carl Cleveland, *et al., India's Roots of Democracy; a Sociological Analysis of Rural India's Experience in Planned Development Since Independence.* Bombay, Orient Longmans, 1965.

Tekumalia, V.N., *Village Plans at Work Bombay,* Khadi and Village Industries Commission, 1958.

Tewari, Ram Chand, *Village Level Worker and the Cooperative Movement.* Faridabad, Govt. Press, 1963.

Turner, Roy, ed., *India's Urban Future; Selected Studies From an International Conference Sponsored by Kingsley Davis etc.* University of California, 1962.

Umrao Singh, *Community Development in India,* Kanpur, Kitab Ghar, 1962.

United Nations, *Civic and Political Education of Women.* New York, Author, 1964.

——, *Rural Development Workers.* New York, United Nations, 1962.

——, *Study Kit on Training for Community Development.* New York, United Nations, 1957.

——Bureau of Social Affairs, *Social Progress Through Community Development.* New York, United Nations, 1955.

——Deptt. of Economic and Social Affairs, *Community Development and Related Service; a Report by the Secretary-General.* New York, Author, 1960.

——, *Community Development in Urban Areas; a Report by the Secretary-General.* New York, United Nations, 1961.

——, *Report on the World Social Situation.* New York, United Nations, 1963.

——, Economic Commission for Asia and the Far East. *Report of the Working Group on Development of Indigenous Teaching Material for Social Work.* Bangkok, Author, 1964.

——, Secretary-General. *The Social Training of Frontline Rural Development Workers; a Report by the Secretary-General.* New York, United Nations, 1962.

Vakil, C.N., *Poverty and Planning.* Bombay, Allied, 1963.

Wilner, Dorothy, *Community Leadership.* New York, United Nations, 1960 (*its* series of Community Development).

# INDEX